My Kitchen Cure

How I Cooked My Way Out of Chronic Autoimmune Disease
with Whole Foods and Healing Recipes

Mee Tracy McCormick

Foreword by Joan Borysenko, Ph.D.

Introduction by Carolyn Coker Ross, M.D.

LeeMee Publishing

Published by LeeMee Publishing
Los Angeles, CA • Nashville, TN

Interior design & layout: Gary A. Rosenberg • www.thebookcouple.com
Cover design & illustrations: Ted Raess • www.raessdesign.com
Photographs courtesy of Heather Muro at Muro Photography

Printed in the United States of America

10   9   8   7   6   5   4   3   2   1

Contents

PART THREE: Let's Get Cooking!

This book is dedicated to my family: Bella, Lola, my momma, my adopted adult parents Peggy and Ted, Nicole, Tylor, Gina and Lalo, Momma Joan, Carolyn Ross, Maryalice, Nely, Renee, Gil-Ben Ami, the Tomlinsons, Heather Muro and family, the Hamiltons, Virginia Harper, Dr. Sheng, Kerri, Justice, Lauren, and all the REAL FOOD Angels in Nashville, Tennessee, who came to cook with me.

So many others have supported me along the way and I just want you all to know that I appreciate your love and kindness.

They say blood is thicker than water. However, I believe that relationship is what binds us. Lee Richard McCormick, thank you for eating my food when it tasted terrible and for believing in me when I didn't—and most importantly, for choosing to say yes to an adventurous life with Mee.

Foreword
by Joan Borysenko, Ph.D.

Get ready to go on an adventure. A real magical, mystery tour through your cupboards to your heart, your mind, your body, and your community.

Your leader on this tour is a sassy, brilliant, and refreshingly out-spoken young woman on a mission. And that mission is healing through food—and healing of the food supply itself through changing the way we grow and raise it. In the process, Mee is healing whole com-munities through her outreach to schools, churches, and well, all of us, through televised cooking lessons that are so delightful you'll want to run right out and round up the ingredients.

I first met the Amazing Miss Mee just a few weeks after she gave birth to Lola, her second daughter. As a Harvard-trained medical scien-tist I can affirm what every mother knows. The growing fetus is a deter-mined scavenger. It will feed off your last reserves, of which Mee had precious few. She was deathly ill with a mysterious type of autoimmune digestive disease that defied diagnosis and refused to yield to treat-ment. She was skin and bones—mostly bones—when we met. Baby Lola on the other hand was a bruiser, weighing in at over 9 pounds.

Mee is one fierce mama, devoted to her children and to the well-being of all children. And she is devoted to you, which is what this book is all about. You will read about that devotion in action—how she goes into people's homes, listens to their stories, cleans out their cab-inets, creates a healing kitchen, takes them shopping, and teaches them how to cook. The best part is that they heal.

> Your leader on this tour is a sassy, brilliant, and refreshingly outspoken young woman on a mission.

Chronic illnesses that were being "managed" through pharmaceuticals often disappear outright. No more pills. No more pain. And people love the food, food that you don't have to be rich to eat. Mee can and has made a delicious, healthful dinner for forty to fifty people for under fifty bucks. That's hard to beat. And it cuts right through the excuse I hear over and over again from people: that it costs too much to eat a healthful diet.

America is a nation where some people are starving outright, without enough food, and others are starving in a nutritional sense while eating too much. Without question the plague of chronic disease that is sapping the vitality of millions of people—obesity, diabetes, heart disease, hypertension, gastrointestinal problems, and autoimmune disorders—is created in large part by the food that we've grown accustomed to eating. "Food" that is often more chemicals than nutrients. Refined carbs that create inflammation—the final common pathway in diseases as diverse as diabetes, cancer, coronary artery disease, and osteoporosis.

When we hear about the necessity of revamping the healthcare system, it is really too little too late. What we really need to do is to revamp our own health naturally. Health is a birthright for most of us, but the majority of healthcare practitioners don't know much about nutrition and therefore don't teach us enough about how to guard that treasure.

While I'm a seasoned cancer researcher and pioneer in psychoneuroimmunology (that's a big word that means the study of how thoughts and emotions affect the nervous system and immune system and from there every cell in the body), Mee is one of my go-to experts for nutritional information. She is a master.

Whether you're vegan, vegetarian, or like me, omnivorous, you'll find that living a real food life is much easier than you thought and inspires you to find a cure in your own kitchen. I've had the pleasure of staying at the home of Mee and her husband, Lee, several times. I've learned a lot about efficiency in the kitchen from watching her plan the delicious meals. She cooks up something new every day and pairs it with dishes left from the day before. No waste in food, effort, or taste. And everything is fresh, local, and vital. I swear there's nothing in a package in any of Mee's cabinets.

Perhaps the most amazing thing is that Mee's girls have learned to eat healthy, too. And as any mom knows, bucking the junk-food tide in this culture is no easy thing. If they can do it, so can you!

Enjoy. Heal, and go out and spread the word!

Introduction

by Carolyn Coker Ross, M.D.

I have known Mee Tracy McCormick for many years and watched her struggle with her health during that time. On many occasions I wished I could have used my medical background to help her. But, from my own personal experiences of dealing with a medical problem that had no specific "cure" or even any reasonable treatments, I knew that illness is a call to action. Illness is a call from the deepest parts of our selves to change what is not working in our lives and to begin a journey of discovery. Mee's book describes the journey she took and how it has changed her life and the lives of many people with whom she has shared "real food" and her story.

Mee has written a book with heart and soul that takes us through the colorful pages of her adventurous life. The book shines a light on the pain and suffering she endured for years from her undiagnosed and poorly treated digestive disorder. This pain led her on a search for answers. Even though the answers were found and even though many who read her book will be looking for the "magic pill" or the one thing that will help them if they have a similar issue, the most important part of her story is the journey. Her journey is about the desire to be whole and healthy, not just pain free. Her journey is about how pain can be transformed to purpose. Her journey catapulted her from being a mother and the founder of meetracy.com into her community and the world with a passion for teaching people about the healing power of food.

Mee's book is remarkable for its honesty and how it showcases her

> Mee has written a book with heart and soul that takes us through the colorful pages of her adventurous life.

True healing happens when we listen to the still small voice in our hearts that leads us to our own personal path to healing.

own strong, resilient personality. Her book is also remarkable because it shows that the path to TRUE healing doesn't start and end at your doctor's office or with a prescription. True healing happens when we listen to the still small voice in our hearts that leads us to our own personal path to healing, even when it deviates from what may be considered the norm or takes us to places that challenge us to look outside of conventional authorities on healing. Her book questions the status quo and her own intuitive voice frequently takes her onto new paths that eventually lead her to what worked best for her.

Mee's journey to healing is fun to read about and chock full of useful information that will help many who read her book. You will learn things about food you never knew. But behind the fun and knowledge is an invitation. If you accept Mee's invitation to live a real food life and find the cure in the kitchen, your life will never be the same.

A Note from Mee

Every day I seem to learn more and more about food, cooking, and healing. When I first embarked on this grand cooking adventure, I thought it was only to heal my own body . . . to get well enough to live pain free and to be able to eat whatever I wanted. I had no idea that I would not only learn to heal my intestines but also unveil the great secret to healing and preventing disease. This secret is that our intestines and their wellness are the key to balancing our immune systems. Therefore, *everyone* would do well to embark on a real food diet that strengthens the digestive tract, balances healthy bacteria versus unhealthy bacteria, and produces healthy, whole, and long shadoobies daily.

As I began to share with the world what I'd learned, the e-mails began to pour in from all over the country via my website, www.meetracy.com. I found myself digging for answers for folks who were suffering from autoimmune diseases and cancer. I knew that if food could heal a hole in my intestines, then for certain it could help others get well from an array of different illnesses.

What I found were tons of stories of food miracles. This hunt to understand our health and what makes us well expanded my own healing, and I found the "red thread" that connects all of us on the road to better health—real food. I hope my journey inspires you to shift your relationship with life and *know* that you have a choice in what you eat and how you feel.

With age and experience, you will be happy to know, growth becomes a conscious, recognized process. Still somewhat frightening, but at least understood for what it is. Those long periods when something inside ourselves seems to be waiting, holding its breath, unsure about what the next step should be, eventually become the periods we wait for, for it is in those periods that we realize we are being prepared for the next phase of our life and that, in all probability, a new level of the personality is about to be revealed.

—Alice Walker

PART ONE
Journeys & Adventures

We Said Yes!

I've been living my life as if it were a giant adventure from the moment I arrived in this world. I'm someone who sits comfortably on the edge of the next. I guess I learned at a very young age that change is part of the deal, so instead of putting my dukes up, I might as well find an easy spot where I can bend, shift, and mold to whatever comes my way.

This trait is the thread that binds my husband, Lee, and me together. He fully believes in living a big life—not to be confused with big stuff. Over the years we've lived in some pretty groovy little surf shacks and rockin' double-wides.

When our second daughter was born we were living in four places: *Nashville* on our working cattle ranch, *Sausalito* in a fabulous apartment overlooking the San Francisco Bay (Lee was hired to develop a holistic drug and alcohol treatment center there), *Malibu* where Lee built a treatment center, and *Teotihuacán, Mexico,* where we built the Dreaming House, a happening little blue casa and boutique hotel at the foot of the pyramids.

As Lee finished his project in Sausalito, we were really living in Malibu because we were so in love with our lives there. But neither of us had a real reason to be there, and dang, we were spending some serious cash to "live" there. We had several conversations revolving around "What are we doing here?" and one afternoon, we finally decided to go to lunch, raise our glasses to the sea, and make a pact with life: *If an opportunity for adventure presents itself, we will take it.* Lee loved to surf, and I'd dreamed of writing a book, so we agreed that Sayulita, Mexico, was the ideal place to check out.

A few weeks later Lee and I flew down to Mexico for forty-eight hours to find a place to live. A week after that, we arrived in Sayulita, Nayarit, a tiny surfing and fishing village on the pacific coast, north of

Puerto Vallarta and about an hour from the mouth of the jungle. We had fallen in love with Sayulita a year earlier while on vacation. This time we checked into Villa Amore: a groovy, open-air, palapa palm leaf–style condo/hotel. The condo we rented actually belonged to a pro surfer. It was the first time Lee and I had been away from our babies. I was a wreck. My recent nightmare was haunting me daily.

Someone shot me. I could feel the bullet move through my chest, and the force of the impact pushed me into another place. I closed and opened my eyes, peering into a town that was not my usual realm. I stood still, grasping my chest and looking around as people I'd never seen before began to pop into this place, all of them grabbing their chests. It was clear to me that they had been shot in the same place. Within seconds they diverged. I was conscious of being killed. I had arrived on the other side, and the direction we went in was congruent with the path that we were on before dying.

Suddenly, my good friend and man of honor at my wedding, Alphonso, popped over. He had been shot. A dream guide appeared, someone you can't really see with your eyes but know he or she is there in front of you talking and directing. He loaded Alphonso and me into an SUV, and we started to drive. As we rode through the new land, the dream guide explained that we had died and needed to cross over, so that we could return or be reincarnated at a time when our value would be appreciated, allowing us to become our greatest selves.

Alphonso was fine with this. I was as well until I saw an image of Lee, Bella, and Lola playing on the beach in Bermuda without me. I began to panic, and the air left my body. NO WAY was I going out like this! NO WAY was I going to leave my girls!

> Someone shot me. I could feel the bullet move through my chest, and the force of the impact pushed me into another place.

I searched the dream frantically for an exit, losing my witness point of view. Gasping for air, I reentered my bedroom and touched Lee's back to see if he was real. Then I flew from my bed, rushing into Bella's room, kissing her, and then to Lola's crib, lifting her into my arms and smelling her neck as a momma bear would do. This dream shook me for weeks. I couldn't figure out what it meant. Little did I know, I was fix'n to be reincarnated and face my death. Like in the dream, I would have to *choose* to shift the direction of my waking life.

I was reminded of this dream before dozing off to sleep.

Our first morning in town, we walked to Choco Banana, a wonderful brunch joint located in the center of the village and owned by a British woman who had migrated to Mexico many moons ago. Our plan was to find a local realtor to look at a few places. Lee struck up a conversation with an older expat who'd spent winters in Sayulita for years. Lee told him our story, and the guy said, "Hold on a second, my friend owns a real estate office right here, next to Choco Banana. Let me see if he is in."

A few minutes passed and a handsome Canadian dude in his thirties appeared. His name was Neil. Lee explained again what we were looking for, and the guy's eyes lit up. "You won't believe this, but I have a house that I'm managing on the North side in one of the better areas of town. It's on the beach. The real big deal is that it is the *only* long-term beachfront rental available in the entire village. Owners make more money renting short term during the high season than if they rent by the month. The downside is that it's still under construction. Wanna see it after breakfast?"

We did. We finished our grub and loaded into our rental truck, heading away from town. He wasn't kidding. The house sat directly on the beach. It was definitely in need of some work; it was one of the oldest houses in the village. The owner had taken an old concrete house and had the kitchen redone and updated the bathrooms. There were three bedrooms; two ocean-view rooms had sliding doors, which opened onto a deck. The other could be turned into an office. We were sold and immediately filled out a lease. Before leaving Sayulita, we met with the contractor who was working on the property. The final work was to paint the inside. We wanted a groovy Mexican pad, and I had practice decorating the Dreaming House in Teotihuacán. My house in Malibu was lovely, but mainly white walled. Mexico meant moving into a colorful, vibrant world with a lively house to match!

> Like in the dream, I would have to choose to shift the direction of my waking life.

Saying Good-bye to the "Bu" and Hello to the Mexican Jungle

Immediately upon our return to Malibu, we began to pack the house. Our Guatemalan household helper/nanny thought we were nuts to want to move to a third-world country. She'd worked her butt off to build the life she had in the U.S.

My most difficult good-bye was to Ted and Peggy Raess, aka Nanny and Bubba. I'd met both in my early twenties when I first arrived in LA. I was introduced to them through Gabrielle, one of my closest friends. Ted and Peggy didn't have any children of their own, and since I was an orphan, we were a perfect fit. We formed a family rooted in love, not blood. They'd introduced me to my husband. Ted gave me away on my wedding day, and they were present for the arrival of my girls. Leaving LA meant leaving them for the first time in ten years.

Within three weeks of finding our beach house in Sayulita, we were moving in, and with the same quick rhythm, we fell into the arms of this magical Mexican village.

> Life in a rural Mexican town was challenging, and most tasks required skills that neither of us possessed . . .

Life in a rural Mexican town was challenging, and most tasks required skills that neither of us possessed: like how to locate the gas delivery man who supplied weekly gas to our casa's gas tank, and the electricity to the house was an on-and-off event; the storms in the jungle came on a regular basis and with them the loss of power. The hardest task was paying our phone bill. We had to pay by cash. It took days because we learned we had to drive to Bucerias, the closest city where an ATM-like machine was located. The problem was that the road leading to Bucerias was known as the "death road" because every day someone was getting killed on it, which led to major traffic jams. Whenever we headed into town on the death road, I'd bless the car and imagine a giant red heart protecting our Mexi-Rig.

However, our life wasn't complicated emotionally; we had returned back to basics, and worrying about anything seemed far off and otherworldly. My daily focus was the kids, eating, and keeping the lights on. Oh, and avoiding snakes, deadly scorpions, land crabs, and iguanas.

I'd enrolled Bella in a small preschool, and I made friends of my own. I call these women "The Mango Mommas." They are made up of four young Sayulitan women in their twenties and thirties, educated women raising young children and attempting to maintain corners of themselves, much like me. We had playdates and Mommas' nights out, and we cried and laughed together. They became the base of our family's community, and through them, I began to truly understand Mexican culture. However, no one was or is as important as Senora Gina. The day I met her, I knew I'd found "My Person" and truly the reason our family had moved to Mexico. *To find her.*

Senora Gina is not only the matriarch of the village of Sayulita, but one of the most sophisticated, generous, kind, intelligent, faithful, loyal, and beautiful women I have ever met. To call her *friend* is not enough as she fulfills the role of so many titles. Sister, aunt, grandmother to my children, mother to my Mexican self, guide, teacher . . . the list goes on and on.

Our little house was on the sand, and the ocean moved underneath my bedroom with the rising tide. Sleeping with the waves opened our minds. Some scientists have even proven that sleeping near waves can change brain patterns.

. . . we had returned back to basics, and worrying about anything seemed far off and otherworldly.

Sleeping with the waves opened our minds.

My mind began to let go of the constant list-making from my Malibu lifestyle. My inner workings began to shift quickly, calming down as I let go of who I thought I was meant to be on the outside and embraced the re-creation of the inner Mee. I found myself looking forward to climbing into bed at the end of a long day, not because I was exhausted, but because I was looking forward to what dreams would fill my night. These dreams were vivid and always full of people I'd never seen or people I hadn't thought about in a while. I would awake to self-reflective thoughts of who I had been during our relationship, and these thoughts traveled with me throughout the day. When I returned to sleep, my dreams would bring me to another time in my life. Sayulita helped me recapitulate who I had been. It served as a resting place. The Huichol Indians believe that Sayulita is the place of "in between the worlds." This is where the veil is thin, and it is easy to spiritually connect to the other side; it is also from where our creativity stems.

These memories compelled me to evaluate who I was and how my reactions shifted outcomes. My favorite visitor was my momma. She visited my dreams the most, and on one particular occasion, I heard her whisper into my ear, "Check the baby."

> The Huichol Indians believe that Sayulita is the place of "in between the worlds."

I sat up, searching the room for whoever had spoken. Lola was sleeping alone in her crib. Suddenly, I heard the sound of Lola fighting for air. I ran into her room and switched on the light, thrilled that the electricity was finally working. I lifted my baby from her crib and was thankful that she was fine. Something had been stuck in her throat, but it had cleared. Thank goodness my momma woke me, and I was wide-eyed and alert. I also dreamed that my momma walked into the room with a new haircut and a fabulous straw bag. She brushed away the fear and sadness I felt for her death by telling me to stop worrying. I woke with the scent of her skin in my mind. It had been a while since I'd dreamed with her.

Life in the jungle was challenging and exciting. Every day we were connected to the outside world and nature. This connection fed our souls like never before. Our minds were challenged with learning a new language and cultural rights and wrongs. We were seen as immigrants by the natives, and I began to understand what my momma's family had felt when they immigrated to the United States from Italy.

I was expanding my life's perspective, and what neither my husband nor I knew is that the journey we'd embarked on was going to shift the direction of our lives forever.

◆ ◆ ◆

I'd always thought of Mexican food as being covered in cheese and sold at Taco Bell, or worse: Chi Chi's, a chain restaurant in the 1980s where all of the Oberlin and Cleveland–area school kids would go for their Spanish class field trips. First of all, none of us knew that *chi chi* meant "titty"! The name of the restaurant was a clear indication that whoever was running it either had a sense of humor or zero relationship with Mexico and its cuisine, 'cause Lord knows, not even strip joints in Mexico are given such crass names.

> I couldn't cook without the assistance of a box or jar.

I had a crew of helpers in our little casa, and one of them, Angel, came every afternoon to cook. The menu was usually freshly caught fish: dorado, a type of mahi mahi, corn tortillas, salsa, and whatever veggies were available at the market. One never entered a market with a list; I'd learned this early on as my first few trips into town armed with a list were pointless. I had a hope that maybe what I was planning to cook was in stock, but the tiny village relied on the vegetable man who drove around the streets blasting loud music from his shabby truck and screaming through a microphone to come out and buy fresh produce.

We ate what was seasonally available. Lots of zucchini, carrots, onions, garlic, potatoes, cabbage, and occasionally, I'd come across ginger and sweet potatoes, and in June, papayas and lychees. There were very few processed foods available besides spaghetti. I was thankful for this because on Angel's day off that's what we ate. I couldn't cook without the assistance of a box or jar.

My Food History
and the Constant Burn

Food and I had never really danced well together. I came into the world with a damaged intestinal track, and the day I was born I was rushed to Pittsburgh Children's Hospital where I underwent a surgery that removed three inches of my small intestines and then reconnected them. The doctors told my momma that I would not make it and a priest was brought in to baptize me immediately.

Well, I survived and spent the first few years of my life struggling with food, as it was difficult for me to digest. My momma said I screamed and screamed in pain nonstop for the first few years of my life. At age five, I was finally able to eat well enough. Then my parents divorced, leaving my momma alone with three children, earning $1.75 per hour, with zero child support. There wasn't any money to buy food, so I spent the next few years going to bed hungry.

Around the age of nine, my momma had troubles of her own. She was diagnosed with Crohn's disease, a condition where the lining of the intestines is basically eaten away by unstoppable bacteria. The immune system goes into overdrive in an attempt to attack the bacteria, but ends up hurting the body. The human is left suffering horrible pain and bleeding bouts, without the ability to digest food or absorb nutrition. There is *no* cure and no *known* drug to really help. It breaks my heart knowing my momma suffered the way she did.

Needless to say, I was raised on a less-than-healthy diet: canned corn, peas, green beans, chipped ham sandwiches served on white bread with Hellman's mayonnaise, Cheerios or Wheaties, and pasta with marinara sauce. I barely remember eating chicken or beef, except on special occasions. We spent summers with my grandparents in Appalachia where my Italian grandma cooked relatively fresh foods, rigatoni and sauce, meatballs, rolled oats for breakfast, and frittatas. Canned corn and peas were again the vegetables of choice. During the summer, we ate watermelon and fresh corn on the cob.

> The doctors told my momma that I would not make it and a priest was brought in to baptize me immediately.

In January 1989, my life changed. On New Year's Eve, my momma was in a head-on collision; she was thrown 500 feet from her vehicle and suffered severe injuries. On January 7, one week later, my best friends Gina DeMarco and Holly Velky were killed instantly in another car accident. On January 12, my momma passed away. Five days later, my great-grandmother Lloyd died in her sleep.

I had no money and nowhere to go. With the kindness of Lynn and Ray Muro, who loaned me twenty dollars, I filled up "The Peach" (my orange Chevette) and drove to my grandparents' house in the mountains. After Grandma Lloyd's funeral, my grandfather took me to a convent to study. I pondered the idea of becoming a nun and then decided it wasn't for me.

> I pondered the idea of becoming a nun and then decided it wasn't for me.

With ten dollars left, I drove to Maryland to live with my momma's brother, Uncle Mike, and his wife, Aunt Melinda. They told me I could live with them, but I had to make my own way. The next morning after arriving, I combed *The Washington Post*. Never having seen so many want ads, I knew I would be fine. By the time my aunt and uncle returned home from work that day, I'd found my way around and landed a job as a receptionist in a small office. Eventually, I saved enough money to return to college (I'd left Kent State mid year after my momma's car accident).

While I was going to school, I worked as a waitress on the weekends. The benefit of that job was a free meal. When I wasn't working, I ate canned peas and pasta or stopped by a fast food restaurant to buy something off the dollar menu. Wendy's Jr. single with cheese was my favorite.

After leaving school, I moved to New York City with the intention of attending FIT (Fashion Institute of Technology), and then on to Los Angeles, where a summer job as a stylist led me to a new world that I was destined to remain in for a few years, as this world was far away from the sadness of my past. Now, in my early twenties, I was in my first adult relationship, dating a young and handsome Israeli diamond dealer, Kapara (Hebrew for "most important one"). Kapara *loved* to eat out at all the fancy hot and hip spots. I was introduced to Middle Eastern foods and fine dining and loved eating every bit of it.

Today, I think back to my last supper without fear: One evening, Kapara and I went to Matteo's, one of the best Italian restaurants on the West side. I ordered a steak with Italian-styled roasted potatoes, a side of pasta, garlic spinach, and red wine—oh and fo'sho, a cannoli for dessert. I remember this meal so well because it was the last time I ate without fear.

Later that night an awful set of spasms gripped my abdomen. I felt as though everything had frozen inside of my body; not even my blood was moving freely. My tummy grew as if I were six months pregnant, and after hours of nonstop pain, Kapara thought it best to take me to the hospital. He waited with me for hours until he had to leave for an appointment, so I stayed there by myself. Finally someone came for me and put me in an examination room in the emergency room. I must have been there for hours. My last memory was vomiting and falling off of the examination table. When I opened my eyes, my good friend from college was standing over me and calling for a nurse. The spasms did not let up, and soon a team was working on me, stuffing tubes down my nose and into my abdomen (used to pump the stomach of everything, including air). They hooked me to an IV, which pumped morphine into my veins. They believed I had suffered a partial bowel obstruction from scar tissue from my surgery at birth. Before I went home the next day, I was told to eat low-residue food for a few days. A low-residue diet virtually has no vitamins in it and is made up of carbohydrates and sugars.

Soon after this episode, the "burn" began. It was a slow-building fire that seemed to come from somewhere deep inside my intestines. At first it didn't last for very long, but over time, this burn became a part of my deal. I lived with it like a codependent woman with an addict. I accepted the pain as part of me. I suffered a few more partial bowel obstructions, doing my best to avoid going to the hospital by finding ways to get through them. Usually once I threw up four or five times, they would subside.

However, I never resumed my fine-dining food partying; I was afraid. I began to monitor what I ate and how much I ate. One of the

> A low-residue diet virtually has no vitamins in it and is made up of carbohydrates and sugars.

doctors advised me to avoid almost all vegetables, grains, beans, and salads. So I ate tiny portions of chicken, and I was basically left with pasta and cheese.

By the time I met Lee six years later, the burn was constant. Everything I ate hurt me, and I was living on "paste." When I did eat, my food was virtually devoid of most nutrition. A friend had introduced me to a health-food product that was prepared much like cream of wheat. I lived on it. Sweet Lee married my stomachache and me. It was part of the deal.

When I was pregnant with my first daughter, I suffered a partial obstruction that landed me in Cedars-Sinai Medical Center in LA. Lee was away at The Ranch in Nashville, and I was alone. I'd thrown up at least twenty-five times and almost passed out. My neighbor called the ambulance. After many hours in the ER, I was checked into a room to face my immortality as a surgeon explained the situation to me. He told me that if I didn't undergo immediate surgery to cut away the scar tissue, I risked the possibility of a total bowel obstruction, which could kill my baby and me. (This is how I found out I was pregnant, as I didn't know before meeting the surgeon.) With the shock of this information, I was then blasted with a choice: If I underwent the surgery, I would lose my unborn baby.

I prayed.

I said no to the surgery, and once I'd made my mind up about that, an OBGYN was sent to my room to take my case. Her name was Dr. Divine.

However, it wasn't a smooth road ahead. I ended up back in the hospital soon after, once again with another partial obstruction, this time in Nashville. That was the first time I heard my daughter's heart-

> Sweet Lee married my stomachache and me. It was part of the deal.

beat. I was determined to get through the partial bowel obstruction, and we did.

When it came time to deliver Isabella, I almost didn't go to the hospital. I thought I was suffering from the flu with the usual symptoms: a headache, a stomachache, fever, and pain. Lee convinced me to roll forward with the plan, and I met Maryalice, my dear friend who was serving as my doula, at Baptist Hospital.

As the nurses were prepping me for my scheduled C-section, one of them said, "Girl, you should have gotten here sooner; your contractions are two minutes apart. You're about ready to bring this baby into the room."

This was a testament to how much pain I lived with; I didn't even notice I was having contractions. An hour later, Isabella was born, a healthy beautiful baby. We'd made it.

I left the hospital, and packed deep into my intestinal luggage, the constant burn remained. I decided to investigate. The doctor I went to see didn't think it was scar tissue causing the burning pain, so I underwent tests and began to take a pill for IBS (irritable bowel syndrome). Nothing changed. I played around with the idea of giving up gluten, dairy, and sugar, as I'd heard giving up those things could help ease digestive distress; however, I was never diligent for long periods of time. Truth is, I wasn't very good at sticking to it.

Then Lola came into our lives. Baby number two. Luckily, this time I stayed out of the hospital. The only issue I had was low iron, extremely low. I was put on intravenous iron transfusions twice a week for the last few weeks of my pregnancy. Lola rolled onto the scene a whopping 9.4 pounds with a full head of hair and wide awake. It looked like she drank all the iron!

After she was born, I underwent a few more tests. My doctor had a hard time finding out what was the cause of the burn. He thought the obstructions were the result of scar tissue but that surgery would put me at risk for more problems. I was going to have to deal.

> This was a testament to how much pain I lived with; I didn't even notice I was having contractions.

Burning in Mexico, So Back to LA

Six months into our Mexican adventure, the "burn" returned with a vengeance. I found myself almost faint from the heat; I couldn't stand the sun to touch my skin. This was strange, as I'd always loved to be outside and on the beach. Some days I couldn't get out of bed because the burn seemed to radiate from my belly button to my fingertips. I hadn't eaten a full plate of food in months. I was wasting away.

One weekend Lee was out of town, and I was home alone with the girls. My helper, Maria, had gone home for the night and would not return until Monday morning. I felt my tummy begin to "shut down," and the spasms that signify danger began to move through my back and abdomen. I got the girls into bed and climbed into mine, praying that it wouldn't be an obstruction, and tried to drift off to sleep.

At 4 a.m. I'd fallen onto the floor trying to get to Lola, who was crying in her crib. The pain was out of control, and I couldn't stand or move. I lay in a ball on the floor in the doorway talking Lola into calmness and breathing my way through the spasms. The phones were out due to a recent storm, the closest hospital was an hour and a half through the jungle, and the only hospital that could help me was five hours away in Guadalajara. The road to Guadalajara was dangerous in the daylight and a death wish in the evening as the drug cartels ruled the roads. Trying to navigate the drunken drivers made it even worse. Who would find me? Was I going to die in the jungle?

After some time, I mustered up enough strength to make it to the back bedroom with both of my babies, as Lola was eighteen months old and Bella was just five. Bella helped with snacks for Lola, and we watched movies on the computer. Twenty-four hours later, the pain stopped and I was safe, but I knew I needed to return to the States. With the phones working again, I called Lee to tell him that I'd suffered another attack, and this time it was different. I knew I'd barely made it through. Something was wrong, and it wasn't scar tissue.

I got on the phone with my doctor in LA and told him I was coming back ASAP. I needed him to schedule every test he could; I wasn't going to leave the hospital until we knew *exactly* what was going on.

> Some days I couldn't get out of bed because the burn seemed to radiate from my belly button to my fingertips.

We were in LA the following weekend, camping out at Ted and Peggy's house. The sky was full of smoke! Once again, parts of Los Angeles were burning. A year before, while living in Malibu, we had awoken to fire and smoke, soon followed by police on motorcycles who were going door to door telling the residents that we had twenty minutes to load our stuff and head out. We headed to the Loews Hotel in Santa Monica, along with most of Malibu's evacuees. We lasted only three days in that hotel because the smoke was so brutal we all had sore throats and headaches. Finally, Lee had enough, and we fled to the Ranch in Tennessee. I'd been in love with Malibu until then, but those fires were close to home and revealed the unsustainable life there. My love affair with Los Angeles had gone through a huge shift and the journey to the jungle was even more attractive, untethering me from my LA life.

I know what you all are thinking: *A love affair with that smoggy, superficial dry city?* Los Angeles is where I came into myself, found myself, and created a life of my own. However, the jungle had changed me; it fed me and grew me like one of its giant green leaves!

Upon arrival in LA, I began undergoing a series of tests. I told my gastroenterologist that I was not leaving until we knew exactly what was wrong with me. Returning to the jungle would be life threatening, and I was ready to investigate.

The worst part of the tests was the prep for the colonoscopy. For this test, you have to drink a huge gallon of nasty-flavored water that helps move all the shadoobie from your digestive tract. Even drinking a glass of water was incredibly painful, so I barely finished it. By this time, I was hardly eating or drinking at all, and those few gallons of nasty really pushed me over the edge. The doctors also decided to implant a camera inside my stomach while I was under for the colonoscopy. Since swallowing was almost impossible, placing the camera deep into my stomach was the best plan of action.

My first series of tests were to see if I had a Crohn's disease gene. Why my doctor waited ten years to test me for this gene since my momma had the disease I don't know. Either way, the test came back negative. When my blood work came back, we discovered that I was *severely* anemic.

> I wasn't going to leave the hospital until we knew *exactly* what was going on.

"Dangerous," they said. It was a sign that I was definitely hemorrhaging somewhere inside my body. The camera was going to make its way through my intestines in search of ulcerations, holes, inflammation, and hopefully not find any narrowing of my intestinal wall and get stuck.

I arrived on time for my colonoscopy with Lee as my driver. When I awoke from the anesthesia, they told me that I had so much old, undigested food in my digestive tract that they had to do the test twice! They found very little in my colon and would have to wait for the camera to come out in my shadoobie. They sent me home with a battery pack strapped to my tummy; the pack/film receiver would last up to eight hours, and then I would return to the hospital where they would be able to watch the footage. All was good until that night when the doctor's office ran the camera test. They called to say that the film revealed that the camera must have hit a narrowing halfway through me and was stuck!

> If the camera didn't find its way out, they were going to have to open me up to remove it.

OMG, I was a wreck. If the camera didn't find its way out, they were going to have to open me up to remove it. That would not be an easy surgery, especially in my condition. I started drinking mugs of warm water with lemon, which is a great way to get the pipes flushing. After two days, the doctor's office called to check in and said that it must have found its way out or I would be having big-time discomfort. Whew, I was relieved.

My next test was an MRI. I had no idea I was claustrophobic until I lay down in that bizarre machine. Good grief, it was awful! I felt like my body and my mind were at war. I tried hard to focus on my breathing and on my mother's voice. I closed my eyes and saw her standing at the head of the tube trying to distract me with memories of my childhood. The memories were encouraged by the fact that the technician chose old rock 'n' roll to blast through the headset. I felt like I'd eaten a pot brownie, half nauseous and half dizzy, trapped on a ride at the Lorain County Fair in Ohio with a funky old carnie running the ride and refusing to stop it. . . . I was tripping with every thought!

My next stop was a CAT scan in search of tumors. It wasn't bad, but it was odd having the dye shot into my veins. I remember being cold and completely worn out by all the machines.

The last day of my tests I drank another nasty drink, a barium chalky drink that moved through my intestines while I flipped from side to side under a big x-ray machine, as they searched for a narrowing. The not knowing was the worst. The doctors needed to review the eight hours of the camera tests. They hadn't found any ulceration, just a few tiny dots that seemed like they could turn into them, but that was it, leaving the doctors perplexed.

Senora Gina, who had a connection in LA, hooked me up with a doctor who came highly recommended. She said you should always have two opinions and two people looking at a puzzle from two different directions. It's more likely to solve the mystery. Since her family was highly connected in the medical world, I took her advice and made an appointment with Dr. Leo, who immediately made a spot to fit us in. He was a young fellow in his thirties, attractive and open-minded. As I sat with him, he started investigating like crazy, asking me many questions no one had ever asked me before. I felt like I was with Dr. Gregory House from the TV show, and I *knew* he was going to help me. That night he texted me twice with more questions. Then he organized different tests than my main dude had. Once again, I felt like a lab rat!

Once all the tests had been run, all we could do was wait for the results. I enjoyed catching up with Ted and Peggy when I wasn't in the hospital. Once the girls and Lee turned in for the night, I would pour out my fears all over their rug, as I had done in my early twenties. However, now my fears had shifted. I was perplexed by my health and the fear that I was going to suffer forever, as my mother had. I watched Isabella and her tiny frame and saw myself. The word "hereditary" flashed through my mind.

> I felt like I was with Dr. Gregory House from the TV show, and I knew he was going to help me.

Peggy always helped me find my way off the floor of being a victim, making sure that I went to sleep empowered in some way, by showing me that I had a choice in my reactions to what was going on in my life. Ted was the best father I could have ever had; he listened and saw my greatness. I was scared to death, and leaving my girls was my greatest fear.

Peggy had started out as my teacher in the desert. I'd attended women's workshops with my friend Gabrielle, and that's how we were first introduced. Peggy soon became the most amazing guide and adult mother I could have had. I'm certain that life played out perfectly; my momma was a great momma to the child I was, and Ted and Peggy were a gift of amazing adult parents. I became *me* on my own terms, and they have held a line without judgment. The best part of gaining adult parents is that there is no history of blame to distract from the moment; there is only now. This builds a wonderful future based on a clean present. We have spent every holiday, birth, and preschool moment together. Bella and Lola know them as their grandparents and my family. Being with them while going through so many medical tests was a great gift of support.

I enjoyed being in LA, but I couldn't wait to return to the jungle. I hoped that the doctors could give me some drug that would ease my troubles and our journey would get back underway.

> I became *me* on my own terms, and they have held a line without judgment.

Bodies and Souls

After two weeks in Los Angeles, the doctors still did not have a full diagnosis. They knew that my small bowel was swollen, and according to them, the only way to bring the inflammation down was with a series of medications. The CAT scan didn't show the aortic syndrome* that had appeared a few years earlier, which was great news.

We were still uncertain about what was causing the severe anemia. I returned to the hematologist who I'd worked with during my preg-

---

* Before becoming pregnant with Lola, my doctor had run tests and believed that I suffered from superior mesenteric artery (SMA) syndrome. This is a very rare, life-threatening gastrovascular disorder characterized by a compression of the third portion of the duodenum (the connector of the stomach and small intestines) by the abdominal aorta (AA) and the overlying superior mesenteric artery. This syndrome has a high mortality rate; one out of three people die as a result.

nancy with Lola. He was freaked by my lack of iron and immediately ordered a series of transfusions.

It's always eye-opening to spend time in the chemo-infusion center waiting room. Watching how many people have cancer, I sat and imagined their lives, their families at home, and who they were. Cancer does not discriminate. On one particular day, an old, sweet woman sat with tears in her eyes; she was frightened of what was to come. She told me that she had been diagnosed with ovarian cancer. Seeing her as a mirror of my poppy, who was at the Mayo Clinic undergoing lung surgery to remove cancer, I held her hand and told her to imagine a red heart in front of her, which is what the Hopi Indians do whenever they are scared. The heart represents love, and when we switch our mind from thoughts of fear to thoughts of love, the outcome is positive. I held back tears of compassion, and I thanked God for every day I was here.

The hematologist decided to jack up the type of iron I had taken before because he wanted to get as much in my body as possible. He warned me that I could be allergic. The craziest thing was that once he said it, I *knew* I was allergic. Not wanting to seem crazy, I went ahead with the plan. The nurse sat me down in my "chemo" chair and gave me more tips on what to do if I should feel anything strange. Hearing my inside voice once again, I picked up my cell phone and called Peggy, wanting to ask her to come. No one answered. I tried Lee's phone. No one answered. Then, I tried Ted in the office. No answer.

The IV drip began, and within less than four minutes I felt hot, flushed, and stopped breathing. I could not get air. I'd had asthma as a child so I understood the tightening of the chest, but this was different. There was NO AIR IN THE ROOM. Then came *severe* pain in my back. I've never stopped breathing before, and it was the worst, most frightening thing I have ever experienced in my life. Within seconds there were ten people surrounding me. Oxygen and antihistamine were plunged into my IV and ass. I could hear the nurses talking to me, but all I could think about were my girls, Lee, Ted, and Peggy. I had gone into anaphylactic shock.

Slowly the pain in my back lessened and I began to breath, but the shaking from the antihistamine was intense. Lee finally appeared. Poor guy, he was worn to the bone with my illness, doctor appointments,

> The heart represents love, and when we switch our mind from thoughts of fear to thoughts of love, the outcome is positive.

and being cooped up in someone else's house. My fear of death had found its way into his mind, and the two of us were clinging to hope.

During this fast and frightening moment, I had some kind of ultra-aware moment. There I was, fighting for air, scared to death, wanting to scream from the pain in my back, and all I could do was see my own soul for the first time. I literally saw all the lives inside of my body and how desperately they wanted out! I could see the panic of my deepest self, squirming and clawing to escape. While this was occurring, the medical team, trying to keep my heart pumping and lungs breathing, was kind and gentle. They were talking to my physical body, my soul, and us . . .

> I had faced my greatest fear and arrived on the other side of the mountain.

"This will pass, stay calm, we are here, and you are going to feel better soon."

I could feel warm, sweet hands on me, and someone telling me to breathe slowly. As my lungs reopened, I felt my body and soul realign and work together.

When I returned to Peggy's and saw the girls, my heart broke. I had faced my greatest fear and arrived on the other side of the mountain. I felt like a part of me died that day, the part of me that had any doubt that we are greater than our bodies. The following day I returned to the "chemo" ward to attempt another type of iron, and as I sat in my seat, I felt fear when the drip started. But this time I was fine and remembered my own advice, look for the RED HEARTS!

My regular doctor said he thought that I'd created major inflammation in my small intestines by taking too much ibuprofen, as I suffered upwards of 3 headaches a week. The camera revealed very little. It was decided that I should take steroids for a while to help with any inflammation that might have been causing my digestive distress. Dr. Leo was still doing research, and he sent me back to the jungle with a promise to keep in touch; he was not giving up. There was nothing the doctors could do except wait and see how I responded to the steroids.

Arriving in the jungle, the warm, humid air immediately wrapped her arms around us. We released the deep breaths we'd been holding for more than two weeks. Senora Gina prepared a meal of loving food, and we inhaled it and then climbed into bed by 7 p.m. The sound of the ocean rocked us to sleep, and dreams flooded my mind. Once again, I found my place within the veil. I was home.

Two weeks after returning from Los Angeles, I was back at work in my little office. I still did not feel well, and the burning continued. One night I hit the floor. I could barely swallow water, and those horse pills the doctors had given me were the majority of what I'd been feeding my body each day. They had to have something to do with it.

Senora Gina made an appointment for me with one of the leading gastro doctors in all of Latin America, who was working in Guadalajara but was originally from Italy. We loaded the Mexi-Rig and headed out. This doctor had worked at the Cleveland Clinic and thought I had Crohn's disease. He explained that in Mexico they were experimenting with stem cells and that I could possibly be a candidate. However, the process to undergo this procedure was brutal. It would involve completely wiping out my immune system, then keeping me isolated like the Boy in the Plastic Bubble. The procedure would last six months, and it could kill me. That was not an option.

One afternoon I sat in my tiny office in town writing when I got a call on my cell phone from the States. It was Dr. Leo; he asked if I was sitting down. He told me that he had attended a conference for intestinal disorders and saw a slide of a really bad ulceration that consumed the total circumference of the intestinal wall. When he checked the patient's name, it was mine! My main doctor had missed it on the camera roll. I had a HUGE gaping hole deep in my ileum, the final section of my small intestine. I was hemorrhaging.

Dr. Leo told me that I needed to return to Los Angeles pronto. He wanted to try a new procedure called a "double balloon" in which they would inflate my intestine and take a biopsy. He said that the ulceration had a fifty percent chance of being cancerous or Crohn's. I was sitting alone in my groovy office in the jungle, and I hung up the phone and sobbed. All I could think about was my momma and how I'd done everything in my power to create a different outcome for my life. I'd focused on making different choices, and yet here I was about to walk in her shoes.

> The procedure would last six months, and it could kill me.

I heard that familiar voice—my God voice—whisper inside of my head: *Your outcome is your own; it will be up to you. You decide whom you will choose to become with this and whose shoes you will walk in.*

Dancing with Destiny in Nashville

We had been living in Sayulita, Mexico, full time for a solid year when we closed up our little casa and packed up our suitcases to board a plane for Nashville. On December 13, 2008, around 10 p.m., we arrived at the Ranch in Tennessee, slightly culture and climate shocked. It had been seven years since I spent any real time in winter. I usually only returned to the Ranch in late March along with the warmth and green of Southern Spring.

Bella summed it up best when she woke up the morning after we arrived, looked out her window, and said, "Momma, hurry up, come here and look out my windows. Something is wrong with the trees. They are sad and skinny without leaves. Are they sick?"

She'd never seen naked winter trees. Moving between the worlds is tough, and it's not the climate that changed. Lola wept for HOME every night, the beach, and Maria, and it made me wonder, *Where exactly is our home?*

Hearing Dr. Leo in my mind, I felt the urgency of his words: "You must get to a doctor soon. I will arrange a connection for you with someone in Nashville."

Ted and Peggy had moved from their house of thirty-three years. They headed north to the Bay Area to be close to Ted's family and to escape the congestion of Los Angeles. We were uncertain of how long I would need to be under medical care, and Lee thought it was best if we went where the girls had their belongings and he could run the Ranch and treatment center. I sat at the window wondering what was next, and as I prepared breakfast in my double-wide kitchen, I found myself searching for my ant friends who had covered my kitchen in the jungle. I missed the jungle immediately.

I found myself searching for my ant friends who had covered my kitchen in the jungle.

I soothed the girls' worries by reminding them of our plan: We would spend the Christmas holiday at our ranch house, and I would meet with doctors at the medical center in Nashville. Hopefully those doctors could perform the double-balloon procedure and decide whether to operate or give me medication to cope with the condition. Healing my body any other way seemed out of the question. A pill seemed way easier for me; all I had to do was take them, and then I could return to eating what I loved.

I'd thought I'd feel a great sense of relief being so close to doctors who could help me if I went down. However, the transition of going from Sayulita to Nashville was downright shocking. It was one thousand times more difficult than moving to the jungle. The gray sky and icy rain kept the girls locked up in the house, and Lee couldn't seem to let go of his love affair with the ocean and the strong waves that had rocked all of us to sleep. Speaking of sleep, none of us had slept since returning to the still world of a landlocked life.

Being that we were living in Mexico and had barely returned to Nashville in over a year, the treatment center had been using our double-wide as a group meeting place a few days a week. Clients processed their crack-smokin' days and heartbreak that led to these crazy moments in their life on my sofa and left the energetic mess behind on the rug. The combination of shifting worlds and chaotic energy had us dreaming dark and heavy.

When Lee and I were first married he was living in what is called the Lake House, a beautiful custom-designed house on the Ranch full of floor-to-ceiling windows overlooking a small lake where all of our newly born foals and mare mommas resided. The double-wide offered me such freedom when we first moved out of the Lake House. It felt like a free pass into a world that was *Mee and Lee*—not his history or his family's. His momma didn't decorate the double-wide. We did.

I've always been someone who prefers small spaces to live in; I like feeling connected to my tribe. But now with the cold weather keeping us inside, I felt trapped, and the plastic sinks had lost their novelty. Lola would tell anyone who would listen at least four times a day, "I wanna go home!" I had even heard her whisper to Bella while they were playing, "Let's go home, Bella." Like the two of them could grab their bags and *adios!*

> I was back in the medical cycle, visiting with doctors who lined up different prescriptions to treat what I "possibly" had.

I understood it was eleven degrees outside the first morning I pulled away from the double-wide in my Porsche. Lee had her shipped across the country from Los Angeles where we had her in storage; her attitude was as shitty as Lola's about being dumped into bitter weather.

I was headed to my new hangout, the oncology ward at St. Thomas Hospital. I was to go there every couple of days for iron transfusions. In the transfusion center were seats full of folks receiving their chemo treatments. They were a friendly bunch, but the underlying feeling of gray swarmed the walls at times. By "gray" I mean the in-between area, not knowing what's next or what it all has meant.

I was back in the medical cycle, visiting with doctors who lined up different prescriptions to treat what I "possibly" had. Thoughts of cancer in my intestines weighed on my mind, and my only social interactions occurred in this chemo ward. I listened to the horribly sad tales of young men and women trying to beat death. I kept asking myself, *Why are we all so sick?*

I hooked up with a great hematologist, although "great" does not include the horrendous rectal exam he gave me during my first appointment. I liked him; he read a lot and shared the books he'd been reading with me. I began to ask him questions about his clients: Who were they? Where did they come from? What was their social class? Were they educated? Did they have life patterns?

According to the hematologist, "The majority of my cancer patients come from rural areas and farms." The doctor explained that many years ago high levels of smoked meats resulted in higher incidences of stomach cancer. Now, however, he was witnessing purely chemical driven cases of cancer from exposure to pesticides, fake foods, and thousands of assorted chemicals.

Most farming land is covered with some type of pesticide that can affect the well water people drink. Chemicals and dusting powders blow with the wind and affect others living nearby, flooding their drinking water and wells too. Even city tap water is suspect because water-cleaning centers don't know how to rid the water of the invisible pharmaceuticals and chemicals that are contaminating humans. These substances are being found in people's urine at higher rates than ever. An ironic relationship has developed: instead of fueling us, our food is aiding in our destruction—from mass production to consumption. If you ingest a grape covered in pesticides, the benefits and value of the natural grape fly out the window. That the medical community can argue this is just plain wrong.

> An ironic relationship has developed: instead of fueling us, our food is aiding in our destruction

Meanwhile, Dr. Leo was doing his best to get me in for the double-balloon procedure. There was only one doctor in Tennessee who performed the test. He was at Vanderbilt University Medical Center, and there was a major waiting list to get in to see him. The bad news was that I wouldn't be able to get in to see the double-balloon dude for twelve weeks.

I was glad I'd gotten an appointment because as soon as we'd arrived in Nashville, I'd gone to see another gastroenterologist at a smaller hospital, and he failed to listen to me. As I sat across from him I could tell that he had already decided what was going on with me and was going to use his recipe of cocktails. This threw me off after dealing with Dr. Leo, who had heard every word I'd said, understanding that each patient is an individual. Instead, this tiny hospital doctor handed me a prescription of drugs aimed at attacking all the "possibilities." I didn't have a full diagnosis, and already I was looking to take an array of cancer and Crohn's drugs? What if I didn't have one of these diseases? I was also not comfy with the idea of wiping out my immune system with these drugs. Didn't I need an immune system to fend for my body? How could I EVER get well without one? Wasn't autoimmune illness the imbalance of immune support and therefore flipping the crazy switch? Hmmmm . . . Here was the giant question: *How in the world was I going to swallow twenty-five pills a day when I could barely swallow water?*

> Didn't I need an immune system to fend for my body?

That night I lined all the drugs up on the countertop. As I filled a glass of water to begin my protocol, I once again heard the same whispering voice I'd heard before leaving the jungle when I wept about wearing my momma's shoes. It was God for certain. . . . "'Cause if you don't believe in being able to hear God's voice, why are you going to church and praying?" is what my poppy always said.

My God voice asked, "What's in that stuff you are fix'n to take?"

I walked over to the kitchen table, sat down in front of my laptop, and began researching what was in the drugs. I couldn't find the list of ingredients on most because of the patents on them, but I did find a ton of side effects and forums where people shared their horrific stories of what it felt like to be on these drugs. *What to do?* I put the pills back in their containers with a plan to go to the bookstore and to the library in the morning. I was about to embark on another adventure, one that would save my life.

Lee and I knew we were going to be in Nashville for a while, so we made the decision to enroll Bella in a kindergarten class in the city of Nashville, and we rented a house in town. After two weeks in our new house, I sunk into a pit of sadness. It was the dead of winter; I was alone in a giant house and sick.

I called Bill Attride, one of the top astrologists in the United States. I wanted a reading. I started the conversation by filling him in on the details of my life. I told him we were back in Nashville full time so that Lee could be closer to the Ranch to oversee operations and that I thought it was important to support him. Also, in Nashville, I could get the needed medicine or surgery for my intestines.

Bill started to giggle and said, "I hate to break it to you, but you are not there to support Lee. Your family is there to support *you*. Nashville is your place of dharma. Also known as your destiny, this is where one finds their purpose and life's work. You will only form poignant relationships [there]."

I felt as if the room was spinning. *How in the hell could my place of destiny be in Nashville?* It was cold and dreary and lonely. Shouldn't my place of destiny be where I have a world packed with close friends, sunny skies, and the ocean? Clearly, he was wrong.

Maryalice (my doula with the birth of Isabella and my dear friend) lived a few minutes from our house in town, and we picked up right where we'd left off. Maryalice's body-alignment practice in Nashville was still going strong, and she was even more of a wizard than when I'd last seen her. A body connected with the spirit does its best work. The work it is meant to do. In other words, she helps people get out of their own way so they can hear God/spirit and trust the messages that are specific to them. She doesn't speak for God; she only guides/counsels people through their blockages—both emotional and energetic.

> A body connected with the spirit does its best work. The work it is meant to do.

Maryalice, the great connector, introduced me to three of my life's greatest teachers: Gil Ben Ami, whose name means Happy Son of My People, Virginia (Ginny) Harper, and Dr. Sheng.

The first was Ginny Harper. When I'd told Maryalice all about my health situation, which she had known about since my pregnancy with Isabella, Ginny Harper came to her mind immediately. She'd had a client whose son had suffered for many years from Crohn's disease. He'd been diagnosed as a child. Finally, at fourteen years old, he met Ginny Harper. She guided him with healing foods and shifted his diet. By his high school graduation, he'd returned to Vanderbilt University Medical Center for a colonoscopy, and they found his intestines to be one hundred percent healthy.

I called and spoke with her assistant, and soon I met with Ginny Harper, who was hosting a cooking class. Ginny had been diagnosed with Crohn's disease nearly thirty years earlier, around the same time my mother was sick. Her story was horrifying because, at the time, the methods for healing were brutal, although today's standards have sadly not improved much. I clearly remember the day I drove to Ginny's center: it was raining, my tummy was burning, and I wondered what in the world I was doing. However, when I walked in, my mouth dropped at a clear sign that I was in the right place.

When I married Lee and did a redecoration of our bedroom in the Lake House, I found a large roll of amazing fabric that Lee's mother had bought in Aruba. I dropped two old, tired wingback chairs at a shop to reupholster them. When we returned to pick them up, the shop was closed because the owner had gotten sick. But there, in the corner of Ginny's clinic, sat my chairs from seven years earlier, covered in my mother-in-law's unique vibrant Caribbean embroidered fabric. I took this as a sign. I had a place to sit at this table.

Ginny was already cooking by the time I'd arrived. There were at least thirty people seated—women, men, and children of all ages. Each shared stories about what they had experienced and how they healed not only from digestive disease but also from a variety of illnesses, including diabetes and breast cancer, under Ginny's guidance for following a macrobiotic diet. Some of them had been so sick they were forced to use wheelchairs because the pain in their legs was too intense to stand. Some of these folks had suffered from different forms of cancer. However, everyone there had fantastic success stories. I also met the woman Maryalice told me about, and she shared her son's story with the rest of the room. He'd been diagnosed with severe Crohn's disease in eighth grade, and they initially went the medical route. That only led to more suffering from the horrible side effects of the drugs. Then they'd found Ginny, and immediately began Ginny's process of changing his diet and going back to the roots of food. As a result, the entire family's lives changed for the better, especially his.

My mind spun in circles as I watched Ginny prepare miso soup for the first time. How could I ever do this? I didn't know what half the

> I took this as a sign. I had a place to sit at this table.

ingredients were, let alone what to do with them when I found them! I pushed back my insecurities about cooking and struggled to be present, not allowing fear to run all over me.

The cooking lesson lasted an hour, and then we all gathered in a circle and ate. I was so hungry and thrilled to know that the food I was eating wasn't going to hurt me. I GRUBBED! Everyone left, and I sat quietly while Ginny poured through my medical records, looked at my tongue, and felt my pulse. I kept thinking how similar she was to my momma: they had both been sick in the eighties and experienced the same horrific medical path. Ginny and my momma share the same tiny frame and similar features as both were of Latin descent.

I felt an overwhelming amount of emotion wrap around me, and I knew my mother had guided me to that moment. I was on my own path and wearing my own shoes, not hers. Ginny and I discussed my medical records, and she explained what I needed to eat and how often. I had *never* heard of most of these foods nor knew where to get them or why I needed to eat them for that matter, but she had gotten well and helped others so I trusted her. I told her that my double-balloon test was scheduled for May. Ginny explained the danger of this procedure; it could cause my inflamed, swollen intestines to rupture, which the doctors had told me was a possibility. Expanding them would definitely cause more damage. It didn't take a doctor or food specialist to understand that much.

I also understood the fear of cancer that weighed on my mind—"The Big C" lingered. Dr. Leo's words, "There is a strong possibility, I'd say a fifty percent chance of you having intestinal cancer; the ulceration is huge and you've had it a very long time, at least ten years. Crohn's ulcerations that have been left for this long lead to cancer."

The only way I could find out if I had intestinal cancer or Crohn's was to undergo the double-balloon procedure so that the doctors could biopsy the tissue.

When I explained to Ginny that there was a possibility I had intestinal cancer, she looked deep into my eyes and asked, "Well, if you did, would you treat it any differently?"

I reacted immediately. "I have little girls, and I can't mess around with this food thing and die!"

> I was so hungry and thrilled to know that the food I was eating wasn't going to hurt me.

Ginny looked right at me and asked again, "If you do have cancer, would you treat it any differently?"

I was spinning and defensive. "Yes, for sure. I've got to do everything in my power to survive. I've got two little babies. They need me."

Ginny calmly asked me again, "But would you still do this diet?"

From my heart, I responded, "Yes."

If I have cancer or any other awful illness and do go the route of medicine, I *knew* that I would still need to do *my* part and support my body with REAL food.

"Good," she said. "Now you can really give this process a shot, see how you feel in a few weeks, and then you can revisit the double-balloon test idea."

It was as if God were giving his food a shot by my not being able to get in for the procedure for three more months, allowing me this time to get on the "good food foot."

As I was leaving, I glanced across the room and spotted what looked like a book I'd found on the Internet when I was living in Mexico. Life in the jungle is free of mailmen; I'd not been able to order it. When we returned to the States, I'd forgotten the title and believed the author to be living somewhere in Maine. I walked over and picked it up. Holy cow! It was the book, and Ginny was its author. She didn't live in Maine but spent half the year in Spain, serving as the director of digestive disorders for the SHA Wellness Clinic.

I left Ginny's center with a menu of what I was to eat and when. I only heard a quarter of what she said; I felt as if I was in a cloud of *What the hell do I do next?* I was overwhelmed yet excited that there was a path for me to follow, but completely intimidated by the fact that I didn't have a clue about what to do, how to cook, or where to find the majority of the ingredients. What I did hear was to start with miso soup twice a day and umeboshi twig kuzu tea.

I'm not someone that you can say, *Eat this, don't eat this.* I need to *understand* why. Ginny had told me to avoid three main things: DAIRY, WHEAT, and SUGAR. These ingredients were the staples of my meal supply and giving them up was gonna take some serious reckoning. Again she left out the WHY. When someone is changing his or her entire lifestyle, the WHY is a big deal. She knew why, but with all of

> I knew that I would still need to do my part and support my body with REAL food.

the information she shared, breaking down the WHY was a lot for one sitting, or maybe she assumed I knew. I left her house, stepped into the rainy day on a mission: how to cook the food on the menu and why to eat it.

Upon my arrival home, Lee asked a million questions that I didn't have the answers to. I called Maryalice, sharing my feelings of being overwhelmed. She calmed me down.

"Meme, it's one step at a time. Go to Whole Foods and ask a worker there to shop with you. Start Googling and order some cookbooks."

I hung up the phone and hunted "macrobiotics" on the Internet like a crazy lady. I found very little and what I did find seemed over my head or the info was available only via paid counseling. I was SERIOUSLY INTIMIDATED.

The following day I went to Whole Foods and the bookstore. Whole Foods was great. Someone helped me out, and I left the store with a bunch of items to start my new life. The bookstore was less helpful. When I asked for books on cooking with whole ingredients and sea veggies, the lady looked at me as if I were speaking Chinese. Like when I was eighteen, after my momma died, and I was left with twenty dollars to start my life with, here I was clinging to a metaphoric twenty-dollar bill once again, building the foundation of my future. Life was asking me to go back to the basics and build my way up through poignant relationships and a city destined to guide me.

Putting the Puzzle Together

I was on my own. Ginny Harper had led me to the idea that food could heal me, and she gave me a menu, but it was up to me to put the puzzle together. I'm not someone who is comfortable with leaning on others, so I had to find a way to stand on my own two feet in my very own kitchen. Learning about these new foods—from what they looked like and where to get them—was incredibly important. I started at Whole Foods, Trader Joes, and my local markets. Anything I couldn't find in a store, I found online.

The first few months were a training ground, and I did a lot of things wrong. My taste buds were accustomed to so much over-flavored fake food that I fought cheating and adding in crap, chips, French fries, cookies, and occasionally a fish sandwich from McDonalds. I often failed to bring everything on the list into my kitchen and my body, because I was overwhelmed with pain. I was still healing, and fear of my sickness could catch me up in a debilitating spin cycle of doubt; however, even doing the minimum on this diet helped my body begin to heal!

I started with miso soup, umeboshi twig kuzu tea, and brown rice mixed with cooked veggies and aduki (aka adzuki) beans. At times, this food was run through a food mill to aid in digestion. We ate this for months. *We* meaning my husband, my kids, and my dear friend Mary-alice, who cheered me on and supported the process. Lee and Mary-alice "raved" about my newfound cooking abilities, inspiring me to move forward. I didn't have the energy to cook two different meals (one for me and one for them), and I didn't need the food temptation either. Plus, if my mother and I were susceptible to this illness, so were my girls. Our new way of life was about both healing and prevention.

I searched for new recipes and danced with different flavors. I first learned what flavors complemented one another. Once I figured this out, I learned how much of each was necessary. Most of my food for the first six months looked like rice bowls that had been overcooked, but I didn't care. I was finally able to eat, and after fourteen years of being hungry and suffering when I did eat, I loved every bite I cooked.

> The first few months were a training ground, and I did a lot of things wrong.

It's not only about cleaning the body but about strengthening the digestive track in the same way one builds an old out-of-work muscle. I'd NEVER eaten REAL food packed with fiber and nutrition before. My digestive muscle was hitting the gym!

I checked in with Ginny every couple of weeks and attended a grand total of two cooking lessons. The truth was it came down to me. If I wanted to get better, I had to learn to cook the food, find the time, and take my life back into my own hands, one meal at a time. I watched cooking shows on TV to learn little tricks, how to chop properly, and different techniques, but I was amazed to see how little REAL foods most of the chefs on the shows cooked. I was in search of learning about *real* whole grains (not processed grain products that use whole grains) and beans. I wanted to know what food did in the body, not only what vitamins were found in them. I was forming a *relationship* with my food and my body.

> I was forming a relationship with my food and my body.

In the beginning, the constant burn was still with me and I was super sick. I found the entire process of this new way of eating and cooking overwhelming. Through a momma at Bella's school, I met a lady who had healed her body with food eight years before with the guidance of Ginny Harper. She had a blood disease that was treated medically with chemotherapy without guarantee of cure. She had learned to cook with Ginny's help, and within a few years, had a miraculous shift in health and had no trace of illness for eight years. I immediately contacted her.

The woman came to my house for tea and shared her journey. She was a pleasant person and very Southern in her mannerisms. Her eyes were very clear, but she had a severe case of rosacea, a skin disorder related to inflammation. I remember this hooking my questioning mind, *Why, if someone had been living so clean for eight years, would she still suffer from severe rosacea?* Either way, her shiny eyes and big white-toothed smile hooked me. I saw her love of grinning as a good sign.

She was looking for part-time work and thought it would be great to cook for me a few days a week. I jumped at the opportunity, and Lee wanted me to feel better and thought that if someone with experience could help us out it was worth the money. My food was the out-of-network prescription we were paying for monthly.

I loved having enough food dropped off to last two days, and every delivery, I was introduced to new foods and different ways of preparation. The woman who cooked for me introduced two dishes that I had not been preparing: collard greens and burdock root made with carrots and onions known as kinpira. Both of these dishes are blood supporters. Once I began to eat these foods on a regular basis, I began to crave them. I also turned a corner. I had more energy and felt better.

All was well as I began to expand with the food support. However, after a few weeks, I had tremendous gas pressure, which I'd never experienced before. I felt as if the gas was ripping through me. I spoke to my cook, and I reminded her that when one has a digestive disease the manner in which the food is prepared is very important. Beans must be soaked, and grains, tofu, and tempeh (a meat substitute made from fermented soybeans) must be steamed before cooking. She assured me she was preparing my meals this way.

Around the eighth week of this arrangement, Lee and I loaded the kids up along with my cook, and we all headed to Mexico. Lee was leading a journey through Teotihuacán and Senora Gina was going to join us there.

The next morning we left my house at 4 a.m. . As we pulled away from my house, the cook was weepy and emotional. I knew that Teotihuacán was pulling on her. It is a place of personal power. If any type of emotional crisis is going on, Teotihuacán can serve as a giant magnifying mirror for all to see—most importantly, demanding that the individual see himself or herself.

Our first flight to Atlanta was the longest hour ever. The cook cried the entire way. I had to keep telling the girls that she was fine and was just remembering sad events in her life. Actually, she was going through a tough divorce and her husband had kept the kids. She was forty-three years old, and her world had come crashing down. I felt great compassion, but I needed some boundaries. My body was so very weak, and the burn in my abdomen was constant. I was doing all I

> Once I began to eat these foods on a regular basis, I began to crave them.

could to keep it together physically and tend to my two small girls in the airport and on the plane.

We had a two-hour layover in Atlanta, and the cook busted out breakfast. It was millet porridge with dried cranberries, which I had specifically asked her not to make because it wouldn't travel well. On top of that, she wanted to share it with me from the same container! I reminded her that I must be very mindful of what I put into my body, as healing the digestive tract bacteria and a weakened immune system requires paying attention to bacteria from other people too. Plus, I reminded her that she had a ton of emotion that day, and I truly believe that our emotions are a part of our body, mixing in with our saliva and affecting everything we touch. I ate something else.

When we landed in Mexico City, I found myself racing to see Senora Gina. I felt as if I were going to burst through customs. There she was, standing in an elegantly tailored raincoat and lovely black leather loafers with her makeup tastefully applied. I clung to her with the same tenacity as a young child who'd been separated from her momma. Quickly, Senora Gina seemed to swoop my girls and me up, leaving Lee in the background (he had arrived in Mexico City a week earlier). Having Senora Gina in front of me, I felt as if I were standing before a clear channel. My eyes drifted toward my cook as I prepared to introduce her to Senora Gina. I gazed upon her with a new perspective. Man, I hadn't been seeing clearly in Nashville at all.

Mexico City was in the midst of a giant flood. The streets were full of water, and sewage had spilled everywhere. The ride from Mexico City to Teotihuacán went from its usual one-hour-long ride to a four-hour journey. Luckily, Senora Gina and Maryalice (as she had flown into Mexico City by another airline to join us) kept the girls and me giggling. I was starving, but eating that nasty old porridge wasn't gonna happen!

The next few days, my cook became immersed in the journey with the others. I had wondered if she was going to offer to cook at all, which was supposed to be our arrangement. Each afternoon she returned from the ruins exhausted. The ladies in the kitchen of our Dreaming House Hotel were master chefs; they cooked *only* ancestral foods, and they would rather soon die than open a can of anything or

> I reminded her that I must be very mindful of what I put into my body . . .

a box of something. I explained to them the way I ate and my condition. They said not to worry; they could handle cooking for me and set to creating a menu. Soaked beans, a smoothie with fresh aloe, teas with herbs to support digestion, steamed and sautéed veggies, homemade corn tortillas, and fresh fruit—mainly papaya as it contains digestive-enhancing enzymes that help to break food down. (I only eat small portions of papaya because I watch my sugar intake.)

After a few days of eating Mexican ancestral cooking, I could begin to understand what Carolyn Ross, MD, MPH, had meant when I explained my diet to her: that I shouldn't just rely on certain foods to heal my body.

Dr. Ross and I had first met in Teotihuacán three years earlier. She'd come on one of Lee's journeys, and we'd clicked immediately. We remained great friends, and when I moved to Nashville, she had taken a job at the Ranch as a consultant with the eating-disorders program.

Dr. Ross is a trained medical doctor. She also trained under Andrew Weil, MD, through his integrative medicine program at the University of Arizona. Dr. Ross ran her own women's clinic in Tucson, Arizona, and has an expansive perspective when she sits with patients. When she'd come to Nashville for consulting and would visit me for dinner, I'd work out my recipes and she'd cheer me on. Plus, she kept an eye on me medically. If I had any questions, I'd save 'em up for her visit.

Dr. Ross continued to bring to my attention that healthy eating is about eating real food, like our ancestors did. Her support kept me from getting too rigid with the macrobiotic diet that Ginny Harper was trained in. She kept my sights on the total potential of *all* original foods and their healing abilities. Healing our bodies with food isn't something "new." It's old school. Most cultures don't and didn't have access to many of the particular ingredients on the macrobiotic diet, and people still got well. She also told me that moderation of REAL foods is important too, like avoiding tomatoes if my pH was out of balance or if my body felt acidic. Balance was key.

Being in Mexico and eating the ancestral food, I now understood Dr. Ross's point of view BIG time. All cultures minus ours still have a relationship with their food. I was on a kick now, y'all. I wanted to study

> Healing our bodies with food isn't something "new." It's old school.

cultures, cancer incidences, and global disease statistics to find the food connection! One more very important piece of my journey to Teotihuacán—the place that teaches through energy—was to mind *who* was handling my food.

I'd fallen into an authentic world with Senora Gina, my dear friend Emily who lives at the Dreaming House, and Maryalice, while my cook jumped knee-deep into the Teotihuacán experience. I watched from a distance as all of her masks crumbled away.

I also watched as she smoked cigarettes. Oh, man, I couldn't believe it! How could someone be macrobiotic, survive a terminal illness, and still puff on a nasty cancer stick? This was hypocritical, and now I understood why I was having so much gas. She was cooking my food with a mind full of unresolved thoughts and taking smoke breaks between handling my food. Smoking cigarettes means one is handling toxic sticks all day, and you can't wash this toxicity off. Our food is not only the ingredients we chop and peel, but also the feelings of the chef who is preparing it.

Two of the women in the kitchen also serve as the town's curanderas. Curanderas are the medicine women of Mexican villages. They aid the villagers in staying well emotionally, energetically, and physically with local herbs and remedies. Yep, ancestral folk are aware of energy/feelings and how they affect one another. This is nothing *new* age.

Yolanda, the main cook, pulled me aside two days before we were leaving and said that I needed to pay better attention to who I was allowing to handle my food. She thought that my cook was not the best choice for support, as her negative situation was sabotaging my progress, although not intentionally. I heard her, not only about my cook, but also when it came to eating in restaurants where the vibe is negative and the staff is underpaid and disgruntled. Fast food restaurants are notorious for negative energy. How many times have you ordered something and you suspected that the people working there would spit in your food if you pissed 'em off?

I also thought about eating animals that are mass produced and sold to feedlots where they are piled on top of each other and slaughtered in awful ways. If we are what we eat, then, dang shawty, I needed to pay attention to what I was eating!

> Our food is not only the ingredients we chop and peel, but also the feelings of the chef who is preparing it.

On the last day in Teotihuacán, I told my cook that I didn't need her help anymore. I felt I needed to take back my kitchen and really get it together for myself. Suddenly, she lashed out at me. All of her unresolved anger came out and I saw the big old gas bubble that had been moving from her claws to my intestines through the food I'd been eating. I did my best to let her anger roll off of my back, but I got a little bit of spice to me, and when someone sprinkles me with chili, I sho'do kick back!

I felt awful that I bit back and didn't hold an aerial point of view. But, hey, I'm heavily flawed, too. I flew home more determined than ever to learn what I didn't know, once again taking back my kitchen and feeling gratitude that my former cook had empowered me to do so.

My Spirit's Resilience

After eight months, my new way of eating—as minimally as I was doing it—helped me stabilize my body and clear my mind. As I simplified my foods, a door opened that allowed me to look at the other parts of me that were affecting my health and immune system. I'd heard many times over that when our emotional selves are exhausted, our immune system is directly affected. This is when a cold or flu attacks. Long periods of time of being emotionally worn-out taxes our immune system in a giant way, opening a door that lets in many major diseases—from cancer and heart disease to autoimmune disorders.

A few years before I knew just how sick I was, I'd attended a workshop in Charleston, South Carolina, led by an amazing woman: Dr. Joan Borysenko. I'd first met her over dinner with Lee and our good friend Gary Seidler. (Gary is a dear friend of ours and a fantastic man who owned a publishing house that specialized in health-related titles.) The moment I sat down across from Joan I knew she was one of the brightest women I had ever met and that she was going to teach me many, many things. I felt like a little sponge soaking up every word that fell from her mouth.

> The moment I sat down across from Joan I knew she was one of the brightest women I had ever met and that she was going to teach me many, many things.

Dr. Borysenko earned her doctorate in Medical Sciences from Harvard Medical School, where she completed postdoctoral training in cancer cell biology. Her first faculty position was at Tufts University School of Medicine in Boston. But after the death of her father from cancer, she became more interested in the person with the illness than in the disease itself, and she returned to Harvard Medical School to complete a second postdoctoral fellowship, this time in the new field of behavioral medicine. Under the tutelage of Herbert Benson, MD, who first identified the relaxation response and brought meditation into medicine, she was awarded a Medical Foundation Fellowship and completed her third postdoctoral fellowship in psychoneuroimmunology. What she is known for, in a nutshell, is being one of the first cellular biologists to study the effects of faith on cancer cells.

As I listened to Dr. Borysenko, I heard her detail her experience with cancer. She believes that cancer is part genetic, part emotional/stress, and hugely environmental. I was sitting in an old church turned into gathering center in the old part of Charleston when I heard this last part: emotions and stress affect our cells.

Four years later I started to read Joan's books, particularly *Minding the Body, Mending the Mind.* I was going to have to look at myself from a new perspective, one that got my mind right. I also called Joan, and our bond solidified. I'd met her for good reason. Like Dr. Carolyn Ross, Dr. Joan Borysenko joined my team, encouraging me and agreeing that this is a lifestyle change that I would need to implement for the rest of my life. Like Dr. Ross, she reminded me that I must be careful not to cling tightly to a specific regimen and to remain expansive in my food point of view, eating organically as often as possible, including all animal foods. I also switched all of my cleaning supplies and shampoos to be as "go green" as possible.

> I was packing all of my worries, sorrows, anger, and frustration deep into my body's root— the intestines.

I soon saw that I was an intense person, holding tight to life. I was packing all of my worries, sorrows, anger, and frustration deep into my body's root—the intestines. In Chinese medicine all of the body's organs are broken down into couples. The intestines are a couple with the heart, as the intestines protect the heart. Intestinal issues are all about vulnerability. I'd fought for so long to hide mine. It was time I came undone, letting go of all that I thought needed protecting.

Joan came to Nashville to give a talk and stayed with us as our guest. I sat in the back of the Belcourt Theatre listening to her and laughing and marveling at one of my heroes. She guided the audience inspirationally, reminding them that they had a choice in their reactions to what life dealt. She shared her theory on resilience, which is explained further in her book *It's Not the End of the World: Developing Resilience in Times of Change*. Joan's idea is that our resilience is a muscle that can be developed half by genetics and half by choice. Resilient people have certain traits in common: 1) they don't wear rose-colored glasses, 2) they have a grand sense of humor, 3) they complete things, 4) they take action in times of crisis, 5) they are masters of improvisation, and 6) they go into the world and give back to their community.

I will never forget our walk home from the theatre that evening as I rattled off that I had these six traits. I clung to the idea of not only building my intestinal muscles and my body's immune system but building my spirit's resilience as well!

I was someone who lived in my head with my thoughts swirling around. However, holding on to life with a pensive grip had to stop because the body cannot receive nutrients when it is bracing itself for the worst. I'd been preparing myself for the worst since I was at least five years old, and as I grew older, it only intensified.

One day, Lee pointed out that I was clenching my fists as we rode in the car. "Look at your hands, are you in pain?" he asked.

I wasn't; it was how I held myself.

I began practicing to rest flat on my back every day for ten minutes to allow my adrenal glands to balance themselves, while letting go of the fear I'd been clinging to. I'm not a nap taker nor do I sleep in. Even when my babies were tiny, I was up at the crack of dawn cleaning and cooking before they woke up, so taking time for relaxation did not come easily for me.

I had lost nearly twenty-seven pounds in four months. I couldn't get my weight above ninety-nine pounds. Everyone was concerned about my weight, and some people were downright rude about it. I was embarrassed by my thinness and those people who stared or were rude didn't want to hear that despite my appearance my pain was dissipating and that I wasn't losing entire days to my bed. I'd cut all

> I'd been preparing myself for the worst since I was at least five years old, and as I grew older, it only intensified.

processed foods and high-fat foods out of my diet, and I was only taking in foods with nutritional value. My food had a job to do. Each bite was going to work instead of hanging out on the side. After the first four months, I introduced natural supportive oils into my diet, such as sesame, tahini (sesame butter), almond butter, avocados, coconut milk, and coconut oil. Again, there was a key component: finally I got that when I relaxed and opened myself, my body would receive love and nutrients and I began to absorb nutrition, bringing me back to a healthy weight.

> It is not about treating the symptoms, but about rebuilding the mind, spirit, and body.

Healing with food is not an overnight process. It is not about treating the symptoms, but about rebuilding the mind, spirit, and body. This process goes to the core, removing the damaging factors and knocking out the cause. Once this is complete, the rebuild begins and the time frame required depends on how sick one has been, how many drugs have been taken, and how committed they are to their wellness.

I see this way of living and eating as a complete makeover, and I'm not going back. When our mind is right, our table is right. My taste buds don't even like the old way of eating. Now, when I eat fake food, I can feel the nasty buildup on my tongue. No thanks.

Searching for Positive Results and Experiences

After twelve weeks on my new path, I went to a major Nashville hospital for my checkup to prepare for the double-balloon procedure. On the door was a sign that read: GASTROENTEROLOGIST AND PHARMACOLOGIST. While I sat in the waiting room I asked anyone who would answer how they were doing, why they were at the doctor, and what methods were working for them.

To my disbelief, almost all of them were suffering from Crohn's disease or colitis. They were on heavy pharmaceutical cocktails, and some of them had been through a number of surgeries to remove their damaged bowel sections. NONE of them were doing better.

One young man who was about eighteen years old stood out: his face was completely swollen due to a side effect (known as moon face) of the steroids he was on. He was carrying a *huge* grocery bag full of the medicines he had been taking for the past year. I was shocked. I also learned that he'd been on OxyContin (a super-addictive pain medicine) for almost a year. I asked him the ultimate question: "Well, can you eat whatever you want?" He told me he had a lot of discomfort and that the steroids interfered with his sleep and the sleeping pills made him nauseous and that he could barely eat.

> Compared to these people, I can honestly say I was feeling great!

Compared to these people, I can honestly say I was feeling great!

Before I met with the gastroenterologist, I had to first meet with a nutritionist and a psychiatrist. Finally after some time, a very large woman drinking a huge fast-food soda called my name from behind the reception desk. The nutritionist was ready for me.

The nutritionist's first questions were fairly basic: *What do you eat on a daily basis? How many calories do you take in? How much dairy do you consume? How much meat and poultry?* And so on. I started by telling her that I ate greens three times a day and that my menu consisted of green beans, broccoli, sweet potatoes, cauliflower, peas, onions, garlic, ginger, turmeric, bok choy, cabbage, carrots, okra, zucchini, squash, miso soup, and sea veggies. In addition, I explained that I ate only whole grains such as brown rice, quinoa, or millet, and that I consumed beans a couple times a week and ate fish an average of three times a week. I told her that I also sometimes ate eggs and that I cooked with coconut oil, olive oil, sesame oil, avocado oil, or ghee (clarified butter from which irritants and allergens are removed from the butter. Seriously ancestral, ghee has been commonly used in Africa, India, and the Far East for over 2,500 years and is believed to help in the healing of digestive ulcerations).

Once I finished, the nutritionist had some concerns, including my source of calcium. I explained to her that dairy creates mucus in the lining of the intestines, which covers the villi and inhibits them from grabbing nutrients in other foods. I told her that I needed to make sure my villi are free and clear to do their work. So, I eat quinoa, I explained, which has more calcium than dairy. I also told her that my greens and broccoli are full of calcium. To top it off, I explained that my blood work had indicated that I was not lacking nutritionally.

"There were *no* signs of illness or deficiencies anywhere in my blood," I told her.

"Oh," she said.

Her bigger concern, she said then, was my calorie intake. So I began breaking it down again.

Why are we more concerned with the calorie content of food than with nutrition? What would happen if restaurants and grocery stores advertised the effects of each ingredient in their foods rather than the calories in each bite? What if we found out that we have been eating fake foods that were calorie dense but nutrition poor?

I told her that if everyone approached food the way our ancestors approached it—as something to fuel the body and keep it healthy and strong—weight loss and calorie counting would be a thing of the past, 'cause we'd have nothing to lose.

Next she expressed concern over my protein consumption, so I gave it to her old-school style: "First of all, let's focus on history. As few as seventy-five years ago, manual labor was part of our culture, but around five hundred years ago, there was *only* manual labor. A thousand years ago most folks didn't have a cow, a spare chicken, or numerous species of fish to choose from. They worked longer, hotter, harder hours and consumed a tiny amount of animal protein each week. Instead, they cooked with ghee, ate eggs, and drank small portions of *organic unpasteurized or fermented* dairy. We think that we need bacon for breakfast, deli turkey for lunch, and a burger for dinner. It's WAY TOO MUCH!"

Then I reminded her that there is a lot of protein in plant, grains, beans, tofu, tempeh, fish, and eggs. I was well covered in the protein department. My protein sources were easily digestible, which meant my body could ABSORB it without worsening inflammation or acid levels, which meat sources of protein are known to do.

This lady's mouth was wide open. She wanted to know how it was possible for me to eat all of the foods that folks with digestive disorders were told to avoid. Keep in mind that gastro doctors suggest eating a

> What would happen if restaurants and grocery stores advertised the effects of each ingredient in their foods rather than the calories in each bite?

low-residue diet composed of potatoes, milkshakes, burgers, bread, and so on. These foods have almost NO nutritional value for the body: they are full of sugar and yeast, which feed the bad bacteria in the intestines. They also lack fiber, which is important for cleaning out the stagnated mucus lining in the intestines. Toss in the added fat and salt and dang, her suggestions were equivalent to the *Titanic.* With this sort of direction, folks don't have a shot at surviving.

"Well," I said, "it's a process. I started out by slowly reconditioning my body to eat the way it was designed. Our creator designed our bodies for whole grains. And when I say *whole grains,* I don't mean whole-grain bread, whole-grain pasta, snacks made with whole grains, etcetera. I mean whole grains bought in bulk and soaked overnight with kombu."

When she admitted to not knowing what kombu is, I had to explain to the nutritionist the importance of consuming the trace minerals found in sea veggies, such as kombu. I talked about how kombu breaks down the gas-causing carbohydrates in the whole grains and beans and adds to them the minerals magnesium, calcium, iron, and selenium—a major immune booster. It also contains iodine in its most natural state, which fights the effects of radiation. (We are exposed to more radiation than ever before!) Iodine is also a natural antifungal, which was prescribed long before there were chemical/pharmaceutical antifungals for sale.

I told the nutritionist that soaking grains and beans with the kombu overnight, cooking them thoroughly, and then chewing (*really* chewing) is vital to successful digestion. If we rush through our meals by standing up and eating fake food, how are we supposed to get better?

The lady asked me if I had a website so that she could learn more, and I handed her my card.

My next stop before seeing the gastroenterologist was the psychiatrist. He was an older, bizarre gentleman from Brooklyn, New York, who told me at least twenty times how important and intelligent he was. I thought he was going to ask me questions about my emotions, fears, and doubts living with a chronic illness. I was actually looking forward to this part of the day, because Lord knows, I could have used a nice couch to cry on.

I started out by slowly reconditioning my body to eat the way it was designed.

I made it as far along in my story as, "We moved here from the Mexican jungle," when he went off about his fear of snakes. He could not understand how I lived so close to snakes! He told me that he went to many seminars to get over his fear but was still a nervous wreck. The more he talked, the more jumpy he became. Then he asked me one of the only two questions he asked during the entire session: "How about you? Are you afraid of snakes?"

"Nope," I answered, and I told him a story about when the Witness, a great friend of mine who always seems to show up in my life when an opportunity for my expansion occurs, was visiting us and sat on the toilet to make her morning movement. When she turned to flush, she jumped. She had been sitting on top of a very poisonous snake, which had wrapped itself around the seat! It was staring dead at her, angry and hissing!

The psychiatrist was frozen in his chair, white as a ghost, and again asked, "You sure you aren't afraid of snakes?"

Nope.

Then he asked me the second question: "Would you be opposed to taking a series of pills that could prevent you from getting cancer, because, you know, you are a candidate for cancer."

I looked at him as though he was fo'sho off his rocker. "What are you talking about? Aren't you supposed to make me feel better? Help me cope with the struggles that I am facing? Don't inject more fear and tell me I'm gonna get cancer."

Then he went on a tangent: "Well, you people baffle me. You refuse to take these drugs that could possibly save your life."

I looked right back at him and said, "Listen, dude, I'm not gonna argue with you. I don't have cancer. I'm not gonna be your guinea pig and take some pills because if I don't have cancer now, I'll get it from your cocktail of choice. I'm not looking for a pharmacologist but an actual doctor. If I wanted to hang out with a pusher, I'd pick up the guy on the streets because at least he's gonna be straight up."

As I was walking out of the office he yelled, "Snake!"

I jumped, because who does that? His response: "I thought you weren't afraid of snakes."

I left his office shaking my head. *What was going on here?!*

> *She had been sitting on top of a very poisonous snake, which had wrapped itself around the seat!*

The fast-food receptionist told me I could see the next doctor, but an intern, who asked all the regular questions, including what my shadoobie looked like, greeted me first. I told him it was really nice, came out in one full-sized log, connected, and smooth, not skinny and S-like.

"Uh huh," he said, and then wanted to know what I ate that day.

I told him what I had for breakfast and lunch, and he responded, "Wow, does that take a lot of time to prepare?"

I said, "Yes, it does, but it's worth it; it's for my body."

He told me that neither he nor his wife cooks and most of the time they eat at restaurants or make convenience foods. When I asked him why, he responded that they work a lot and spend time doing errands, like going to Target and Costco.

"I understand, but it's about value, and we must ask ourselves what we value and what is our own value?" I responded.

By the way, he was also overweight.

FINALLY, the gastro came into the room, and again, I noticed that he was not the picture of health. He read my chart and asked me how I was doing. I told him I was fine, but he might want to look into finding a better psychiatrist. I asked about getting cancer and his response was the same, "It's always a possibility."

I explained the success of my new diet to him, but he told me I should still have the double-balloon procedure.

"Well, if I have inflammation in my intestines, and you blow it up with a balloon, won't that, number one, be dangerous, and number two, cause more irritation?"

He said yes to both, but felt that after the procedure, he would better understand my state of health. When I asked him if ulcerations could be healed, he told me that it is possible. He sees it often, he said, and they call this remission.

I explained my theory: if we only eat food devoid of nutrition, we won't get better. However, if the food we eat is full of nutrition and we eat things that heal the body, we support the immune system and aid the healing process. Adding probiotics to fight bad bacteria helps grow healthy bacteria.

"First of all," he began, "studies have not shown that any of this

> "I understand, but it's about value, and we must ask ourselves what we value and what is our own value?"

works, and while you are right about a lot of it, most people won't take on this time-intensive diet. They want a pill or a surgery, and they want to eat what they like. I'm glad this is working for you and you are taking your time and learning new things."

He handed me his card and told me that if I ever needed him he would be there. I let him know that I would not have the double-balloon procedure right away. Maybe in a couple years to prove that I was well. My only question was, "How come we aren't studying the *positive* effects that foods have on the body, instead of only spending millions on drug studies?" He had no response.

I left feeling good about my path because I knew there was no way I was ever going back there. I saw what the doctor's idea of help looked like, and I had a CHOICE. My personal nobility was on the line. I was going to have to stick this one out and give Gil Ben Ami a call . . . Happy Son of My People was the piece I was missing.

> "How come we aren't studying the *positive* effects that foods have on the body, instead of only spending millions on drug studies?"

Gil Ben Ami
(Happy Son of My People)

The first time I walked into his office two years earlier, I weighed 90 pounds, and all I could do was lay on his acupuncture table and cry. I hurt so badly. I was afraid and completely broken.

Gil Ben Ami's voice rang of immediate trust; his face was round, like a teddy bear. Before I climbed onto the table, Gil sat with me and we talked. He explained to me how acupuncture works. I had to process his words, and then take the time to figure it out.

Here is my take on it now that I've been going for years: It's like fine-tuning our electrical systems. If the passageways of our inner electricity are blocked, our natural electrical current gets backed up and causes blockages; these blockages can lead to illnesses. Acupuncture opens these blockages; when our bodies are flowing, they are in an optimal state of health. Our blood is moved throughout the body through this electrical current, much like river water flows along its path. If the water stops moving, sitting in one place for a long period of time, it gets funky, smelly, and full of disease-causing bacteria. The same happens to our blood.

I told him all I knew about my health, and he listened. I was shaking as we spoke, shivering from cold. No matter how many layers I applied, I couldn't warm up. Gil set moxi (ground mugwort herb rolled up like a tiny cigar) on my kidney points. (Moxi is used to warm up the body and release dampness by stimulating energy in the body.) Within minutes I was warm. Once the moxi was lit, Gil began to place the needles, starting at my feet and working his way up my legs and to my abdomen.

Acupuncture *does not* hurt. Sometimes there's a short pinch, but the pain stops quickly. With each needle, tears poured from my eyes. I was embarrassed because the tears were not from pain but from emotion. By the time he placed the final needle on the top of my head, I was crying without restraint. I sobbed, and Gil held my hand, speaking to me in a calm, solid tone.

I'd entered his office in a swarm of black butterflies; this cloudy darkness kept me spinning by what propelled and created it: the hook in my mind that I was going to die and leave my family as my momma had left me. My greatest fear was tapping me on my shoulder.

"Mee, you are going to be okay now; it will be a process. In six months you will turn a corner and one year from now another corner. Be patient and unravel; you didn't get this sick overnight, and you will not get one hundred percent better overnight. Many people want things to happen quickly, but with quickness, a lot is lost. Our bodies heal by allowing the energy inside to move freely. You have been holding on tight for way too long. Begin letting go here. Do not be afraid of death, none of us get out of here alive and this fear will hook your attention, keeping you from living."

With this, he placed one more needle above and between my eyes at the mythical third eye. I felt my head let go and my body drop, as I drifted deep into another world and time. I tried to open my eyes and sit up, but I couldn't. It felt as though I'd been sedated and the only way out was relaxation. I watched my mind run through lists, rants, and

> Our bodies heal by allowing the energy inside to move freely.

conversations. Finally, I stopped listening, and I was in a quiet place. Fear was one of the first themes of my sessions with the Happy Son of My People.

I'd read that acupuncture could trigger memories—even as far back as past lives. For me, I had plenty of current lifetime memories to sort through. For the next two years, Happy Son of My People would load me up with needles, and I'd settle into a deep sleep where all kinds of images of my life would pass. Like most people, my childhood was "flawed" and full of heartbreak. At eighteen years old, a series of car accidents had stolen the lives of three of my closest people—starting on New Year's Eve with my momma. Exactly a week later, my two best friends were killed instantly in another car accident. Then my grandmother died of old age a few days later. I had spent many years working out this grief and loss. The abandonment of my father at age five stung my heart, but what I'd not looked at closely was the effect my momma's illness had on me. A young child takes on a lot of responsibility and fear when their main parent is chronically ill. I'd been through so much that I never imagined how the latter impacted me.

> A young child takes on a lot of responsibility and fear when their main parent is chronically ill.

Happy Son of My People explained to me in his Kabalistic and Chinese medicine point of view: "You were wounded in your root from the very beginning. In Chinese medicine, the intestines compose the human root."

Immediately my mind took in this information and images followed. This was how I saw it: Like a tree, we receive our nourishment through our root. If a tree's roots are bad, the tree will die. From my beginning, I have been living with a wounded root. A mother not only feeds her growing baby food but also passes on thoughts, feelings, and fears, which travel through the soul cord (umbilical cord) into the intestines. Plus, a mother who herself lacks nutrition—primarily vitamin D—passes this on, too. Can you imagine a strong tree without vitamin D?

At the time of my conception, my momma was terribly saddened by my father's extramarital affairs. She'd found out that he had gotten a friend of the family pregnant. I wondered on an energetic level if this sadness that hurt my momma to her core had also punctured mine. I would spend the next two years unraveling the emotions trapped in my intestines. Could it really be true that unresolved sadness and grief

> Like Dorothy, I would find my courage, connect to my heart, and acquire knowledge.

can cause blockages in our human electrical systems? Do our burdens contribute to our illness and disease?

I left Happy Son of My People with my soul floating and less burning pain in my stomach. Each session seemed to help me improve in health.

Chinese medicine didn't treat the symptom but instead hunted for the cause and focused on rebuilding all parts of the body. I was learning about connection.

Like Dorothy, I would find my courage, connect to my heart, and acquire knowledge. Then I'd put on the ruby red slippers, and find my way through Oz, arriving in my own life, not my momma's—a life that I created by reacting to life's situations differently with a more expansive approach and outcome.

Discovering Nashville

Our first year living full time in Nashville was probably one of the hardest years of my life. Being so ill, I had a difficult time connecting. Lee traveled a great deal for work, which left me alone for what felt like long periods. Eighty percent of my days were spent in pain. Yes, I was gradually improving, but I still had tough days. On those days, I would load my two-year-old Lola and six-year-old Bella up with snack trays, and the three of us would live on my giant bed.

The cold weather was super hard on all of us. We didn't know how to "live inside" after so many years in LA and Mexico. We were all craving the feel of fresh grass under our feet. I had Maryalice, and thankfully, I'd met Marielle and her family, who had moved from Mexico City to Nashville. This commonality formed a union between all of us. We carpooled and spent many after-noons at Marielle's kitchen table discussing our life paths. I reveled in our connection.

After a year of friendship, Marielle informed me that she was going to be moving away. Her husband had taken a promotion with Nissan, and they would all move back to Mexico City by the end of the school year. She was happy to live close to her family, but sad to leave Nashville as she'd made so many friends. I was devastated. She had become my close friend and confidant. Aside from Maryalice, I'd not connected with anyone on a friendship level. Coming from Malibu and Sayulita where I'd formed lifelong relationships, for me, Nashville was a lonely place. Isabella was crushed too, as Marielle's daughter, Ines, had become her "person."

Marielle gave me a great piece of advice. She said, "Meme, get out there and discover Nashville."

I noticed there was a theme here. Since moving to Nashville and opening up my office (a converted old convent), three different assis-tants I had hired to work with me moved away. So Marielle wasn't the only one leaving me. But there was more.

> The drugs had kicked his butt, and then he met Ginny Harper and changed his life.

Ginny Harper was spending half the year in Spain; before leaving again for a seven-month stretch, she came to lunch to check on me. I was doing well, yet growing bored with my recipes. She recommended that I have Luke Williams come by a few days a week to teach me some of his recipes. I was excited by the idea 'cause Luke Williams meant a lot to me. I'd first met him a month into my new way of cooking.

Luke worked hand in hand with Ginny. One afternoon he came to my house for lunch. He was a very handsome guy in his early thirties. At one point he'd been into extreme sports—from rock climbing to wind surfing. He also owned his own green building company. The afternoon we met, Luke shared his life story—all of his travels and then his fall with sickness. He was diagnosed with colitis, ulcerations in his colon. He'd gone the medical route and couldn't get better. The drugs had kicked his butt, and then he met Ginny Harper and changed his life. When we met, he'd been cooking and healing for two and a half years. He said he had hit some rough patches on the path to getting well but that he was holding steady.

That afternoon he became the person I held in my mind's eye whenever I doubted the path I was on. If I hit a rough patch, I thought of him and knew it would pass. Luke was one of those people who brought a bright light to the room. I was super excited to have him teach me some tricks, as he completely understood my condition. I called him, and we made a plan; he was going to start working with me the first of April. I had been cooking this way for a year and a half.

One afternoon just before Luke was to start cooking with me, I was on Facebook when I saw a post saying how sad someone was that Luke Williams was gone. I went to his Facebook page and read his wall. Oh my goodness, he had died. This was crazy, but how? I sent Ginny an e-mail. I then called Maryalice, who didn't know anything and said she would call her good friend who knew him well and would get back to me.

Later that day, Lee and I were at the bank in the drive-thru line; my cell phone rang and it was Maryalice's friend.

She asked, "Are you sitting down?"

I said, "Yes, I'm in the car with Lee. I can't believe that he is dead. What in the world happened? Was he sick?"

The other end of the line was quiet; I recognized this silence from many years before. "From what I understand he had been very sick again; he'd had a flare up with his colitis. He got very sad about it. He drove himself to the hospital parking lot and shot himself in the head."

My heart fell into tiny little pieces. This person had been the rock in my mind's eye. I clung to the idea of his good health like a life raft, and now he had jumped to the other side. I hung up the phone. Lee drove me home where I curled up into a little ball. All I kept wondering was, *Can this happen to me? Can I get super sick again? Can I get so sad that I could take my own life?*

I understood on such a deep level the desperation one can feel when they live with such chronic pain and suffering. When I would suffer partial bowel obstructions, I would pray for God to take me, to not allow me to suffer this way. The only difference is I have a family, little girls who need and love me, a husband who adores me, and a life I love.

> I understood on such a deep level the desperation one can feel when they live with such chronic pain and suffering.

Luke Williams was single, never been married, and had no children. Regardless of the many friends and family who supported and loved him when he wasn't well, all his mind could focus on was the suffering; it's all he knew.

A month after his death I had a dream. I was at my mother-in-law's house sleeping on the third floor in a room we called the jungle room. The walls are covered with one of the most well-done murals I've seen of an actual safari, and there is even a giant wooden giraffe parked in the corner!

In the dream, the room began to fill with water. I first felt panic, as the water was rising quickly. Suddenly, a little animal appeared; I was afraid of it. The little animal turned into an angel and told me not to be afraid. He asked if I had any other questions. I asked about Luke Williams. The angel said that he was now doing God's work very well and happy, that he chose to jump and landed with grace. The angel reminded me that God gave us free will to make our own choices. The angel turned to face me head on, and I could see his face clearly; it was Luke Williams.

He then said, "Don't give up, keep going forward and don't be afraid. You will make it through this time in your life, then you will guide others."

I awoke.

I heard this as a warning. I needed to maintain this lifestyle for the rest of my life, always monitoring my intake of sugar and yeast (as everyone should do).

After my momma and my two friends, Holly and Gina, died, I read every book I could find in which someone had picked him- or herself up off of the ground. I was hunting for stories of resilience. Maya Angelou was my favorite. She'd come from nothing and created a life built around being her authentic self. Many, many years later, I kept Maya in my mind when I sat down to write the first few pages of this book. She told me to write with the voice in which I speak. Luke Williams's death meant to me that it was time for *me* to become the person I'd been looking for.

> I was hunting for stories of resilience. Maya Angelou was my favorite.

Washing Away What Was

I first came to the Ranch kicking and screaming November 29, 2001. I thought there was no possible way that "My Angus"—the man of my manifestation dreams—could live in Tennessee. And to top it off, there was no way I could live here with him!

Soon after I met Lee, I had my first reading with Bill Attride, the astrologer. He told me that Nunnely, Tennessee, was my place of challenge, but not to worry, because I was ruled by Mars and Mars always rises to the occasion, never letting a challenge get the best of it. I said this was good 'cause most of the land Lee and I owned was in Nunnely. Actually, we owned most of the land in Nunnely.

I'd done my best to shift my attitude toward the Ranch. Like Eva Gabor in *Green Acres,* I had been uprooted and plopped down on a farm.

I was born in Appalachia, attending school in a tiny town in Ohio. I equated success with living a cosmopolitan life. At fifteen years old, I knew I was leaving my rural community for New York City. By the time I met Lee, I had lived in major cities for so long that I didn't know what to do if there were no coffee shops, stores to walk to, or people to look at. I didn't know how to sit on the porch and dream; my life was all about distraction and the exterior.

The first time Lee took me to eat at the Homestead Buffet, it was a scene right out of a movie. I walked in with my long blond hair, wearing low-waisted, hip-hugging brown corduroy's, a fitted T-shirt, and high-heeled boots with Oliver (my mini Maltese) tucked in my Gucci bag.

The music stopped.

I looked around the room, eyein' up the crowd to see the style of the place. I whispered into my purse, "Oliver, we are not in LA anymore."

The fashion movement at the Homestead Buffet was (and is) all about overalls, cowboy boots, and Wranglers. The sign outside said the buffet theme was seafood. However, when I approached it, I found nothing from the sea but everything from the pond. Frog legs, crawfish, catfish, and chicken fingers. I thought my days of eating at

> I didn't know how to sit on the porch and dream; my life was all about distraction and the exterior.

Dan Tana's on Santa Monica Boulevard were dead. I thought this was hell.

Luckily, I met Patsy Davidson, a tiny little red-haired woman with a serious tan (she loved her tanning bed). She owned a little hair salon, Cuts and Curls, located in the basement of her house. (I think it's the only hair salon near the Ranch.) I was glad to know her, 'cause once I was there and parked at the Ranch, growing that baby inside my belly, I sho' did need a place to get my hair did.

Patsy was always so sweet to me. The first time I went to see her for highlights, she put all of my hair into a cap and then pulled pieces through the little holes using a metal hook that looked like a crocheting needle. I'd never had my hair highlighted like that before. I'd grown accustomed to having it painted with a brush, a process done in Beverly Hills called Balayage, which originated in France.

Sitting in that chair with the cap on my head and listening to Patsy Davidson chatter to me about the local goings-on, I felt as if I'd really landed inside a movie script. Patsy knew I was lonely out on the Ranch, and she always was sure to drop me a card in the mail or leave me a kind message checking on me. That same summer I listened to Eva Cassidy nonstop singing along to the tiny baby in my tummy. No wonder Bella was born with the voice of an angel, for certain Eva's sound was imprinted on my baby. Eva Cassidy's voice and its freshness went hand in hand with the view from my bedroom window—nothing but rolling hills, cows, and horses.

Lee and I got married in a fever. We met, fell in love, and that was it: baby on the way. It's a funny thing marrying someone you've only known a few months; the journey unwinds once you're both so intertwined. I was more committed to Lee after a month of knowing him than I'd ever been to another human. Lee had been through a lot and he'd ruined a lot, too. When I met him, he was doing his best to give his life staying power, and when I'd pitch a fit and lock myself in the closet, stuffing all I could fit into my suitcase, threatening to leave, he'd hold tight, giggling on the other side of the door, explaining to me, "Darling, in life you gotta have staying power, and I've learned the hard way. So even when you wanna give up, I'll hold on and wait on the other side."

> It's a funny thing marrying someone you've only known a few months; the journey unwinds once you're both so intertwined.

This is exactly what he has done, as I have for him. I didn't have a clue what it meant to really be married, what it meant to be a rancher, what it meant to go to rehab, or what it meant to own a rehab. Over the past eleven years, I have grown leaps and bounds by witnessing our Ranch life as well as from watching the thousands of clients check in heartbroken and lost, and then seeing them leave connected with a sense of knowing that their life is theirs to decide. All of this living has rubbed off on me in a big way. I've been learning that freedom is something we create within ourselves. Expansive and wide living is the way.

> I've been learning that freedom is something we create within ourselves.

The Ranch has allowed me to expand, to spread out, as Peggy Raess likes to say. I love watching the baby cows be born in the spring and driving through the pastures in Lee's truck with my own kids hanging out the window. We all marvel at life as it reminds us of the magic of creation. Over the years, life at the Ranch grew on me.

Moving to Nashville full time, I'd begun to appreciate it even more. Now that I was into eating real food, I appreciated having the land to produce it. Lee had gotten in on the food-education act and shifted our cattle company to grass fed. He'd watched me heal my body, and after years of ranching, he knew that feedlot meat was harmful to humans. I've learned to value the people who work the ranch, too. Those cowboy-boot wearing and overall-clad fellas and fillies understand what is truly sustainable; they understand the earth and how to not only support the humans, but also her.

Jane Ellen and Rusty had become important people to me. When we first arrived from the jungle, Rusty, our foreman for the cattle company, had always been someone I respected. He'd worked as a deputy sheriff before becoming a rancher, and the combination of truth-telling straightforwardness and downright rough cowboy talk made him one of my favorites.

Within the first two weeks back from Mexico, Lee traveled to Peru, and there was a mix-up with money being transferred from Lee's account to mine. I didn't have access to any cash; it was the dead of winter. *What if I got stuck on the side of the road or worse?!*

I called Rusty, and he immediately pulled money from the cattle company and delivered cash to my doorstep, but what else he gave me was priceless. As he stood in the foyer of my double-wide, he brought to my attention something I had been avoiding: our businesses.

When I married Lee, I was careful to keep separate what was his and what was mine. I'd come into the marriage with clothes, some diamonds, a little bit of cash, and a lot of experiences . . . oh, and Oliver. I also knew how little I understood about ranching and rehab, so I stayed out of the way and let Lee run his own show. But after years of not knowing, I knew I had to step up and participate. My marriage was a partnership, and if Lee went down so did I. I'd married my husband with the energy of a young girl, not wanting to step where I wasn't invited. I'd returned to live on the Ranch not as a guest but as an owner. I was now a woman, every day discovering my capableness in the kitchen and reclaiming my health. I'd become empowered, and the Ranch was not my husband's but ours.

Rusty knocked on the door. I invited him in, and he stood in the foyer dropping bombs: "Ms. Mee, I don't mean to do you no disrespect, but I was wondering if you knew how many tractors we got over there at the headquarters?"

I shrugged my shoulders in an I-don't-know kinda way.

He went on, "How about cattle? You know how many head of cattle you own? How many horses? How about how many clients are at the treatment center?"

Again, I shook my head no.

"I don't wanna scare you or wish you all bad luck, but what would you do if Mr. Lee dropped dead right now and you were left with all this to care for? I tell you what—so many people would be up there stealing you blind, 'cause they know you don't know what you got or what to do with it."

Damn shawty boy was right. The "what's in it question" was circling me again on another level. I didn't have a clue as what in the world I would do. As Rusty said good night, climbing into his truck, the young woman I'd arrived as long ago left with him.

That night the room spun with *what ifs* and the realization that I really and truly didn't have a clue what I would do if something did happen to Lee. Then, on another level, it was time Lee and I became

> When I married Lee, I was careful to keep separate what was his and what was mine.

partners in all aspects. I pulled my weight in our life. I'm the organizer and the grounder. I can run a household, Lee travels like mad, and I keep the girls on a schedule and do all that they need. I wasn't the maid or nanny, and Lee had never asked me to be. It was Mee that took on the role.

Lee returned from Peru, and I got involved. I think he was glad that I was interested and wanted to support the Ranch in whatever way I could. Jane Ellen, who runs our cattle company office, and I had become good friends. Spending time on her farm with her kids inspired me. They are six, eight, fourteen, and sixteen and run things. A ranch life creates capable people. I was about to see how capable rural people are.

It was May 1, 2010. Lee and I were home watching TV and enjoying the rainy spring day. It had been raining for about a full day when Rusty called to say that the water was really rising and one of the young cowboys was stuck in the loft of one of the barns. This meant that the water had already risen more than ten feet. It was surreal. We clung to the TV as Nashville was divided up into islands, and we were trapped in town while the Ranch—close to fifty miles away—was floating down the Piney River.

After two days, Lee was finally able to drive out to Hickman County. He arrived to find complete devastation. The flood was soon to be called the Thousand Year Flood, as no one had seen this much water in that many years. That night, Lee came home in tears; his heart was broken and the businesses he'd built were underwater, literally. Worst part is we didn't have flood insurance and FEMA was nowhere in sight. People were living in tents, and drinking water was sparse.

For the few days that I sat in town waiting to be able to travel to the Ranch, I prayed that all would be well. My mind raced with where we would go next if we lost everything. I'd learned to cook foods that heal and support the body: I could start a cooking business and cook for the sick. We could move into an apartment or get another double-wide. I started to see how little we needed to live. I was well and no longer dying slowly. I thought of the things we'd lost and prayed for the things I couldn't replace: our wedding picture, Bella's birth pictures, the old bed in the girls' room that was passed down through Lee's sister, our antique bed. Everything else had lost its value. I wanted memories.

> The flood was soon to be called the Thousand Year Flood, as no one had seen this much water in that many years.

Finally, I was able to make the trip out to the Ranch. The main office of the rehab center was destroyed. The "shed" (as it was called), which was serving as offices, and group rooms with a new kitchen that we'd recently added were destroyed. The "Spirit Building"—a beautiful group room building where gatherings were held—was also destroyed. We'd finished it, and it had been amazing!

The farm was hit hard: Four hundred goats were killed, eighty cows were killed, and all of our trucks, tractors, pick-ups, cars, equipment, and miles of fences were lost. The horses were all safe, as they'd made their way to high ground. A ranch the size of ours, a few thousand acres, has many barns and small work areas with many small houses— all were hit with damage.

Lee first moved to the Ranch twenty-five years before. It was his life and our future. Everything we had was invested in it. One of the cowboys drove up alongside and was talking to Lee. He looked across the cab of the truck at me and said, "I sure am sorry, Ms. Mee."

I felt tears well up in my eyes; I caught a bubble in my throat, and Lee turned to me and in the strongest voice above a whisper, he said, "Don't you dare break in front of him. We are the bone of this community, and if we go under, a hundred and fifty families go with us and that is NOT gonna happen."

In his eyes, I saw the men before him: cowboys, ranchers, Florida pioneers. He is made of stock that believes in rebuilding, and I am his match. This same energy is behind his treatment center, the journeys he leads to Teotihuacán, and me as I have moved into the community with my message of food and CHOICES. We decide who we become, 'cause Lord knows we can't control what is given to us. But we can decide what we do with it.

We made our way to the end of the long drive leading to our tiny double-wide. The front porch we'd added on was completely detached, and the house seemed to be floating. Wearing my Hunter rain boots, I carefully navigated my way toward the entrance. The house looked as if some giant had come and turned everything upside down, tossing the kitchen appliances as if they were doll furniture. A foot of mud covered the rug, and our fine furniture, which we'd moved a few years back from the Lake House, was covered in swamp particles.

What was most interesting was that, although our bed had shifted in position, the bedspread (white chenille) was virtually untouched. The same in the girls' room. Both beds were still made perfectly, and all of the throw pillows sat in place. I heard a whisper, "Meme, don't

> We decide who we become, 'cause Lord knows we can't control what is given to us.

spin in fear. Come out of the world of doubt and KNOW you will be fine, as you always will have a place to rest your head."

My eyes filled with tears, not for what we had lost but for what we still had. I was reminded of our daily bread. For many, many years, people survived on their daily bread, and only now, we needed more. Our simple lives, simple foods, simple needs had become not enough.

I worked for days alongside a handful of people, hosing down furniture, attempting to save what we could before mold and rot set in. Jerry Peele, our friend and partner in the cattle company, drove down from Upstate New York to help. We'd first met Jerry and his wife, Iva, years before in Bermuda. They'd lived in Bermuda in one of the most amazing estates built in the 1700s, Ardshield. We'd traveled there a few times as Lee led workshops through my favorite therapist EVER, Sara White. Iva and I became fast friends, as our lifestyles were a total match and mirror. They also own a farm in Upstate New York, two hours past New York City, where they raise organic cattle, chickens, and lamb. By day, Jerry Peele is a highfalutin investment banker, and by afternoon, he is a downhome British dude, raising healthy meat for humans. Iva is actually the person who had first introduced me to the macrobiotic way, as she has been eating and cooking macrobiotic foods for years. When we'd first met and I'd told her how I suffered she'd recommended I find a macrobiotic counselor. Jerry, who himself has been on a healing diet for what was believed to be multiple sclerosis, has been eating an ancestral diet and doing well for years.

The cowboys and we saw him as the cavalry. Yep, he was one man, but he showed up when we all felt lost, alone, and scared; we were drowning. Jerry Peele worked for hours building fences and cleaning up. He brought a refreshing energy, motivating all of us. He'd return to our house in Nashville late in the evening exhausted, and I'd cook for him, as this was my way of saying thank you. I'd become a rancher's wife and a person who understood the old ways. The simplest way to say thank you is through a meal . . . that heals.

Meanwhile, Lee was making a deal with a corporation that had wanted to buy into our treatment business. We'd pushed this corporation/group of investors back, but as the Ranch was underwater, our partner in the rehab did what most people do in times of crisis and

> Our simple lives, simple foods, simple needs had become not enough.

showed her ass, refusing to support rebuilding. Lee and this partner had been close for twenty-five years; she'd been a great friend to him for many years, and she'd worked hard handling the money side of things. However, the past few years, things had gotten twisted between her and Lee, and now this twist was fix'n to take us down.

Lee made a deal. She was bought out, and the investor came in. We felt as if we were swapping one evil for another, and it was only time that would show us the outcome. We were taking a leap of faith that God/Universe had brought these people to us to help and keep the Ranch doing what it does best: helping people.

We rebuilt with our own money earned from the big buy in. However, Lee gave up controlling interest in the treatment center. This ain't an easy thing for a daddy to do with his baby. However, the shift in the treatment center brought Lee's focus back to the cattle company. Had Rusty, the other cowboys, the local ranchers, our neighbors, and Jane Ellen and her kids not stepped up and formed a bond, a lot of hearts would have been broken. A farm is the backbone of rural communities; everyone works together for hay to be cut, animals to be fed, and food to be grown. I realized I was part of something huge; again, my nobility—what I chose to be—was my choice. I also understood something about my mother-in-law; she'd been married to big-time ranchers, and she'd held her ground running her part of things.

Soon after the floods, I briefly met a woman who influenced me deeply. Her name was Frances Lewis, and she and her husband had been ranch managers for my in-laws on their giant ranch out in Colorado and in Tennessee before Lee took over. Lee's stepfather, Mr. Artemus Darius Davis, along with his father and brothers, were the pioneers of chain supermarkets; they were known as the "Beef People," as they founded and owned Winn Dixie. The family ranches that I am speaking of were the main producers of the Winn Dixie beef.

The Lewis Family worked noble jobs on these ranches, feeding their families, putting their children through school, and paying for weddings; they built their lives by running and supporting our ranches. Frances Lewis had worked side by side with my mother-in-law, Ms. Pauline. They'd been a team through lots of dramas and natural disasters. I met Ms. Lewis at a ranch party. She'd come out with her

> A farm is the backbone of rural communities; everyone works together for hay to be cut, animals to be fed, and food to be grown.

husband, as she'd not been out in a long time due to pancreatic cancer. She filled the table with stories of the past and who Lee's people were. I was moved beyond belief, understanding the honor I'd been given marrying into such a family. I wanted to do right by Ms. Lewis so I offered to cook for her in an attempt to support her body through the chemotherapy. I knew she'd cooked for Ms. Pauline, and had Ms. Pauline known Ms. Lewis was so very sick, she'd want to take care of her, too. That night, Mr. Lewis cried when he hugged me good-bye, and I saw Lee in his eyes, realizing how hard it had been for my very own husband to watch me suffer. Soon after our meeting, Ms. Lewis passed away. I'd not been able to support her, but I knew what I had to do. She'd inspired me on many levels.

I fell deeply in love with Nashville as I watched people connect across the city, rebuilding their lives with ease and grace after the big flood. Suddenly, the country music I heard on the radio told a tale that was mine, and it was time for me to give back. My resilience was fix'n to be fortified, and we all know resilience and participation are medicine for the soul.

> I was moved beyond belief, understanding the honor I'd been given marrying into such a family.

Jumping in With a Grin

I was no longer a passenger in my Nashville life. I'd watched the city pull itself up by its bootstraps, and I knew these were folks I wanted to dance with. Like a girl in love, I had no fear of rejection or failure. I could only see the light.

I felt better than I'd felt in almost twenty years. It was time to see how I was doing medically. I made an appointment with Dr. Reisman, MD, who had a private practice that specializes in treating the whole person, both holistically and scientifically. I handed over my medical records and underwent a series of blood tests. We were going to hunt for signs of cancer, nutritional deficiency, and bacterial overgrowth in my stool. We'd also be checking my levels of B vitamins, calcium, iron, and all the other big ones, including hormones, as well as checking my adrenal function.

I returned to Dr. Reisman's office two weeks later, nervous, scared, and shaking. *What if I wasn't well? What if I'd fooled myself into thinking this "food thing" was working?* My biggest fear was that my anemia had returned. I'd not had an intravenous transfusion in over two years, and the hematologist had told me that I'd need to remain on them for the rest of my life . . . that I'd never be able to absorb iron from foods, especially if the hole in my intestines was still leaking blood.

Dr. Reisman sat before me and read my results: *everything* was normal and healthy, including my levels of vitamin D and iron. They were PERFECT. I cried as I confessed my doubts to him. I was healthier than I'd ever been, probably in my entire life, and there was only one direction I was going, and that was up. I was now convinced: if we are sick, we must support ourselves and work with our doctors. If they give us a treatment, pills, or surgery, it is our responsibility to do our own parts at home: in the kitchen.

The more I moved into the world, the stronger my resilience became. Early on, I'd shifted my blog from being that, "a blog," to a website: www.meetracy.com. The website opened doors in the community for me to share what I had learned about health through food. I was offered an opportunity to appear on the local FOX morning show,

> I was now convinced: if we are sick, we must support ourselves and work with our doctors.

Tennessee Morning. The producer, Debra Williams, gave me a shot to cook on her show. I'd never done this before. I was as nervous as could be, but once I walked on set, I knew exactly what to do: tell the audience WHY they wanted to eat real food, and then show them how to make it.

I have no idea how I knew to prep things in advance and have the prepared final product ready, but I did, and my brain rambled facts like Rain Man as I watched the playback video. I was amazed and knew that there was a higher power bringing me to the television screen. The beginning of my next incarnation had rolled on the scene with a gangsta lean. I was acquiring TV cooking skills, and bringing WHOLE GRAINS and my old-school farm-to-table diet to Nashville's table. I wasn't a fancy chef cooking complicated food; I was a regular person who taught herself to cook, and in the process, healed my body. Nashville was receptive.

One day my assistant at the website, Abi, told me about the Art Outreach Program at Vanderbilt University, which she was the head of. Once a week, she and a handful of other students would drive to a Church in North Nashville, a lower-income African-American neighborhood, and teach art. The pastor who led the congregation at the church (and still does), was active in implementing as many positive experiences for the neighborhood as possible, including this program.

Abi knew my history because I had shared with her my tales of being a hungry child, much like the kids in her program. She expressed her concern that most of the kids who attended her art program would leave there and return to houses devoid of dinner. She asked me if I would prepare food for the children on Wednesday afternoons. Without hesitation I said, "Absolutely."

However, it would have to be REAL food. And I didn't want to cook for them; I wanted to teach them how to cook for themselves. This was a shot at influencing kids and a large group of folks in a neighborhood located in a "food desert"—meaning there is no market that sells whole foods within three to five miles. Most folks living in food deserts don't own a car or have access to public transportation that will deliver them to full-fledged markets. I had lived as a child in food-desert neighborhoods, riding my bike from the age of six with a pocket full of food stamps and only a little room in my tiny basket for groceries. My momma had to bum rides to get our big shopping done.

I called the pastor and we met, immediately agreeing that this was a *doing* project, not a talking one. He'd had plenty of folks come to him with ideas. He was ready to implement this one. I returned to my office where I set out to lay a game plan. I would first need to hook up the kitchen at the church with plates, bowls, glasses, cups, and silverware that was not made of plastic, paper, or Styrofoam. They were also in need of pots and pans.

For certain, years ago, this church's kitchen used to serve meals made of real food. The only way to prepare this real food was by

using real dishes and pots. My idea was to host a kitchen drop off where people from all over the city could bring used or new kitchen items. My next step was to meet with a group of members from the congregation to introduce the Real Food Makeover, a Community Kitchen Project. I met with twenty people between the ages of forty and seventy years old, the backbone of the church. Everyone received me well as I told my tale of healing my body and learning what food can do for the body. To top it all off, I started the evening by introducing everyone to tortilla chips, veggies, and homemade hummus. This was the first time any of these people had eaten hummus. I was amazed. I'd assumed everyone in our country, especially folks in a major city like Nashville, had eaten hummus before. I left the church *knowing* that the Community Kitchen Project was about more than food. I was fix'n to cross community and cultural lines for the first time!

The next time we all met was at my house; my sister, Nicole, drove down from Ohio to help, and the two of us spent the evening before preparing food to teach our first full-on class. The menu was a black-eyed pea croquette, a "veganaise" (a heart-healthy mayonnaise) dressing with turmeric and dill, fresh spinach salad, and miso soup. My goal was to reintroduce foods that everyone's ancestors had a relationship with. Black-eyed peas were a Southern staple until recently. Now they are found typically only on New Year's Day and are usually poured from a can.

Nicole and I had been working together in the kitchen since we were young girls. Because she was older, she prepared the food and I got cleanup duty. Now the roles were reversed. I was the lead cook. At one point, I looked over at my sister and grinned. I thought how happy our momma would be if she could see us—working together to heal my body and to influence others to see food as a way to empower themselves and their families. I also thought how wonderful it would have been to cook for Patti Cakes. My eyes welled as this thought crossed my mind. All a child of an ill parent wants to do is to be of assistance. I knew I needed to reach kids, too.

> All a child of an ill parent wants to do is to be of assistance. I knew I needed to reach kids, too.

Before eleven in the morning, a caravan of cars parked in front of my house. The church group was here, and we were fix'n to have some fun! I moved through the cooking demonstration. Cooking on the morning shows had taught me to have everything prepared, so that I would only need to make small portions for the lesson. Then, while the instruction was fresh, the students could give it a try. WE ALL GRUBBED. The table was full of conversations revolving around childhood memories of gardens and fresh foods. My plan worked! I had ignited a spark that connected a flame to a relationship with real food!

The next few weeks revolved around getting the kitchen drop off going. My plan was to involve the city of Nashville in helping to revive the kitchen at the church. The drop off was held on Music Row at the Integrative Life Center. I returned to the morning shows to cook and talk about the project. I made flyers and hit every grocery store and coffee shop across the city. Everyone has an old pan, spatula, or set of dishes they don't use. I appealed to them to donate these items.

The morning of the drop off, I was blown away by the turn out. All the local news channels showed up, and we had enough items dropped off and shipped to me at my home address through my website followers. We were ready to turn the church kitchen into a functioning heart, pumping out real food to the congregation. The pastor thought it would be a great idea for us to cook with the kids after school and then serve the bible study group that gathers every Wednesday. Our plan was for at least eight adults and whatever kids we could gather to help prepare the meal that heals. The first few times I was the one who prepared the meals. I'd roll into the kitchen and get to work cleaning, chopping, and preparing while the pastor walked the neighborhood in search of hungry kids. I'd been trained for this as a child: I knew how to clean and now cook, and now here I was building a community kitchen. I was filled with unbelievable joy over having something of value to contribute to my neighbors. I'd dreamed of finding an old woman out by the Ranch to teach me the old ways, and here I was in my thirties and I'd become her. I felt such giant gratitude that a year before I could barely stand long enough in my own kitchen, as the pain in my abdomen was so severe and my body too weak to cook.

I remember one afternoon I'd showed up to cook. I was alone, working away in the kitchen as the rain was pouring down. I propped the side door open so I could hear it and smell it. The choir was in the main chapel practicing, and dang, they could blow! I listened as they sang, and without knowing it, my spirit had joined in as the entire building filled with a timeless and true old hymn. It grabbed me by my heart.

> *I was filled with unbelievable joy over having something of value to contribute to my neighbors.*

I am on the battlefield for my Lord.
I am on the battlefield for my Lord.
And I promised him that I, I would serve him till I die;
I am on the battlefield for my Lord...

I'd gone to the Basilica of Guadalupe in Mexico City with Senora Gina, torn with pain and praying on my knees for a miracle. I swore that if she helped me, I would help others. The miracle was granted. I was shown God's food, and it was up to me to choose to heal myself. There I was, a Catholic girl, cooking real old-school food and learning Baptist hymns. I was reminded that there is one God, and he loves us all. (The word *church* in Latin simply means "a gathering of people.")

Eventually, each week that I showed up and cooked, someone else would join me. Mattie, a member of the congregation in her fifties, had been right there from the beginning when I first came to speak. She'd heard my story and started on her own path to change her relationship with food. I liked this lady very much; she is one of those people who silently hold a line, praying and believing that all will be right. We'd work in the kitchen, and she'd sing and I'd tear up. I'd found a fantastic place to grow. And like my momma who'd explored many churches, I was connecting in different churches this time, not looking for God but being with people and bringing God's food to the table. 'Cause that's the thing: all the food I eat comes from the earth and God. To support our human bodies, God created everything grown on the earth.

Each week someone new joined the Real Food Makeover team—folks who followed the blog and a few kids who had grown accustomed to my being there on Wednesday nights. Fred, the husband of Bella's second-grade girl's basketball coach, became my right-hand man, besides Abi. Fred was the most reliable helper and still is. He'd been on blood pressure medicine since he was sixteen. He's now in his forties. Since changing his food ways, he's cut back from three to four pills a day to none! His son, Jack, a teenager at a local Catholic high school, came too. When I'd first met him, he wanted *no* part of eating real food. He bragged about drinking a liter of soda a day. I told him I could tell 'cause his skin was reflective; it was covered in acne. I let him know that if he cut out the sugar/soda and added burdock root to his diet, his face would clear up. Within two months, his skin was clear and he was showing up to cook with me.

I'd always thought that I would one day participate on an "activist level." Being from Oberlin, we were encouraged from a young age to take action when social injustices presented themselves in our line of

> The miracle was granted. I was shown God's food, and it was up to me to choose to heal myself.

vision. Once I launched the Real Food Makeover, the world of food activism, which had slowly been setting up camp in Nashville, came to my attention. The most influential of the food activists was a large community of advocates who focused on getting the government and corporate grocery stores to open up in food deserts. I think their idea is a good one. It is definitely an injustice that there are no nearby markets that sell fresh veggies and whole grains in these neighborhoods. However, my argument to them is that we first have to face some issues, and the main issue is the relationship humans have with fake food.

It's an ADDICTION. Like drugs, people want to keep their crap food. It's also a physical dependency, too. Sugar, fat, salt, and caffeine are addictive. I found this out firsthand. 'Cause if the people can't afford to buy the food, and more importantly, don't have an interest in cooking real food or have the education of how to prepare it, they are not going to buy it, and then the grocery store isn't going to sell it any more. Winn Dixie had a large market in one of the food deserts here in Nashville, located next to a huge area of projects. Not only didn't they turn a profit, but folks didn't buy the real food items and the processed foods were expensive. On top of it, the store lost again due to a high incidence of robbery. I told this to one of the food advocate ladies I met. Afterward, she didn't invite me to any more food advocate play dates. I wasn't participating with her in finger-pointing and adding to the victimhood of the people in the communities of food deserts.

My intention is to empower and aid in the forward movement of a healthier culture. I'd bumped into a bunch more food advocates, but it was the same deal—someone looking for a soapbox, while I was busy standing in the kitchen and running out of dish soap after teaching and introducing people to real food. I'd even hit up local farmers to see if I could use their old wasted scraps. Once again I hit a dead end, so I just kept creating my own path.

After dabbling with these food activist groups, I decided I wanted no part of it. I don't dress the part in more ways than one, and I don't talk the victim jargon. Truth be told, we have to take care of ourselves. If we want to eat fresh food, all we need is a bucket and some seeds. Plant it on a porch, a patio, or a balcony or borrow a garden hoe and

> Like drugs, people want to keep their crap food.

> My intention is to empower and aid in the forward movement of a healthier culture.

plow. After living in a third-world country, I'd watched the poorest of the poor raise food to feed their families. There are no government food stamps given out for buying fake food. Don't get into a tizzy; I believe food stamps and government assistance are super important for those in need. But I want to empower people to take action.

The Real Food Makeover was getting tough on me. Every week I'd show up and find myself convincing folks to try an avocado, hummus, black beans, salad, and fresh-fruit smoothies. Yep, they were afraid to try smoothies made with real blueberries, strawberries, and a banana! Each week I'd leave the kitchen shocked by the realization that most people don't even *know* what a fresh veggie looks like. Once I made oatmeal with real oats in their whole form. It wasn't instant out of a package and it was not quick cooking—but oatmeal made the way my grandma did (and still does), the way I now do. Out of twenty-two people, not one of them had eaten real oatmeal. This isn't about introducing agave sweetener or some fancy rare health food. This is REAL ancestral food, the food this country was built on.

The kids were the easiest to reach. Because they were already in a learning mode at school, they appreciated the attention and time. They were proud they had learned something new. The elders of the congregation were also open 'cause they had a memory of eating real food. The problem was the parents of school-aged children; they were completely uninterested. One woman would drop her daughter off, crinkle her nose, and say flat out "NO way, I'm not trying it." But her daughter would eat every bite on her plate. From the parents' point of view, it was about convenience and time. Some parents would way rather drive to Target and take the kids to extracurricular activities than be with them in the kitchen—parents and kids cooking alongside each other, listening to music, and answering homework questions. This is not something that's missing only in low-income households; it is also missing in the wealthiest households; the more money, the more distractions. I can't tell you how many people I know who spend their days driving their kids from class to class, returning home after seven with nothing prepared to feed everyone, stressing out, and heating up crap. Their intentions are fantastic: to give their kids what they didn't have, to expose them to amazing things, but in truth, what is the value

> The kids were the easiest to reach. Because they were already in a learning mode at school, they appreciated the attention and time.

if their bodies are fed crap, and the heart of the home, the kitchen, beats at a trickle?

I came up with a plan to create a garden down the road from the church. Jane Ellen rolled into town with our tractor from the Ranch to till up an empty lot; however, it turned out that the lot wasn't useable for farming. Next I brought Fred to the table, who was going to build raised-bed garden boxes. However, the church needed to pay $50 for the supplies, but it never happened. I had to be mindful not to become the congregation's champion, being sure they participated in taking action to support their own health and wellness.

The good news is that the Health Department in Nashville invited Abi and me to a meeting. We'd applied for a grant that would pay for the food, the gardening, and also a stipend for those who wanted to learn to cook with me. (Yep, folks could actually get paid to learn to cook meals that heal!) The Health Department wanted to do their best in guiding us to fulfill the requirements needed to receive a grant. We'd left that meeting completely blown away. The women we'd met with completely believed in our approach. They had also been following my website, cheering me on with a goal in mind that we could possibly take the REAL Food Makeover citywide; the major requirement was that the church implement a food policy.

The following week I returned to the church super excited to share my news. I was so flattered that the Health Department believed in the project that I immediately blurted out the good news. However, when I told the pastor that the grant did not cover remodeling of the kitchen and that there had to be a food policy in place, he changed his entire demeanor and said he didn't want it. I was bummed. He'd come up with the idea that the kitchen needed a total makeover. I kept telling him that once we got the program rolling, the congregation would be on board. At this time, only about three adult members were showing up to cook. I said that life would provide and a makeover would be easy, but FIRST we needed to keep cooking and get folks to actually eat the food.

Then the issue of the food policy came to the table. I'd cleaned out the Kool-Aid and the powdered spaghetti sauce envelopes that filled the cabinets when we'd started, but slowly they found their way back

> I had to be mindful not to become the congregation's champion, being sure they participated in taking action to support their own health and wellness.

in along with the disposable tableware. Seemed no one wanted to do dishes, even though a man named Mark Francis from Australia had offered to pay for an industrial dishwasher. However, once again, no one took action to pick one out. That same evening a handful of kids came running up to me to tell me that the pastor himself was in his office eating pork skins while the kids and I were chopping and cutting veggies for the Meal That Heals. I giggled. However, when the pizzas and sodas were delivered another time through the college kids who tutored there as I was cooking with the kids and attempting to inspire them to try what I was making, I began to see the struggle.

One Wednesday afternoon I'd gone to the market and bought my regular amount of food, spending between $40 and $50 dollars per Real Food Makeover, which would feed, mind you, an average of forty people. That's right, y'all, buying nothing in a can, box, jar, or freezer section, real whole foods and half the items were organically grown. Eating this way is doable; it's the best way to shop and cook on a tight budget.

I arrived at the church along with one of my assistants and Fred. We got to cooking: lentil soup, mixed greens with spinach salad, freshly made miso-ginger-tahini (sesame butter) salad dressing, and fresh fruit for dessert. For a drink, we always served lemon water with fresh lemons and sometimes cucumbers.

Usually we started cooking around 4:30 p.m. and served around 6 p.m., but by around 6 p.m., no one else had shown up. Finally, a girl and her momma came in, asking if we'd seen the note on the door. Fred walked to the door and found a small note under the iron bars saying that Bible Study was cancelled. The note made no mention of the Real Food Makeover. So the five of us all sat down together to eat. I left the church wondering what to do next.

That night I received an e-mail from a food-service program that organizes meals for families in need of meal support due to childbirth, surgeries, illness, or other situations. I saw the list of meals that people were going to prepare each day and I *knew* I had to get involved; a body healing from ANYTHING, including childbirth, needs support. Cheesy shrimp grits casserole with cheesecake for dessert isn't going to do much but fill the belly. I picked a night and submitted my recipe:

> Eating this way is doable; it's the best way to shop and cook on a tight budget.

aduki bean tacos, corn tortillas, fresh guacamole, homemade salsa, brown rice, vegetable kale miso soup, and sliced watermelon. It would be easy to do because my dear family friend (DFF) was going to be driving down for cooking lessons with me.

DFF and I had been friends since the fourth grade. Her family was one of the only four Italian families in Oberlin. I'd spent most of my time at her house. Her momma made foods similar to mine growing up: pasta, tomato sauce, and lots of peas! When DFF was about nineteen years old, she'd undergone surgery. The doctors had found a large tumor growing on her ovary. It was the size of a small watermelon and had been growing since her conception. The biopsy showed the tumor to have hair, bone, teeth, and nails. It was a twin that had been feeding off of her for her entire life. There were also signs that she had vitiligo, a condition that causes depigmentation of patches of skin. It occurs when melanocytes, the cells responsible for skin pigmentation, die or are unable to function. Research has shown that this is usually tied to autoimmune issues. Also, she had severe scoliosis and many other health problems.

When the autoimmune system is screaming at us, we should listen. Part of the "WE" is health practitioners; they must pay attention whenever *anything* autoimmune comes up. This is the basis of our *entire* health and wellness, the alarm system that there is imbalance, and imbalance that is left untreated leads to disease.

Well, the doctors told her since the tumor wasn't cancerous she was fine. They sent her on her way, and she carried on with her American lifestyle and diet. In her early thirties she came down with what she thought was a horrible flu: vomiting, fever, chills, aches, night sweats, and weight loss. This flu did not go away after a few days or weeks. Finally, her doctor performed more tests and found out that her body had created another large tumor, but this tumor had ruptured inside of her. It was polluting and poisoning her body, especially the liver, as the liver serves as the organ that *everything* flushes through.

Once again, my friend was told that all would be fine and was sent home. Once again her body made more tumors, and these ruptured. For six years, she had constant dull pain in her back and under her rib

> When the autoimmune system is screaming at us, we should listen.

cage. The doctor decided to do a scan of her gall bladder, finding it to be fine. Then she started to itch constantly; there was no rash or visible sign of illness. The itching was inside of her body.

She'd been following my site and seeing me get well, so she called me. I told her to come visit me and to make an appointment with Dr. Sheng. Dr. Sheng is a Chinese medicine doctor here in Nashville. I'd been seeing Gil Ben Ami for two years when I decided I was ready to take my healing to another level. Gil Ben Ami had gotten my blood flowing and had helped me shed my fear of death. Now I needed a doctor. I'd heard that Dr. Sheng was off-the-hook good and super-medically oriented as she had studied medicine in China, where she had been the head of a hospital. Vanderbilt University Hospital was studying her work, as she was having fantastic results with stage-4 cancer patients.

The word around Nashville was that there was a five-week waiting list. I made the call and left my name and number. An hour later the receptionist called me back telling me that she was Lee's niece through marriage. Since I was like family, she wanted to get me in as soon as possible.

Shazam, shawty!

The door flew open, and I was on Dr. Sheng's table within a couple days. She is the cutest person EVER. She can't be five-feet tall, dark short hair, pearl earrings, and the clearest of eyes. She sat down next to me asking me questions and then listening to my pulse and looking at my tongue, as Gil had. Without telling her much, she seemed to know exactly what I was feeling symptomwise and when she looked into my eyes I *knew* she could see me, all of me. I began to see her once a week. After six months, my health had turned another corner. Her technique was different from Happy Son of My people. She loaded me up with 100 needles at my weakest points! She also custom-made Chinese herbal blends, which I began to take immediately. They eased the last of my digestive distress. I was (and am) progressing.

DFF made herself an appointment to see Dr. Sheng and began her monthly journeys to Nashville, which was a ten-hour car ride. I wanted to understand which foods would help support the liver and be easily digestible by someone with liver issues. It seemed my DFF was encouraging to me to learn even more. We got into the kitchen and cooked

Without telling her much, she seemed to know exactly what I was feeling symptomwise and when she looked into my eyes I knew she could see me, all of me.

nonstop. She called the tiny bowls of soup and food I served her "Bitch Bowls," and our giggles began. (DFF had very little appetite, and she could barely eat; since food was her medicine, it was important that she eat small bowls of food. So every couple of hours, I'd sit her down and place a Bitch Bowl in front of her.)

Her first appointment with Dr. Sheng was scary; Dr. Sheng poured through her records and then her human body, announcing that she believed DFF had Hodgkin lymphoma and that she'd probably been sick for at least seven years. This was congruent with the information DFF had recently received from the Cleveland Clinic. Dr. Sheng said that the constant itch was definitely inside; it was her connective tissue—that is, her muscles.

That night DFF and I sat on my sofa, looking down the path of "what ifs." Dr. Sheng had said that her chances of turning this around were maybe 25 percent, as the disease was strong in her body. We sat eye to eye, facing our immortality together. I'd been in her shoes, understanding the moment at hand way too clearly. We were brought together for a reason. Holly (my dear friend who died along with my closest childhood friend Gina in a car accident a week after my momma) had been DFF's best friend. Holly's death had broken her heart and affected her deeply.

I know we were brought together at this most crucial time in our lives by our friends. It was as if they were there in the room with us sitting beside us, as DFF got her mind right with her choices. Gina and Holly had died young. Both DFF and I had almost climbed into the car with them the night they were killed. They had stopped by our houses to see if we could go with them to Ohio State for the night. They died on the way home. As we were looking into the face of illness and death, our friends had returned in spirit. It felt as if the world had stopped, and we were surrounded by the desire to live.

I asked DFF what she wanted to do. She said that she wanted to eat real food for as long as she was alive. I reached across the sofa to hold her hand, and like schoolgirls piling palms on top of one another, I saw the hands of our dead friends cover our own. We were walking this path together, as we had walked as children.

Our cooking sessions were fantastic. DFF inspired me to learn more

> I'd been in her shoes, understanding the moment at hand way too clearly.

> We were walking this path together, as we had walked as children.

and to try new recipes. She also reminded me to eat simply. DFF had come to some of the Real Food Makeovers, jumping in and inspiring others to make healthier choices so that they could take preventative action toward avoiding chronic disease.

After just ten months of eating foods that support the body, taking Chinese herbs, and having monthly acupuncture sessions, DFF was doing better than ever. The constant itch stopped and her pain lessened greatly. She even lost 20 pounds and looked like a brand-new person. (Even today, she continues to do well. Every time she gets scared, she gets into the kitchen to take action to support her body, and this calms her mind.)

There we were, working in the kitchen yet again, preparing the aduki bean tacos for the food service, hoping the lady who received them would like and appreciate the food. When we pulled into the driveway, a lovely blonde woman immediately came to the car, and excitedly introduced herself.

"I am Cookie, and I am so very excited for your food. I saw on the list what you were delivering and couldn't wait! My son is in your daughter's class, and I've been following what you are doing here in the city. We deeply appreciate all the food that has been sent to us, but most of it was incredibly unhealthy. I've had a double mastectomy; the hospital released me two days later as there was a "glitch" with my health insurance. I'm in an awful spot and *know* that I need to eat food to support my body."

I gently hugged her and told her that I would do my best to connect with her, encouraging her to come to the Real Food Makeover classes when she was well. Then I introduced her to DFF, who was sitting in the front seat. She was glowing at how perfect life can be and shared her success story with Cookie. Her beauty was the proof.

As we pulled out of the driveway, I knew not to get discouraged by the church's failure to get all in. I knew that life was going to open another door and that the Real Food Makeover would roll on, and this is what happened.

The Integrative Life Center (ILC) on Music Row, which was founded by my husband, Lee, as an alternative approach to outpatient drug, alcohol, and eating disorder treatment, would be the new Real Food

> I knew that life was going to open another door and that the Real Food Makeover would roll on, and this is what happened.

Makeover location. The train was moving on, and I was taking the Noble Food Makeover on the road, spreading it around the city.

The pastor never contacted me again after the no-show at the church. I had no hard feelings; life is a giant choice and God gave us humans free will. I sent an invitation for his congregation to join me at ILC. In the meantime, I was asked to teach a cooking class through the University School, one of the top private schools in Nashville, that also offers a bangin' lineup of adult evening classes.

I'd spent an evening chatting up a local gastroenterologist at my friend Marielle's going-away party. Our conversation had centered on healing Crohn's disease and colitis through diet. He was into what I'd been up to and my positive outcome. He got my theory that killing off the bad bacteria, strengthening and balancing the immune system, rebuilding the digestive muscles, and balancing the pH of the body would bring about positive changes in one's health. He said that if every one of his patients, including his father who suffered from Crohn's for years, would take action to support their bodies, he'd have less business. The grand finale of our conversation was when he asked me about my shadoobie and its formation. I told him long, connected, and log-like. Not skinny, never runny, and never with mucous or blood.

This was fantastic! His amazing wife had been sitting alongside of us and joining in. A professor at Vanderbilt, she had finished a giant long-term study on the effects of sugar substitutes in the body. She said she was convinced that food has an effect on our health, both positive and negative. The two of them recommended that the University School of Nashville seek me out to teach a class for their adult evening learning program.

> Dr. Thomas Lewis also began referring patients to my site to see if I could help influence their food choices.

Dr. Thomas Lewis also began referring patients to my site to see if I could help influence their food choices. So much for recommending the low-residue diet for life if you are suffering from a digestive disease. Once the flare-up has passed, there is a healthy way to eat to build back the intestines better than ever. A low-residue diet that lacks nutrition is only packed with calories.

I signed on to teach the class through University School, and before I knew it, I was standing in one of the most beautiful homes in

Nashville. A momma in her late thirties served as the hostess. She was pretty, sweet, physically fit, and kind. Her house, which was super modern in a minimal style, was located in one of the most elite gated communities in the city. It was full of country music celebrities. The kitchen was Italian-style, with the latest imported gadgets and gear. I was so excited to get cooking. A bunch of folks had shown up for the lesson, and my meal was planned: tofu schnitzel, gluten and dairy-free millet mash, kuzu shiitake mushroom gravy, collard greens with olive oil and garlic, and apple kuzu for dessert.

Everyone loved the meal and was excited to learn how to prepare it. The hostess, on the other hand, was a nervous Nelly in the kitchen. She kept saying how she never cooks and was constantly disappearing from my side. Finally, at the end of the night, after everyone else had left, she asked if I could sit awhile and chat. The hostess had found a confessional for all of her eating and cooking habits (seems she wasn't kidding when she said that she didn't cook and was intimidated). According to her story, this was an understatement. She was absolutely terrified of following a recipe or preparing anything other than pasta, hot dogs, or chicken breasts. Then she showed me what was in her pantry, and I made a huge connection: the majority of the wealthiest homes as well as the middle class in every major city in this country have a common thread with the poorest: They are FOOD DESERTS. The processed foods that fill their pantries, cupboards, and bellies are full of the same poor ingredients. Yes, the food had different names and different price points; however, the effects of these foods were the same—harmful, high in calories or chemically altered to be low in calories, devoid of REAL nutrition, and loaded with sugar, salt, and fat.

> The hostess had found a confessional for all of her eating and cooking habits.

After showing me her pantry, she let it all go: "I *know* what I'm feeding my kids is unhealthy, but no matter how many books I've read, I can't seem to get into my kitchen and take my family table back. The fear of convincing my family to expand and eat real food is way more overwhelming than the fear of chronic disease and cancer."

I saw Mee in her. This was Mee on many levels. I'd not EVER cooked real food before. I was the princess of processed foods, and my knees shook when Ginny Harper had rattled off the list of foods to bring into my diet. I felt no judgment of the hostess. Instead, it was a kinship. She'd done nothing wrong; she just didn't know how to take action.

I left my first University School cooking class confirmed in my real-food position and determined to continue to guide people into a new way of looking at life and their health.

When I hosted the Real Food Makeover at ILC, it was a HUGE success. Standing room only. People took notes and ate up every bite they could. NO CONVINCING, as they'd made the CHOICE to be there. Not having a full kitchen—only a small area with a sink and refrigerator—I set up card tables with butane burners. Each table was stocked with a recipe and ingredients. I was creating a community that cooks together, because the only way we will all get well is together.

A handful of people had driven from over an hour away and from out near our ranch to participate. Two of these people were a mother and her teenage daughter. The momma had just gotten out of the hospital after suffering a severe flare-up of Crohn's. She was in bad shape. She'd tried all the immune-suppressing drugs, and they were no longer working, leaving her immune system in an even more weakened state. The bacteria in her intestinal track was wreaking havoc and running major game on her gut.

I sat with them afterward, listening to this momma's story, watching her fourteen-year-old daughter fight back tears. I pushed back in my chair, once again seeing my own lineage: my own momma suffering; me a scared girl. This woman was gonna die, and her daughter was unable to help her with her pain. I imagined Bella's and Lola's faces passing across this young girl's face; then I saw myself in this momma. I too had once sat there, needing to be convinced to give real food a try.

Isn't it amazing that we are more afraid to try new foods that have ZERO negative side effects than we are to take a pill that has a patent on it not revealing WHAT'S IN IT? However, the list of horrible and deadly side effects associated with the pill seem to not scare us. I took a deep breath, fully feeling the emotion of the situation. Again, I heard the familiar internal whisper say to me, *Keep cooking, Meme, keep cooking and keep sharing what you know and learning what you don't.* See, the best thing my poppy ever taught me was that I could hear God if I listened. My direction will always be known.

As I loaded my car with the ten bags, pots, and pans that it takes to host a community kitchen, I knew there is no such thing as MEE and them—there is only *we* and *us*. We are each other; no matter how strong I get healthwise, I am a member of this human race, and only through connection can WE conquer what holds us back from becoming our greatest selves. Seeing *Mee* in *You* is the way. And the only way to see each other and ourselves is without judgment.

> Isn't it amazing that we are more afraid to try new foods that have ZERO negative side effects than we are to take a pill that has a patent on it not revealing WHAT'S IN IT?

Toasting to Another Adventure

In August 2011, Lee and I again were faced with a choice: I'd written a trilogy of books: *The Adventures of Princess Know It All.* A buzz was building, and Los Angeles was calling as I'd given the manuscript to a longtime friend (and Lola's godmother), who is a major television producer. She'd known that I was "trying to write a book," but once she read it, she flipped and said get here now!

Lee and I raised our glasses, once again toasting to adventure. We flew out to Malibu, bringing with us only two suitcases each. We enrolled the girls in school and found us a highfalutin, fully furnished double-wide, overlooking Zuma beach, complete with a Viking kitchen.

Nashville was home, but life was asking me to step up and fulfill my dreams as a writer, and Lee was supportive. I knew it was a crapshoot, but I had also learned that death dangles mighty close. When my life comes to an end, I want to know that I lived fearlessly and gave everything I dreamed of a chance while attempting to do my best. Surprisingly, it was me who was hesitant to leave Nashville. I'd fallen in love with the South and flourished in Music City. I had a world of friends and fantastic neighbors. Isabella loved her school, and Lola was enrolled for the fall. I felt great guilt watching them adjust to a new school environment and community. Even if we'd lived here before, it was now to a different beat and a new set of drums. Lee had been the roamer in the past, and I kept the solid footing under our feet. But here I was pulling the rug from underneath "those people's" sweet little feet.

One morning I spent twenty minutes sitting on my couch watching the morning fog roll in off of the Pacific. Its cool dampness crept through the cracks of the double-wide. My fancy vintage designer swivel chairs that came with the casa seemed to twist unattended with the thickness and chill. I loved living out there on the edge of Point Dume. Our double-wide sat at the back of the club, as locals call the trailer park. It offers an ocean view. Native American Indians used Point Dume as a place to send smoke signals to other tribes up and down the coast, as it sits way out in the ocean (sort of like an attached island).

> When my life comes to an end, I want to know that I lived fearlessly and gave everything I dreamed of a chance while attempting to do my best.

There is something to this for me. The combination of thick fog, giant sky, and never-ending ocean felt like a blank canvas full of electricity to power my imagination as I worked at becoming a better communicator. What's really fantastic is dreaming way out there on the edge. I'd sleep deeply with the windows open, allowing that chilly fog to rest on top of my down comforter, filling my sleep with fantastic and crazy dreams. One night I dreamed that Lola and I were breaking into a friend's house and stealing sweaters! We weren't doing it out of malice but instead with giggly mischievousness. Simultaneously, there was a second dream occurring, like a split screen in a theater. I kept seeing this woman working like a mad scientist trying to find the formula for my work. My dream guide was there (you know the one you can't see, only hear). He kept telling me not to worry, "she" was working behind the scenes and would connect the dots. I'd then jump to the other half of the screen and return to my crazy escapades with Lola. Then back to the mad scientist—each time reassured that destiny was at work.

I woke up thinking about this dream, and there was a peace as I rested quietly in the early hours. Suddenly my mind grabbed a name: Eleanor Coppola, Francis Coppola's wife. I crept out of my bed, made some coffee, and hit Google search. What I learned about her is that she not only kept a home during their life together, but she also connected the dots, making a documentary based on home movies shot while her husband filmed *Apocalypse Now*. She also wrote *A Memoir: Notes on a Life*. I'd never thought about Eleanor until moving here. Our phone number was one of her old numbers (whenever I called someone, her name would pop up on the caller ID). About an hour later the phone rang, and Bubba and Nanny (Ted and Peggy) called to tell me about their night out. The highlight of their evening was that they'd sat next to Eleanor Coppola and Francis at a restaurant up in wine country!

I quickly told them about my dream and how I'd spent the morning reading about Eleanor. I knew what was happening; she was a mirror for me, and I'd never have to meet her to feel her influence. When I was young, I thought someone outside of MEE would connect my dots, tie it all together, find the formula, and make things happen—thera-

> What's really fantastic is dreaming way out there on the edge.

pists, friends, boyfriends, managers, bosses, doctors, acupuncturist, healers, writing partners . . . thinking it would take someone else to make what I do good enough, as if someone else held the key to my value. I relied on assistants, friendships, and family. Even as I approached marriage, I saw my husband's position and life as the one giving us importance.

I LOVE getting older 'cause, with age, has come my growth and confidence. There sitting amidst the fog, I was seeing life differently. Instead of seeing the mad scientist as someone else, I see her as MEE. I married a man whose world was big, and TOGETHER, we created a huge life. Like Eleanor and Francis, we had moved around the globe like gypsies. I'd been taking notes, making funny home videos, and now put it all down. With each thought and reflection through Eleanor Coppola, I saw with clarity that I am indeed the mad scientist in the dream, constantly looking for the formula for a happy life, cooking up a recipe to feel better, and carving a path for not only my own personal success, but also for the success of my family, all in effort to save time.

> Instead of seeing the mad scientist as someone else, I see her as MEE.

I'm someone who has never gone backwards. I know when things have finished and it's time for a change, so moving back to Malibu was undefined to me. In Mexico and Nashville I'd returned to work, committing myself to writing full time. My previous lifestyle in Malibu, I'd been a straight-up stay-at-home momma, and I wasn't certain if my friendships were going to remain intact. Plus, renting an office space in Malibu was an absurd experience. After life in the Mexican jungle and Nashville, I'd gotten real about finances.

Malibu's cost of living shook me down to my boots, especially when the real-estate person had taken us to find an office space. One spot in particular was off-the-hook wacky; the listing said it was garden level and included a/c. When we arrived, I knew it wasn't going to be good when the realtor took the elevator to the basement, opened up a door leading to a windowless hallway, and then opened up another door where a mop and broom came crashing down on us. He quickly switched the light on to reveal a JANITOR'S CLOSET, for $1,300 per month! I burst out laughing. He stared at me. I apologized and explained we were from Nashville, and the prices were shocking us.

I did find a spot pretty quickly, as I'd immediately found a local acupuncturist—Dr. Asha Randall, a beautiful woman of Indian descent. She runs a holistic healing center at the south end of Malibu and happened to have a spot available: above the gardens with two large windows (and not a broom closet)!

Within the first few weeks, I was asked to start a Real Food Makeover in Malibu. I was super nervous, more so than in Nashville, as I assumed that people in Malibu would already know what I know and possibly not have an interest. I was also returning to Nashville every six weeks to appear on the morning shows and lead the Real Food Makeover there. I did it: I put together an e-mail and sent it out through Deanne Rollins, the owner and founder of the California Ocean of Learning Pre-School in Malibu. Isabella had attended her school years before on our first dance with Malibu, and Deanne had watched me get well. She wanted to educate and inspire parents at her school, feeling that it is a moral obligation to guide the parents of the children who attend the school. Within fifteen minutes of sending out the invitation, the class was packed with forty RSVPs. I'd presented the Real Food Makeover as a series of monthly classes, which would end in a community meal that heals. Right off the bat, a handful of people registered for the entire series.

I'd thought that I'd moved to Malibu for the sake of my writing, but after the first food makeover, I saw that maybe that's just how life had gotten me to come here. I was no longer in this cooking thing alone. There was a team of women and men in Malibu *and* Nashville who were coming together because they were yearning to feel better and wanted to feed their families healthier nonprocessed foods, real foods.

It wasn't all ease and grace. Early on in the year, a big old pot of stew was stirring at the girl's school; sugar and unhealthy food were the main ingredients causing the boil.

> There was a team of women and men . . . who were coming together because they were yearning to feel better and wanted to feed their families healthier non-processed foods, real foods.

Finding My Voice
Through My Dreams

As you know by now, I'm someone who works out my "stuff" through my sleeping dreams. I always know when I'm fix'n to step in a pile of shadoobie by what goes down in the dream world. One week I had three dreams in a row, predicting the future:

The Dreams

I was in a car driving toward a large body of fresh water. The road was hilly, and I could physically feel the road as it dropped in my tummy. We arrived at an old-folks home where we were greeted (*we* being my friend Gretchen and I) by a nurse.

She said, "You need a reading, girl. Come this way, they will see you next."

We made our way down a dimly lit hallway, stopping at the last room on the right. A woman, well I think she was a woman, she seemed to be both or neither, I guess 'cause it didn't matter. Her skin was brown and her eyes were round chocolate saucers. She tapped at a chair for me to sit in and then took my hands and the world disappeared. I couldn't take my eyes off of her chocolate saucers and her ever-spreading face. She was expanding.

Then she said, "You are growing into a very big person; you are becoming the person you wanted to be, and if you want, you will grow very much. Don't worry; it is only time and time is moving quickly."

Suddenly I looked into those eyes of hers and saw that they were mirrors. It wasn't her who was spreading out before me, but it was really me that I was seeing! She dropped my hands, and I caught my breath, the room returned along with the nurse.

She said, "The Oracle is tired now. You must leave."

I woke up.

The next night I dreamed again. This time I was with some kind of priestess. She was pushing and pushing me to answer her questions.

> She tapped at a chair for me to sit in and then took my hands and the world disappeared.

But her questions were difficult because the answers were locked deep inside of me, in a room without a key, far away from the Mee that I am. This is 'cause they were placed there by the girl that I had been—the one who was afraid to speak her truth. I looked around, and there were Indians hunting in the marsh, and the woman priestess said, "Life here in Alaska is very difficult." Then she went back to pushing me with questions.

Finally, I opened my mouth and a huge amount of truth came flying out. My truth was so very big that it caused a tidal wave that washed the priestess away. As she was pulled back into the sea, her eyes danced with joy, and I felt free. I heard her say she was proud of Mee.

That same morning, I woke up choking. In my dream, a walnut was lodged in my throat. I know why I dreamt this. A few days earlier, one of the mommas from the girls' school sent around an e-mail regarding the student store, which is run to raise school funds. The only problem with the store is that, in addition to selling pens, pencils, and erasers, they sell crappy JUNK—that is, candy and other unhealthy snacks. Her point of concern was that the school coach tells the kids to remind their mommas to give them a few bucks so that they can be sure to buy something from the store or from one of the frequent bake sales (again to raise money). So the little boy comes home asking momma for a dollar, and she tells him, "No, I don't want you to eat any of that stuff," and then he feels as if he's letting his beloved coach and school down.

I jumped in on the e-mail with my opinion:

> I wanted to support the student store, and then I saw what my girls were choosing and were eating and thought, OH NO. I work very hard to keep the sugar and processed foods from our house. When we go into the world, it's like walking through landmines. The worst place to have to do food battle is within the school grounds, where peer pressure has more power than parental guidance. Unfortunately, young children don't have the ability to completely understand what a "healthy choice" is. If they are offered Chips Ahoy or an apple, they want the Chips Ahoy. Bake sales can still exist, but with healthier guidelines. Feeding our children real

Unfortunately, young children don't have the ability to completely understand what a "healthy choice" is.

food is the greatest gift we can physically provide, and REAL food leads to better focus, balanced hormones (young children have hormones that affect the thyroid and adrenal glands, which affect emotional reactions), and stronger immune systems as sugar weakens the lining of the digestive track. Finally, by providing real food, we are sending a message to our children that we CARE and to our community that we are a group of parents who take ACTION.

—Mee Tracy McCormick

Well, my response fueled the momma fire, and before I knew it, I received two e-mails from teachers who were concerned about what to serve the kids for after-school classes and holiday parties. A TIZZY was brewing now. The Sugar Pushers were fix'n to rumble with the Healthy Mommas.

A few days later at after-school pickup, two of the Healthy Mommas were chatting about how they'd danced with the colonel (aka the principal). (This is what I call the principal because he'd dressed up as the KFC colonel for Halloween and lugged around a bucket of fried chicken!) The two Healthy Mommas were in full-on spinning mode. Seems their curbing the sugar efforts were not being well received by the administration, who said bake sales and the student store are part of the school's history—and ain't NOBODY down with letting go of the crack (aka sugar)! One of the women was even wondering if she should remove her child from the school.

I knew I was fix'n to dance when they told me that they had been told (one of the DUMBEST responses): If your child is fed healthy foods at home, they will make healthy choices at school.

Okay, I gotta call bullshit when I sniff it. My kids are amazing eaters, but if a trusted person in authority dangles a cookie made with hydrogenated oils and covered in crappy pink frosting in front of them, they are going to buy it!

Later, when I told this to Lee, he said sarcastically, "Why don't we put cigarette machines all over and see what the upper kids choose?"

After listening to these disappointed Healthy Mommas tell their tales, I said, "Nah, don't worry. I got this. I know these people are not so stupid. California is supposed to be health conscious and Malibu,

> A TIZZY was brewing now. The Sugar Pushers were fix'n to rumble with the Healthy Mommas.

the upper echelon of our society, for sure should know that candy and refined sugars sold during school hours is a total sabotage to the entire school community, the kids and teachers. I'm gonna go have me a chat with the colonel."

Funny thing happened along the way; I'd picked up on the fear of one of these momma's, and it had me balling my fists, and I was reacting from a place of assumption. As I approached the office, God moved through me, shifting my energy and realigning me with my heart's intention: TO PREVENT KIDS AND ADULTS FROM GETTING SICK and going through what I went through.

I walked into the colonel's office, and I saw a man who was worn out by the end of a long day full of dealing with issues, complaints, and concerns. I felt a huge wave of compassion for him especially 'cause I was fix'n to take his bucket of chicken.

I said, "Hey there, how are you today? I know everyone is in a big old tizzy about the sugar situation, but I wanted to let you know that I'm here to help. I know you don't know who I am or what I do, but helping folks shift their relationships with unhealthy processed foods is my forte."

I gave him not a second to even share his opinion on the subject or deflate my blimp. I was running on jacked up air. I continued, "I'm super busy right now, but I'm going to come in and teach your upper classes to bake real baked goods using REAL ingredients with unrefined sugars and even toss in some things that support the body instead of breaking it down. Then the upper kids can sell their healthy baked goods to the younger kids and inspire the entire community to try new things and shift out of the old paradigm. 'Cause I mean it's plain crazy that folks would actually want to keep feeding their babies things that harm them."

The colonel then told me there was going to be a meeting regarding the sugar situation on January 10, and he asked me to be there.

I said, "Fo'sho, shawty, and even better, I will come with a tray of yummy healthy goodies. 'Cause it ain't the kids who are hard to change, but the mommas and poppas who will not let go of their traditions and addictions. On the other hand, children always want to improve, and school is the most appropriate place to educate."

> I gave him not a second to even share his opinion on the subject or deflate my blimp. I was running on jacked up air.

That sweet old colonel stood up and hugged me good-bye. As I walked outside, it dawned on me that most folks don't know what healthy is and are so afraid it's gonna taste bad. They are even more afraid that they will be judged for how they have been eating and feeding "those people," so they remain in an unhealthy rut.

My dreams were making sense. I was once again about to expand. The next night, I dreamed I was choking on a walnut 'cause Lord knows what my truth-releasing did was put more work on my plate. I was nervous and asking myself did I really want to take on another community's poor food addictions? Y'all know where I've been with folks who don't wanna change, and it's a heck of a hike uphill. But it is worth it. I closed my eyes and made a promise that as long as I've got my health, I shall be of service. I call this gratitude in action.

> . . . it dawned on me that most folks don't know what healthy is and are so afraid it's gonna taste bad.

Tarred in Sugar and Feathered at the Community Forum

I had a private conversation with myself on the way to the school food forum meeting: *Meme, you are going to sit back and watch. DON'T VOLUNTEER for anything. You are slammed already with life and work. As it is we are not in Malibu to redo a school's food policy.*

I was pleasantly surprised at the number of people who showed up at 8 a.m. Not to mention the wonderful introduction the colonel and the coach gave, as the administration was 100 percent in favor of shifting the school's food policy and creating a much healthier environment. This was a relief because I'd thought they were going to be the difficult part in the equation. Turns out the colonel himself had dealt with diabetes and had shifted his health in a positive direction with food awareness. The coach who runs the student store battled the same issue and came out on top. He brought in an example of what he sells at the student store and one of the Healthy Mommas read the ingredients, giving us a breakdown of what unhealthy stuff was in it—

or as I like to call it *FAKE versus REAL,* 'cause to me, it's not about good food versus bad food. That is a thing of the past and doesn't get us anywhere. We need to educate people to eat real food.

Immediately one of the Sugar Momma's got in the ring, defending the crap: "I teach my kids what to buy and not to buy, and they know better. So I don't give them any money to buy it if I don't like it. It's all about you and how you're parenting. I have no problem with this stuff."

Well, you know where that went for ten minutes: to the battlefield. This Sugar Shark had pointed the all-deadly finger of judgment at *this* Healthy Momma.

Feeling a little bit stunned, I got in the game and asked if we were all there to create a healthier student store and bake sale? The answer? NO! A handful of these people were so dead set against giving up the Pringles, damned cookies, and birthday cupcakes that you'd a thought the Healthy Momma's were trying to pass out condoms rather than whole grains!

Then the Diet Soda Warrior went off and not in the Healthy Mommas favor! She'd introduced herself earlier in the meeting as a doctor and the mother of two children at the school. I'd assumed she and I were on the same team. NOPE. Waving a diet soda with a big old SPLENDA written across the top, she carried on about how once in a while a little red food dye isn't enough to give her kid cancer. And besides, she added, we all have cancer in our bodies. (This point is true; studies have shown weakened immune systems are linked to high incidences of cancer.)

What I wasn't able to say was that sugar weakens the immune system, and every 4 grams of sugar is equal to 1 teaspoon. The cookies in question had 18 grams—that's over 4 teaspoons! So I say this is not a positive snack choice for a midday school break. Do kids need 4 teaspoons of sugar, especially since we know sugar intake is linked to lack of focus? The Diet Soda Warrior's rant continued, as she waved the diet soda some more. Mind you, her reference to cancer came after I'd finished telling my story about having faced a diagnosis of intestinal cancer a few years back and another woman's story (the mother of two young children) about having stage-4 breast cancer. This lunatic's rant stung like a bee.

> What I wasn't able to say was that sugar weakens the immune system, and every 4 grams of sugar is equal to 1 teaspoon.

Finally, I pushed my chair back from the table. "I'm shocked" slipped from below my breath.

I couldn't and can't believe that in Malibu, California, there was a room full of women and men fighting to keep the damn cookie in school! I don't know of an elementary school that sells crap on the playground anymore. I could feel all the invisible energetic daggers thrown my way. I stumbled with my words, having lost my footing. Of all the places I've taught, I had *never* experienced such rage and anger regarding shifting a food policy. My goodness, even in the deep South where many people I'd spoken to believe that macaroni and cheese is a vegetable, they UNDERSTOOD the need to remove processed foods and sugar, especially when it comes to our kids.

I tried to express myself, but all I could do was pick my jaw up off of the ground. Then I had a thought: *These people are the parents of my children's peers. If I get in the ring with them, then our strained relationship will affect my girls.*

It's a tiny school, and y'all know hate can spread. I want my girls to be happy and supported. I don't have a dog in this hunt. I *am* running my home kitchen, packing lunches, and as much as I'd like to support a student store and eighth-grade bake sale, I *can* say no to my girls when they ask for a dollar. Sugar Ray I ain't.

Even when I told the people at the meeting that I would teach the kids to cook and that implementing a food policy and creating a HEALTHY student store could influence future enrollment (especially since I'm teaching the preschool mommas in the community to cook real foods), they still threw their daggers at me.

> WHAT?! How dare you try to feed our kids beans! We want refined sugars and flours! How dare you try to add fiber to their diets!

Then I gave them more fuel when I said, "Hey, we can even make cupcakes using black or white beans instead of flour." (This recipe is in Part Three.) The crowd roared, and they have been blasting me with bombs ever since! *WHAT?! How dare you try to feed our kids beans! We want refined sugars and flours! How dare you try to add fiber to their diets!*

The big concern was that kids like to eat things that are bright and playful with sprinkles and sparkles . . . SERIOUSLY?

So I told 'em I got a tip: If you want food to be more appealing to your families, tell them that it will help them focus, remain calm, learn easier, keep colds away, help them grow, and allow them the opportunity to grow old and not miss out on life due to suffering from a preventable disease. Explain to them where food comes from, visit farms, cook fresh produce with them, hold a line with them, and be the ADULT. This is about parenting first. Making them happy because it sparkles is a sign of our culture's values.

Why are we as adults PROJECTING our issues and unhealthy traditions and food cravings onto our children? Why do we have to decorate food and make it pink and pretty? Have we not learned from the cereal aisle in the grocery store where this thinking leads us?

Finally, the meeting came to an end. A handful of folks lingered; they were the ones on the Healthy Momma's teams and the colonel, who truly believed in foods that support the body as opposed to those that crash it. The Sugar Sharks snarled at me and left immediately.

I left in a spin cycle. *What had happened? What was I going to do? I'd offered to teach, but at what price? Becoming the target for anger and fear?*

> That night, tucked under my down comforter, my mind spun in circles. Dang, I'd stepped in a big pile of stinky shadoobie.

That night, tucked under my down comforter, my mind spun in circles. Dang, I'd stepped in a big pile of stinky shadoobie. How in the heck was I going to back out and WHY did I think I needed to volunteer to teach folks who don't want to learn? I sent a late-night e-mail to the colonel telling him I was afraid to get involved. His reply was "Let's talk."

I entered the principal's office the next morning and was greeted with a hug. Then I plopped down onto the couch with a jumble and bumble of words flying from my mouth. There he sat high above "the traffic," holding an aerial point of view, calm as a colonel. I stopped my rant and felt God's hand on my shoulder, guiding me back, reminding me of my agreement with life. I'd crawled on my knees before the Tilma in Mexico City, praying to Our Lady of Guadalupe at my sickest and weakest that when I was well I would share my energy and health, that as long as I remain well I will be of service.

As I glanced into the colonel's face, I saw we are the same. He had come out of retirement to resurrect this tiny school, proving that life is about being of service.

I told him my plans. Okay, so I will teach the eighth-grade class five cooking lessons for living a Real Food Life, starting with cooking *whole* grains, moving on to legumes, vegetables (leafy greens included), fish high in omega-3s, a soup, and ending the series with a dessert that the kids can prepare. Preparing "A Meal That Heals" would teach them to look at food from a new perspective, one where food has a purpose and is not just to satisfy hunger.

Like the church in North Nashville, I was seeing the same situation: kids are way easier to ask to expand than adults, especially when it comes to new and healthy foods. I was blown away with how open my community cooking classes were at the school. Each time we gathered to cook, all of them including the boys, grabbed aprons, dove in with openness, and then ate every single bite of what I made!

When I broke out the collards with garlic and olive oil, they cleaned the pans within seconds. I decided to stand clear of the Sugar Sharks (most of them looked through me when they passed me by), and I spent my breath talking to the kids about REAL food and making choices based on supporting their bodies. Each time I cooked, I left inspired and supported as a handful of Healthy Mommas showed up to help me out.

As of the writing of this book, the school still hasn't shifted its snack polices. Cupcakes and sugar show up every day in some form for birthday and holiday celebrations, and yep, some teachers are still rewarding their students with candy: THE WORST THING TO DO. But the student store is better and the weekly bake sales seem to have ended. Maybe next year they will have shifted their food policy . . . maybe the kids will be the ones to request it.

> Preparing "A Meal That Heals" would teach them to look at food from a new perspective, one where food has a purpose and is not just to satisfy hunger.

Where We Are Now

In December 2011 our farmhouse outside of Nashville was finished. We had done it! We worked our way back from the floods and returned to our land. We spent the following summer on the ranch and slept in our own beds. My sister, Nicole, joined us as she relocated her life to the ranch; she had become dedicated to learning about food from seed to table. Nicole is now teaching classes and working as a private cook when she isn't busy running our CSA garden bags and planting seeds. Nicole's son, Tylor, a sophomore at Lipscomb University, joined us as we worked on the seven acres of the biodynamic organic gardens we'd built, digging 2,000 pounds of potatoes! (We will add another acre of food each year.). Together, we cooked and enjoyed food from our own land every day.

The highlight of our summer was when we hosted the largest Real Food Makeover yet, and the best part was that my family and I grew and picked all the food that we cooked, and Stephen Tomlinson, Jane Ellen's husband, shared his story of health and wellness, paying it forward, a true food angel.

You see, in December 2011, Stephen was hospitalized with an acute diabetic attack. He'd been on a handful of medications geared at treating his diabetes and heart issues for a few years when everything hit the fan—his body said, "No more." When he was released from the hospital, he sat in my kitchen and said, "Ms. Mee, I'm ready to make the change." His two teenage daughters—Bailey (15 years old) and Samantha (16 years old)—had been showing up at the Community Food Makeovers since I'd started, and they'd even integrated some of the recipes into their family's meal plan.

For Stephen, it was game on now, and over the next six months, Baily and Samantha would cook to save their daddy's life, inspiring me to understand the effect of food choices on diabetes. We don't have to be doctors to learn to cook and eat the right foods for our individual health—the Tomlinson girls prove this point. Their entire family did just this, and within two months, I received a text from Jane Ellen that the doctors had removed Stephen from all his meds, and by June, he was down 50 pounds!

I have watched as "Those People" (my girls) have formed a relationship with food and the natural world, boosting their confidence as it has mine. One recent afternoon, I jumped on a horse that my girl Jane Ellen was about to ride. She looked at me with eyes that said, "Are you sure?" I nodded *I got this.*

You see, it's been years since I'd ridden, as my body was too weak and my fear too great. As I headed out to pasture following my husband and daughters, I relaxed into the saddle, no longer holding on tight with fear of what might happen.

My Kitchen Cure isn't just about my physical health; it continues to teach me to trust me and to know that I am good enough—and it has helped me to shed a ton of fears I'd been packing around for years.

PART TWO

Getting My Mind & Body Right with Knowledge

Know thy intestines . . .

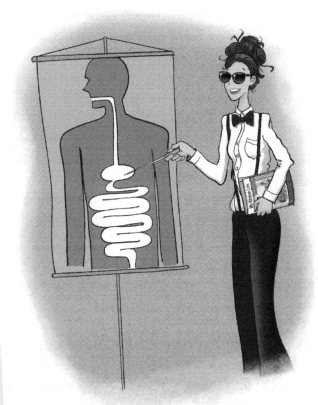

. . . and what you are putting in them.

It All Begins with Change

When I first left Ginny Harper's center armed with a list of what to eat and what foods to avoid, I felt incredibly overwhelmed. I'd never heard of most of these vegetables, grains, or legumes, let alone cooked seaweed! All I could do was focus on what I'd miss: my grand-mother's pork butt sauce with rigatoni and parmesan cheese, Kraft Macaroni & Cheese, Doritos, Taco Bell, pizza . . . the list went on and on, and it went everywhere I went—'cause I was not letting it go!

In the early days of shifting to a real food life, I spent a lot of time missing my old favorites and feeling victimized by what I couldn't have. That is, until one night Lee and I went out to eat. I asked the waitress to be mindful of dairy and wheat, and she said, "Oh, I'm so sorry you can't have the mashed potatoes. They are *so* good with all that yummy butter and sour cream . . . you poor thing."

I stared past her, searching for a blank space to process my thoughts and then rallied from within. Wait a minute! I'm not a victim. I'm a fortunate human being who learned to eat foods that support my health. I spoke with a kind, calm voice: "Please don't feel bad for me. I'm a lucky girl, and truth is, I don't choose to eat food that will hurt me. I feel blessed that I have the education to make positive food choices. Besides, now my world of food is even larger than ever before."

Then the waitress seemed to take a step back, hearing what I'd said, and confessed, "I actually have diabetes and feel left out when people order what I can't have."

Ahhh, she had projected her own food fears and issues onto me like so many people did and still do. Finally, I decided to stop partici-pating.

This was an empowering moment that opened me up to shifting my own perspective regarding my food. I was making a choice to eat foods that heal and support.

From that moment on, if I was tempted to eat something that would hurt me, I'd ask myself, "Girl, who and what are you feeding? Is this bite fix'n to feed a healthy cell or a potential cancer cell?"

> In the early days of shifting to a real food life, I spent a lot of time missing my old favorites and feeling victimized by what I couldn't have.

It was simple: food was my medicine and I was in it to win it; every bite I took had a purpose. Of course I'd gotten sick. I'd *never* eaten with the intention of supporting my immune system, cells, brain, breasts, vagina, hair, skin, or the big one—MY INTESTINES. I ate like most people: for taste, habit, and comfort. The only time I ever ate anything semi-healthy wasn't to support my body. Instead, my mind's ego and vanity were the driving force. I ate healthy food to stay thin. Totally whack intention, 'cause yo-yo dieting with fake foods *never* works, as the body is constantly working overtime trying to process all the fake foods and toxins. Moving to a real food life is the most natural and easy way to keep weight off.

One afternoon feeling lonely and yearning for fake food, I sat sipping my twig tea and staring off into my family's food history. Before Lee and I were married, we had attended a weekend "therapy" session that allowed us the opportunity to look at the manner in which our families did relationships. Known as "Family of Origin Work" the session was led by our good friend Michael Brown, or as I call him, "The Professor." Lee and I had a profound experience as we literally mapped out the history of the marriages, divorces, and parenting on both sides of our families. This gave us a chance to not only understand the map that led us to each other, but the honesty of creating a new map, determined to avoid some of the potholes our families had fallen into. I decided to look at my food history the same way.

At the time, my girls were two and six years old, genetically predisposed to digestive distress and divorce. Once again, I was faced with a truth: before I could move forward, I would have to unravel my past; my emotions were deeply rooted in the foods I'd grown up smelling and tasting. I was paving a new road through my kitchen.

I come from "young women," meaning that they had their babies at a young age. All of my grandmothers, and my momma, birthed their first babies around the age of eighteen years old. The benefit is that I was raised with two great-grandmothers, two grandmothers, and my momma.

My great-grandmother on my mother's side, Nana, immigrated to the United States from Italy in the 1920s. She was a super-great cook. I remember her cooking lentil soup with fresh basil she'd grown on her

> It was simple: food was my medicine and I was in it to win it; every bite I took had a purpose.

windowsill, and her homemade pasta—simple wheat, flour, and salt. Her tomato sauce was made from fresh tomatoes and there was always some sautéed greens and garlic on the side.

My other great-grandmother, who had a Scotch/Irish background, came from a poor rural farming community. She cooked simple foods based on whatever was available in the garden. My momma's momma kept her Italian roots in the kitchen, but by the time I was a kid, she was using boxed pasta and canned tomatoes. She cooked fewer fresh greens, except spinach on occasion. Almost every morning we ate old-fashioned rolled oats—oatmeal with butter and milk. My nana's Italian fruitcake was her favorite holiday baked good and half of it came from a mix, and fo'sho, she wasn't drying out her own fruit like she had done years before.

My paternal grandmother, my daddy's momma, was a total 1950s meat-and-potato cook, and her years as a makeup artist for the dead at the family funeral home added to her ability to present a meal with five-star touches. When I think of her, the comforting smell of beef bourguignon fills the room along with the sounds of Barry Manilow. We didn't see her very often, but when we did, we knew we were fix'n to eat some red meat.

Life in my history of food shifted with the divorce of my parents. My momma was flat broke, and she'd moved three hours away from all of my grandmothers. My momma worked two jobs a day, one of them in a diner where she'd bring us home leftovers if we were lucky. There were periods of time when we didn't have a car or my momma was sick in the Cleveland Clinic, and my older sister (who was only ten or eleven) would be in charge of grocery shopping and cooking. This meant we ate chipped-ham sandwiches on white bread with ketchup. Eggs, orange juice, Cheerios, canned peas, corn, and green beans were a luxury.

Every once in a while, my momma would make a pot of grandma's sauce, and we'd eat pasta for a week. Meat was served on rare occasions, and it was usually meatloaf, chicken served with a can of creamed mushrooms, or a ham on Christmas Day. There were periods when we had no food.

We almost never ate out at restaurants—except for Wendy's occa-

> Life in my history of food shifted with the divorce of my parents.

sionally. My momma thought they served the best burgers. She also enjoyed a fish sandwich from McDonalds. Then there was her favorite, Bob Evans. This eating out was only occasional and usually depended on how her intestines were working. For someone with a digestive disease who was treating it medically and continuing to eat the modern American diet, there are two phases: you can either eat or not.

Like a good daughter, I absorbed my momma's favorite foods as being mine, too, tossing them into my family's origin of food history. We didn't have any of these chains in our tiny town of Oberlin, but if we were out in the bigger cities, we were sure to hit 'em up since they were seen as treats.

Because my momma suffered so badly at the hands of anything she ate due to her struggle with Crohn's disease, food was a doubly twisted issue in our house. If we had it and momma ate it, she seemed to get even sicker.

When my momma and my two friends died, I moved to the University of Maryland where I lived off campus, and once again, food was scarce. I'd become a decent waitress and lived mainly off of the food at work, swinging a morning shift when I could and working double shifts when time permitted. The kitchen in my apartment held one shelf of food: a box of instant white rice, canned peas, corn, and Cheerios.

A few years later, when I met Lee, his first visit to my apartment in Hollywood, California, was a truth-teller; I couldn't cook. All I had in the fridge was a can of salsa, a can of green beans, and water. My cupboard was even worse—one saucepan, a fork, knife, spoon, and two coffee cups. I ate out when my tummy didn't hurt.

Lee's food history was very different from mine. First of all, he was (and still is) deeply Southern; his people were some of the first settlers in the state of Florida. Lee was a "change of life" baby. His daddy was fifty years old in 1956 (the year Lee was born), so Lee had come from a completely different food background. His world didn't include convenience foods. The McCormick's ate from the garden and forest. They even had their own farm. So even though it was the 1950s' era of meat and potatoes, vegetables were still part of their daily meals. Southern folk like Lee's family ate fresh black-eyed peas, collard greens,

> Like a good daughter, I absorbed my momma's favorite foods as being mine, too, tossing them into my family's origin of food history.

and plenty of sweet potatoes. Yes, today those are still traditional foods for Southern families, but instead of being plucked from the backyard garden, they are dumped from a can.

Idora, the wonderful woman who raised Lee and ran his momma's kitchen for close to sixty years (and still does at the age of ninety-seven), was a die-hard foodist. She was born on a Georgia plantation, the daughter of a sharecropper. She only knew how to eat what she'd planted. When I first went to "Tara" (as I call Lee's momma's house), I was blown away by the amount of food that was cooked every day: fresh biscuits, ham, pie, and green beans. However, over the years, Idora has not been able to stand and cook 'cause, as she says, "Old Arthur [arthritis] done got a hold of my hands."

There's a new gal cooking, and dang if she ain't modern. Gone are the fresh collards and in are the cans of Old Glory, biscuits from a tube, and ham from a tin. Idora doesn't like it one bit, but what can she do? Ironically, minus "Old Arthur," she's remained in excellent health—well, that is until recently; her intestines are having a rough go. I wonder why?

People always give me the same old shtick when they want to keep their fake foods: "Well, my granny lived to be ninety."

Yes, I'm sure she did . . . 'cause she ate real food for the first fifty years!

When Lee was a young boy, his momma and daddy split. His momma remarried a major mogul, a pioneer of sorts in the grocery business. His name was Mr. A. D. Davis, and he was the son of the founder of the first chain grocery stores in the United States. A.D. had been instrumental in the building and expansion of the Winn Dixie markets, which was the largest chain of grocery stores in the country at the time. These markets boomed with the explosion of processed foods since now the processed food companies had plenty of shelf space to sell their wares. Processed foods weren't the only food item finding a larger platform. The commercial production and sale of beef and other meats had found a way to reach a larger audience. Winn Dixie became known as "The Beef People," and A.D. owned one of the largest cattle ranches in the United States.

When I was only two years old, Lee was already working as a cow-

> These markets boomed with the explosion of processed foods since now the processed food companies had plenty of shelf space to sell their wares.

boy on that ranch and would later run one of his own in Nashville, Tennessee. Who knew I would grow up to marry into this family, get super sick, and return this family's lineage to a real food life, shifting the feedlot mentality of raising cattle to an old-school way of raising food fit for human consumption? Grass-fed beef and organic produce is *not* a modern thought or movement. It is way ancestral.

    Getting my mind right was half the battle of getting myself into the kitchen. I had a destiny to fulfill and a big life to live, one that demanded I eat and cook real food every day. I was changing my family lineage and attempting to avoid chronic disease in my children. The other half of the battle was learning how to manage my time, which I did by planning ahead and organizing my early mornings.

> Getting my mind right was half the battle of getting myself into the kitchen.

How Long Does It Take to Feel Better?

This is the big question everyone wants to know. I, too, asked upon embarking on this new way of life—*how long?* I felt better within a week. I was a different person within a month. Not only because of the food, but because my faith was restored and I was seeing my body's true healing potential. Each week I mastered a new recipe and each week my intestines gained strength. Within six months the constant burn was gone. A year later, I was back in the game. My major turning point was after two years. I remember running around with the girls at the park and thinking, *Wow, my tummy doesn't burn, and I'm not exhausted at 3 p.m., or crawling into bed at 7 p.m.* I still suffered some hard times; however, they were fewer and farther apart. They were usually triggered by eating out in restaurants where I'd cheat and eat some unhealthy oil, chow down on wheat, or unknowingly get slipped dairy. In the early days, sugar called my name, each time wrecking my new game. What's also been amazing to me is seeing how much healthier I look. My skin is no longer gray and dry. My hair is bouncy and thicker than it's been in years. I've also returned to a healthy weight. I will never talk bad about my body again. I am proud of the few extra

> Each week I mastered a new recipe and each week my intestines gained strength.

pounds as I will also never eat food from a vanity point of view—I eat for wellness and health. I don't eat junk—not because it will make me fat, but because it will make me sick.

These days I feel well 99 percent of the time. I have to remind myself that everyone gets a bout of gas now and again. My intestines are functioning and my shadoobie flows with ease. However, the effects of long-term illness took their toll on the rest of my body, and I am still finding my balance. I see myself in it for the long haul, and with each year that passes, my overall health will improve—creating a superhero out of me!

Know Thy Intestines

The craziest thing is that after all those years of pain and suffering, I never really understood my intestines, how they work, or their purpose. I was sitting with doctors and completely relying on their knowledge. Learning about food led me to understanding what happens once it enters my body. Once I gained my knowledge, I *knew* that food was key to rebuilding Mee.

The digestive tract begins with the mouth and ends at the rectum. From the moment we start thinking, smelling, and preparing food, our digestive system kicks on. Salivation is the first step. Saliva contains amylase, a digestive enzyme. The reason we salivate is to break down the food we are going to eat.

During one of my first cooking classes with Ginny Harper, she had me sit down before my meal and breathe slowly, calming down my body. She then rang a little bell signaling me to take a bite. She told me to chew that one bite until she rang the bell again, signaling me to swallow. The purpose of this exercise was to teach me to eat properly. The longer chewing time increased the amount of digestive enzymes and broke down my food more completely, preparing it for its next stop, my stomach.

The main job of the stomach is to turn the chewed food into a soft

I don't eat junk—not because it will make me fat, but because it will make me sick.

Once I gained my knowledge, I knew that food was key to rebuilding Mee.

mush that is ready for the small intestines. The stomach has three layers of muscles to churn the food and mix it with naturally occurring acid and digestive enzymes. As we age, our bodies produce fewer of these natural enzymes; this is why digestive enzyme supplements are helpful to people with digestive distress as well as those seeking optimal absorption of nutrition.

Learning this helped me understand why chewing gum always hurt my tummy. It's really not very good for anyone, as it activates digestive juices even though there's no food heading down the pipe. This actually increases hunger and can deplete the concentration of enzyme-rich digestive juices.

Back to the stomach: this is also where the beginning of breaking down proteins occurs. Eventually, protein is broken down into amino acids, which can be absorbed and used by the body to build new proteins depending on our individual needs. It takes a few more hours for our food to become what is called "chyme" (mushed-up food). The chyme is moved along into our small intestines, where the greatest amount of nutrient absorption occurs, *and where I had a giant hole (or ulceration), which prevented my absorption of food because it was seeping out.*

When food reaches our small intestines, it is flooded with digestive juices from our pancreas, liver, and small intestine. These secretions also contain enzymes that finish off the job of breaking down proteins, fats, and complex sugars into simple sugars. Bile from our liver breaks down large fat molecules into smaller ones that can be absorbed by the body. The chyme travels through 23 feet (7 meters) of small intestine where it is completely broken down into nutrients that are absorbed into the blood to be used for energy and bodily support and to heal and repair the body. If our intestines are not functioning 100 percent, our body will be weak and susceptible to illness. This is exactly why *all* of us need to get hip to supporting our intestines!

Now that our food is broken down, it hits the villi that line the small intestines—they are little hair-like fingers, which are actually blood vessels. They grab the nutrients and then send it through a vein that leads to the liver. The liver is the MacDaddy of all the organs as it filters all of the blood that drains through the digestive tract.

> If our intestines are not functioning 100 percent, our body will be weak and susceptible to illness.

Certain fibers and water that can't be digested in the small intestines make their way to the large intestine. There aren't any more digestive enzymes in our large intestines. However, there are bacteria that metabolize some of the remaining nutrients in the chyme. (Some of the gas we experience is a byproduct of this process.) A benefit of this process is that this bacterium makes vitamin K and some B vitamins. Our large intestines main gig is to absorb these vitamins, some ions, and any remaining excess water. Our colon (large intestine) can experience slow-moving waves of contractions three to five times a day. These contractions force our digested food, now "fecal matter," toward our rectum. Fiber in our diet increases the strength of contractions and softens our shadoobies. A well-supported and functioning digestive tract should ideally produce at least one to three soft, but not loose, shadoobie movements per day.

Fiber in our diet increases the strength of contractions and softens our shadoobies.

I cannot tell y'all how many mommas of young children have come to me complaining that their youngins don't pooh for days. When they've gone to their doctors, they were told to put the kid on MiraLAX, a stool softener. I tell them to feed them real food, packed with fiber and water, and all will be good; real food is what we were created to eat, I tell them. If we start our already nutrient-deficient children on MiraLAX, how will their intestines function twenty years from now?

Feeding Our Kids Real Food Every Day

There is not a week that goes by that some momma doesn't come up to me in the park, at the kids' dance studio, or in car line for after-school pickup, asking me this question, "How can I get my kids to eat real food?"

First I ask, "Do you eat real food every day?"

This is huge, because if they see you eating real food, then they will do as you do—not as you say. Whenever I teach, I focus on the person learning. Don't worry about your husband and kids, worry about mastering your new real food life. Once you are totally on your own team, it's easy to get your crew on board. Kids love a leader; they want a parent to take the time to prepare them real food, as they naturally want to be nurtured and supported. I explain to the girls constantly what I'm making and why.

I had a huge moment early on in my food journey; I'd mastered cooking, and I was on board, fo'sho, when one night I sat down to eat with my girls. In front of me was an incredible meal packed with highly nutritious foods: kale, miso soup, quinoa, and a sautéed white fish. On the girls' plates there was their most favorite meal of all: boxed organic mac and cheese.

What the hell was I doing: This is parenting? I suddenly saw the absurdness of my actions. If any of us sat down in a fine restaurant and watched a man get served a complete steak dinner, baked potato, salad, steamed veggies, and a glass of wine while his children were served a warm bowl of water, we'd scream out, "Child neglect! Abuse!"

I was no different. I was taking the time to prepare amazing food and making sure I fed each healthy cell in my body, while my kids were eating nutritionally devoid foods—all the time at almost every meal. Whew, I had to get it together. This wasn't about the food; this was about parenting. If I didn't start guiding them with food, how in the world was I going to be able to hold a line with big things like drugs, sex, unhealthy friendships, and grades? It is up to me to teach them to make healthy choices.

Once I sorted it out, I had to get in the game and shift the rules around, and what I did is what I tell parents now: *I'm the parent, they don't have ATM cards, keys to my car, and fo'sho, they can't run to the market unattended. And here is the big one: They don't know. They have absolutely no idea about the health benefits of real food and the consequences of being raised on fake foods. So, why are they permitted to dictate what they are fed?*

After I had this awakening, I was determined to make the shift from a half real food household to a complete one. I cooked the same meals for them; if I ate it, they ate it. My husband included. If he wanted something else, he was responsible for buying it, making it, and cleaning it up. I served them tiny little plates of food and asked that they try it. If they didn't want it, I never forced it. I don't believe in forcing chil-

> This wasn't about the food; this was about parenting. . . . It is up to me to teach them to make healthy choices.

dren to eat, nor to eat everything on their plate, and then rewarding them with sugar—this imprints on a child's young mind that the real food is a punishment as opposed to a luxury.

Instead, I'd say, "Fine, you are excused." However, when they returned to the kitchen later asking for a bowl of cereal or a sandwich, I'd hand them their dinner plate from earlier. This is what my nana, grandmother, and momma did—there were never two meals served.

The worst thing I've ever seen is a commercial for one of those nutritional drinks used as a replacement meal for elderly adults, which is now being marketed for kids who just don't like to eat healthy foods. I roll around on the floor each time this thing airs! This is so dang wrong I can't stand it! This liquid kids are drinking is not food and can never replace the value of real food. To me, it's a sign of poor parenting and lack of family structure. Not to mention how unfair it is to give to a child. *Ughhhhhh*!

Of course it wasn't always easy at dinnertime in my house: there were tears, fits, tantrums, and stomp offs. I held my ground, not reacting, remaining calm and kind. If they flat out refused to eat that night, I'd toss the food, and in the morning, serve a healthy breakfast. They always ate it. Eventually they learned, like training a puppy to not beg and eat their own food. Now my girls eat it all. Some things they like better than others, and I know when to pick my battles. When we attend birthday parties or outings, they eat what they are served, and I don't make a squeak about it—unless it's plain old nasty crap like uberprocessed packaged dyed foods; then I say no.

Now when they go to someone's house where the kids get fed crap, they come home and say, "Momma, poor Susie eats nothing but moon pies all day long!"

They know that what we eat keeps us healthy, and there is nothing more I can ask for. When they grow up and leave my house, I'll know I fed my kids real food. Even better is when they ask me to make them a special soup if they have tummy aches or a cold. They love the umeboshi plum balls and guzzle aloe vera juice (see recipes in Part Three)! My husband, too. If he's been away from us for a few days, he always comes home and gobbles up everything I make.

> I don't believe in forcing children to eat, nor to eat everything on their plate, and then rewarding them with sugar . . .

What Is Autoimmune Disease?

There are well over one hundred documented autoimmune diseases, and every day new ones are being diagnosed. An autoimmune disease occurs when our body's disease-fighting cells mistakenly attack healthy cells, the very cells that these warrior cells were created to protect! Many scientists now believe that our environment is causing the increase in autoimmune diseases, as we are exposed to more than 80,000 man-made chemicals on a daily basis. This makes it hard for our warrior cells to tell the difference between what is a toxin and what is not. When these fighter cells are inundated daily, they begin to shoot at everything because they can't tell the friends from the enemies. Never before in the history of humankind have we been inundated with such a large number or amount of toxins. When we slather lotions on our skin, shampoo our hair, spray down our kitchen counters, sprinkle flavorings on our food, wash our clothes, or fill our gas tanks, we are breathing in chemicals.

In a 2005 study,* researchers found 287 industrial chemicals, including pesticides, phthalates, dioxins, flame retardants, and the breakdown chemicals of Teflon, in the fetal cord blood of ten newborns from around the country. These chemicals were transmitted to the infants by their mothers, who had been exposed to them before and during pregnancy.

Our mattresses are not safe either; we spend upwards of eight hours a day sleeping on and breathing in flame-retardant chemicals. If you live in California, for instance, you should know that state law requires that all furniture and mattresses sold in the state must contain this fire-retardant chemical, which is so toxic that it's scary. It has even been linked to cancer and autoimmune disease. The governor of California has tried to revoke this law; however, the chemical lobbyists have deep pockets and a reach to match. Fortunately, you can order organic mattresses, and they are NOT any more expensive!

> An autoimmune disease occurs when our body's disease-fighting cells mistakenly attack healthy cells . . .

*In *The Autoimmune Epidemic;* article written by Donna Jackson Nakazawa; study noted by Dr. Douglas Kerr, MD, PhD.]

The number of autoimmune-disease sufferers is scary: one in twelve Americans (and one in nine women) will develop an autoimmune disorder at some point in their lifetime. Charting these numbers is tough, since there is no record-keeping database for autoimmune diseases.

To give you an idea of the beating the immune system of an average American takes over the course of a normal day, take a look at the following:

> one in twelve Americans (and one in nine women) will develop an autoimmune disorder at some point in their lifetime.

7:00 a.m. Box of cereal with food coloring added, processed and GMO (genetically modified) grains. *Immune system kicks in to fight the fake ingredients in the food.*

8:00 a.m. Go for a walk and pass by where a lawn-care specialist is spraying a neighbor's yard. *If a chemical can kill an insect, it can kill a cell and pollute ground water.*

9:00 a.m. Grab 3G cell phone, which now makes us the "tower" and hits our hips with small doses of radiation all day long (hello, thyroid issues). Swing by the dry cleaners to pick up clothes and place garments not yet off-gassed into car, roll up windows, and run air conditioner, recycling the dry-cleaning chemicals. *Off gassing is when building materials and chemically treated products from new clothes to countertops release chemicals in the air through evaporation. This evaporation can continue for years, meaning we are breathing them into our bodies while we walk, sleep, drive, work, and sit.*

10:00 a.m. Hair appointment at the salon—just roots. *Studies have shown that women who color their hair are three times more likely to come down with lupus.*

12:30 p.m. Stop to get gas; don't wash hands after pumping, and grab a handful of pretzels. *Benzene and bacteria—immune system is working overtime!*

1:00 p.m. Lunch at favorite restaurant—big salad, chicken, and sweet tea. NONE of the meal is organic because all-organic restaurants are rare. *Salad wasn't washed well and a small amount of bacteria seeps into the intestinal tract, further taxing the immune system. Pesticides are all* *over the food, and the chicken has enough antibiotics in it to kill a urinary tract infection.*

4:30 p.m. Take a nap on the brand-new sofa (as it off-gases), while the baby sleeps in her flame-retardant car seat after noshing on a handful of kiddie snacks packaged in phthalates. *Phthalates are estrogen mimickers, which have been linked to cancer and autoimmune disease.*

5:00 p.m. Cook dinner; boil water in a large nonstick pot for pasta; kitchen fills up with steam. *No need to worry about the pasta absorbing the seeping chemicals from the pot because the entire family is now breathing them in via the steam in the air.*

8:00 p.m. Vacuum house after spraying the carpet with chemical air freshener. Finish up laundry by adding a dryer sheet for that extra fresh scent. *The dryer sheet adds another chemical for the skin to absorb via tomorrow's T-shirt.*

9:00 p.m. Climb into your top-of-the-line $2,000 flame-retardant bed.

No wonder we are so tired! That is just a brief example of how the average American's immune system spends the day fighting foreign chemicals and fake foods.

So, you see, when the FDA says small increments of these ingredients are harmless, I'm sure they are right; however, our common lives are packed with small increments twenty-four hours a day, 365 days a year, making these small increments LARGE increments over time.

A major player in the fight against autoimmune diseases, Dr. Gerard E. Mullen of Johns Hopkins Hospital, recommends eating a whole real foods diet that supports and rebuilds the digestive tract, avoiding any fake food that further stresses the immune system. Dr. Mullen knows that foods can heal because he too used food to come back from a grave autoimmune illness.

> Dr. Gerard E. Mullen recommends eating a whole real foods diet that supports and rebuilds the digestive tract, avoiding any fake food that further stresses the immune system.

What Are Crohn's Disease and Colitis?

Crohn's disease is an autoimmune disease that causes inflammation, or swelling, and irritation of any part of the digestive tract. The inflammation leads to ulcerations, wounds that may eventually become holes, allowing nutrients, other particles, and blood to seep out of the intestines. This throws the entire body off. The part most commonly affected by Crohn's disease is the end part of the small intestine, called the ileum.

Colitis affects the colon in a very similar way, while Crohn's disease can affect both the small intestine as well as the colon.

I see Crohn's disease and colitis like this: a family of four goes out to dinner, and everyone comes down with a slight bout of food poisoning. One of them takes a while longer than the others to recover. This person maybe had a weakened immune system at the time, and the bacteria causing the illness gained power. Then, over the course of a few years, if the diet of this person is rich in sugar, yeast, processed foods, and large amounts of mucus-causing dairy, the bacteria is further fortified. Along comes another outing and a new batch of food poisoning. Within a few more years, if that long, this person becomes incredibly ill and is diagnosed as having inflammatory bowel disease (also known as Crohn's or colitis).

> The surgery I had at birth made my intestines and immune system highly susceptible to threats.

The surgery I had at birth made my intestines and immune system highly susceptible to threats. I can very clearly remember coming down with food poisoning a few times; each time was worse than the time before. I'm very mindful to eat at home as often as possible. Whether or not we have Crohn's or colitis, it is IMPERATIVE that we keep our kitchens clean, cook in clean kitchens, and be mindful of kitchen bacteria—not only from animal products but also from our produce. I do not eat at community potlucks as I have found most people no longer tend to their kitchens with the same care and steadfastness that our ancestors did. I feel we have lost the teachings of how to run our homes. Also, I *never* eat raw foods when traveling, and I steer clear of eating in any place that serves food if it doesn't seem clean. I do not eat raw fish or medium-rare meat either.

Symptoms of both Crohn's disease and colitis range from common to extreme bouts of gas, bowel obstructions, bloody stools, chronic diarrhea and/or chronic constipation, abdominal pain (constant/frequent), and anemia. All I had was constant abdominal burning, anemia, and occasional partial bowel obstructions. It took the doctors ten years to diagnose me, and I am thankful. Had they diagnosed me earlier, I would have become a walking pharmaceutical cocktail, as I was not yet in the space to take my health back via my kitchen. I believe that not having taken the drugs allowed me to heal at a faster rate. My body didn't have to first combat the side effects of the harsh pharmaceuticals. The healing foods went right to work on my weakest link—the intestines.

Doctors don't know what causes these awful digestive diseases, nor do they know what heals them. For the most part, they believe food has NO influence over the disease: Obviously I disagree.

What I think and KNOW is that food definitely plays a crucial part in healing these diseases. The only way to get the body back in balance, in my opinion, is to support it with highly nutritional foods and avoid chemicals and toxins, including sugar. If there is an overgrowth of bad bacteria, then we need to balance and boost the immune system to fix that. Suppressing the immune system with immunosuppressant drugs will NEVER make us well. I have yet to meet ONE person who got well solely on the meds.

> Doctors don't know what causes these awful digestive diseases, nor do they know what heals them.

Tips for Aiding the Digestive Tract & Easing Digestive Distress

I've put together a list of tips that have helped me get well and made eating less painful and more enjoyable. Of course this is not medical advice. Always check with your doctor for medical advice. This is what I did and still do on a regular basis.

1. **Take a digestive enzyme before each meal.** OMG, this has been key for Mee! In the beginning, I would take 2–3 before each meal and sometimes after. If you drink wine or coffee with your meal, take an extra. The only side effect of taking too many digestive enzymes is that they can increase bowel movements.

2. **Take probiotics.** It is believed that if you are suffering bouts of bad gas, frequent yeast infections, or bloating and pressure after you eat, you are possibly suffering from "dysbiosis." This means that you don't have enough healthy bacteria in your digestive tract. Adding probiotics to your diet is believed to aid in balancing this bacteria battle. Probiotics come in many forms, including capsules and even powder. I personally had a very difficult time taking probiotics in the large doses required. Instead, I ate my probiotics (see below). Any foods sold with added probiotics are a wash if they are also loaded with sugar.

Bitch bowls are small bowls of food eaten seven times a day with a break in between.

3. **Chew your food!** Before you sit down to eat, take a few breaths. Calm down, and chew as many times per bite as you can—until your food is "mushy."

4. **Eat "Bitch Bowls."** Bitch bowls are small bowls of food eaten seven times a day with a break in between. If you've got any digestive distress, take it easy and ease up on your intestines by following the old saying, "Don't stuff your mouth!"

5. **Increase your intake of fermented foods, such as sauerkraut.**

6. **Cut out questionable foods.** I stopped eating hard to digest foods that are also high in fats such as gluten, dairy, beef, chicken, sausage, bacon, sugar, and processed foods (with the exception of brown-rice pasta once a week). Now that I am well I eat occasionally small amounts of grass-fed organic beef, grass-fed organic lamb, and eggs.

7. **Eat miso soup.** I made a fresh pot of miso soup every day and ate a bowl of it twice a day—once in the morning, and once at night. (See recipe on page 00.)

8. **Soak grains.** I soaked brown rice overnight with kombu seaweed. I cooked the brown rice with extra water until it was super soft (the same with quinoa and millet). (See the recipe in Part Three.)

9. **Soak Beans.** I also soaked aduki beans overnight with kombu. (See the recipe in Part Three.)

10. **Steam vegetables.** I steamed all kinds of veggies and sometimes also sautéed them in water. Occasionally, I'd use olive oil or sesame oil.

11. **Soak Oatmeal.** I soaked organic oatmeal overnight with kombu and ate it for breakfast.

12. **Drink kuzu with apple juice.** This calms the nervous system and stops spasms and cramps. This also aids in easing the constant burning pain associated with digestive disorders. (See the recipe in Part Three.)

> Studies have shown that low levels of vitamin D are not only linked to flare-ups of Crohn's disease and colitis, but also cancer . . .

13. **Take aloe vera juice.** I had 2 to 4 ounces of organic aloe vera juice twice a day. It is excellent for the skin and intestines, as it soothes inflamed intestinal tissue.

14. **Adapt to a real food breakfast.** My diet became incredibly simple as I ate collards and kale for breakfast, changing my craving and palate to adapt to a real food breakfast.

15. **Cook with high-quality oil.** I only cooked with sesame oil and olive oil for the first few months, adding in some coconut oil and then ghee (there's more info about oil later).

16. **Try acupuncture.** I began acupuncture sessions up to twice a week.

17. **Take vitamin D.** I took vitamin D3 (5,000 units per gelcap) once a day. Studies have shown that low levels of vitamin D are not only linked to flare-ups of Crohn's disease and colitis, but also cancer, as vitamin D is a major ingredient in creating and sustaining a healthy immune system.

18. **Take fish oil.** I took fish oil for omega-3 fatty acids (healthy fats). Studies have shown that omega-3 intake has a direct effect on

lower inflammation levels in the body. Plus it's excellent for skin—beautiful skin is a direct link to low inflammation, and skin irritations and rashes are linked to a poorly functioning liver according to Chinese medicine.

19. **Eat umeboshi plums, plum balls, and medicinal teas.** They are considered extremely alkaline, aid in digestion, and fight acid—so perfect with a glass of wine or after a cup of coffee. (See recipe in Part Three.)

20. **Try Chinese medicine.** After two years with an acupuncturist, I switched to a Chinese medicine doctor who formatted specific herbs to support my body's rebuilding efforts. Immediately, I felt even more relief.

21. **Try talk therapy.** I began seeing a therapist weekly so that I would have a place to process my stress and anxiety. For years, I carried it around with me, afraid to show it and let go of it. So it piled up in my gut, adding to the ache.

> I began seeing a therapist weekly so that I would have a place to process my stress and anxiety.

22. **Eat smaller portions.** I'm all about "Bitch Bowls" (see #4) and so are the Japanese, as they have a rule I live by: eat until 80 percent full. You know when your there 'cause we've all said, "I can't take one more bite." Well, listen to your own personal knowing.

23. **Consider more raw veggies.** If your digestive tract is in good shape and you're not suffering any dis-ease, then add in more raw veggies as they contain natural digestive enzymes.

24. **Simplify your meals.** My good friend, Iva Peele, said it best one day: "Mee, people with big dreams need to eat simple foods." It's true; every meal doesn't have to be complicated with thirty different ingredients. I am sure that if I make lasagna with tofu ricotta, that the next day I eat a "Bitch Bowl" with brown rice, cabbage, and carrots (see the recipe in Part Three). This gives my body a break in breaking my food down. Our lives are so super busy and complicated, I find that eating simply calms not just my physical body, but also my emotional body. I think clearer and react more calmly. When you are stressed, simplify.

25. **Drink lemon water.** Warm lemon water is a great way to keep the intestines moving. First thing in the morning, squeeze half a lemon into a mug of warm water (see recipe in Part Three).

26. **Don't drink while you eat.** If you fill up your stomach with water or other liquid, it's unable to begin the digestion process. When you do drink, drink only 4 ounces at a time. Chugging big bottles of water causes bloating and gas, not to mention that our bodies can't absorb it all.

27. **Try massage.** For the first year of my healing, I would get a massage once a month from a local massage therapist who really understood all parts of the body. I told her that my weak link was my intestines, so she would spend twenty minutes working on my intestines and the reflexology points on my feet associated with the intestines. She taught me to do this very massage on myself; by using two fingers, you gently massage your abdominal area, starting at the lower right side of your belly. Then, massage up to the bottom of your rib cage, then across your upper abdomen, and then down the left side, in clockwise motion around your belly button. I taught Lee this technique, and now when I suffer a bought of gas or feel blocked, he helps. It's a great tool if you have small children who suffer from constipation or digestive disease.

> For the first year of my healing, I would get a massage once a month from a local massage therapist who really understood all parts of the body.

28. **Use a hot water bottle.** I'm not talking about a heating pad but an old-school rubber bottle (they can be found at almost any drugstore). I fill mine with hot water from a kettle and let it rest on my tummy or back if there are spasms there. The heat brings circulation to the intestines.

29. **Try Di-Gize oil.** Obsessed! It smells so good, calms every one down, and seriously aids in circulating the intestines. I put a few drops on the bottom of my feet and the palms of my hands while massaging my abdomen. It's a little pricy, but a bottle lasts a long while. Here is the link to order on line: www.youngliving.com/essential–oil–blends/Di–Gize.

30. **SHADOOBIE!** Constipation is a terrible, horrible thing—not because it's uncomfortable, but because it's highly toxic. Chronic constipation can definitely lead to colon cancer.

31. **Breathe from deep within your belly.** It's no joke! Oxygen is something we all need; shallow breathing is a modern bad habit. Not only does breathing properly ease digestive distress, but it also calms our emotional selves. When I get in a tizzy or right before I eat, I breathe!

> Not only does breathing properly ease digestive distress, but it also calms our emotional selves.

32. **Avoid drinking ice-cold beverages.** Cold beverages contract the body. Think about how your body contracts when you get an outside chill; the same thing happens inside when you pour icy liquid into a 100-degree container. Contraction causes digestive pain. I'd eaten ice for years and could only drink ice water, so I thought. My poor tummy!

33. **Don't eat any nuts or corn kernels until inflammation in your digestive tract has passed.** The little particles are abrasive and can add to discomfort.

34. **Take rest breaks and get enough sleep.** Sleep is such a big deal to help the body heal. I'm not much of a napper, but once my Chinese medicine doctor stressed how much better I would feel if I'd rest for 10 minutes a day by laying down flat on my back, I tried it and realized she was right. This 10-minute rest gives my adrenals a chance to recharge. I also make sure that most nights I'm in bed by 9 p.m. and up at 7 a.m., giving my body 10 hours of sleep. This way my cells can reboot, baby!

Our digestive tract needs to rest too. I try not to eat past 7 p.m., which in a city like LA is tough since most folks don't go out to eat until 9 p.m. I curb this by eating at home and having a cup of tea or soup at dinner.

Killing the Bad Bacteria and Feeding the Good

Where does bad bacteria come from? Well, this is my theory: We all have bad bacteria from dirt, water, foods, and of course, not all bacteria is bad. We need the good bacteria for healthy gut function. However, when we get a really nasty strain, like a tummy virus or food poisoning, some of these bacteria linger behind and wait to be fed sugar and yeast. Over a period of time, these bacteria grow.

Now that large populations of Americans suffer from small bacteria overgrowth in their small intestines, intestinal issues are on the rise and are becoming "common." Indications of this condition include tummy aches, bloating, loose stools, and bad breath. Irritable bowel syndrome (IBS) is a red-flag diagnosis of this truth, as it is screaming there is sensitivity and inflammation in the digestive tract—all a precursor for inflammatory bowel disease IBD). If bacteria is left to fester and be fed, it will lead to the weakening of our intestinal walls, which can become bowel ulcerations and categorized as IBD. Imagine having a scraped knee; you would do all you could to keep the area clean and protected. The same should go for wounds and scrapes (inflammation) in the intestines.

Here in the Southeast of the United States, the *Clostridium difficile* (C-Diff) superbug is surpassing staph infections in hospitals in number of incidences. The C-Diff superbug is an antibiotic-resistant bacterium found in the colon and can cause diarrhea and other more serious intestinal conditions, including colitis (a bacteria-driven inflammatory disease in the colon). C-DIFF is spread by spores in feces, and the spores are difficult to kill even with most conventional household cleaners or alcohol-based hand sanitizers. In fact, some of the disinfection measures used against staph infections are not successful with C-DIFF. If you have a previous bacteria overgrowth and one of these nasty bugs gets into your gut, your intestinal lining is defenseless. The immune system tries to fight this bad bacterium over a period of time, but we keep feeding the bacteria and eventually our immune system

We all have bad bacteria from dirt, water, foods, and of course, not all bacteria is bad. We need the good bacteria for healthy gut function.

can't keep up. This leads to the breakdown of our immune systems and the land of autoimmune disease. If our immune systems are strong, disease cannot live in the body. It is a fact that the base of our immune system is found in the intestines. If you want to keep your kids healthy, spend less money on doctor bills and instead consider what bad bacteria is going into their mouths.

Eating at home as often as possible is another way to support your immune system, and if you already have digestive or major health issues, eating at home should be a priority, fo'sho. I was a waitress in both nice restaurants and dive diners; I *know* the state of cleanliness and bacteria. Lemons used for water and ice tea are usually downright nasty as the servers grab them with unwashed hands, after handling checks and money. These nasty lemons hit your ice water or tea. I say pass on the lemon when eating out.

> If you want to keep your kids healthy, spend less money on doctor bills and instead consider what bad bacteria is going into their mouths.

Probiotics

After beginning to remove the sugar and yeast that was feeding the nasty bacteria, I was told that I needed to take things a step further by adding probiotics and prebiotics to my diet. Probiotics are found naturally in fermented foods such as sauerkraut, miso, pickles, yogurts, and kefirs. I began to take a probiotic pill once a day before bed, and a prebiotic pill in the morning before breakfast. Probiotics kill the bad bacteria, and prebiotics feed the NEW good bacteria. A side effect of probiotics is gas, as one theory is that the good and bad bacteria are doing battle—be patient and wait it out, or try taking your probiotics with food (this is what I was advised to do over and over). Or, as I was told, "If you have increased discomfort while taking these, lesson the dose, cut it in half, and do not take it every day."

Every acupuncturist, naturopathic doctor, and food guru has told me this and now even some medical doctors advise their patients to take probiotic pills. In my case, probiotics never stopped hurting me. In fact, I have *never* been able to take probiotics in a pill or powder form. What I have done is eaten my probiotics in the most natural way via the foods that they are fermented into. This creates a gradual colony of healthy bacteria and becomes a part of one's body organically.

I ate and still eat, kimchi, sauerkraut, natto, umeboshi plums, coconut kefir, and miso soup twice a day.

This past summer I spent the afternoon with our livestock mineralist, Mark Bader. He has PhDs in nutrition and chemistry. I was fascinated by the connection between Crohn's disease/colitis in humans and John's disease in cattle, which similarly affects the lining of the intestines. The University of Florida believes it to be exactly the same disease. Mark too believed it to be similar, with different bacterium found in cattle than in humans but attacking the system in the same manner. I asked him how he worked with the sick cattle, and he said he balanced their bodies' pH levels, and then fed them specific probiotics. When I told him I could not take probiotics, he said of course I couldn't. For one, the probiotics weren't a match for my diet, because most over-the-counter probiotics are formulated for people with a high-sugar diet. He was right. I'd totally cut out sugar and sugary foods, only eating brown rice occasionally. Yet, I was filling my belly with bacterium that I didn't need, like *Lactobacillus acidophilus*. This is one of the main strains of bacterium found in the majority of probiotics. It is beneficial for those on a high-sugar diet. Plus, Mark agreed that the reason eating my probiotics helped me was because I had gradually added them in via my diet. Mark is currently creating a probiotic specifically for my diet, and I can't wait to try it!

Now I have a healthier flora of bacteria in my intestines and I don't crave sugar or yeast in the ways I used too, but when I do, I find it really easy to curb it. A dried fig is like eating a chocolate bar, as my body has found its balance not only in my digestive tract but also in my mouth. My taste buds are no longer covered in a layer of fake sugar, fat, and salt. They are now more like a young child's, and I can actually taste the flavors of real foods.

> In my opinion digestive diseases are not hereditary; they are preventative!

In my opinion digestive diseases are not hereditary; they are preventable! *What* we eat is hereditary. We can change what we eat to create a healthier outcome for our future generations.

Fermented Foods

The only time I ever ate anything fermented was if my grandmother on my daddy's side made her famous sauerkraut with apples and pork. I had no idea that fermented foods were ancestral globally, and it's only fairly recently that they were removed from our American dinner plates. When I started on this food journey, sauerkraut and pickles were on my list to be eaten with every meal. The stipulation, however, was that they not be modern made, because modern pickles are prepared with vinegar instead of the traditional method of lacto-fermentation, using salt.

Back in the day, bread and pasta were made with naturally leavened wild yeast (sourdough) as well. Beer, wine, and cheese are also made differently now, through a process that kills off what many believe to be beneficial bacteria.

Humans all over the world have been fermenting food since ancient times. The earliest evidence of winemaking dates back 8,000 years in the Caucasus area of Georgia. 7,000-year-old jars, which once contained wine, were excavated in the Zagros Mountains in Iran. There is evidence that people made fermented beverages in Babylon around 5,000 BC, ancient Egypt circa 3,150 BC, pre-Hispanic Mexico circa 2,000 BC, and Sudan circa 1,500 BC. There is also evidence of leavened bread in ancient Egypt dating back to 1,500 BC, and of milk fermentation in Babylon circa 3,000 BC.

One theory is that lack of fermented foods is why so many people suffer dairy sensitivity and allergies; that ancestrally the only way people ingested dairy was if it was fermented.

Here are six reasons to eat fermented foods:

One theory is that lack of fermented foods is why so many people suffer dairy sensitivity and allergies

1. **Fermented foods improve digestion.** They are broken down during the process of fermentation; therefore, they are easier to digest, which improves absorption. For example, some people can eat yogurt, but not any other type of dairy because the lactose (the primary allergen in milk) is broken down in the fermentation process.

2. **Fermented foods aid in restoring healthy bacteria.** They are total probiotics!

3. **Fermented foods are packed with natural digestive enzymes.** Immediately, I began eating a scoop of sauerkraut or a small teaspoon of natto (fermented soy beans) with each meal.

4. **Fermented dairy products contain good amounts of folic acid.** This vitamin is crucial to producing healthy babies.

5. **Fermented foods last for months in the refrigerator!**

6. **Fermenting food is inexpensive.** You can find fermented food starter kits online and in health food stores. If you are dairy free, you can make your own coconut kefir probiotic drink. I actually prefer it to dairy, and it's known as a hangover cure.

The following is a helpful list of store-bought probiotic foods:

- **Bubbies brand sauerkraut or pickles**—they are fermented the old-school way.

- **Umeboshi plums**—found at health food stores, Asian markets, or online.

- **Natto**—fermented soybeans; they are like eating pungent cheese. I LOVE them! They can be found in Asian markets, some sushi restaurants serve them, or you can buy them online.

- **Homemade coconut kefir water**—starter kits are found in almost all health food markets or are easily purchased online. It's easy to do!

- **Miso paste**—only buy organic; if you are avoiding soy, then try the chickpea soy free. You can find miso paste in Asian markets, international food stores, or online.

> Fermenting food is inexpensive. You can find fermented food starter kits online and in health food stores.

The Benefits of B Vitamins

Everyone wants to know if I took tons of supplements right away, and the answer is no. My goal was to rebuild my digestive muscle by eating food. It was hard enough for me to eat already, and I was told by Carolyn Ross, M.D., that my body probably wouldn't even absorb vitamins until my intestines were functioning properly.

I run into lots of folks who live on supplements and vitamins instead of eating a balanced diet. I'm not down on these things; I just believe that food was created to support the body, and we should start there.

Besides vitamin D and my omega-3 gels, I do get a shot of vitamin B. It's a crazy-good thing getting B-vitamin injections. They have shifted my healing journey. Once I started these injections my energy levels improved, my periods got easier along with my PMS, and my digestive dis-ease lessoned. I found out that many doctors and gynecologists recommend different cocktails of injections depending on individual issues. There are studies that have shown that people who have inflammatory bowel syndrome (IBS) have fewer flare-ups and discomfort when they get these injections. B vitamins are absorbed in the small intestines, so if you've suffered from digestive issues that affect the small intestines, it's a guarantee you've not been able to absorb enough vitamin B. Here's an overview of what each one does and the foods you can eat to get them!

> I just believe that food was created to support the body, and we should start there.

Vitamin B1

Vitamin B1 maintains energy supplies. It aides in the coordination of muscle and nerve activity, helps heart function, and (my favorite for my issue) supports hydrochloric-acid production—natural digestive enzyme.

Foods to Eat: black beans, Brussels sprouts, eggplant, green peas, cantaloupe, mushrooms, romaine lettuce, sunflower seeds, sesame seeds, tuna, navy beans, pinto beans, lima beans, tomatoes, and spinach.

Vitamin B2

Used for the production of cellular energy!

Foods to Eat: legumes, millet, sea vegetables, sunflower seeds, wild rice, small amounts of asparagus, broccoli, organic soybeans, yogurt, collards, and spinach.

Vitamin B3

You can get this alone in an injectable form from your doctor, especially if you have high levels of the "bad" cholesterol (LDL). It also stabilizes blood sugar, stimulates circulation, and increases hydrochloric acid production.

Foods to Eat: almonds, asparagus, avocado, cantaloupe, collard greens, cremini mushrooms, dark rye, spelt, peanuts, halibut, salmon, shiitake, calf liver, tuna, and grass-fed beef.

Vitamin B5

Ooh, this is a big one, especially if you are a big-time coffee drinker as our adrenals are taking a hit with all of our high-stress lifestyles topped off with large amounts of caffeine consumption. Vitamin B5 supports healthy adrenal glands (it's the antistress vitamin).

Foods to Eat: avocado, broccoli, cantaloupe, cauliflower, green peas, mushrooms, peanuts, sunflower seeds, sweet potatoes, turnip greens, cucumber, eggs, corn, shiitake mushrooms, and cremini mushrooms.

Vitamin B6

Vitamin B6 is required by the body to manufacture dopamine, one of the mood neurotransmitters. Research into the effects of vitamin B6 on PMS have been mixed, but I personally have found it to help BIG time!

Foods to Eat: chickpeas, wild salmon, lean grass-fed beef, organic chicken breast, white potatoes (with skin), oatmeal, banana, pistachio nuts, and lentils.

> What I have found is that B12 calms me down and gives me energy to keep going.

Vitamin B12

What I have found is that B12 calms me down and gives me energy to keep going. Instead of jacking me up like caffeine and whacking me out, B12 supports the nervous system and also the production of red blood cells, preventing anemia. I was so severely anemic for so many years that I get this shot twice a month and try to eat foods that contain it naturally.

Foods to Eat: tempeh, spirulina, nori seaweed, sprouts, nutritional yeast, clams, oysters, mussels, caviar, lamb, beef, crab, lobster, Swiss cheese, and egg yoke.

Selenium

Selenium is a mineral not a B vitamin, but I am including it here because it is a major player in healing, and I'm all about getting it into my body and my family's bodies. It protects cells from free-radical damage, enables the thyroid to produce thyroid homes, helps lower the risk of join inflammation, and supports glutathione metabolism.

Foods to Eat: asparagus, barley, blackstrap molasses, garlic, shiitake mushrooms, oats, rye, sunflower seeds, tofu, and the big one—sea vegetables!

Everything You Need to Know About Sugar

Sugar is sugar, whether it's agave, honey, brown sugar, cane sugar, fruit sugar, or grain sugar.

Here's the deal: Sugar is sugar, whether it's agave, honey, brown sugar, cane sugar, fruit sugar, or grain sugar. Our body registers it all as one big old group—sugar. It feeds the unhealthy bacteria living in our intestinal tracts. In our country, there is a huge surge in small intestinal bacterial overgrowth—an overabundance of unhealthy bacteria in the intestinal tract. When there is an overgrowth, our immune system (which depends on the health of our small intestines for its strength) suffers. The immune system is not only connected to cold and flu, but also to cancers and autoimmune diseases.

Tummy aches, bad breath, gas, pressure, yeast infections, and frequent colds and tummy bugs are signs that our intestinal villi are covered in bad bacteria, mucus, or plain mowed down (unable to grab the nutrients from the food).

Kids are huge victims of small intestinal bacterial overgrowth. First of all, their immune systems are not completely developed, and they are fed foods sweetened to please them, all day long. This explains the rise of digestive disorders in young children beginning at age four and up. Once one of the really bad gastro bugs find its way into these little digestive tracts, they are fed and grow, taking control of the child's immune system. Look at it this way: we bring our infants home with a message from the doctor to take good care of the baby since his or her immune system is not yet built, but by nine months old, the baby is introduced to sugar on a high-intake level—apple juice—which immediately suppresses the undeveloped immune system.

> Kids are huge victims of small intestinal bacterial overgrowth.

When we have too much bad bacteria, disease on all levels sets in. Every time you get that thing halfway through the day that says, "Oh, man, my sugar dropped. I need a soda or a cookie," it's not your sugar; it's the junky bacteria in your gut jonesin' for more dope! It's also the imbalance that has been created in the brain by an excessive abuse of sugar. (If you are diabetic, your sugar issues are different.)

Inflammatory bowel disease is definitely related to an overgrowth of sugar, yeast, and unhealthy bacteria. If you suffer from digestive disease, cut back on your sugar and yeast for at least *four* months to see a difference. Cutting back on sugar for a few weeks won't matter much; that bacteria has been growing like crazy for years by the time it's giving you trouble.

Here is my personal perception of what happens to sugar inside the body: When we take a teaspoon of sugar that's been sitting in our kitchen at room temperature (65–75°F) and add it into a hot pan on the stove (around 98 degrees or hotter), the sugar begins to sizzle as it heats up. This is the same process that occurs in our bodies: the sugar heats up the blood, literally creating acid. Most folks consume 160 pounds of sugar a year. One 20-ounce bottle of soda contains 27 grams of sugar. Every 4 grams equals 1 teaspoon of sugar. Thus, every time you drink a soda, you are drinking 6.75 teaspoons of sugar!

Imagine getting a glass of water and scooping 7 teaspoons of sugar into it—or even worse, imagine doing this to your children's water! Did you know that most folks who are living on a theoretically low-sugar diet are still averaging 40 teaspoons per day? Not to mention, sugar is food for the unhealthy bacteria growing rapidly in the digestive tract of people who eat diets high in yeast and sugar.

Every time I crave a sweet, I stop and think, *Oh, that's not my body craving sugar; that is the bad bacteria calling out for more.* And instead, I eat something to support the healthy bacteria that strengthen my immune system, such as miso, fermented foods, probiotics, coconut kefir, or veggies rich in vitamins. By supporting our cells, we literally decide which cells we are going to feed—cancer cells or healthy cells. You see, everyone has cancer cells in their bodies, so when I take a bite of food, I've got a choice in what I'm feeding my body and how I'm supporting my body's immune system.

Upon my first meeting with Ginny Harper, I swore I didn't have a sugar problem. The truth is, I didn't know that I did. I'm not a candy gal; I don't care for sweets and processed cookies. A nice piece of cake now and then and 2 teaspoons of sugar in my coffee (8 grams) were all I needed, and an ice-cold soda a couple times a week—until the plug was pulled. When I started reading labels and observing how much processed food I was eating, while attempting to stop taking in any sugar, I began to realize the truth behind my consumption. Once I started reading labels and I couldn't have any extra sugar aside from what is naturally found in beans, grains, and veggies, I started jonesin' like a junky, shawty!

Let me tell you, I was rationing bites of cookies to get a fix. Thank goodness for the sweet vegetable juice recipe I learned (see Part Three). It was on Ginny's list, and I needed it for my sweet tooth. The other naughty side to sugar is that it feeds the bacteria that cause ulcerations. If we view ulcerations as a physical wound, it helps us pay attention to how we are healing. Imagine a large cut on your leg; you wouldn't add harmful bacteria or creams that feed the harmful bacteria to the cut. You also wouldn't allow dirt to get into the cut. Instead, you would try to kill the bad bacteria and feed the healthy bacteria.

> Every time I crave a sweet, I stop and think, "Oh, that's not my body craving sugar; that is the bad bacteria calling out for more."

Sugar is food for bad bacteria. When we are craving it, that's a sign that we have plenty of it. I see the bacteria as a parasite, so when it wants more food I say, "Hell no, Joe."

Sugar, Cancer, Heart Disease, and Addiction

If your intestinal relationship with sugar isn't a concern, then check out some other facts that definitely apply. In April 2012, Dr. Sanjay Gupta did a story for *60 Minutes* on CBS in which he referred to sugar as a toxin, proving medically and scientifically that:

1. **Sugar is a feeder of cancer.** Harvard professor and head of the Beth Israel Deaconess Cancer Center Lewis Cantley says when we eat or drink sugar, it causes a sudden spike in the hormone insulin, which can serve as a catalyst that fuels certain types of cancers. Nearly one-third of some common cancers, including breast and colon cancers, have insulin receptors on their surface. Insulin binds to these receptors and signals the tumor to start consuming glucose. Every cell in our body needs glucose to survive. The trouble is, these cancer cells need it to survive and grow too.

2. **Eating and drinking sweetened foods and drinks can be as bad for our hearts as cheeseburgers.** When the liver gets overloaded with fructose, some of it is converted into fat. Some of that fat ends up in the bloodstream and helps generate a dangerous kind of cholesterol called small, dense LDL particles. These particles are known to lodge in blood vessels, form plaque, and are associated with heart attacks.

3. **Sugar is proven to be one of the most addictive substances; it triggers dopamine in the brain like drugs do.** Eric Stice, a neuroscientist at the Oregon Research Institute, says that by scanning hundreds of volunteers, he's learned that people who frequently drink sodas or eat ice cream or other sweet foods may be building up a tolerance to sugar, in much the same way drug users build up a tolerance to their drug of choice. As strange as it sounds, this means the more sugar you eat, the less you feel the reward. The result: you eat more than ever.

> . . . people who frequently drink sodas or eat ice cream or other sweet foods may be building up a tolerance to sugar, in much the same way drug users build up a tolerance to their drug of choice.

My concern is how this sugar consumption is affecting young children's brains. Considering they are consuming more sugar now than ever in the history of humankind, it can't be good.

Healing with food is not an overnight event: it takes time. What I know is time goes by either way, so doing something proactive is the way to go. It's funny now to think that I'd ever return to my old way of eating. When I do try heavily processed foods, my mouth swells up from the oil, and I honestly don't enjoy it 'cause all I can taste is "fake."

White Sugar: Understanding It

We are constantly told not to eat white sugar, but I thought it would be helpful to share exactly why. The white crystalline substance we know as sugar is an unnatural substance produced by industrial processes (mostly from sugar cane or sugar beets) by refining it down to pure sucrose, after stripping away all the vitamins, minerals, proteins, enzymes, and other beneficial nutrients. What is left is a concentrated substance that the human body is unable to handle—at least not in the quantities that are now being ingested as part of today's accepted lifestyle.

> The white crystalline substance we know as sugar is an unnatural substance produced by industrial processes

White sugar is addictive. The average American now consumes approximately 160 pounds of sugar per year. This is per man, woman, and child. The damage sugar does is slow and insidious. It takes years before it ruins our pancreas, damages our adrenal glands, throws our whole endocrine system out of kilter, and produces a huge list of other damage.

Overconsumption of sugar is the main cause of diabetes, hyperglycemia, and hypoglycemia. It is either a significant or contributory cause of heart disease, arteriosclerosis, mental illness, depression, senility, hypertension, cancer, and I believe a major contributor to digestive illnesses.

Natural Sugar Alternatives

The world of natural sugar is super sweet! When I was being raised, it was normal to scoop teaspoons of white sugar into my cereal and to sprinkle brown sugar and cinnamon on my toast. On top of that, the only syrup I'd ever used was Aunt Jemima's—a totally processed version of maple syrup.

My appreciation of brown rice syrup wasn't immediate. I was so used to the extreme sweetness of fake foods that I had to take a sweetener hiatus for a few months. Now that I'm off the "hard" stuff, I love the healthy stuff—or, as I call it, "the good stuff." Still it is best to use natural sugar alternatives with low glycemic indexes. However, know that sugar is sugar no matter what kind. All of it feeds unhealthy bacteria and causes inflammation.

The following are descriptions of some of "the good stuff" and the amounts of each to replace 1 cup of refined white sugar:

. . . know that sugar is sugar no matter what kind. All of it feeds unhealthy bacteria and causes inflammation.

Agave Nectar

Agave nectar is similar to honey in taste, but it is not as sweet and floral tasting. It's also processed as it comes from the blue agave plant. The core of the plant contains the *aguamiel,* or honey water, as it is called in northern South America and Mexico. The Aztecs mixed it with salt and used it to treat skin infections and wounds. The aguamiel is the substance used for the syrup production.

There are two types of agave: a dark amber or light color, and a consistency much like maple syrup. The light-colored nectar resembles maple syrup or honey in flavor, but the taste is more delicate, lending to its popularity in drinks, teas, and other snack goods. It actually has more calories than table sugar, 60 compared to sugar's 40, but because agave is about 1.5 times sweeter than sugar, you can use less of it—meaning you can get the same sweetness for the same amount of calories. When buying agave, purchase organic to be sure it is free of unnecessary pesticides and chemicals. And remember, it's a sugar, so use it wisely.

Agave nectar is similar to honey in taste, but it is not as sweet and floral tasting.

Amount to replace 1 cup of refined white sugar: 3/4 cup. Reduce liquid in recipe by 1/4 cup for every cup of agave used, as agave is a liquid.

Glycemic facts: 2 tablespoons of agave nectar has a glycemic index of 30.

Barley Malt

Barley malt is a sweetener produced from sprouted, or malted, barley (as this specific process has become known). It contains approximately 65 percent maltose, 30 percent complex carbohydrates, and 3 percent protein. Malt syrup is dark brown, thick and sticky, and possesses a strong distinctive flavor that can only be described as "malty." It is about half as sweet as refined white sugar. Barley malt syrup is sometimes used in combination with other natural sweeteners to lend a malt flavor without overpowering the flavor or texture of what is being made.

Amount to replace 1 cup of refined white sugar: $1\frac{1}{4}$ cups. Reduce liquid in recipe by $\frac{1}{4}$ cup. If a recipe calls for honey, molasses, or rice syrup, barley malt can be substituted measure for measure, but substituting barley malt for molasses may not work, as molasses has a very strong taste. Barley grains are treated with enzymes that digest the grains' complex carbohydrates into a more simple sugar-producing sweet, maltose-rich system.

Glycemic facts: 2 tablespoons of barley malt has a glycemic index of 42.

Brown Rice Syrup

Brown rice syrup, aka rice syrup, is a sweetener derived by culturing cooked rice with enzymes to break down the starches, then straining off the liquid and reducing it by cooking till the desired consistency is reached. Be mindful if you are totally gluten free as barley sprouts are used as the enzymes.

Amount to replace 1 cup of refined white sugar: Use $1\frac{1}{4}$ cup of brown rice syrup in place of white sugar and reduce the amounts of added liquids to the recipe by $\frac{1}{4}$ cup. (Use in the same way as barley malt.)

Glycemic facts: glycemic index of 25—SUPER LOW.

Barley malt syrup is sometimes used in combination with other natural sweeteners.

Brown rice syrup, aka rice syrup, is a sweetener derived by culturing cooked rice with enzymes

Maple Syrup

Maple syrup is made from the sap of black, red, or sugar maple trees. The sap is boiled to evaporate its water content. Since it comes from trees, it's not a surprise that it's packed with antioxidants, zinc, calcium, and potassium. It is also believed to ease digestion issues resulting from regular table sugar.

Maple syrup has a versatile flavor so it can be used in salad dressing, fish, or on pancakes. It's super sweet in taste so a little goes a long way. My favorite thing about it is it's *ancestral*—folks have been tapping trees for this sweet stuff for eons.

Amount to replace 1 cup of refined white sugar: 1 cup. Reduce liquid by 1/4 cup for every cup of maple syrup used. If a recipes calls for honey, molasses, or rice syrup, but you want to use maple sugar, it can be substituted measure for measure.

Glycemic facts: Pure maple syrup has a glycemic index of 54, while flavored maple syrup has a glycemic index of 68.

> It [maple syrup] is also believed to ease digestion issues resulting from regular table sugar.

Molasses

Molasses contains significant amounts of a variety of healthy minerals (iron, calcium, copper, manganese, potassium, and magnesium). It is made from the liquid left over after the first crystallization of sugar from sugar cane juice. This liquid is boiled again to produce light molasses, but further boiling makes the liquid darker and more bitter, as more and more sugar is extracted. The second boiling produces dark molasses, and the third, blackstrap molasses.

Amount to replace 1 cup of refined white sugar: 1/2 cup. Reduce liquid in recipe by 1/4 cup.

Glycemic facts: Molasses has a glycemic index of 55.

> Molasses contains significant amounts of a variety of healthy minerals.

Rapadura and Sucanat

Rapadura is made of sucrose crystals that have been coated in mineral-rich cooked cane juice. Sucanat is made the same way and has a molasses-type taste, which can be too strong for some recipes. Jiggery, gur, piloncillo, and panela are other names for rapadura or sucanat. In Mexico, piloncillo is used in coffee, juices, and desserts.

Amount to replace 1 cup of refined white sugar: 1 cup.

Glycemic facts: Sucanat has a glycemic index of 47; rapadura, which is exactly the same as sucanat but ground smaller, is the same.

Stevia

Stevia, an extract from the stevia plant, is much sweeter than sugar and therefore less needs to be used; it also has very few calories. Many Western health authorities have yet to acknowledge stevia as a safe sugar substitute, stating that there are not enough studies on the plant. However, stevia has been used in South America for centuries, and there have been many studies reporting that stevia is a safe and useful sugar replacement, especially for people with diabetes or hypertension (some folks feel that this lack of support may have something to do with pressure from the artificial sweetener companies). Stevia is available at health food stores and some grocery stores.

Amount to replace 1 cup of refined white sugar: $1/8$ teaspoon whole leaf powder = 1 teaspoon sugar; $3/8$ teaspoon = 1 tablespoon sugar; amounts differ if using liquid or white powder form. See product's label.

Glycemic facts: Stevia is believed to have zero glycemic index.

Be Aware of Parasites!

Life in Sayulita, Mexico, taught me lots of interesting things, but learning about parasites was downright fascinating in that *oh-tell-me-more-but-do-I-really-wanna-know?* kinda way. Our housekeeper immediately notified me that every Mexican family in the village takes Vermox (anti-worm medication that kills parasites) every six months. It's so common that it is marked on their family calendars. It's not just the Mexicans who are aware of parasites; most cultures acknowledge that they are a common occurrence. Only here in the states do we believe we are so very clean that it's not even a possibility that we will get them. It is debatable if Vermox and other chemical parasite removals are healthier for us; however, on the box it says if you have digestive disease or ulcers not to take it.

In Japan people eat tons of raw fish; however, they have a way in which to eat it, always with wasabi—freshly made with real horseradish as it kills parasites; they eat daikon and traditionally fermented pickled ginger, which creates digestive enzymes that kill parasites. They also drink tea made from Corsican seaweed (a foxtail-like plant that grows beneath the warmer waters of the Atlantic and Pacific) to relieve intestinal parasites. In Japan, this tea seaweed is known as makuri. Schoolchildren in Japan are given makuri tea once a month to safeguard their health. You can order this tea online or purchase at a Japanese market.

When we came back from Mexico, I couldn't get my pediatrician to give the girls anything to rid them of parasites. I knew they'd acquired them as they both suffered tummy aches and gas centered around the full moon—a direct indication, as this is when parasites hatch new eggs and cause discomfort.

Dr. Sheng gave me a natural remedy: 2 tablespoons of ground pumpkin seeds with lemon juice and olive oil every night before bed. Dr. Sheng says, "Don't eat any foods that smell yummy while eating the pumpkin seed remedy." You only need to do this once a month for four nights in a row.

I also gave the girls papaya digestive enzymes every day. They taste like sweet, chewable candy. Tending to our parasites is an ongoing process throughout our lifetimes, as we are constantly exposed, and of course, it takes a very long time to get rid of an infection—sometimes years. Every six months I drink the tea and eat the pumpkin seed mix for a few days in a row. Just like unhealthy bacteria, parasites thrive in acidic and sugar-fed bellies. I take regular digestive enzymes at least three times a day, and this helps to rid them from my body too.

> *Tending to our parasites is an ongoing process throughout our lifetimes, as we are constantly exposed.*

Let's Talk About Wheat and Gluten

Processed wheat is incredibly difficult for anyone's intestines; our bodies were never meant to eat it every day. Wheat is very irritating to the intestinal tracts of healthy people, and those with weak digestion struggle even more.

Plus the big whammy: processed wheat contains pesticides. Chemicals are hitting the wheat crops with a vengeance. U.S. demand for wheat has tripled in the past few years, making nonorganic wheat a chemical nightmare as it moves through the body. Many believe that all of these chemicals and additives are wearing down the immune system as it tries to combat these foreign agents, leading to high numbers of wheat allergies, such as celiac disease, and wheat sensitivity.

One theory regarding the rise in wheat allergies and sensitivities focuses on the 1961 debut of high-yield grains. This was when American-born agronomist Norman Borlaug created a new variety of wheat that could handle heavy doses of fertilizer; you see, the more fertilizer one uses, the smaller the pest problem, but the more harmful for humans. Some plant life is more delicate and too much fertilizer hurts it. Because this new grain was heartier and easier to mass-produce, this wheat found its way around the world, with the promise to wipe out starvation. This new and stronger grain of wheat opened the door to more industrial methods of production. This tougher wheat now had to withstand the handling of machinery and worldwide shipping. Stronger glutens were created to produce fluffy breads out of dough that took beatings in big machine mixing bowls.

> . . . the more fertilizer one uses, the smaller the pest problem, but the more harmful for humans.

Raising wheat became more about mass production than it did about quality of grain and ease of digestion. We were moving away from the concept of "Our Daily Bread," at a time when food was looked upon for its health and digestibility. Now, it was about the dollar and quantity. Ancestral grains were no longer chosen for their ease in digestion.

Another problem is that the mass-farming process, with its highly commercial fertilization, has wiped the soil of nutrients, such as iron, zinc, and selenium. When yields go up, nutrients go down. Today's "Daily Bread" has turned into glue filler for our tummies. Add to that all of the sugar and fake sweeteners, and it is not long before the body goes downhill.

Instead of wheat, some folks choose foods baked with spelt flour or emmer flour. These are softer, less abrasive "ancient grains" that were consumed in biblical times. In a word, they are ancestral. A new trend is to hunt for these softer, ancient grains and get them into local bakeries, since people with wheat sensitivity seem to be able to digest them. However, once again, it is important to monitor how often and how many times they are eaten.

I see wheat like this: bleached sandpaper moving through an already inflamed intestinal tract, scratching and peeling as it finds its way out. White bleached baked goods are super scary; the bleaching agent that creates the "white" color has been associated with stress upon the pancreas, as the "white baked goods" turn directly into sugar.

All flourmills that produce white flour use chemical agents to bleach baked goods to a white color. Here is a list of a few of these chemicals: oxide of nitrogen, chlorine, chloride, nitrosyl, and benzoyl peroxide mixed with various chemical salts. What this process does is strip the wheat of its nutrition. Yes, when it says, "fortified," four of the removed nutrients have been unnaturally replaced, but this is compared to the *fifteen* that have been taken out.

White bread and pasta are staples in an American child's diet. This means that these little folks are being hit at least once a day with bleaching chemicals, allowing them to pile up in their systems. Little kids are targets for small intestinal overgrowth bacteria. Their diets are all about snacks—crackers, sandwiches, cookies, chips, fruits, fruit juices, yeast, wheat, and sugar, baby. That's right: fruit juices and fruit still contain sugar that feed the bad bacteria.

I cut total consumption of wheat for a few months, but in my case, I had eaten so much of it that there was a buildup, which was causing sensitivity, almost like an allergy. Aside from testing for full-on celiac disease, there are now tests for "wheat and gluten sensitivity." You see, wheat wears on the adrenal glands, our natural alarm system in the body. Too much can shut 'em down, leading to total fatigue and exhaustion. (If you are sick, find a doctor who looks at the whole body and runs these sensitivity tests.)

> I see wheat like this: bleached sandpaper moving through an already inflamed intestinal tract, scratching and peeling as it finds its way out.

I grew up on pasta and bread, and when I was hungry, I craved wheat. It was a triple whammy for my ulceration, because these foods have sugar and sometimes yeast in them too! To top it off, I piled my pasta or bread with cheese, butter, or tomato sauce. Tomatoes are packed with tons of vitamins; however, when the digestive tract is slammed by acid already, tomatoes are not the most supportive food to eat. I stopped eating them for a year, and I am happy to say I have reintroduced them without a problem!

Wheat is everywhere and hard to avoid if you are eating complicated foods, but it is easy if you cook simple foods at home. Most children eat more processed flour than anything else on a daily basis: sandwiches, cookies and crackers, breaded chicken nuggets, pizza, flour tortillas, waffles, and pancakes. Remember, "whole grains" mean unprocessed. However, when you are feeding yourself or your child "whole-grain bread," it is still complicated and not truly a whole grain.

Eating anything dry or crunchy too often is not good for the intestines. Baked means dry. Here's the way I see it: put a tortilla, chip, or pretzel in a bowl of water, and it absorbs the water. They will do the same thing in our intestines. Our intestines need moisture to function and move the poo. When we are filling ourselves up on dried goods, our digestive tracts become devoid of this needed moisture, leading to constipation, and old backed-up putrid food that sits blocking absorption. Plus, they are "complicated" foods. If you are in a digestive-healing phase or walking a preventative health path, stick to simple grains cooked on your stovetop as often as possible.

Cutting Out Gluten

It's not that gluten is "bad"; it's that we are totally inundated with it. Gluten is best compared to glue, 'cause that is what it does naturally in breads and grains containing gluten; it keeps it all together. Too much slows down the intestinal tract and irritates it. Removing it from the diet has been known to help folks with attention deficit disorder and inflammatory conditions such as arthritis and asthma, as well as autoimmune diseases. Again, the basis of our immune systems is in our digestive tract. If my foods are slowing down and irritating things,

Our intestines need moisture to function and move the pooh.

It's not that gluten is "bad"; it's that we are totally inundated with it.

then I'm not absorbing the nutrients, which knocks the rest of my body off.

I'm typical: What I did was immediately cut out gluten and shifted to gluten-free products, ignoring "what was in them" because I was psyched they didn't contain gluten. However, what *is* in most gluten-free products is sugar, yeast, and some dairy. If one has suffered from gluten sensitivity or celiac disease (an autoimmune response creating an allergy to gluten), it shows itself by creating irritation of the intestinal lining, causing tummy aches, gas, bloating, pressure, constipation, and diarrhea. I personally believe this autoimmune response is triggered by all of the fertilizers and chemicals we are exposed to when eating large amounts of wheat.

After a period of time, celiac left unattended leads to ulcerations —that is, Crohn's disease or colitis, which is severe inflammation and ulcerations of the digestive tract. (People with Crohn's and colitis don't themselves have celiac but can have a difficult time digesting glutens and particularly wheat.) The culprit here is that most folks just remove the gluten and don't know to take steps to heal the damage that the gluten sensitivity has done. Once the intestinal walls are weak, sugar, dairy, and yeast are still in abundance. The immune system is compromised.

Gluten-free products, if they are full of sugar, dairy, and yeast, are still doing damage. I moved right on to the gluten-free muffin along with gluten-free bread "plan," at first not realizing that the majority of gluten-free foods are super unhealthy too, as they are packed with fiber-less starches, xanthan gum, refined sugars, and baking soda packed with aluminum. (They are referred to as the "soda pop" version of bread.) Now, I still eat gluten-free foods; I just learned to read the labels. If they are packed with sugar and unhealthy gluten-free grains, I pass or limit my intake. If you're healing your digestive tract, be mindful to purchase gluten-free products that are organic to avoid pesticides and genetically modified organisms (GMOs).

Technically, some form of gluten is found in all grains, so it's not really correct to refer to other grains as "gluten-free." Wheat, barley, and rye contain gluten. What "gluten-free" customarily means is that the product is free of wheat, barley, rye, and their derivatives. Grains

> I personally believe this autoimmune response is triggered by all of the fertilizers and chemicals we are exposed to when eating large amounts of wheat.

that are safe for people with gluten sensitivity and celiac disease include corn, rice, amaranth, millet, quinoa, sorghum, and teff. Almond flour, which is not made from grains, is a good alternative to regular flour. Once I found the recipe for almond-flour bread, I was in it to win it. I love it! First of all, it's made from almonds, and almond butter contains no yeast, is low in sugar, and is perfect for anyone who is trying to clean up their digestive health . . . which should be everyone.

If you are not able to completely let go of dairy, wheat, yeast, and sugar, begin by simply trying to cut them back. It is a gradual process, and occasionally I do get some excess sugar in my body, and I can feel my belly swell up with pressure. That's when the healthy bacteria start doing battle to knock out the bad. Now, I know when enough is enough. I don't mess with dairy because it takes me down hard, and too much sugar immediately hurts my stomach. The sugar high is not worth missing out on life because of a terrible stomachache.

Sourdough: The Best Choice When Wheat Is Okay

For those who are on the road to a healthy digestive tract and can handle wheat, the best choice of bread, if you want to have it, is sourdough bread. There are many benefits to consuming sourdough bread: higher moisture, longer shelf life, and better digestibility because it is naturally leavened. Sourdough is created using a symbiotic culture of lactobacilli bacteria and wild yeast. The wild yeast, which acts as airborne spores, naturally results in digestible bread. Other breads rely solely on carbohydrates, which act as a brick wall in the digestive system and are difficult to break down. However, according to the Canadian baker and scientist, Shasha Navazesh, these wild yeast spores produce a relationship of enzymes in the intestinal tract, making the breakdown process smoother and easier. Additionally, research conducted by Professor Terry Graham of the University of Geulph in Canada exposed that sourdough bread consumption resulted in lower blood sugar levels than whole wheat breads for the same amount of insulin. Like Navazesh, Graham believes that the fermentation process of sourdough bread changes the nature of the bread starches, creating a more beneficial bread.

Many people who are sensitive to commercial breads are able to eat fermented sourdough breads.

Rising Agents: Baking Soda and Baking Powder

While paying attention to how much gluten is going into our bodies, it's also a good idea to be mindful of rising agents used in baked goods, such as baking soda and baking powder. Of course, I recommend purchasing only aluminum-free products, but I also know that an abundance of these rising agents in our diets can also weaken the lining of the digestive tract. Overexposure to them has been known to cause allergies. If you're healing any part of your body, be mindful of your intestinal wall.

Many people who are sensitive to commercial breads are able to eat fermented sourdough breads. If you don't have digestive distress, or have recovered from digestive distress, I recommend that you find a local baker who makes his or her own sourdough the old-fashioned way and give it a try. Some folks swear that eating fermented sourdough has actually aided in their healing!

The Problem with Yeast

Yeast is another item on the list that can irritate the digestive tract and feed unhealthy bacteria. It is found in everything from bread, premade sauces, pretzels, and pizza to baked goods. Again, we are eating so many yeasty foods that yeast allergies are on the rise.

Lots of people ask me about nutritional yeast, and here is the skinny: it's still yeast. Yes, it is a source of vitamin B12 and protein and also lends a cheesy flavor to foods, so it is great for creating vegan mac-and-cheese dishes or vegan cheese sauces. However, it's yeast, and if we are trying to clean up our intestinal tracts and support our immune system, then I say pass or at least be mindful.

My personal experience with yeast is that for months after cleaning up my "dinner plate" I couldn't figure why I was still having moments of pressure and blocked gassy attacks; yeast was the answer. I'd never

Yeast is another item on the list that can irritate the digestive tract and feed unhealthy bacteria.

had a plethora of yeast infections or signs of yeast overgrowth. However, I did eat foods with yeast, and foods that were feeding my already existent colony of digestive yeast. An example was my move to gluten-free foods, most of which contained a fair amount of sugar. Once I cut these items out, I was pressure free and now the gas is flowing in a healthy, pain-free way.

Dairy—To Eat It or Not to Eat It

When I was born, the doctors sent me home after my surgery with instructions for my momma to be sure to avoid all dairy when feeding me; I was unable to process it, and they felt it would lead to an allergic reaction. I guess I drank soy-based formula. I don't remember having milk until I was about seven years old. When my momma was short on cash, if pizza, mac and cheese, or cereal was on the table, I ate it. The only time I can remember getting a stomachache was after eating one of these items—oh, ice cream too. By the time I was in my midtwenties, I was a regular dairy eater; I'd learned to like it, and in fact, I even craved it! I'd heard, like most people, that if you are craving something, it's your body's way of communicating that you need it: Not true.

Carolyn Ross, M.D., explained to me that our body's immune system gets worn down from doing such a thing; eating foods that we have allergies to day in and day out takes its toll. A dairy allergy doesn't only show up as bowel problems but also as headaches, joint aches, skin irritations, and other disorders. In her practice, she deals with many overeaters; she finds that most of them eat the same five things that they are allergic to every day . Once she gets them off of these foods for three to four months, and then reintroduces them, they are able then to identify the allergy or sensitivity, because symptoms are obvious and usually more intense.

I'd completely stopped all dairy immediately for five months until we flew back to Sayulita for a short visit. I totally jumped ship, hopping

A dairy allergy doesn't only show up as bowel problems but also as headaches, joint aches, skin irritations, and other disorders.

back on the condensed milk (condensed milk is loaded with sugar) and coffee boat upon my return to the jungle. Within twenty-four hours I hit the floor, my intestines cramped from inflammation. I'd done a great job of eating simple foods and sticking to my food list. The condensed milk was the only time I'd strayed.

There is a great deal of controversy around human consumption of dairy. Here is what I discovered:

◆ Just like all other species, the average human mother stops producing milk for her offspring after the age of three years (of course, some mommas do milk for longer).

◆ We are the only animals to consume another animal's milk.

◆ A cow's milk is packed with enough nutrition to grow a full-sized cow upwards of 600 to 2,500 pounds. (The average American living in the U.S. weighs 190 pounds for males and 164 pounds for females.)

◆ Humans can absorb plenty of calcium from greens and whole grains. (Quinoa is said to contain *more* calcium than dairy.) Cow's milk is NOT the only way to absorb calcium.

> Humans can absorb plenty of calcium from greens and whole grains.

◆ Compared to human milk, cow's milk is deficient in vitamins B1, C, E. Vitamins A and D are added. Milk is no longer processed in an ancestral way; there is some argument around the process of pasteurization as it removes not only the harmful bacteria but also the helpful. It is also true that pasteurizing milk reduces the nutritional profile of milk. There are many people who are pro raw milk. Jordan Rubin, who healed his intestines from severe digestive disease and is the author of *The Makers Diet,* recommends using raw dairy products for the healthy cultures. Many people who are lactose intolerant or dairy sensitive claim to be able to consume raw dairy products with no digestive distress. The FDA insists that unpasteurized milk has no probiotic effect and cannot explain this phenomena. However, an informal survey of over 700 families conducted by the Weston A. Price Foundation determined that over 80 percent of those diagnosed with lactose intolerance no longer suffer after switching to raw milk products.

◆ When mucus-related problems exist—discharges from the nose or other parts of the body, frequent colds, asthma, allergies, sinus problems, tumors, cysts, constipation, colon troubles, small intestinal problems, growth of *Candida albicans,* or excess weight—it is a good idea to consider eliminating the consumption of dairy.

I believe that my overconsumption of dairy was very harmful to my small intestines. "Overconsumption" does not mean I was drinking four glasses of milk a day or eating cheese smothered all over my food. How I came to the realization that I was overconsuming dairy was by really reading the labels of my typical foods, which I had been buying for years. I knew they weren't on "the list," but I still wanted to know if they were "okay." For the first time, I was reading the labels not for calories, salt, and fat, but instead, I was in search of what was *really* in it. What I found was a common thread: dairy, wheat, sugar, and words I couldn't pronounce.

> For the first time, I was reading the labels not for calories, salt, and fat, but instead, I was in search of what was really in it.

Milk, whey, and casein are all dairy and are found in just about every processed food—from potato chips to salad dressing. These small increments add up and soon aid in the creation of mucus that filled up my intestinal tract. I compare this slimy lining to when I have a head cold and swig a big old glass of milk. What do you get? More snot. Imagine "snot" filling up your intestinal tract, covering the tiny villi that are trying to absorb the nutrition from the food you consume. If these villi are covered in mucus, then they cannot absorb nutrients. Instead, the food passes through and exits the body without lending an ounce of nutrition.

If your body is in optimal health, then fo'sho, dairy in small increments is totally fine. The small increments are because we must always watch our acid levels, and dairy is considered an acidic food.

Lots of folks ask me if I'm into raw butters, which are included on diets like the Maker's Diet and other diets for digestive health. My thing is I'm not down with risking adding any more dangerous bacteria to my body. Not at this point in my game.

Where's the Vitamin D?

Vitamin D is not naturally found in cow's milk; it is added in because without vitamin D our bodies cannot absorb calcium. Calcium is found naturally in quinoa (more than in milk) and leafy greens such as kale, collards, broccoli, and spinach. If we mix a quinoa/spinach salad with some sunshine, we are giving our body what it needs in an authentic manner. Vitamin D grows with the grains and the greens; the two are perfect dance partners. Mushrooms are also fantastic sources of vitamin D.

Vitamin D is found naturally in fatty fish, mushrooms, red meat, and the sun! Yep, ten minutes of sunshine a day on your face and hands without sunblock can do the trick; the darker the complexion, the longer the need for sun exposure. All kinds of studies have shown the connection of lack of exposure to sunshine and low levels of vitamin D. One such study that struck my fancy was this one:

John White, an endocrinologist at the Research Institute of the McGill University Health Center, led a team of scientists from McGill University and the Université de Montréal. They presented their findings about inflammatory bowel disease in the *Journal of Biological Chemistry*: "Vitamin D, in its active form (1,25–dihydroxyvitamin D), is a hormone that binds to receptors in the body's cells." Dr. White's interest in vitamin D was originally in its effects in mitigating cancer. Folks with cancer have a tendency to have low vitamin D levels and cancer thrives in a poor immune system.

Because his results kept pointing to vitamin D's effects on the immune system, specifically the innate immune system that acts as the body's first defense against microbial invaders, he investigated Crohn's disease. "It's a defect in innate immune handling of intestinal bacteria that leads to an inflammatory response that may lead to an autoimmune condition," stresses Dr. White. Vitamin D is a preventive health plan for family members of cancer or digestive diseases and autoimmune diseases.

Parathyroid glands are the small endocrine glands found in the neck and located behind the thyroid. They produce parathyroid hormone, and this hormone keeps a groove in which the two dance. Therefore, they are a huge part of our body's balancing act when it comes to calcium and vitamin D absorption, via the small intestines. If we have too much calcium, we can't absorb vitamin D, and if we don't have enough vitamin D, we can't absorb calcium.

Every time the pediatrician tells me to give my girls milk, I school him! As far as nondairy milks such as soy, rice, or almond milk products, I try to make my own or only buy organic brands, being sure to not overuse these processed products.

By the way, I make sure to avoid any products with carrageenan, commonly used as a thickener in dairy and nondairy products. It is made from a red sea vegetable also known as Irish moss. According to Joanne Tobacman, professor of Clinical Internal Medicine at the University of Iowa, there is evidence of human trials that might show carrageenan to be a danger for human consumption. In lab animals, carrageenan is used to induce ulcerative colitis. What this told me is if I have an already weakened digestive lining and my diet is full of carrageenan (found in tons of processed foods) then for sure it can't help me and will only add stress to my situation.

Figuring Out Oils

Over the past few years I've watched my body get better and better. I've picked out my triggers that can set my intestines into a swollen hot mess—sugar, dairy, wheat, and any additives. What took me the longest to figure out was oil!

On a recent trip to Florida I'd had a tough time with my tummy; I couldn't understand why. We'd stopped at a few places on the drive from Nashville, but I'd avoided eating the trigger foods. Even after making healthy choices, I still found myself super bloated and extremely gassy. I told my sister, Nicole, who was vacationing with us, that I was going to avoid eating out the remainder of our stay. I did just that. Three days later I was back to my comfy digestive self. Our grandparents were visiting us, and Nicole and I had loaded them up to drive them home two and a half hours away.

When we were kids they'd take us to Perkins for special occasions, and here we were all together and passing a Perkins; of course they wanted to stop. I thought, *Okay, I will find something to eat.* Here's what went down between the waitress and me:

> **Mee:** "May I please have two scrambled eggs with olive oil, as I have a dairy intolerance?"

> **Waitress:** "I'm sorry, ma'am, but we don't have olive oil or butter here."

> **Mee:** "Oh, well how about a salad, and I'll just use this olive oil and vinegar here on the table."

> **Waitress:** "Oh, that's not olive oil, that's cottonseed oil; like I said, we don't have olive oil here. Only oil we got is cottonseed oil."

> **Mee:** "Oh, okay, I'll just have a plain baked potato, nothing on it."

What took me the longest to figure out was oil!

A light bulb had gone off; cotton is not a food. Even the FDA agrees since they don't monitor it. Therefore, it is one of the most heavily pesticide-sprayed crops. Also, when you press it to extract the oil, you're pressing out the chemicals. They all can't be removed, especially the *naturally occurring* toxic oils found in cotton. Yep, that's why it's not a food: 'cause it's naturally toxic, and it is meant to be worn not eaten.

Lee says when cows get into cotton fields and eat too much cotton, they go blind. And Dr. Andrew Weil says it's a super-unhealthy oil that is high in saturated fat. We all know that saturated fat leads to heart disease and diabetes (which is technically an autoimmune disease). Cottonseed is also hard on the intestines and liver. The liver flushes toxins, and if it's working hard breaking down fats, look out intestines! When one organ is off, the others are too. If the intestines are busy dealing with oil, they are unable to absorb nutrients—their main purpose. So, if you are suffering or recovering from any illness, support your intestines by protecting them from future distress by watching your oils!

Oh boy, I was on a mission. I wanted to know what kind of oil I was eating so I hit my research hard—palm oil is another tricky one. Yes, it is a plant that bares an oil-producing fruit; the only way to extract this oil organically is to steam it like they do in Africa and then crush the oil from the pit of the fruit. When it is done via a machine for mass production, the oil is said to be oxidized, which of course makes it toxic to the organs (hard to digest and high in saturated fat). The big kicker with palm oil is the environmental messes these plantations and farms create—wiping away much of Malaysian and Indonesian rainforests.

The next oil I found to be dominating in restaurant foods is soybean oil. We all know that there is too much soy in our diets, and we are eating tons of processed soy—meaning if you read a label and it says "soy" in the ingredient list, it is processed. This overindulgence of soy in our food is leading to soy allergies, and some doctors believe it is linked to estrogen dominance in both men and women, which can lead to cancer. (Of course, there is a difference between eating processed soy and fermented soy. Fermented soy changes the game 'cause it's packed with health benefits!)

The real scary deal is that soy is massively produced, heavily sprayed with chemicals, and a GMO (genetically modified organism).

> We all know that saturated fat leads to heart disease and diabetes.

Most vegetable oil can contain palm oil and soy oil without mentioning it on the label, as they fit under the category of a vegetable. Cotton-seed oil can be mentioned on labels as "may contain," which means it does!

There, I did it. I found the missing link in my intestinal issues—the oil! I traced my journey back, and everything I'd eaten leading up to my tummy's meltdown was linked to the oil. You can Google most chain restaurants and find out what type of oil they cook with. Each place we'd eaten on the way to Nashville and the drive down to Florida cooked with these oils, and understandably so—they are cheap. Just like most folks can't afford to buy organic foods, neither can small restaurants, and it's not a priority for the big chain restaurants, because we don't demand it.

Fresh organic foods and healthy oils are pricey; however, it's a question of value. Do we want it cheap or do we want it real? 'Cause when it comes down to it, what you eat is directly related to how you feel. There you go. If you are wondering why you get gassy or bloated after a meal out, it could be that you weren't eating real food.

Confirmation of my oil findings came a few months later. I was having dinner with Dr. Joan Borysenko (Harvard cellular biologist) and sharing with her my latest discovery. She quickly chimed in that she had done a major study on the effects of oils and cells. She said that unhealthy oils, many of which I'd listed, definitely weakened healthy cells. In Joan's studies, she found that olive oil actually has a positive effect and supports healthy cells while combating breast cancer.

> Do we want it cheap or do we want it real? 'Cause when it comes down to it, what you eat is directly related to how you feel.

The Dirt on Canola Oil

Most people choose to use canola oil as a healthy alternative to vegetable oil. However, studies that date back as far as the 1960s and 1970s have proven otherwise. In fact, the costs of consuming this new "low-fat" oil far outweigh the benefits. For starters, let's take a look at the origination of the product. Canola oil is a genetically modified plant from Canada (hence its name). It is produced using the rapeseed plant (a plant that is so poisonous it is used as an effective insect repellent).

Not only used as an insecticide, rape oil was also the source of mustard gas, a weapon that has since been banned because of the horrific blistering of lungs and skin that resulted after its consumption. There is simply too much hard evidence against canola oil to ignore it. In fact, canola oil has been classified as a biopesticide by the Environmental Protection Agency (EPA). Like mercury and fluoride, canola is not eliminated from the body.

Canola is found in almost all snacks and processed foods; because of its low erucic acid rating, it's a big favorite in most "healthy recipes." However, research has shown that a side effect of canola consumption in animals is an accumulation of fatty deposits around their hearts, thyroids, adrenal glands, and kidneys. The fatty deposits disappeared when the canola was removed from the animals' diet, but scar tissue remained. Another interesting fact I learned is that rapeseed oil is an acetylcholinesterase inhibitor. This is a big-time player in the body's message system when it comes to transmitting signals from the nerves to the muscles. Lots of folks are talking and performing research to see if there is a relationship between rapeseed oil and the rise in cases of multiple sclerosis and cerebral palsy.

Canola oil is produced using the rapeseed plant (a plant that is so poisonous it is used as an effective insect repellent).

In addition to genetic modification, the process of making canola oil is troubling. The procedure involves a combination of high-temperature mechanical pressing and solvent extract, usually using hexane. Hexane! Even after considerable refining, traces of the solvent remain. (Hexanes are significant constituents of gasoline. Yep, you can easily find it coming out of your tailpipe. So, eating something that has been treated with it is not a good idea.) Like most vegetable oils, canola oil also goes through the process of bleaching, degumming, deodorizing, and caustic refining at very high temperatures. This process can alter the omega-3 content in the oil, and in certain conditions, bring the trans fat level as high as 40 percent.

On the other hand, olive oil is the gold standard and has been documented with extensive research. Quality olive oil (extra virgin, cold-pressed) is manufactured by this simple process: the olives are pressed, and the oil is collected. Yet, the food oil industry promotes canola oil as an equally healthy twin to olive oil. This is deceptive, as there are few studies involving canola oil and human health. (Numerous animal studies, such as the one mentioned above, point to serious and dele-terious effects of canola oil.) To learn more, visit:

◆ www.naturalnews.com/031550_canola_oil_side_effects.html #ixzz2BkrGcMgB

◆ www.ehow.com/list_7427295_harmful-effects-canola-oil.html

◆ www.rense.com/politics5/dare.htm

◆ http://organicyogamama.com/canola-oil/

◆ www.ehow.co.uk/about_5414785_dangers-canola-oil.html

◆ www.cantola.com/Tricky_Foods.html

What About Natural Oils?

I use olive or coconut oil for cooking. According to Mayo Clinic nutri-tionist Katherine Zertasky, olive oil in its least processed form (indi-cated as "extra virgin") is the most heart-healthy oil because it contains the highest levels of polyphenols, strong antioxidants that promote a healthy heart. Additionally, moderate consumption of olive oil can lower the risk of heart disease by lowering the total and low-density lipoprotein cholesterol levels in the body.

> Coconut oil is another alternative that is sometimes referred to as "the healthiest oil on earth."

Coconut oil is another alternative that is sometimes referred to as "the healthiest oil on earth." Coconut oil is unique in its chemical properties because it is composed of shorter fatty-acid chains than most other fat consumed. These shorter chains, known as medium-chain triglycerides (MCTs), are more easily metabolized by the body and often found in infant formulas, according to the author of *Nutrition for Endurance Athletes,* Monique Ryan. The MCTs in coconut oil also raise the level of "good" cholesterol (HDL), promoting heart health. The big perk for coconut oil is that it has a natural antifungal and anti-bacterial effect, once again aiding in kicking the unhealthy bacteria in our digestive tracts to the curb!

Balancing Our pH
and Cleansing Our Blood

Almost all foods that we eat, after being digested, absorbed, and metabolized, release either an acid or an alkaline base (bicarbonate) into blood. Grains, fish, meat, poultry, shellfish, cheese, milk, and salt all produce acid, so the introduction and dramatic rise in our consumption of these foods meant that the typical Western diet became more acid-producing. Consumption of fresh fruit and vegetables decreased, which further made the Western diet acid-producing. When we eat a diet heavy on the veggies, our inflammation rates drop quickly, so if you've got a serious disease tied to inflammation get sautéing, steaming, and raw-fooding.

Yep, dairy is acidic. Hard to believe, but if you were to dump cow's milk into a pond, the water would lose its alkalinity. Jane Ellen, my BFF at the farm, schooled me on this little fact. So, you see, when you've got acid reflux, drinking milk is not the best idea—instead, grab an umeboshi plum and suck on it.

Our blood is slightly alkaline, with a normal pH level of between 7.35 and 7.45. The theory behind the alkaline diet is that our diet should reflect this pH level (as it did in the past) and be slightly alkaline. Proponents of alkaline diets believe that a diet high in acid-producing foods disrupts this balance and promotes the loss of essential minerals such as potassium, magnesium, calcium, and sodium, as the body tries to restore equilibrium. This imbalance is thought to make people prone to illness.

Although conventional doctors do believe that increasing consumption of fruit and vegetables and reducing one's intake of meat, salt, and refined grains is beneficial to health, most conventional doctors do not believe that an acid-producing diet is the foundation of chronic illness. In conventional medicine there is evidence, however, that alkaline diets may help prevent the formation of calcium kidney stones, osteoporosis, and age-related muscle wasting.

My thoughts are that when our blood is full of acidic chemicals (fake food ingredients aka complicated ingredients and fat), it

> When we eat a diet heavy on the veggies, our inflammation rates drop quickly, so if you've got a serious disease tied to inflammation get sautéing, steaming, and raw-fooding.

> Our hormones are located in our blood, and when our blood is loaded with acid, chemicals, and crap, our hormones become out of whack.

becomes a toxic stream flowing through our bodies. If there is an ulceration deep in the intestines or even just plain irritation, it is important to make sure that the blood flowing over the sensitive area is healing, not burning, the intestinal tract. If we are trying to support our cells, then we would not want to cover them up in this funky concoction of crud, right? For anyone who has any type of autoimmune disease or cancer, keeping acid levels under control is key to balancing the immune system.

I started balancing my pH by consistently eating sea veggies, daikon radish, shiitake mushrooms, and aduki beans—vegetables that are known to flush the fat and toxins from our blood. When I added collards, turnips, kale, and mustard greens, my energy and healing increased rapidly. I didn't just turn a corner; I turned a block! Once I learned to make kinpira, burdock, and carrots, I stepped up my blood's level of cleanliness. I immediately had more energy, less pain, and a clearer mind.

Our hormones are located in our blood, and when our blood is loaded with acid, chemicals, and crap, our hormones become out of whack. When our hormones are out of whack, our reactions to life's challenges are usually whacky. I am a big beauty gal; I love to discover new ways to keep my skin clean and clear—I see these foods as the inside beauty tips. If our body has a balanced pH level, then our skin glows! Acne and skin conditions are the body's inside struggles showing up on the outside and calling for attention. Cleaning up our blood cleans our lives too.

ALKALINE FOODS AND DRINKS

- Herb teas, green tea, and lemon water
- Olive, flax seed
- Wild rice, quinoa, and millet
- Almonds and chestnuts
- Raw spinach and lettuce

- Soybeans, peas, and green beans
- Sweet potatoes and potato skins
- Asparagus, broccoli, and onions
- Lemons, limes, oranges, and grapefruit
- Watermelon, mangos, and papaya
- Stevia, maple sugar, and raw sugar

Watching Our Estrogen Levels

The big question is to soy or not to soy? The truth is that we do have way too much soy in our diets because it has become the fabric of our processed foods. If we eliminate processed foods and eat soy in its healthiest form: organic, non-GMO (genetically modified organisms), and pesticide-free miso, tofu, tempeh, tamari/shoyu sauces, and black soybeans (all of which are fermented), it can be good for us. Fermented foods aid in digestion and support healthy bacteria. Japanese women are proof that eating soy in its fermented form is supportive to the body, as they have incredibly low rates of heart disease and breast cancer.

I watch my soy intake, because my liver was overloaded for years with everything that my intestines couldn't process completely. This created a weak liver, which then had a hard time processing excess estrogen. This lead me to develop fibrocystic breasts. After my diagnosis, I immediately got in my kitchen and switched around the way I was cooking. I swapped out my soy miso to chickpea, which is soy free; I used coconut aminos in place of soy sauce, and I cut back on all fermented soy products. My acupuncturist, Dr. Sheng, modified my treatment and tailored my herbs. Immediately I noticed a change, as the many cysts began to dissipate. I also experienced less PMS systems. Gone were my estrogen-dominant menstrual headaches along with excess breast swelling.

Paying attention to our estrogen levels is huge, 'cause we now know that estrogen dominance is linked to breast cancer as well as to testicular and prostate cancer. So, along with monitoring soy, be sure to pay attention to how much plastic you are exposed to. Bisphenol A, commonly known as BPA, is a byproduct of petroleum, which is linked to increased estrogen levels. BPA is found in most plastics, unless the product states specifically that it is BPA-free. This is another reason to avoid processed food and the containers it comes in. Canned goods are also filled with BPA because the liners are made of this material. Some exceptions are Eden Organics, Native Forest, Vital Choice, and some of Trader Joe's branded canned goods. Most cans of tomatoes

So, along with monitoring soy, be sure to pay attention to how much plastic you are exposed to.

are packaged in BPA-lined cans due to their acid level. Avoid it by purchasing tomatoes sold in jars.

Phthalates are chemical compounds of phthalic acid that are mainly used as plasticizers. They increase flexibility and durability in products. They are found in *everything*—including enteric coatings on medications, adhesives, glues, electronics, toys, packaging, detergents, shampoos, cosmetics, almost all personal-care products, food packages, and textiles. BPA is a type of phthalate. If we eat well, stop using foods in plastic containers, and cut out all soy, but still slather our skin—our largest organ—with phthalates, we are exposing our blood and hormones to strong levels of estrogen mimickers. Many studies have found that skin-care products are absorbed even quicker and at a much higher content level than eating foods that contain these same ingredients.

There are plenty of cosmetics that do not contain phthalates or parabens (another chemical to avoid); just do the research! Also be sure to pay attention to what your children are washing their bodies with too; many baby products contain large amounts of estrogen-mimicking ingredients, hence the rise in early onset puberty.

That's a Wrap!

Aluminum foil and plastic wrap are two great inventions, but I always try to avoid my foods' contact with them as both are questionable regarding our health. Therefore, I always wrap my food in parchment paper first then cover with plastic wrap or aluminum foil.

What's Real & What's Fake in the Food World?

Understanding the effects of sugar, wheat, and dairy was only the beginning for me. I'd opened Pandora's box, and everywhere I turned there was something for me to learn. I was hunting for a single thread that pointed to overall ill health. No longer focusing on just digestive diseases, I heard the same question in my head, *What's in it?* I had asked the same question regarding pharmaceuticals, but now I was questioning our food and trying to figure out what is real and what is fake.

I'd opened Pandora's box, and everywhere I turned there was something for me to learn.

"Real Foods" are any foods that are found in their unique and original form—for example, all fresh produce straight from the farm, legumes, organic meats, raw milks, yogurts, cheeses, and whole grains (in their original form). Whole-grain bread, waffles, cereals, and pastas are healthier choices of these products, but they are not considered whole, as they've gone through a major process to be created.

When I have a question, I follow my rule: If nature created it, then I can eat it. I'm not so hard core, as I do eat small amounts of processed products. I do my best to balance them with simple, natural foods. Even though I don't eat dairy or most meat, I believe if you are in good health and eat these foods in moderation, you are in alignment with nature.

All animals need to eat real food, too. If animals are fed pharmaceuticals or processed foods, they do not fall under the "Real Food" category.

Understanding the definition of "processed food" is key. Processed food is any food or animal that has been added to, preserved, and put through a machine in a factory and modified in anyway—including all GMOs (genetically modified organisms). If it came from a lab, then hell no, it's not a food. All boxed, canned, jarred, and frozen foods are processed in some way. Even organic foods found in jars, boxes, and cans are processed.

I totally understand the issues with choosing healthy foods over unhealthy. I always assimilated them as "good and bad." The good I believed didn't taste good, and the bad tasted really good. After eating a bout of "bad food," I would be struck with vanity-based fear, afraid the yummy bad food was going to make me fat. I'd then hit the healthy food with the same vengeful diligence as I'd grubbed on the bad food. Only problem was that I saw the healthy food as punishment for my eating sins. I've had to shift my food perspective and I now see REAL food as the new gourmet and as a luxury item.

Today I know that it has nothing to do with food's being "good" or "bad." Instead, it is a matter of its being real or fake.

> Today I know that it has nothing to do with food's being "good" or "bad." Instead, it is a matter of its being real or fake.

So Many Healing Diets: What Is What?

When I first heard the term "macrobiotic diet," I had no clue what it meant. I'd heard the word in the press when Gwyneth Paltrow raved about it and somehow I equated it with geometry and thought it was tiny little squares of food. Crazy, I know, especially 'cause "macro" means "big" and biotic means "life"—Big Life. There is nothing small about it, as it's a nutritional plan based on whole grains, legumes, seasonal vegetables, seaweeds, and small amounts of fish. The concept behind a macrobiotic diet is that food can heal the body if it is balanced and alkaline.

George Ohsawa was the founder of the macrobiotic diet in Japan; however, Michio Kushi, one of his many students, brought it to fame in the United States in the 1960s. There are a lot of superstitions to macrobiotic cooking, as they believe in the energy of certain foods and also in the way things should be cut. I personally never got into this, and I cut the food the way it felt natural to me, and I got well. In my opinion, it's about the intention of the cook: if we are cooking for love, it's all good regardless of the chopping angle.

Many of the foods cooked in this diet are based on Japanese recipes and remedies. There's one main difference between vegetarian eating and macrobiotics: "macro" eaters do eat fish and don't eat nightshades, as they are believed to prevent and slow the healing of our bodies. Nightshades are any plant from the family of Solanaceae vegetables. People with arthritis are said to be the most negatively affected as these nightshades are believed to cause joint inflammation. Examples of nightshades include:

it's about the intention of the cook: if we are cooking for love, it's all good regardless of the chopping angle.

- Potatoes (not sweet potatoes)
- Tomatoes
- Eggplant
- Sweet and hot peppers (including paprika, cayenne pepper, and Tabasco sauce)

- Ground cherries
- Tomatillos and tamarillos
- Pepinos and pimentos
- Garden huckleberry and naranjillas

I had the toughest time eating eggplants and tomatoes. Before getting well, they would burn my tongue. For the first year, I completely avoided all nightshades. Making my own tomato-type marinara from a combo of beets and carrots gave me that pasta sauce fix from my childhood. Now I'm mindful with how often I consume nightshades, and they no longer bother my body because it's finally back in balance. In fact, I can tell if I'm out a whack if I eat eggplant and it bothers my tongue!

The best part of starting out macrobiotic is that I was taught to be incredibly mindful that I ate a balance of everything plant based and didn't fall into the trap that some vegetarians do and eat anything as long as it does not contain animals. Macrobiotics explains the importance of sitting down to a plate at every meal or soup that is packed with nutrition. A great many people have healed completely on the principles of macrobiotics.

Once I mastered macrobiotics, I wanted to know more. I hit the books big time, starting with the Gerson Theory, based on the studies of Dr. Max Gerson, who treated people with cancer and chronic illness with a series of fresh vegetable juices, coffee enemas, and raw foods. People all over the world have claimed wellness. (Today his daughter Charlotte Gerson runs his center in Mexico.) Of course there has been all kinds of controversy surrounding his treatments, but what I found as a common thread was the importance of ingesting high levels of nutrition via juicing and removing all toxins by detoxing via foods. This is similar to Kris Carr's approach. Carr wrote a wonderful book called *My Crazy Sexy Cancer* about her adventures with liver cancer. She too forged her own path, one based on eating lots of greens, removing processed foods, and juicing along with green smoothies.

The Maker's Diet, written by Jordan Rueben, a man diagnosed with severe Crohn's disease, returned to a very ancestral diet where he sprouted grains, ate legumes, ingested only organic animal products, and also included raw dairy as well. Having read these books, I knew the world of healing foods and diets was bigger than macrobiotics and that all of them were about living a real food life. I was inspired and wanted to know more, so I kept learning. Here's more of what I learned:

> A great many people have healed completely on the principles of macrobiotics.

What the Hell Is a Vegan?

Veganism is a plant-based vegetarian diet that excludes from the diet all types of animal meat and all animal products, including eggs, dairy, and even honey. The term "vegan" refers to both the person and the diet itself. Vegans do not eat any processed foods that contain animal products. They also avoid using any products that have been tested on animals or are made of animal byproducts—such as leather and fur.

> The term "vegan" refers to both the person and the diet itself.

There are many reasons why a person chooses a vegan lifestyle. Eating a plant-based diet has proven to lower cholesterol levels as well as the risk of heart disease, and of course, cruelty to animals is a major reason for many.

What vegans do eat is anything plant based; such as grains, legumes, vegetables, fruits, and every combination of the above. Nowadays, there are a ton of processed vegan foods such as vegan hotdogs, vegan ice cream, and vegan cheese. The only downfall I've found in my vegan journeys is that it's just as easy to fall into a fake food—i.e., processed food—rut as it is on a modern American diet. If you are eating vegan, it's super important to be mindful of how much wheat and sugar you are consuming, as these throw off the body's pH and are harmful to the intestines.

The difference between vegans and vegetarians is that some vegetarians eat cheese and other dairy products, including eggs.

Paleolithic Eating Does Not Include Dinosaurs (As I Thought)

The Paleolithic diet is also known as the Paleo diet, Caveman diet, Stone Age diet, or Hunter-Gatherer diet. It is a modern nutritional plan based on the way humans ate during the Paleolithic era. The diet consists mainly of fish, pasture- and grass-raised meats, vegetables, fruits, and roots and nuts. It excludes all grains, legumes, and dairy products, as well as salt, refined sugar, and processed oils. Again, eating foods in its simplest form has been proven to improve health substantially. My problem is that I cannot digest meats well. I can only eat it in small doses—which is pretty true to this diet if it's followed the way people really ate back then. 'Cause we all know that hunting didn't always

> The Paleolithic diet is a modern nutritional plan based on the way humans ate during the Paleolithic era.

mean one returned with a kill; therefore, more fruits and vegetables were part of a Paleo person's meal.

Raw, Y'all

Okay, y'all, here is the real deal on raw! Raw foods contain live probiotics and enzymes. They are binder- and filler-free. They are uncooked, untreated, and unadulterated! Raw foods are just that: raw and real.

Raw foods are "living foods" because of their active enzymes, which are considered the life force of the food. People who eat "living foods" believe they greatly benefit the body, and that cooking fruits, vegetables, legumes, nuts, and seeds above 118°F kills the enzymes. Then you got the folks whose opinion is that heat activates the enzymes, and food needs to be cooked in order for the body to assimilate most nutrients. Science has not proved either side.

One afternoon while cooking at the Church in N. Nashville, a raw food activist came by the church, as she'd heard about the Real Food Makeover. She was talking to the pastor and Mattie about raw foods and the health benefits. I could see from their faces that she was speaking a foreign language. She then went on to tell them that eating cooked food was killing Americans. I had to jump in the ring; sharing my journey with food and that the first year of eating my real food life, I was unable to digest raw foods, cooking my vegetables until they were soft. I had my blood work run after a year and the doctor found that for the first time in fourteen years, I was above board in my absorption rate—completely balanced nutritionally. This is a huge deal for someone with a hole in their intestines. Also if we look at global diets and ancestral cooking, almost all of them eat cooked foods—as a way to avoid parasite and water contamination. I'm not protesting raw food, I'm actually a huge fan now that I'm able to digest it: It's about the individual's health and choice.

There is no argument that "living food" is get-down, grubbing good! That is my stance; going raw is within reach if that is what you're choosing. There is nothing wrong with eating a bunch o' fruits and veggies all day—then there is the big question that everyone asks. . . .

Everyone always asks where the protein comes from when one

> Raw foods are "living foods" because of their active enzymes, which are considered the life force of the food.

chooses to go raw. Most raw eaters get their protein from plant-sourced proteins. Protein is made of amino acids, several of which are essential and must come from your diet. Anyone who eats a diet of plants needs to include a wide variety to get all the essential amino acids the body needs.

Incorporating raw meals into your diet can be a good thing. With just a little focus, a supply of fresh and organic ingredients, and a small time investment (most of the food is made in a food processor), you can enjoy nourishing, delicious, "living foods" that leave unhealthy options in the dust, baby! Peep out my raw choice section in Part Three. The Juicy Raw Wrap is off the hook!

My favorite raw food restaurant is in St. Augustine, Florida: The Present Moment Café. They get down, and every time I'm there visiting my mother-in-law, I am sure to stop by—not only for a great meal, but also for a dose of inspiration.

What Is Juicing and What Do I Juice?

Fresh juicing is the process of extracting the liquid from fruits and vegetable by pushing the fruit or vegetable through a juicing machine, extracting only the juice. The liquid/juice contains most of the vitamins, minerals, and plant chemicals (phytonutrients) found in the whole fruit or vegetable. The remaining pulp is the fiber of the fruit/vegetable. The benefit of juicing is that these nutrients enter into the body with ease, as they don't have to be extracted via the digestive process. This is great for someone who has had digestive distress and absorption is an issue. For me personally, I juice twice a week and only drink 4 ounces of juice at a time, as to again assure absorption and avoid gas and bloating. I am also mindful to juice mainly vegetables, specifically those low in sugar and high in nutrients, adding only a few select fruits such as apples and pears.

> The benefit of juicing is that these nutrients enter into the body with ease, as they don't have to be extracted via the digestive process.

Proponents of juicing believe that it can reduce the risk of cancer, boost the immune system, and help remove toxins from the body, which can lead to weight loss. The difference between fresh juicing and buying juice from a carton is not only the freshness but also that there is nothing added and it isn't pasteurized.

What Is Organic and Why Eat It?

I remember thinking a few years back that organic had to be a selling gimmick, and of course, it wasn't something I needed to spend my money on. Understanding the definition of "organic" has not only influenced my shopping, but everything that is grown on my farm.

Organic produce and other ingredients are grown without the use of pesticides, synthetic fertilizers, sewage sludge, genetically modified organisms, or ionizing radiation. Animals that produce meat, poultry, eggs, and dairy products do not take antibiotics or growth hormones.

The USDA National Organic Program (NOP) defines "organic" as follows:

> *Farmers who emphasize the use of renewable resources and the conservation of soil and water to enhance environmental quality for future generations produce organic food. Organic meat, poultry, eggs, and dairy products come from animals that are given no antibiotics or growth hormones. Organic food is produced without using most conventional pesticides, fertilizers made with synthetic ingredients or sewage sludge, bioengineering, or ionizing radiation. Before a product can be labeled "organic," a Government-approved certifier inspects the farm where the food is grown to make sure the farmer is following all the rules necessary to meet USDA organic standards. Companies that handle or process organic food before it gets to your local supermarket or restaurant must be certified, too.*

The USDA has identified three categories for labeling organic-products:

◆ 100% Organic: made with 100% organic ingredients

◆ Organic: made with at least 95% organic ingredients

◆ Made with Organic Ingredients: made with a minimum of 70% organic ingredients with strict restrictions on the remaining 30% including no GMOs (genetically modified organisms)

> Understanding the definition of "organic" has not only influenced my shopping, but everything that is grown on my farm.

Products with less than 70 percent organic ingredients may list organically produced ingredients on the side panel of the package, but may not make any organic claims on the front of the package.

Is organic food healthier? At this time, there is no definitive research that makes this claim. It is extremely difficult to conduct studies that would control the many variables that might affect nutrients, such as seeds, soil type, climate, postharvest handling, and crop variety. However, some recently published studies have shown organic foods do have higher nutritional value. For example, researchers at the University of California, Davis, recently found that organic tomatoes had higher levels of phytochemicals and vitamin C than conventional tomatoes. My rule of thumb to follow is that if the plant has been reared with chemicals, it's not supportive to our body, so I avoid it.

> My rule of thumb to follow is that if the plant has been reared with chemicals, it's not supportive to our body, so I avoid it.

Does organic food taste better? Taste is definitely an individual matter, but hundreds of gourmet chefs across the nation are choosing organic food because they believe it has superior taste. I personally can taste the difference, especially when eating tomatoes and watermelon.

Because organic food is grown in well-balanced soil, it makes sense that these healthy plants have a great taste.

What's in Pesticides and Chemically Produced Pesticides?

> Before World War II, almost all food was organic. Only natural fertilizers were used.

Before World War II, almost all food was organic. Only natural fertilizers were used (manures mixed with soil). Farmers worked in partnership with nature to avoid pest problems: they would plant companion crops that naturally repel insects (we do this on our farm as well). Yes, this takes more time and more land, but in the end, the food is free and clear of chemicals and able to do its job. There were still plenty of problems; famines resulted after droughts, but the level of chronic disease and autoimmune disease were way less. After World War II, scientists brought petroleum-based fertilizers and pesticide products to the farming table. Farming became big business and was no longer about feeding humans healthy products to support their bodies: quantity ruled over quality. We bought into this, as food was cheaper and more accessible than ever before. We are now paying a price with our lives and our time, because chronic disease is stealing it.

Irradiation: What Is It?

Irradiation is the process of radiating foods with low levels of radiation emitted from a nuclear source to destroy bacteria and insects, giving food a longer shelf life and decreasing the risk of their carrying disease-causing pathogens. Organic farmers are not allowed to radiate the food grown.

Is it safe? I say hell no. I'm not a rocket scientist, but I know that exposure to radiation, even low levels over a period of time is a bad idea. Food advocacy groups that have studied the research, upon which the World Health Organization (WHO) and others based their claim that it was safe, have proven that WHO was wrong. Food advocacy groups are concerned that eating radiated food can affect cell growth and damage chromosomes and may also not be as nutrient–rich because vitamins and enzymes have been nuked! The worst is that studies have shown that irradiating food does not kill bacteria; we still have to wash our foods "Third-World style."

My deal is that we are exposed to high levels of radiation like never before in the history of humankind. Our cell phones' 3G networks have made *us* the tower. We are "pinged" every day, all day. Add to that the wireless connections in our homes, televisions, computer monitors, and microwaves emitting radiation, and toss in the recent nuclear power plant disasters (i.e., Japan), and we are cooked!

The thing is, our air doesn't go away, and now it's full of radiation.

> The worst is that studies have shown that irradiating food does not kill bacteria; we still have to wash our foods "Third-World style."

Check out the great movie *I AM* about the history of our air and how it can be traced back to the time of dinosaurs; we are breathing in the *same* air the dinosaurs breathed—proving the point that air, and unhealthy toxins in it, don't go away. Thyroid issues are through the roof. It is expected that they will increase to even larger numbers in the near future—particularly thyroid cancer, which can be directly related to radiation exposure. Small amounts of radiation over a period of time add up, and *Bam!* it comes in the form of thyroid issues.

The Dirty Dozen and the Clean Thirteen

> My personal rule is if I eat it or drink or feed it to my kids every single day, I make sure it's organic.

If you don't have access to organic foods and want to know which conventionally grown food is safest to eat, then peep these two lists. The U.S.-based nonprofit organization, Environmental Working Group (www.ewg.org), has developed a list of common fruits and vegetables ranked according to the amount of pesticide residue consumed when you eat them. Peaches, which are sprayed the most, are given a ranking of "100," and onions, which have the least amount are given a "1." These lists were comprised from tests done by the U.S. Department of Agriculture and the Food and Drug Administration. (*Source: Environmental Working Group, Washington, DC—foodnews.org*)

My personal rule is if I eat it or drink or feed it to my kids every single day (for example, coffee with cream in the morning or Lola's apple juice or milk in the girl's cereal), I make sure it's organic. Three hundred sixty-five days a year times five years is a lot of pesticide to ingest. So the tiny increments add up!

DIRTY DOZEN*	CLEAN THIRTEEN**
1. Peaches—100	1. Onions—1
2. Apples—96	2. Avocados—1
3. Bell Peppers—86	3. Sweet Corn (frozen)—2
4. Celery—85	4. Pineapples—7
5. Nectarines—84	5. Mangoes—9
6. Strawberries—83	6. Sweet Peas (frozen)—11
7. Cherries—75	7. Asparagus—11
8. Lettuce—69	8. Kiwi—14
9. Imported Grapes—68	9. Bananas—16
10. Pears—65	10. Cabbages (remove outside layer)—17
11. Spinach—60	11. Broccoli—18
12. Potatoes—58	12. Eggplants—19
	13. Papayas—21

* Meaning y'all want to buy these items organic!

** This is conventional produce that is least contaminated through possible GMO seeds that have blown into crops. Irradiation isn't accounted for or factored in as these conventional items may be irradiated.

Concerns About GMO Crops and Agriculture

A simple definition of GMO foods according to the 1996 Organic Trade Association definition of Genetically Modified Organisms is those, ". . . made with techniques that alter the molecular or cell biology of an organism by means that are not possible under natural conditions or processes." As such, GMOs may contain substances that

Organic Farming

Many farmers are growing their foods organically and naturally but cannot afford the cost of being certified or the complex process that comes with getting certified organic. Get to know your local farmers by forming relationships; this way you can buy local and do not have to pay for the organic price tag.

Converting land to organic status is a three-year process. There is a two-year conversion process consisting of building up the fertility of the land. Produce grown in the first year cannot be stated as organic. In the second year, produce may be stated as "in conversion." It is not until the third year that produce may be stated as fully organic. Soil and natural fertility building are important parts of organic farming.

Organic food doesn't always cost more. Some items, such as coffee, cereal, bread, and even hamburger, may cost the same or even less than their conventional counterparts. And, as the demand for organics continues to grow, the cost will continue to come down. When the cost is higher, consider these facts:

- Organic farmers don't receive federal subsidies like conventional farmers do. Therefore, the price of organic food reflects the true cost of growing.

- The price of conventional food does not reflect the cost of environmental cleanups that we pay for through our tax dollars—I'm just sayin'.

- Organic farming is more labor and management intensive as it takes way more time.

- Organic farms are usually smaller than conventional farms and so do not benefit from the perks larger growers get.

have never been part of the human food supply. Yep, that translates to man-made veggies and animals. In Mee language: a definite "Fake Food."

The governments of the United States and Canada have approved GMO crops for commercial use based on safety studies conducted by the same companies who developed the organisms. In thirty other countries around the world, including Australia, Japan, and all the countries of the European Union, GMOs are not considered to be safe and are therefore significantly restricted or banned outright. Recently, Peru placed a ten-year ban on all GMO foods, keeping them out of their country not only to avoid risk of contagion to their many strains of ancestral potatoes and corn, but also to avoid risk of contaminating the humans who reside within the country. Concerns about the health and environmental impacts of GMO foods are growing, including concerns about food allergies.

According to an American Academy of Environmental Medicine Position Paper in 2009, lab animals fed GMOs showed reproductive disorders, immune dysfunction, cellular and metabolism changes that may be linked to premature aging, GI problems, and insulin and cholesterol issues. The paper urged all physicians to avoid GMO food when possible. The scary deal to me is that corn is engineered to produce a pesticide called Bt-toxin, which breaks open the stomach of insects and kills them. The manufactures swear that the pesticide doesn't affect humans; however, a February 2012 study confirmed that Bt-toxin did break down the membranes of human embryonic kidney cells, meaning it is likely to do the same to other types of human cells. My personal belief is that if a food contains an ingredient that ruptures the stomach of a tiny insect, and we eat these same ingredients every day for 365 days a year for thirty-five years, we too will have accumulated enough Bt-toxin to rupture the tissue of our digestive tracts.

Farmers who have fed their animals primarily GMO grains have seen a huge decrease in fertility, not to mention thousands of farmers worldwide who have lost herds of animals to death and digestive distress after ingesting GMO grains.

The theory that GMO seeds will save the world from massive starvation is just not true. These seeds have a suicide gene in them, meaning each year a farmer must buy a new round of seeds to plant. This goes against every old-school rule of farming, as farmers save their seeds, replanting them each season. Seeds are a farmer's saving account; having to buy new seeds is not only extremely expensive to American farmers but also virtually impossible on a global level in Third-World farming.

Another argument that the pro-GMO folks tell us is that because GMO crops have pesticides built into the seeds, it lowers the use of agricultural chemicals. The problem with this is that they are herbicide tolerant; in other words, they can survive deadly doses of herbicide. A result of this is a huge increase of herbicide use, hundreds of millions of pounds, according to USDA data. Monsanto Roundup is a major culprit and found in large doses in fresh water that animals raised for human consumption are ingesting.

> These seeds have a suicide gene in them, meaning each year a farmer must buy a new round of seeds to plant. This goes against every old-school rule of farming . . .

Here's the deal, y'all: if the pesticide is woven into the fabric of the food, you can't wash it off. I suggest if you are suffering from any illness, especially a digestive disease where the only thing that touches the inside of the intestines is food, then avoid GMO foods.

If you are interested in more info regarding GMO seeds check out *Seeds of Deception* by Jeffrey M. Smith.

Politicians in our country are still arguing whether to label GMO foods or not. In the meantime, there are a few tips that you can follow to lessen your exposure to them:

- **Buy Organic.** Certified organic farmers are not allowed to use GMO seeds. The only problem is that cross contamination is a possibility if there are nearby GMO crops—the wind carries seeds.

- **Avoid nonorganic products,** especially those items containing corn, soy, canola oil, cottonseed, and sugar from beets, as these are the big-five GMO crops.

- **Look for the NON-GMO stamp.** This is a symbol that the farmers and food producers have taken all measures to insure that there are no GMO products in the food. Currently, Whole Foods has committed to certifying its entire store-brand products (called 365 Everyday Value) to not contain GMO.

A great way to double-check what you are buying is go to www.nongmoshoppingguide.com. There are lists of what to buy and also an app to download.

> If the pesticide is woven into the fabric of the food, you can't wash it off.

Breaking Down the Meat

Grass-fed beef first! My husband has taken on the task of switching our cattle ranch from a grain-fed farm to a completely self-sustainable grass-fed beef operation. It was simple for us really; once we realized that the key to my health was eating foods found in nature, we knew it was just as important to raise animals that also ate real foods.

Cows, sheep (lamb), bison, moose, elk, yaks, water buffalo, deer, camels, llamas, antelope, pronghorn, and nilgai are known as ruminant animals (mammals that digest plant-based food by initially softening it, then regurgitating the semi-digested mass—known as cud—then rechewing it). The process of rechewing the cud is to further break down the plants and stimulate digestion.

Studies have shown that eating the meat of ruminant animals is an easy shift to a healthier body as these meats contain less harmful fat and more omega-3s. Omega-3 fats are known to fight inflammation and prevent heart disease. I'd always thought the only way to get my omega-3s was via salmon: Not true. In grass-fed beef, for example, a 3-ounce serving contains 35 milligrams of the heart- and brain-protecting omega-3s: EPA and DHA. Compare this with the same serving of meat from grain-fed stock that has only 18 milligrams. According to Dr. Ronald Hoffman, "EPA and DHA are vital nutrients and may be taken to maintain healthy function of the following: Brain and Retina— DHA is a building block of tissue in the brain and retina of the eye. It helps with forming neural transmitters, such as phosphatidylserine, which is important for brain function. DHA is found in the retina of the eye and taking DHA may be necessary for maintaining healthy levels of DHA for normal eye function."

> In grass-fed beef, a 3-ounce serving contains 35 milligrams of the heart- and brain-protecting omega-3s: EPA and DHA.

Steers that munch on pasture also have twice the conjugated linoleic acid (CLA) per serving (26 milligrams, compared with 13 milligrams in grain-fed). According to Kate Clancy, Ph.D., a senior fellow at the Minnesota Institute for Sustainable Agriculture, early research in rats has linked higher CLA levels with easier weight loss and a reduced risk of heart disease as well as certain types of cancer.

Another positive reason to eat grass-fed beef is that grain-fed cows are believed to be linked to food illnesses. The *Journal of Dairy Science* has reported that levels of *E. coli* are usually higher in grain-fed cattle. The leading theory, says David Pimentel, Ph.D., professor of ecology and agricultural sciences at Cornell University, is that grain creates an environment in a steer's stomachs (they have four of them) that's more hospitable to the nasty bug, adding to the likelihood that the meat of a grain-fed animal will be contaminated with *E. coli* during processing.

Cattle farms leave giant footprints on our air quality, but that can't all be blamed on their methane-emitting toots. The problem is found in the growing of the corn needed to feed the cows, a process that produces a load of greenhouse gases and takes a ton of energy. The U.S. produces 1.5 billion bushels of it each year—just to feed cows.

Pasture-Raised Pork, Chickens, and Eggs

Here's the thing, if you're going to eat pork, chicken, or eggs, follow the same real food rules: pasture raised is natural and ancestral. Eating any type of animal products that come from a mass-produced environment is just wrong: ethically, environmentally, and of course healthwise. All it takes is for y'all to watch *Food Inc.,* a fantastically done documentary on our current food system.

> Eating any type of animal products that come from a mass-produced environment is just wrong: ethically, environmentally, and of course healthwise.

What is pasture-raised pork and why should we eat it? Pasture-raised pork is higher quality, healthier, tender, and delicious pork. It's naturally lower in fat and higher in omega-3s, vitamin E, beta-carotene, and conjugated linoleic acids (CLAs). Pasture-raised pigs enjoy a varied diet combining grass, alfalfa, clover, and bugs from the pastures in combination with an organic feed mix. The pigs spend a great deal of their time outside in the fresh air and are free to root and graze. They have indoor areas for shelter from the elements, or if the animal decides to go inside. They are raised without the use of subtherapeutic antibiotics or artificial growth hormones. This is how pigs were raised back in the day. If you want to know more on the tragic rearing of commercially raised pigs, check out *Food Inc.,* which I mentioned above. This documentary will aid in shifting you to a real food life.

As far as what I think about chicken, well, chicken has many health benefits. It has more amino acids than almost any other foods, and we need aminos for brain development; it's packed with niacin, which is a cancer fighter, and selenium. The problem I see is that we eat too much, and it becomes an inflammatory in our bodies. Then there is this little piece of information regarding nonorganic chicken.

One of the first questions Ginny Harper asked me was how much chicken I'd eaten. "A ton" was my answer. I'd been avoiding red meat, thinking it was harder to digest and less healthy. I decided to find the link between eating chicken and digestive bacteria and here it is.

Federal statistics show that cases of antibiotic-resistant *campylobacter* are rising (*campylobacter* is bacterium found mostly in chicken). An FDA investigation proved that the use of antibiotics in chicken production is a significant cause. The FDA's Center for Veterinary Medicine has proposed a ban on using these drugs in poultry because of evidence that the drugs used in chicken can cause people to get sick from drug-resistant bacteria. Hence, there is a rise in women suffering from urinary tract infections that fail to be treated with antibiotics, as doctors have found this same antibiotic is what chickens are fed. Once again, we have eaten our dose of antibiotics in our food, and we are now resistant to them!

A big issue is a family of antibiotics called *fluoroquinolones.* Some *fluoroquinolones* are sold to treat animals, but others are a leading treatment for humans who get food poisoning from *campylobacter.* Humans have used *fluoroquinolones* since the 1980s, but resistance didn't begin significantly increasing until veterinarians started using the drugs in the mid-1990s, according to data from the Centers for Disease Control and Prevention. So if we are eating chicken, non-organic chicken, then our already weakened immune systems can't fight the bacteria that is present. We can't go to a doctor and get an antibiotic either 'cause it won't work, 'cause we've been eating our antibiotics a few times a week.

I've been told over and over again by my children's pediatrician that it's not a good idea to take antibiotics more than once a year. So, fo'sho, we have no business eating them every day in our food source . . . I'm just sayin', y'all.

> It has more amino acids than almost any other foods, and we need aminos for brain development.

> Once again, we have eaten our dose of antibiotics in our food, and we are now resistant to them!

Food Additives to Avoid

A food additive refers to virtually any substance added to a food, but according to the U.S. Food and Drug Administration (FDA) definition, a food additive is "Any substance intended use of which results or may reasonably be expected to result directly or indirectly—in its becoming a component or otherwise affecting the characteristics of any food."

There are currently more than 3,000 food additives found in foods in the United States. If you are on a preventative health path or are rebuilding your body from any ailment, then I suggest avoiding anything added to your food that isn't food. Many of these additives have been linked to cancer and other chronic diseases and exacerbate all digestive diseases.

> I was blown away when I started discovering how many ingredients we've been eating that are linked to cancer and chronic illness.

I was blown away when I started discovering how many ingredients we've been eating that are linked to cancer and chronic illness. Of course most studies show that tiny amounts of these ingredients are not harmful, but if you're like I was and you ate something every day with a drop of this stuff in it, you would be creating a toxic environment in your body.

All of these items listed below are linked to possible ill health:

◆ **Acesulfame-K**—This is an artificial sweetener contained in baked goods, chewing gum, gelatin desserts, and diet soda. It is a newer sweetener used in soft drinks and some baked goods. The FDA approved it in 1998 for use in soft drinks. Acesulfame-K—the "K" is the chemistry symbol for potassium—is considered 200 times sweeter than sugar. There is a general concern that testing on this product has been scant. Some studies showed the additive might cause cancer in rats. I'd avoid this one regardless of the studies because it's just not natural. I'm sticking to our real food life.

◆ **Ammonium Sulfate**—This is a salt compound comprised of nitrogen. It can be found in some fertilizers and some bread, like the rolls at some fast-food restaurants. Chemicals with ammonia are typically added to neutralize a food that is too acidic, which can affect texture. Again, we are told that it's safe in the amounts it is used in foods, but here's the deal: if you are eating these foods every day or a few times a week, then these amounts add up and the amount of ammonia that rests in our bodies is not good.

- **Artificial Colorings**—A variety of foods are unnaturally colored. Research on animals suggests that these food additives may cause cancer. This includes six artificial food colorings: blues #1, #2, and #3; green #3; red #3; and yellow #6. Also, some red #40 side effects are attention deficit-hyperactivity disorder (ADHD), oppositional defiant disorder (ODD), and obsessive compulsive disorder (OCD). Red #3 is used in cherries (in fruit cocktails), baked goods, and candy. It causes thyroid tumors in rats and may cause them in humans as well. Artificial food and supplement colorings are made of coal tar and petrochemicals. Who'd knowingly eat that?

- **Aspartame**—This artificial sugar substitute is found in "diet" foods, including soft drinks, drink mixes, gelatin desserts, low-calorie frozen desserts, and packets. It is so harmful that my OBGYN in Nashville told me to avoid it during my pregnancy. If it's unhealthy during creation, then fo'sho, it's harmful while healing or living a preventative life. Lots of folks don't like the aftertaste of NutraSweet or Equal, produced by the Monsanto Corporation—big GMO folks. Aspartame is added to over 9,000 food products. This toxic poison changes into formaldehyde in the body and has been linked to migraines, seizures, brain lesions, and vision loss as well as symptoms relating to lupus, Parkinson's disease, multiple sclerosis, and other autoimmune diseases.

Aspartame actually contributes to weight gain by causing a craving for carbohydrates. A study of 80,000 women by the American Cancer Society found that those who used this neurotoxic "diet" sweetener actually gained more weight than those who didn't use aspartame products. Peep this little fact I found: aspartame/NutraSweet (aspartylphenylalanine-methyl-ester) breaks down to its poisonous constituents at 86 degrees (aspartic acid 40%, phenylalanine 50%, and methanol 10%). Remember your stomach is at 98.6 degrees; therefore, you should never use aspartame/NutraSweet in

Aspartame actually contributes to weight gain by causing a craving for carbohydrates.

hot beverages or cooked foods such as Jell-O. How the FDA allows this remains a mystery. There is mounting evidence that the "Burning Mouth Syndrome" experienced by the Desert Storm troops was actually methanol poisoning from drinking Diet Coke that was exposed to desert temperatures.

- **Azodicarbonamide**—This is a processing agent traditionally found in plastics, e.g., yoga mats and the soles of our shoes. According to *TIME's* Heathland, it is also found in hamburger buns.

- **BHA and BHT**—BHA and BHT stand for butylated hydroxyanisole and butylated hydroxytoluene, respectively. They are used as preservatives to keep food from spoilage. BHA and BHT can be found in butter, meats, chewing gum, snack foods, dehydrated potatoes, and even beer. These additives are approved by the FDA as safe for human consumption; however, they are proven carcinogens. There is proof that some people have difficulty metabolizing BHA, and this can result in health and behavioral changes. For certain, this is affecting the behavior of young children. "The structure of BHA and BHT will change during this process [of preserving food], and may form a compound that reacts in the body," says Christine Gerbstadt, M.D. "BHA and BHT are not stable or inert. They're not just hanging out and being excreted by the body." Gerbstadt says that they are obviously not added for the purpose of giving people cancer, but for some people, some of the time, there may be that risk. When it comes to my kids and myself, I'm not going to risk it; I'll just assume we are "some of the people" and avoid it.

> There is proof that some people have difficulty metabolizing BHA, and this can result in health and behavioral changes.

- **Carmel Color**—found in soda and foods. A big shocker is learning that "caramel coloring" in Coke, ginger ale, and Pepsi isn't made from melted sugar, but rather produced using ammonia and sulfites in conditions that form carcinogens. Yep, that caramel color is linked to causing cancer.

- **Cellulose (wood pulp)**—Yes, wood pulp is found in nature but humans are not meant to eat it. Where is it found: in shredded cheese, salad dressings, chocolate milk, and more according to the

Wall Street Journal. It's added to foods to keep them from clumping by blocking moisture and can thicken foods in place of flour or oil, as they cost more money.

* **Meat Glue**—Meat glue, which is technically called powdered or liquid enzyme fibrin, transglutaminase or TG, are enzymes that bind formerly unconnected pieces of meat to make them look like one solid chunk: yep, reconstructed pieces of meat made to look like perfect filets. The worst is that it compromises food safety when the meat is cooked rare in the center. You see true whole cuts can safely remain rare in the center because their centers have never been exposed to air or bacteria, but glued pieces can't. Also, meat glue contains pig and cow blood. I tell EVERYONE not to order or eat their meat rare or medium rare—**especially don't order it for young children who don't have fully developed immune systems.**

> You see true whole cuts can safely remain rare in the center because their centers have never been exposed to air or bacteria, but glued pieces can't.

* **Monosodium Glutamate (MSG)**—MSG is an amino acid used widely as a "flavor enhancer" in frozen dinners, salad dressings, chips, and restaurant food: It is commonly found in Chinese food. I know when I've eaten it 'cause I feel totally bloated for days. It is definitely hard on the intestines. MSG is now so ubiquitous in our food chains (East and West) that you would be very hard-pressed to go MSG-free. As you would expect, junk foods and instant foods like soups and other mixes contain MSG. Prepared food in your grocery stores and at fast food outlets (KFC chicken skin is massively loaded with MSG) and fine-dining restaurants alike are awash in MSG.

  When you see the word "citric acid" in prepared food ingredient lists, think MSG. Industrial citric acid is not made from citrus fruits, it's made from corn. Why is MSG bad for you? Early on (in the fifties) studies reported significant issues relating to the exposure of mammals to MSG. If neonatal rats were given a single exposure to MSG, the neurons in the inner layer of their retina were killed. It was also reported that certain parts of their brains were injured as well, e.g., the hypothalamus.

  When considering various findings of MSG exposure in the rat,

> MSG is a chemo inducer of obesity, type-2 diabetes, and metabolic syndrome X in the rat. Thus, MSG is used in the lab to induce obesity in rats.

remember that humans are five to six times more sensitive to MSG than rats. At one point, researchers determined that rats would be an excellent model for the study of obesity after the exposure to MSG. MSG is a chemo inducer of obesity, type-2 diabetes, and metabolic syndrome X in the rat. Thus, MSG is used in the lab to induce obesity in rats.

* **Olestra**—Olestra is a fake fat used to make nonfat potato chips and other snacks. Olestra has been shown to bind with fat-soluble vitamins A, E, D, K, and carotenoids—**substances thought to keep the immune system healthy and prevent some cancers**—and to eliminate them from your system. Proctor & Gamble, the company that produces olestra, has acknowledged the problem with vitamins A, E, D, K, and is now fortifying it with them. Olestra has also caused digestive upset in some people, especially when eaten often. If you are suffering any type of digestive distress or attempting to rebuild your body, skip this ingredient, especially as one of the side effects is loose shadoobies.

* **Pink Slime**—Pink slime, also known as lean finely textured beef (LFTB) or boneless lean beef trimmings (BLBT), is a beef-based food additive that may be added to ground beef and beef-based processed meats and cheap filler. It is made of finely ground beef scraps, sinew, fat, and connective tissue, which have been mechanically removed. The recovered material is then processed, heated, and treated with ammonia gas to kill *E. coli,* salmonella, and other bacteria. It's ground, pressed into blocks, and flash frozen for use as an additive in beef products. The key word and ingredient is "ammonia." Cleaning your floors with it is one thing, and even then we are warned against it. We are told to use natural alternatives. But when eating it, we are assured it is safe. Seriously?

* **Potassium Bromate**—Potassium bromate (KBrO3) is an oxidizing agent that has been used as a food additive, mainly in the bread-making process. Although adverse effects are not evident in animals fed bread-based diets made from flour treated with KBrO3, the agent is carcinogenic in rats and nephrotoxic (poisonous to the

kidneys) in both humans and animals when given orally. It has been shown that KBrO3 induces renal (kidney) cell tumors, mesotheliomas of the peritoneum (cancer that attacks the lining of the abdomen), and follicular cell tumors of the thyroid. Experiments aimed to shed some light on the effects of KBrO3 have proven that it is a complete carcinogen—**causing and promoting renal tumors in rats. I say make our own bread!**

♦ **Propyl Gallate**—This is a preservative used to prevent fats and oils from spoiling, which is also believed to cause cancer. It is used in vegetable oil, meat products, potato sticks, chicken soup base, and chewing gum, and it is often used with BHA and BHT.

♦ **Silicon Dioxide**—Also known as silica, it's mostly known as quartz or sand. If you feel like eating some, it can be found in many fast food options such as chili and meat filling. It is added to foods as an anti-caking agent, to keep them from clumping. I personally try not to eat sand while I'm at the beach, so I don't know why I'd want it in my food.

> I personally try not to eat sand while I'm at the beach, so I don't know why I'd want it in my food.

♦ **Sodium Nitrite/Nitrate**—Sodium nitrite is a food additive used as a preservative. It is used to extend the life of meats and to prevent the growth of bacteria. It is found in processed meats, including hot dogs, bacon, turkey bacon, bologna, and many lunch meats. You can avoid it by purchasing organic lunch meats as well as organic bacon and hot dogs. What's the problem with sodium nitrate? It is believed to be toxic. When you eat it, nitrosamines are formed. These dangerous compounds are highly carcinogenic. During lab studies, researchers inject these compounds into lab mice when they want to give them cancer.

♦ **Titanium Dioxide**—This is a chemical related to titanium. It's likely to be found in sunblock because it is a great physical blocker of UV rays. Where it shouldn't be found, but is (due to the fact it works), is in skim milk. After the fat is removed, the milk can appear slightly blue, so this is used as a lightener to whiten it. It may also be used in salad dressings, coffee creamers, and frosting, according to *Men's'*

Health magazine. I look at this way—would you put a drop of sunblock in your water and drink it?

- **Trans Fats**—These are artificial fats that are made when hydrogen gas reacts with oil. They can be found in cookies, crackers, icing, potato chips, stick margarine, and microwave popcorn. About 80 percent of trans fat in American's diet comes from factory-produced partially hydrogenated vegetable oil. Why are they so bad for you? Trans fats pose a higher risk of heart disease than saturated fats, which were once believed to be the worst kind of fats. While it is true that saturated fats—**found in butter, cheese, and beef**—raise total cholesterol levels, trans fats go a step further. Trans fats not only raise total cholesterol levels, they also deplete good cholesterol (HDL), which helps protect against heart disease.

- **Tuna Scrape**—Tuna scrape, also known as Nakaochi scrape, is tuna back meat. It is specifically scraped off the bones, and looks like ground meat or like ground tuna. Tuna scrape is sold frozen to restaurants and supermarkets, which use it to make sushi, particularly spicy tuna rolls. After a recent outbreak of salmonella, 116 people in twenty states and the District of Columbia fell ill; many reported they'd eaten spicy tuna rolls. My personal theory is eat only animal products that are thoroughly cooked to avoid nasty bacteria. Freezing doesn't kill salmonella or *E. coli;* once the food is thawed, the bacteria wakes up. Luckily, it does kill parasites. Because the tuna scrape is ground, it isn't surprising that it is high in bacteria. The same is true for ground chicken, turkey, and beef (compared with solid meat cuts). Pay attention to this little fact if you are healing your body or preventing illness.

Where to Buy Real Foods

I had no idea how to properly shop in a grocery store. Prior to learning to cook real food, most of my food was found in the center aisles in boxes. I, too, had thought buying organic meant more money spent. I'd gone organic shopping but found that buying processed organic food cost a ton more than nonorganic processed food. Yet it still lacked in nutrition in comparison to fresh food. Also, it contained many of the things I was trying to avoid: high levels of sugar, dairy, and wheat. Once I switched our household over, I can honestly say that I've cut my grocery bill in half!

The basis of my cooking is what I call "Foundation Foods." These are foods that are whole and support our bodies. They also serve as a "foundation" for my week's meals. I make a pot of beans once a week and usually two different grains each once a week. One pound of millet is 99 cents and feeds my family for days. A 1-pound bag of beans contains 4 cups; I usually cook a pot of beans for my family of four using 1.5 cups of beans. A 1-pound bag of organic black beans is $2.50. It feeds my family a total of at least six days worth of beans. We eat fish once or twice a week. We do not eat more than 4 ounces per serving. The basis of our plate is vegetables. I make salmon burgers using the leftover grains as fillers or combine the beans and grains to create a veggie burger.

When in Malibu, I shop at the local farmers market where I spend between $40 and $60 on fresh produce and fruit. This way, I'm supporting my local farming economy and eating in season, as they are only providing what is grown naturally according to the time of the year.

It is a lot like living in Sayulita, Mexico, where we only bought what was available. My menu changes with what is grown; this is how I keep things fresh and new on the dinner table. I look forward to what is growing and on its way to the market in the coming weeks.

Because I shop at the farmers market, I make sure that I cook all the produce in my house before stopping at the grocery store; it keeps me on my toes and my grocery bill down. My cooking spices

Once I switched our household over, I can honestly say that I've cut my grocery bill in half!

and standard kitchen pantry goods are in need of purchase only once or twice a month so I may spend $80 at the grocery store. I used to walk out of the market having dropped close to $400. I'd get home and stuff my pantry with crap food that was gone within two days—as it was instant gratification food, i.e., snacks.

There are other options if you are unable to get to a farmers market. You can research online or ask around about local CSA markets—Community Supported Agriculture markets known as "food boxes," in which a group of consumers pay a local farmer or group of farmers for a portion of the harvest and become sort of partners in the farm. Every week the farmer either personally delivers these food boxes or everyone agrees to meet at a certain pickup and drop-off spot. The food boxes are stuffed with whatever crop and vegetable is grown within season to the area of the farm. This is a great way to get your veggies, and the cost is usually between $20 and $50 dollars a week.

Food Co-Ops

The workers and customers at food co-ops (which can be set up like a small retail grocery store or a buying club) are generally committed to educating their members about healthy eating, environmental sensitivity, and supporting local farmers. Think Sam's Club or Costco, but all real foods and a social conscience. There is a co-op directory service (www.coopdirectory.org or www.localharvest.org) to help you find a natural foods co-op near you. I was so into creating a food co-op when I was working in North Nashville's food desert. However, it takes a bit of money to start one and a fee to join. Check out your local area for one and save money while shopping, as they sell whole grains and legumes!

> Think Sam's Club or Costco, but all real foods and a social conscience.

Online Shopping

To make things easy and to get you set up with the specialty items, hit up one of the many online food stores:

Natural Import Company: This is where I got my start. I had my list ready and sat down to order everything I needed: sesame oil, tamari, all of my sea vegetables, and kuzu. Once it arrived and I cooked with it, I formed a relationship with the food, and it became fun to hunt for it at a bargain price in Asian markets and health food stores. Visit www.naturalimport.com.

Glutenfree.com: Hunting gluten-free items is made easy at this one-stop shop. When I move between my houses in Nashville and Malibu, I always order a few things so that when I arrive out on the ranch an hour from a whole foods market, I have the basics. Visit www.gluten free.com.

Bob's Red Mill: This is a brand I really like and they seem to have all the grains I need. Visit www.bobsredmill.com.

Eden Organic: This is the only brand of canned beans that are made with Kombu seaweed (the way I make them) and packaged in a BPA-free can. They are also the only folks processing tomatoes in glass jars. (The acid from tomatoes eats away at the cans.) Visit www.edenfoods .com.

Native Forest: This another healthy canned food company. I buy their coconut milk as its BPA free too! Visit www.edwardandsons.com/native_info.itml.

Shop Organic: This is a great site to buy lots of things, especially beans/legumes, which can be bought in bulk as you can store them in airtight containers, and they'll last awhile! Visit www.shoporganic.com.

Herondale Farms: If you are looking to buy grass-fed beef, organic chicken, pasture-raised pork, and grass-fed lamb, this is your spot as they ship straight to your door. Visit www.herondalefarm.com.

Plant Your Own Veggies!

You can really get your money's worth if you plant your own organic heirloom seeds. I have a feeling in the future these seeds will be worth more than gold. Check out this site, as it's a great place to purchase seeds! Visit www.rareseeds.com.

PART THREE
Let's Get Cooking!

My Kitchen Cure Recipes

U pon returning to Los Angeles I enrolled myself in a professional culinary program, learning the basics of French and American cuisine. The benefit of this training is that I can now Mee'ify any recipe—tweaking it for individual health concerns and allergies. Again I have been amazed that the professional training that one undergoes to become a chef has nothing to do with health and wellness and is geared only for taste and comfort. I quickly found out that most classically trained chefs don't have a clue about how to cook fantastic tasting food that has a healing purpose. Most of my lecture notebooks were full of notes as I would figure out how to swap things out or create a yummy classic recipe with better healing ingredients.

> If it comes from a plant,
> EAT IT.
> If it is made in one,
> DON'T.

I've put together my ideal compilation of made up by Mee or "Mee'ified" recipes from some of my favorite restaurants and cookbooks.

Being that I'm someone who didn't have a clue about how to get started in the kitchen and I was totally "recipe" intimidated, I've put together some helpful little tips, which I've included throughout the first section of Part Three. I'll discuss measuring, what's in my kitchen, cooking terms, cutting definitions, and so on. I found these little bits of information really helped me get comfortable with all the kitchen possibilities. These days, when I enter Williams-Sonoma, my heart goes boom boom, 'cause I covet everything they are selling. I've swapped out my hunt for Prada to Le Crueset.

All of the recipes in this part are real food recipes—from Grass-Fed Beef to Tofu Lasagna! I hope this part of the book inspires you to try something new and that it gives your inner adventurer the go-ahead to research and discover which foods are best for your *individual* health. There is only one rule to follow: *If it comes from a plant, EAT IT. If it is made in one, DON'T.*

May this book serve as a jump-off point to your own personal real food life makeover.

KITCHEN EQUIPMENT

I don't have a ton of crazy kitchen gadgets, and the ones I do have aren't too pricey. My kitchen equipment includes:

Rice Maker—Doing my best to avoid cooking with nonstick & aluminum, I hunted down a stainless steel rice cooker. Miracle Exclusive has the best one yet—it will run you around $60 dollars, but will last years! Target has a great selection ranging from $20 and up. Get one with a steam tray so that you can steam veggies while cooking your brown rice, millet, or quinoa.

The Wand (a handheld mixer/blender)—Ever since I got this baby I don't ever need my blender or old-school mixer. The wand is super inexpensive and saves time. Put it right into the pan and blend your favorite soups! Like the rice maker, the wand is sold at any home goods store from Target to Tuesday Morning!

Mini Food Processor—In the past food processors intimidated me, but now I use mine all the time because it saves so much time! Again, I use one of the least expensive food processors and I've had it for years. You can use it to chop up anything—from carrots to garlic. I use mine to make fish rubs, sauces, and soup bases. Target has a bangin' selection or check out your local home goods store!

Nut Bag—This is a *must* for making home-made almond milk, cashew milk, coconut milk, and brown rice milk. I tried cheesecloth and strainers, but when it comes to separating out the nut from the milk, *none* of them worked as good as a nut bag!

Vitamix—I just bought this machine and I'll admit that it is pretty pricey (around $400). You can find it online or sometimes at Costco. I use it instead of a juicer—plop in your kale, carrots, beets, and so forth, and make a juice without the messy cleanup. The Vitamix grinds the skins up too, giving me all the nutrition that veggies and fruits pack!

Food Mill—The food mill is traditionally used for baby food, but this piece of equipment helps big time if you are healing an ailing digestive system. I used this in the early stages to grind my grains and beans.

Stainless-Steel Mesh Strainers (three small)—I use these for my beans and grains.

Stainless-Steel Colander (one)—For straining fruits, veggies, and pastas.

Pots and Pans—First of all, get rid of all of your nonstick pans! They leak chemicals and

I personally don't believe that there is such a thing as a "green" or "healthy" nonstick pan. We're going old school, shawty! Buy some cast-iron pots and pans. They last for a hundred years, add iron to our food, and food tastes great because the pans hold the flavors! Plus, they can be used on the stovetop or in the oven! I also love the enamel cast-iron. They are pricey but beautiful, hold heat, and cook up some food! The best place to find cheap enamel cast-iron pans is in Marshalls or T.J. Maxx. Here's what I have:

- 2 cast-iron skillets
- 2 Dutch Boy oven enameled cast-iron pots
- 2 large oval Dutch Boy enameled cast-iron pots
- 1 large stainless-steel steamer and wok—I LOVE this and bought it for 39 bucks at Costco!
- 1 medium stainless-steel steamer and saucepan

Bamboo Steamers—These are fantastic, as you can stack them to steam more than one dish at a time. I usually put a piece of fish on the bottom steamer and veggies on the top. They are also inexpensive and can be found at most cooking stores and Asian markets or ordered on line.

Veggie Noodle Spiraler—I LOVE this thing; it's inexpensive (between $20 and $30). I use it to make vegetable noodles. Zucchini noodles are my favorite!

Mandoline—This is an excellent time saver when it comes to fine slicing veggies. Just be careful 'cause the blades are super sharp!

Utensils—NO PLASTIC OR SILICONE! Once again, we don't want to use anything that can melt into our food. I know they "say" silicone doesn't break down in high heats, but truth be told I sho' don't want to find out that it does 20 years from now, so I'm keeping real and old school rocking the wood and stainless steel! Wooden utensils are cheap and don't leak chemicals! I don't recommend putting them in the dishwasher all the time, but once in a while it's a good idea to get 'em really clean.

Cutting Boards—NO PLASTIC OR SILICONE! I use bamboo wooden boards, but they do cost a bit more than plastic. I keep my fish and meat board separate from my veggie cutting board. I only have two boards, and I put them in the dishwasher once in a while for a good cleaning. Setting them out in the sun for a few hours does wonders too!

Storage Containers—NO PLASTIC! Here I go again with the "rid yo'self of plastic." If you are trying to cook healthy, clean food, then you sure don't want to place your hard work in a chemical-seeping container made of plastic. No, sir! I bought myself a set of Pyrex glassware with tops included. There are some BPA-free plastic containers available—a good idea for packing lunches. Toting glass to school at three years old is not a good idea!

KITCHEN STAPLES

What I keep in my spice drawer, pantry, and fridge are equally important, 'cause they all work together to make mealtime both REAL and TASTY.

What's in My Spice Drawer?

Dried spices are great for long-cooking recipes like soups and stews. Since yeast and molds can grow on spices, be mindful of how long you've had these in your spice drawer. I do my best to grind my own spices in a coffee grinder when I can.

◆ **Black Pepper**—I couldn't use black pepper for a long time because it stimulates the bowel and can cause friction. However, now I add a dash for flavor!

◆ **Cinnamon**—I love to add this to my apple kuzu drinks or cinnamon tea to keep intestinal bacteria at bay! Add a stick to a pot of water or sprinkle on your oatmeal!

◆ **Coriander**—This adds a bangin' splash of flavor. If you love cilantro then this is a must.

◆ **Cumin**—Used in everything from Latin to Middle Eastern dishes. Cumin also has been shown to balance blood sugar levels and is excellent for diabetics.

◆ **Curry powder**—A must and goes great with anything made with coconut milk!

◆ **Dried cilantro, dried basil, dried parsley**—If you use fresh parsley, basil, or cilantro and are doing a long cook triple the amount, and add more fresh spices again at the end of cooking to kick up the flavor!

◆ **Nutmeg**—Excellent with any squash dish or lamb. I also use it in my béchamel sauce.

◆ **Organic Adobo**—If I could only have one spice, this would be it. It's fantastic with chicken and beef, in soups, and mixed into almond or cornmeal to kick up a breading. I also mix it into fish burgers and bean burgers.

◆ **Sea Salt**—I order from Natural Imports because they have the highest quality sea salt. However, Trader Joe's or your local market fo'sho carries a good sea salt too.

◆ **Thyme**—Known as a cancer preventative, it is excellent with potatoes, scrambled eggs, creamy zucchini soup, and beef. I use it fresh, freshly ground, and dried.

◆ **Turmeric**—Cuts inflammation in our bodies. Add it to foods cooked with ginger, curry, and basil.

What's in My Pantry?

Two of my shelves are packed with clear glass jars filled with grains and legumes/

beans. If I can see them, I cook them, and I know what I need to buy. My pantry is stocked with:

- Black Beans
- Aduki Beans
- Millet
- Quinoa—Red and White
- White Corn Grits
- Oats
- Brown Rice
- Tahini Sesame Nut Butter (organic in a glass jar)
- Almond Butter
- Almonds, Pecans, Dried Fruits (unsulfured and unsweetened)
- Avocados
- Potatoes
- Sweet Potatoes
- Onions
- Garlic
- Sea Veggies: Kombu, Wakame, Aarame, Dulse, Hijiki
- Dried Seaweed Nori Snacks
- Kuzu (a thickener)
- Arrow Root (a thickener)
- Dried Shiitake Mushrooms
- Dried Daikon
- Dried Lotus Root
- Ghee (clarified butter; heals ulcerations and is dairy free)

- Coconut Oil
- Olive Oil
- Sesame Oil
- Avocado Oil
- Tamari
- Coconut Aminos—a soy sauce replacement (soy free with a richer flavor)
- Mirin (rice wine for cooking)—fructose-syrup free
- Organic Tamari, Organic Shoyu Sauces, and Coconut Aminos
- Umeboshi Vinegar
- Rice Vinegar
- Umeboshi Plums

Yes, I do eat some processed foods. What exactly are processed foods? Processed foods are foods that go through a process to get to you. They are created in a factory, and they are packaged and put in a box. When foods become complicated it is a process. Nonprocessed foods are foods in their simplest form. Our bodies are created to receive simple food.

Some processed foods in my pantry include:

- Organic Marinara Sauce (this is for my quick fix for kids' meals)
- Organic Rice Pasta
- Rice Cakes
- Gluten-Free Corn Cake Mix (Bob's Red Mill)

- Can of Chopped Organic Tomatoes

- Soba 100% Buckwheat Noodles (no wheat)

- Granola

- Cereals—Granola with Flax Seeds (under 10 grams of sugar per serving), Brown Rice Cereal, Low Sugar/Gluten-Free Corn Flakes

- Gluten-Free Corn Bread

- Yellow Corn Masa

- Yellow Corn Meal

- Organic Gluten-Free All-Purpose Rice Crumbs (yeast free)

- Organic Coconut Milk

- Organic Tortilla Chips

- Seasnax Toasted Seaweed Sheets

- Eden Brown Rice Chips—I love these!

- Eden Canned Beans (for when I am in a jam. They are cooked with kombu and no BPA in the can liner; you must rinse well before cooking)

- Canned Tuna in Water (seaweed in tuna salad is bangin')

What's in My Fridge?

I LOVE an uncrowded fridge. The only things on my shelves are leftovers, eggs, almond milk or rice milk, and occasionally apple juice. My drawers are full of veggies ready to be cooked.

- **First Shelf**—Almond Milk, Apple Juice, Aloe Vera Juice

- **Second Shelf**—Leftovers (stored in glass containers), Mochi, Corn Tortillas (home-made when I can get 'em!), Yogurt, Coconut Water Kefir, Earth Balance Butter, Nut Cheese (from Whole Foods, made fresh by a friend of mine)

- **Third Shelf**—Fresh Organic Eggs (from my friend's farm), Whole Grain Organic Bread (for my girls)

- **Drawers**—VEGGIES! Kale or Collards, Bok Choy, Carrots, Portabella Mushrooms, Zucchini, Yellow Squash, Daikon (fresh), Cherry Organic Tomatoes (when in season), Beets, and Celery (sometimes)

- **On the Door**—Salad Dressing, Organic Jam, Organic Ketchup, Organic Mustard, Organic Relish, Sauerkraut, Chickpea Soy-Free Miso, Sweet White Miso, Barley Miso, Vegenaise (the best vegan mayo)

- **In the Freezer**—Meats: ORGANIC ground lamb and beef from Pinewood Farms (thepinewoodfarm.com). Veggies: When I'm not on the ranch and able to eat 100% fresh veggies, I buy frozen organic. They are cheaper than fresh, last longer, and I never have an excuse for not cooking veggies because I've got them on hand! Costco sells *huge* bags of them for $7 and change! I buy these: frozen organic broccoli, frozen organic green beans, frozen organic corn, and frozen organic peas.

How to Store Foods

One of the most important tips after you've spent all this time and money to avoid harmful additives and pesticides is that you don't want to store them in chemical-seeping plasticware. I do my best to store all of my grains, sea vegetables, and legumes in air-tight sealed jars. When I'm away from one of my homes for more than a month, I tuck all my grains into the freezer in BPA-free containers. This keeps the grain/meal moths from growing and totally grossing me out.

THINGS TO KNOW BEFORE YOU GET COOKING

Being someone who didn't cook, I had to learn a new language to understand recipes. I've done my best to put together basic definitions and tips that can save you research time and help you avoid recipe intimidation. Since moving to Los Angeles, I've been enrolled in a professional chef's training program. The best thing I've learned is how to follow a recipe without being pensive.

Dry Ingredients

Flours should be spooned lightly into measuring cups. Do not tap or shake down the contents. Molasses sugar should be packed firmly when measuring. Shortening should be packed a little at a time into a measuring cup and the air pockets pressed out.

When measuring dry ingredients in measuring spoons, scoop up the ingredients so that the spoon is overfilled, then run the flat edge of a knife across the top of the spoon so that any excess ingredient is removed. If a "heaping" spoon is called for, do not remove the excess with a knife.

Liquids and Oils

Fill liquids to the line on measuring cups and view at eye level to ensure measurement is exact. Fill liquids to the top of the measuring spoon. Make sure to use a liquid measuring cup.

Pot and Pan Measurements

Square or rectangular baking pans are measured by length times width times depth, such as 9 x 13 x 2-inch baking pan, or sometimes just length times width, such as an 8 x 8-inch square baking pan.

Round baking pans are measured by their diameter and are usually referred to as cake pans, such as an 8-inch or 9-inch round cake pan.

Stovetop pots are measured by volume, such as 1 quart, 2 quart, 3 quart, or larger. These are what I refer to in this book as saucepans or soup pots. A small saucepan would be a 1 or 2 quart. A medium saucepan would be a 3 or 4 quart; 5 quarts and up would be called a soup pot. Sometimes the size is printed on the bottom of a pot; if not, you can find out by premeasuring water and recording how much it takes to fill the pot.

Stovetop pans are referred to as skillets in this book and are measured by their diameter, such as 6, 10, or 12 inches. They are sometimes referred to as small, medium, or large as well.

EQUIVALENTS

I have this little chart taped to the inside of my cupboard so I always know how to break down my measuring.

3 teaspoons (tsp.) = 1 tablespoon (tbsp.)	4 tbsp. = $1/4$ cup
$5\ 1/3$ tbsp. = $1/3$ cup	16 tbsp. = 1 cup
1 cup = 8 fluid ounces (fl. oz.) = $1/2$ pint (pt.)	2 cups = 1 pt.
4 cups = 1 gallon (gal.) = 1 quart (qt.)	4 cups = 1 liter (L)—roughly
5 milliliters (mL) = 1 tsp.	125 mL = $1/2$ cup
250 ml = 1 cup	946 mL = 4 cups
1.89 L = 8 cups	28 grams (g.) = 1 ounce (oz.)
100 g. = $3^1/2$ oz.	454 g. = 1 pound (lb.)
16 oz. = 1 lb.	

The term "scant" means a scatter or a dash of something.
This is where you get to decide how much something needs based on your intuition.

Cutting Veggies

Here's the deal to living a real food life—we have to take the time to sit and chop. There is no way around it. Now that I've gotten myself some knife skills, I actually enjoy my prep work before cooking. I get into a zone and find the process grounding, a total meditation and time-out for me.

I was officially the worst vegetable cutter *ever*. To top it off I used a serrated knife, which is perfect for bread but a *disaster* when chopping veggies.

When we moved back to LA, I decided it was time to take my knife skills to another level. They had improved a bunch over the years, but I wanted to take them higher, so I enrolled in a knife skills class at a local cooking school. The class was wonderful, but the Chef Rectum was way too full of herself.

Cooking Definitions

Once again I had *no* idea what the difference between boiling and parboiling was. I spent so much time researching and Googling, I thought to save y'all some time, as I'd break it down fo' ya!

◆ **Boil**—when a liquid bubbles; full boil is reached when stirring the liquid can't stop bubbles.

◆ **Parboil**—to cook in boiling water briefly to speed up the cooking process.

◆ **Roast**—to cook uncovered in a pan in the oven.

◆ **Sauté**—add oil to ingredients in a skillet and stir gently while cooking.

◆ **Steam**—put ingredients in a steamer basket over a pot of simmering/boiling water and cover with a lid (only enough water

---

Why Steam?

Steaming vegetables retains more nutrients than boiling vegetables. The food becomes more digestible and fibrous, strengthening our intestinal muscle. If you are suffering digestive distress, cook vegetables a bit longer than the recipe calls for.

Some rice makers come with a steam basket, so you can steam your veggies while you make your rice. Here are some guidelines:

◆ Steam spinach for 30 seconds

◆ Steam bok choy for 1–1$\frac{1}{2}$ minutes

◆ Steam kale, collards, carrots, and Swiss chard stalks for 2 minutes

◆ Steam broccoli, cauliflower, beets, and green beans for 2$\frac{1}{2}$ minutes

◆ Steam Brussels sprouts for 3–4 minutes

◆ Steam squash, sweet potatoes, and corn on the cob for 8–10 minutes

to have it come to a boil; not enough to let it touch the food in the rack or basket).

- **Slice**—cut in one direction.

- **Chop**—cut in two directions to create smaller, bite-sized pieces.

- **Dice**—creates even smaller pieces than chopping.

- **Mince**—creates the smallest pieces; can be done with a knife and cutting board or with a food processor (for vegetables like garlic).

- **Julienne**—creates matchstick pieces.

- **Zest**—removes the outer colored layer of citrus fruits called the peel or rind, which is used for added flavor.

Explanations of Nutritional Value

Fiber—relieves constipation; lowers blood cholesterol levels and risk of diabetes, heart disease, and developing hemorrhoids; reduces blood pressure and inflammation; aids in weight loss; makes meals feel larger and the effects of fullness last longer.

There are two types of fiber:

- *Insoluble* (doesn't dissolve in water); helps with constipation and irregular stools; includes whole-wheat flour, wheat bran, nuts, and certain vegetables

- *Soluble* (dissolves in water); helps with lowering blood cholesterol and glucose levels; includes oats, peas, beans, apples, citrus fruits, carrots, and barley

Protein—75 percent of your weight is protein; found throughout the body (muscle, bone, skin, hair) makes up the enzymes that power many chemical reactions and the hemoglobin that carries oxygen in your blood; gives you energy.

Calcium—aids in maintaining bone health, protects cardiac muscles, promotes dental health, and helps prevent colon cancer and reduce obesity.

Selenium—may reduce the odds of many different cancers, including prostate cancer. It's a *huge* immune booster.

Phosphorous—helps with bone and teeth formation; allows proper digestion of riboflavin and niacin; aids in transmission of nerve impulses; helps your kidneys effectively excrete wastes; gives you stable and plentiful energy; forms the proteins that aid in reproduction; and may help block cancer.

Copper—necessary for proper growth, utilization of iron, enzymatic reactions, healthy connective tissues, hair, eyes, aging, and energy production; supports healthy heart rhythms, thyroid glands, wound healing; red blood cell formation, and low cholesterol levels; helps relieve arthritis symptoms.

Manganese—increases a healthy bone structure and metabolism; helps build essential enzymes for building bones; acts as a coenzyme to assist metabolic progression in the human body; helps form connective tissues, absorption of calcium, and production of sex hormones; helps regulate blood sugar levels and metabolize fats and carbohydrates; alleviates PMS systems.

Magnesium—helps with the transmission of nerve impulses, body temperature regulation, detoxification, energy production, and the formation of healthy bones and teeth.

ALL ABOUT BEANS

Beans are no joke when it comes to being good fo' ya! I had been told by every doctor I'd met that it wouldn't be possible for someone with my intestinal issues to *ever* eat beans. Well that turned out to be a myth 'cause I get down with these little protein packers! Don't forget beans are CHEAP—as in costing you little cash—and they go a long way!

Rules of Beans

Here are some rules for preparing beans:

◆ Beans must be soaked overnight in water with kombu sea vegetable.

◆ They must be drained and rinsed off after soaking, then new water added before cooking (amounts according to recipes that follow).

◆ Be mindful that beans come from the ground, where they are among rocks and dirt. Go through your beans before you cook them, searching for broken beans and tiny stones that could easily have been missed. You don't wanna break your tooth on a rock.

◆ Most beans double in volume from dry to cooked. One cup of dried beans serves about four people. Soybeans and garbanzo beans usually triple, so you are going to have a little extra here.

◆ Remove and rinse the kombu after soaking—I usually chop mine up into pieces before adding it back to the cooking pot.

◆ Don't chop up the onion or garlic or they will get scooped out when you skim the foam. Instead place whole garlic cloves and quarter pieces of onion into the pot.

◆ Bring to a boil, cover, and simmer for 30 minutes.

◆ Remove the spongelike foam that floats to the top of the pot while cooking. This foam is home to the gas-causing carbohydrates. If you don't remove it, your tummy will fo'sho be in a state of methane suffering!

◆ Add salt during the last 10 minutes of cooking. If you add salt any sooner, it will slow the cooking time.

Buy yo'self some nice cast-iron, stainless-steel, or enameled cast-iron pots. For real. They don't leak nasty chemicals into your food, but they do retain the heat, cook your food evenly, and maintain the flavors; some even say that cast iron adds iron to the food. The real perk is that even though they cost a bit more they last *forever*!

So Many Beans to Choose From

Beans can be eaten in different stages. Some are eaten green, either in or with their pod, such as green beans; or shelled and eaten without their pod, such as fava beans, green beans, and fresh soybeans (edamame). The majority of beans are of the dried variety, which can be stored for long periods of time. These need to be soaked and boiled before they are eaten. Pinto beans, black beans, and garbanzo beans are examples of this type.

- Aduki (also spelled adzuki) are small red beans with a sweet and nutty flavor and a firm texture. They are prized in Japan, where they are cooked in both savory and sweet dishes, including a sweetened puree used as a filling or topping. In the macrobiotic world, they are a preferred bean for eating regularly, as they contain less fat and oil than other beans. Cooking time: 1 hour.

- Black beans are native to South America and are also used widely in Central America, Cuba, Puerto Rico, the Caribbean, and Spain. They are sometimes called black turtle beans. Cooking time: 1–1½ hours.

- Black-eyed peas are said to be a Chinese relative of the mung bean. They found their way to India and Africa, and because of the slave trade, ended up in America, where they became a staple of southern cooking. They have a light and smooth texture. Cooking time: 1 hour.

- Garbanzo beans (chickpeas) have a great nutty flavor and a firm texture. They are the most widely grown beans in India, where they are known as *channa dal* and also ground into flour (called *besan* or "gram flour") for making flat breads. The Middle East made this bean famous in a dish called hummus. They are extremely popular in Greek cuisine. Most garbanzos have a yellowish color, but there is a variety called black Kabuli that is quite nice and makes a cool-looking black hummus. Cooking time: 2–2½ hours.

- Kidney beans are indigenous to Mexico and are usually a deep dark red color. They have a meaty texture and are commonly use in chili recipes. Other varieties are red beans, a smaller version of kidney beans, and cannellini beans (white Italian kidney beans). Cooking time: 1–1½ hours.

- Lentils originated in southwest Asia. The most popular in the U.S. are brown lentils and green lentils. French lentils are a variety of green lentil with a tortoiseshell appearance. Puy green lentils are grown in a special small area in France called le Puy and must be grown according to

French regulations that ensure their quality. Red lentils are a beautiful orange color and are very soft when cooked. The smaller *masoor* lentils you see at Indian markets are either the brown or the orange masoor. The brown *masoor* are the orange *masoor* with their seed coats on. They take longer to cook then regular brown lentils. Cooking times: brown and green lentils, 45 minutes; red lentils, 20 minutes.

- Lima beans and baby lima beans taste about the same, the larger being meatier. Native to Central America, these beans eventually reached Peru and were named after its capital city. In North America, the Algonquin Indians made a dish called succotash with corn and lima beans. Cooking time: $1^1/_2$–2 hours.

- Mung beans are beady little olive-green legumes that cook quickly. They are very popular in East Indian spiced lentil dishes (dals). When you buy fresh bean sprouts loose at the market, these are the beans they were sprouted from. Cooking time: for whole mung, 45 minutes to 1 hour.

- Pinto beans are reddish brown with lighter streaks and are popular in Mexican cuisine; and when cooked and mashed they are delicious as *refritos,* or refried beans. Cooking time: $1^1/_2$–2 hours.

- Soybeans contain 35 to 38 percent protein and all the essential amino acids that the body doesn't manufacture on its own.

They've been cultivated for over 5,000 years and have served as the major source of protein for the people of China, Japan, Korea, and Indonesia. Europe has had them for about three hundred years, while the U.S. began using them in the 1900s and is currently the world's largest producer, at over 5 metric tons per year, or about 500 pounds per citizen. Most of these soybeans are fed to factory farm animals. In the Midwest soybeans are also known as sweet beans. Edamame are soybeans eaten green out of the pod, roasted and seasoned, or boiled for stews or healing teas. Most dried soybeans are a yellowish color, one exception being the black soybean. Cooking time for dried soybeans: 2–$2^1/_2$ hours.

- Split peas come in green and yellow varieties. The fresh peas have been allowed to dry, which gives them a sweeter essence. Split peas make a yummy, hearty soup. Cooking time: 40–50 minutes.

- White beans include four types: great northern beans, navy beans, pea beans, and the big marrowfat. Cooking time: $1^1/_2$–2 hours.

BEAN YIELDS

2 cups dry beans = 1 pound cooked

1 cup dry beans = 2–3 cups cooked

1 cup dry beans = 4 servings

Cooking Beans, Lentils & Peas (aka Legumes)

The key to cooking beans is to be sure you've cooked them thoroughly. Where folks go wrong is turning off the stove too soon. If they aren't done in the recommended time, add more water and turn up the heat, bringing them to a boil for another 15 minutes.

Cook legumes in lots of water, then drain afterward (except lentils and split peas).

Legume	Soaking Time	Water: Legumes*	Cooking Time	Nutritional Values and Additional Notes
Aduki (adzuki) beans	2–4 hours	3:1	1–1 1/2 hours	Easy to digest; tones kidneys according to traditional Chinese medicine
Black beans	6–12 hours	4:1	1 1/2 hours	Contains the most antioxidants of any legume
Black-eyed peas	4–12 hours	3:1	1 hour	Protein, minerals, B vitamins, and isoflavones
Cannellini (white kidney) beans	6–12 hours	3:1	1–1 1/2 hours	Molybdenum, folate, and tryptophan
Chickpeas (garbanzo beans)	6–12 hours	4:1	2 hours	Contains more iron than any other legume; protein and molybdenum
Kidney beans	6–12 hours	3:1	1 1/2–2 hours	Molybdenum, folate, tryptophan, and protein
Lima beans	6–12 hours	2:1	1 1/2 hours	Molybdenum and tryptophan
Lentils	20 minutes– 4 hours	3:1	45–60 minutes	Molybdenum, folate, and tryptophan; easy to digest (less gassy); second highest amount of protein of any legume
Navy beans	4–12 hours	3:1	1–1 1/2 hours	Tryptophan, folate, and manganese; controls blood sugar
Pinto beans	6–12 hours	3:1	1 1/2 hours	Molybdenum, folate, and tryptophan
Soybeans	6–12 hours	4:1	3–5 hours	Highest amount of protein of any legume (can be difficult to digest though); molybdenum, tryptophan, and manganese

*ratio of water to legumes

SPROUTING

I had *never* heard of sprouting until I'd read Jordan Ruben's *The Makers Diet*. He'd healed his body of one of the worst cases of Crohn's disease via food. Many of his recipes include the sprouting of his grains. Sprouting is the practice of germinating seeds to be eaten either raw or cooked. Sprouting is great for us because sprouts are more nutritious than the seed, nut, bean, or grain they come from. Plus sprouts have all the essential amino acids, vitamins, minerals, chlorophyll, and enzymes. The greatest benefit is that sprouts from seeds, grains, or legumes are said to be easily digestible. Sprouting takes only a few days and very little effort and can be done in your own kitchen with cheap equipment. It's super easy!

Whatcha Do

Rinse whatever you are sprouting well and then drain immediately. Place in a bowl. Cover rinsed seeds, grains, or legumes with cool or room-temperature filtered water (to about 3 inches or $7^1/_2$ centimeters above seeds, grains, legumes). Soak for recommended time (see package for directions or the chart below) cover with cheesecloth. Drain off and discard water after soaking, as it contains enzyme inhibitors—or as I call them, gas blasters! Then rinse and drain sprouts (no soaking) at least twice a day. (In hot weather, do this three times a day to prevent mold.) Ensure they're really drained well each time by propping jar upside down on dish-drying rack to drain on an angle in a bowl.

Sprouting takes 2–5 days, and sprouts are ready when they are as long as the grain or legumes themselves; small seeds are ready when hulls begin to break away from their two tiny leaves. Once sprouted, place in a container with a folded piece of paper towel on the bottom to absorb any excess water and then store in the fridge. Eat within four days.

Sprouting and Soaking Times for Seeds, Grains & Legumes

Sprouting takes only a few days and very little effort and can be done in your own kitchen with cheap equipment. It's super easy!

SEED, GRAIN, OR LEGUME	AMOUNT TO YIELD ABOUT 4 CUPS SPROUTS	SOAKING TIME	SPROUTING TIME
Aduki (aduzki) beans	1 cup	12 hours	3–5 days
Alfalfa	2 tablespoons	6 hours	5–6 days
Chickpeas (garbanzo beans)	1 cup	12 hours	3–5 days
Fenugreek	1/2 cup	12 hours	3–5 days
Lentils	1/2 cup	8 hours	3 days
Mustard seeds	1/4 cup	6 hours	5–6 days
Mung beans	1/2 cup	8 hours	2–4 days
Radish	1/4 cup	6 hours	5–6 days
Rye	1 cup	12 hours	3 days
Red clover	2 tablespoons	6 hours	5–6 days
Sunflower seeds	2 cups	12 hours	2 days
Soybeans	1 cup	12 hours	3–5 days
Wheat berries	1 cup	12 hours	3 days

BEAN RECIPES

MAKES 8–10 SERVINGS

WHATCHA NEED

2 cups aduki beans

6 cups water

1 strip kombu sea vegetable

1 good-sized chunk ginger
(you decide how much you like)

1 small chunk turmeric

1 tablespoon tamari or shoyu
soy sauce or coconut aminos

1 butternut squash, peeled
and chopped

$1/4$–$1/2$ teaspoon sea salt

ADUKI BEANS
Vegan, Dairy Free, and Gluten Free

Aduki beans, also known as adzuki beans, are the first beans that I was introduced to by Ginny Harper. Aduki beans are the detoxers of legumes. They are also known as the skinny bean because they help flush excess fat from our bodies. The biggest perk for me is that they are the least gas forming of all the beans and they cook quickly! Plus, the nutty flavor mixes up my palate.

Whatcha Do

Peep the Rules of Beans (page 194). Aduki beans are smaller and cook faster, so you only need about an hour of simmering time until the beans are tender. Add all of the ingredients except the squash and salt. The squash is added during the last 30 minutes, and the salt is added during the last 10 minutes.

BLACK BEANS
Vegan, Dairy Free, and Gluten Free

WHATCHA NEED

2 cups black beans

6 cups water

1/2 onion, chopped in half

2–3 cloves garlic,
chopped in half

1 teaspoon baking soda

1 tablespoon dried or fresh basil
(use more to taste if it's fresh)

1 tablespoon turmeric

1 tablespoon tamari or shoyu
soy sauce

1/4–1/2 teaspoon sea salt

Whatcha Do

Peep the Rules of Beans (page 194). Mix all of the ingredients except the tamari or shoyu sauce and salt. Simmer the beans for about 1 1/2 hours on low. You don't have to stand next to them. If they are still not done after the cooking time, then add more water and keep cooking 'em. Black beans take longer than most beans. Cover pot to keep the water in, and add more water if you've removed a bunch while skimming off the foam. Add your tamari or shoyu and salt during the last 20 minutes.

GARBANZO BEANS
Vegan, Dairy Free, and Gluten Free

MAKES 8 SERVINGS

WHATCHA NEED

2 cups of garbanzo beans
soaked with 2-inch piece
of kombu overnight

3 cups of water—
to cover beans while boiling

1/2 onion, chopped small

3 cloves garlic, chopped

1 tablespoon freshly grated
turmeric or turmeric powder

1 cup chopped fresh basil

1 tablespoon organic adobo
seasoning

Pinch of sea salt added
in the end

I love chickpeas! I cook up a batch and use them in hummus a few days later.

Whatcha Do

Peep the Rules of Beans (page 194). Rinse your beans well and cover with water, bring them to a boil, and remove foam. Add all ingredients except salt, lower heat, and cook for 45 minutes or until beans are soft. Add pinch of sea salt.

MAKES 8 SERVINGS

WHATCHA NEED

1 16-ounce package dried black-eyed peas, washed and soaked overnight with 3-inch piece of kombu seaweed

3 cups water—to cover beans while boiling

1 medium onion, chopped

4 cloves garlic, chopped

1 can Eden Organic diced tomatoes with green chilies

1 large potato, peeled and diced

3 tablespoons olive oil

1 teaspoon sea salt

1 teaspoon chili powder

1 teaspoon ground coriander

$1/2$ teaspoon freshly ground black pepper

Fresh cilantro, as garnish

BLACK-EYED PEAS—SOUTHERN STYLE BUT MEE-IFIED!
Vegan, Dairy Free, and Gluten Free

Whatcha Do

Peep the Rule of Beans (page 194). In a large saucepan bring black-eyed peas to a boil, removing foam with a ladle. Chop up kombu and add in with beans once the foam is cooked off. Add the onion, garlic, tomatoes with green chilies, potato, olive oil, sea salt, chili powder, coriander, and pepper. Cover and cook over medium heat for 45 minutes to 1 hour, or until the peas are tender. Add additional water, if necessary. Serve garnished with cilantro.

MAKES 6 SERVINGS

WHATCHA NEED

1 teaspoon olive oil or sesame oil

$1/4$ onion, chopped

2 cloves garlic, chopped

1 tablespoon tamari or shoyu soy sauce or soy-free coconut aminos

$1/4$ cup of water

2 cups leftover cooked beans

REFRIED BEANS
Vegan, Dairy Free, and Gluten Free

Refry all your leftover cooked beans. It's easy!

Whatcha Do

Heat a pan with the oil, then sauté the chopped onion and garlic. Add tamari or shoyu sauce or coconut aminos, and then add in your beans. Heat ingredients together then remove from heat, place in a bowl, and whip them up with your electric hand wand or use a blender or food processor. These beans make burrito night a hit!

MUNG BEANS
Vegan, Dairy Free, and Gluten Free

Mung beans are considered a cooling food in Chinese medicine. They are great for inflammatory issues and excellent to eat in the summertime. I love the name and thought they had to be some crazy bean but they aren't. They are super popular in Asian culture and easy to cook.

Whatcha Do

Peep the Rules of Beans (page 197). Rinse your mung beans well after soaking, cover in pot of water, and bring to a boil. Boil for 14 minutes and remove foam. Chop kombu seaweed and add to pot. Add everything else and cook until beans *and* veggies are soft! Add diluted miso during the last 5 minutes.

MAKES 6–8 SERVINGS

WHATCHA NEED

$1/2$ cup dried mung beans soaked overnight with 2-inch piece of kombu seaweed

2 cups water

5 potatoes, peeled and diced

$1/4$ teaspoon sea salt

1 tablespoon olive oil

1 onion, diced

2 carrots, diced

2 stalks celery, diced

5 shiitake mushrooms, stems removed and diced

1 tablespoon of miso paste

WHITE BEANS
Vegan, Dairy Free, and Gluten Free

I LOVE THESE BABIES! These gems remind me of my Italian grandmother. She used white beans in her pasta e fagioli, so I hook 'em up the Italiano way!

Whatcha Do

Peep the Rules of Beans (page 197). Treat these little babies like the rest—by now you've got a rhythm for cooking legumes! Add the tomatoes in the beginning with everything else, except the basil. The basil goes in the pot once the beans are done since the freshness of the basil kicks up the flavor. These white beans make an awesome dip! All you've got to do is whip out your electric hand wand or pop 'em in the blender.

MAKES 6–8 SERVINGS

WHATCHA NEED

2 cups white beans

6 cups water

1 2-inch piece of dried kombu sea vegetable

$1/2$ onion

3–4 cloves garlic

2 tomatoes, chopped or puréed in a food processer (optional)

2 tablespoons olive oil

$1/4$–$1/2$ teaspoon sea salt

A bunch of basil

ALL ABOUT GRAINS

We were a rigatoni pasta family, and my momma didn't like rice 'cause her momma didn't make it. In fact, I *never* once ate whole grains growing up. As an adult, I never ate any grains other than an occasional side of brown rice. I didn't know what I was missing!

Whole grains are best used in their original form with all of their parts intact: the bran, the germ, and the endosperm. When manufacturers remove the bran and germ to make refined flour, they remove most of the vitamins and minerals—a major no-no if you want to get good nutrition out of 'em.

Rules of Grains

If you follow these rules, grain intimidation is no longer an issue. Take a look! I've tried to make 'em easy to follow:

- I soak all of my grains overnight (except millet and quinoa; see below), and if you are suffering from digestive troubles, it's a good idea to do that. Be sure to add a 2-inch piece of kombu sea vegetable when soaking. The kombu helps cut the carbohydrates that cause gas and it adds minerals to your grains—boost 'em, baby!

- You do not have to soak millet or quinoa overnight. Instead, it is recommended you soak them for 20 minutes and then rinse them. Be sure to toss your kombu into the pot with your grains.

- After soaking, rinse your grains and add fresh water. The soaking water is full of grain garbage: excess gas-causing carbohydrates and dirt!

The Grains I Eat!

In the beginning of my food journey, I only knew about brown rice, and truth be told—I didn't like it. Most people half cook it, leaving it chewy and tough. Once I was on my new food path I was in awe of the bulk foods section at Whole Foods. Literally. A world opened up to me, one that would keep my dinner table from ever becoming drab with the same old white rice.

It has become fashionable to avoid all carbohydrates and grains, as most people are eating from a vanity perspective. Sadly, this theory is wrong. Eating whole grains is the key to balancing the body. Eating them in moderation and rotating them is primary. Avoiding grains is what is unhealthy. You will not gain an unhealthy amount of weight if you are cooking quinoa, millet, and barley, because your focus will be to eat a plate of food that is also full of veggies!

If you are suffering from digestive distress or a flare up, only eat brown rice or millet until your digestive tract has calmed down.

- **Amaranth** is not a true cereal grass but a

weedy plant of the pigweed family. The seed is high in protein and about the size of a poppy seed. The leaves of amaranth can also be eaten as well. The blooms of the plant are unique and beautiful, with colors of purple, orange, red, or gold. In Mexico, amaranth is super common as snack bars, and cookies are made with amaranth. (Tip: Add amaranth when cooking with other grains—about a teaspoon—for added nutrients and to add a mixture of flavors.)

- **Barley** is a strength builder. In Chinese medicine it is said to help in the removal of dampness. Signs of dampness are illnesses or weakness. I eat barley in the depths of winter. It's great for breakfast and in stews.

- **Buckwheat** is a cereal unrelated to wheat. After it has been cooked and prepared pilaf-style, it is called kasha. I love buckwheat for baking. It's super yummy and as a whole grain it has a fragrant, distinct flavor. A great game changer for dinner parties.

- **Oats** are mechanically pressed or rolled for oatmeal. They can be grounded as well.

- **Wild rice** is not actually a member of the rice family, although it is a grain-producing grass. Native to North America, wild rice can still be found growing wild in the ponds and lakes of Wisconsin, as well as in neighboring states. Native Americans were the first to introduce it to the colonists. Like rice, wild rice grows in water, although it tends to require much deeper water resources. The two grains also have taste similarities, both tasting much more nutty with the outer husk left on. (Much of the wild rice crop in the U.S. is still hand-harvested in the traditional manner. Your package label usually states whether the product has been harvested by hand.)

Cooking Grains

The key to cooking grains that taste yummy is making sure you've cooked them long enough (see the chart on the following page). If you are suffering any type of digestive distress or are healing your body and need to aid absorption, add extra water to make them more like a porridge. After you've made these grains a few times you'll have a rhythm for it, and the timing will come naturally.

Brown Rice

I always try to soak my brown rice the night before with a small piece of kombu sea vegetable. But now that I'm well, I can get away with soaking it for 20 minutes.

COOKING GRAINS

GRAIN	WATER: GRAIN*	COOKING TIME	APPROXIMATE YIELD**	NUTRITIONAL VALUES AND ADDITIONAL NOTES
Amaranth	2:1	20—30 minutes	2 cups	Very high in fiber, protein, and calcium; easy to digest
Barley (hulled)†	2—3:1	1—1½ hours	3½—4 cups	Selenium, phosphorous, and copper; warming properties
Barley (pearl)†	2—3:1	30—50 minutes	3½ cups	Fiber, selenium, phosphorus, and copper; supports bowel health; warming properties
Buckwheat	2:1	10—15 minutes	2 cups	Lowers risk of high cholesterol and high blood pressure
Bulgur†	2:1	20 minutes	3 cups	Avoid with wheat allergies
Cornmeal	3:1	30 minutes	3 cups	B vitamins, which support lung health, memory, and energy when under stress
Kamut†	3:1	1—2 hours	2½ cups	A type of wheat but higher in proteins, minerals, vitamins, and unsaturated fatty acids than common wheat
Millet	2:1	20—30 minutes	3½—4 cups	Most alkalinizing grain
Oats (whole)†	2¼:1	½—1 hour	2—2½ cups	Nourishes nervous system
Oats (rolled)†	2:1	5—10 minutes	4 cups	Nourishes nervous system
Quinoa	2:1	15—30 minutes	3—3½ cups	Highest protein of any grain; more calcium than cow's milk; contains vitamins B, E, and iron
Rice, brown	2:1	25—35 minutes	3 cups	Manganese, selenium, magnesium, and B vitamins
Rice, wild	2—4:1	45 minutes	4 cups	Manganese, selenium, magnesium, and B vitamins
Rye berries†	3:1	2½ hours	2½ cups	Manganese and dietary fiber help prevent gallstones
Spelt*	3:1	2 hours	2¼ cups	Riboflavin (vitamin B2) aids in relieving migraine symptoms, and niacin (B3) protects against atherosclerosis
Wheat berries†	3:1	1—2 hours	2½ cups	Shown to have unique benefits in preventing breast and colon cancer; high in manganese; avoid if intolerant to wheat

*ratio of water to grain in cups   **based on 1 cup dry grain
†Contains gluten or is processed in a factory where other gluten-containing grains are processed.

Why Eat Brown Rice Instead of White?

Well for starters, brown rice has $3\frac{1}{2}$ grams of fiber while white rice has less than one! Brown rice also contains nutrients like magnesium, manganese, and zinc. White rice has reduced levels of these nutrients, but is often fortified with iron and some B vitamins. Bringing Bs into our bodies aids our nervous system and can help relieve mental depression. Filling our plates with food in its natural state is a sure way to regain our healthy selves! I love brown rice and now that I've gotten hooked on the full flavor, plain old white rice tastes void of substance. I make brown rice at least once a week. I always make enough of it to last a few days and use it to thicken sauces. This staple makes mealtime a piece of cake—I always have a strong base to build with!

GRAIN RECIPES

BARLEY CROQUETTES
Vegan, Dairy Free, and Gluten Free

Barley is one of my foundation foods. I like to make a bunch of it to use later in the week for other dishes like these croquettes.

Whatcha Do

Peep the Rules of Grains (page 197). Combine leftover barley (mixed with mashed leftover beans if you want to), egg (optional), and tahini (sesame butter) to make them stick. Make little patties, dust them in rice breadcrumbs, and cook on medium low heat in oil until browned on both sides. Any grain pilaf can also be used with leftover beans—mashed together and pattied up!

MAKES 6–8 SMALL CROQUETTES

WHATCHA NEED

2 cups leftover barley

Leftover beans (optional)

1 egg*

1 tablespoon of tahini (sesame butter)

$1/4$ cup rice breadcrumbs (gluten free, yeast free)

3 tablespoons olive oil or organic grape seed oil**

*If you are not eating eggs, leave out the egg.

**Enough to coat the bottom of the pan; you may need more via the cooking process.

MAKES 4–6 SERVINGS

WHATCHA NEED

1 cup barley (pearled barley), soaked overnight with a 2-inch piece of kombu

3 swirls olive oil around the pan

2 cloves garlic, chopped

1/2 onion, chopped small

2 carrots, chopped small

1 stalk celery

1/2 cup shiitake or maitake mushrooms

1 cup frozen organic peas

4 cups of spring water (use 1 cup to dilute barley miso)

1 1/2 tablespoons barley miso, diluted in 1 cup spring water

1 tablespoon tamari

1 teaspoon Eden sea salt— my favorite

chives, chopped (garnish)

parsley, chopped (garnish)

lemon, spritz

BARLEY PILAF WITH BARLEY MISO
Vegan and Dairy Free

Barley removes dampness (inflammation)—excellent for arthritis. Yes, barley contains gluten, but as long as you don't have any celiac issues there should be no problem. Barley is the only gluten ingredient I use. This recipe can also be made using millet or quinoa.

Whatcha Do

Rinse soaked barley and kombu. Chop the kombu fine to use with the other vegetables. Heat pan with the olive oil. Add chopped kombu, garlic, onion, and barley. Toast the barley over low heat. Add the rest of the veggies and cover with water, diluted miso, and tamari. Bring to a boil and boil for 6 minutes. Cover and turn flame to low, cooking slowly for 40 minutes or until soft. Add more water if necessary so pilaf doesn't dry out. Add sea salt and serve with fresh chopped chives, parsley, and a spritz of lemon. These last three ingredients not only add flavor, but they also support the liver and aid in digestion.

MILLET WITH GARLIC AND ONIONS
Vegan, Dairy Free, and Gluten Free

A third of the world has been living on millet for over 2,500 years! When I first introduced it to my family, my husband said, "We can't eat that—it's for cows!" He couldn't be more wrong. Millet is full of mightiness. It is alkalizing and balances overly acidic situations. Millet also sweetens the breath 'cause it retards bacterial growth in the mouth. It is believed to prevent miscarriages and is an antifungal agent. (It is said to be one of the best grains for those suffering from Candida albicans overgrowth.) If you've got constipation, stomach acid, vomiting, indigestion, or diabetes, eat millet! If you are pregnant and suffering morning sickness—make a soup with it or prepare the millet creamy or "congee" style. (Congee is typically Asian rice porridge, but you can make it with other grains, like millet, too.) Millet is a low-carbohydrate grain—an excellent choice for people watching their sugar.

MAKES 4–6 SERVINGS

WHATCHA NEED

1 cup millet*

4–6 inches kombu

1 teaspoon olive oil

1/4 yellow onion, chopped fine

1 teaspoon garlic, chopped fine

3 cups water

A pinch of rocking sea salt
(from Natural Imports)

*Millet does not need to be soaked if you have a healthy digestive process.

Whatcha Do

Peep the Rules of Grains (page 197). Soak the millet with kombu in water in a glass bowl overnight. The next morning, remove kombu, strain the millet, and rinse. Heat the olive oil in a skillet, add chopped onions and garlic, cook the onions until they are clear, and add your strained millet. You can also chop up the kombu and add it in too! Toast the millet with the oil and vegetables in the skillet. Once it's toasty, add 3 cups of water. Bring it to a boil and simmer for 10 minutes, then lower the heat and toss in a pinch of salt. Cover and let simmer for 35 minutes (just like rice).

Note: If you are in the midst of digestive distress don't use the onions and garlic until you are stronger—they may be a bit too much for you.

MAKES 6–8 SERVING

WHATCHA NEED

2 cups millet, rinsed

7 cups water

1 small cauliflower
(about 2 cups florets)

1/4 teaspoon sea salt

Extra water for mashing

Ghee—clarified butter*
(optional)

*Clarified butter is made by melting butter until it separates, then skimming it to remove the milk solids (lactose) from the butterfat.

MILLET MASHED "POTATOES"
Vegan, Dairy Free, and Gluten Free

My girls love Millet Mash and so does my tummy! There are no potatoes in this fabulous side dish, and it can easily replace mashed potatoes in any meal! Combining millet and cauliflower does our bodies good—especially when it comes to fighting tumors. In fact, this combo has been proven to slow the growth of tumors and cancer cells!

Whatcha Do

Lightly toast millet in a pan. Bring water to a boil in separate pot and add millet, cauliflower, and salt. Cover and simmer for 25 minutes until the water is absorbed and millet is soft (like making rice). I like to blend this baby in the pot I cooked it in. Miso can be added just before blending as a flavor enhancer and a probiotic. I like to use my handheld blending wand to mash the cooked millet and cauliflower. I also like to add ghee because it is known to aid in the healing of digestive ulcerations, and it brings a buttery, mashed-potato flavor to the millet mash! Serve with Kuzu Gravy (see recipe).

POT-BOILED BROWN RICE
Vegan, Dairy Free, and Gluten Free

MAKES 4–6 SERVINGS

WHATCHA NEED

1 cup brown rice
(short or long grain,
or brown basmati)

2 cups water*

1 pinch of sea salt

*For larger batches, use less water: 3 cups rice
with 5 1/2 cups water

Whatcha Do

Wash the rice by swirling it in a bowl of cool water. Drain in a large, fine-mesh strainer. Pat the rice with a paper towel to remove excess water, then place it in a pot that has a snug-fitting lid. Add water and salt, and bring to a boil uncovered. Cover and simmer—without stirring or lifting the lid—for 50–60 minutes. Relax . . . dinner is cooking itself.

PRESSURE-COOKED BROWN RICE
Vegan, Dairy Free, and Gluten Free

MAKES 6–8 SERVINGS

WHATCHA NEED

2 cups short-grain brown rice

3–3 1/2 cups water

1/8 teaspoon sea salt

Whatcha Do

Wash the rice and drain in a strainer (as in previous recipe, Pot-Boiled Brown Rice). Place in pressure cooker with water and salt and start on medium-low heat for 20 minutes. Then turn the heat up to high briefly until pressure valve jiggles. Put a flame spreader (the flat burner cover from your stove) under the pot to keep from burning rice on the bottom. Reduce the heat to a simmer and cook for 40 minutes (1 hour total).

QUINOA

The Inca people have known the real deal when it comes to grains. They have been eating quinoa for thousands of years. Wonderfully fluffy, light, and filling, quinoa (pronounced keen—wa) was the main grain of Incan civilizations. Peruvians climbed many mountains eating this dietary staple as a main source of fuel for their bodies. In fact, quinoa packs nine of the essential amino acids necessary for humans, and more protein than any other grain. In addition, it is higher in fat content than other grains, is a good source of iron, phosphorous, B vitamins, and vitamin E, and has more calcium than MILK. FEED IT TO YO' BABIES!

MAKES 4–6 SERVINGS

WHATCHA NEED

1 cup quinoa, rinsed

$1^1/_2$ tablespoons sesame or olive oil

$2^1/_4$ cups water

Pinch of sea salt

OPTION 1

$1/_4$ chopped onion

2 cloves chopped garlic

OPTION 2

2 carrots

1 stalk celery

1 cup shiitake mushrooms

1 cup peas

SIMPLE QUINOA
Vegan, Dairy Free, and Gluten Free

Whatcha Do

To cook, toast quinoa in a skillet with a small amount of sesame or olive oil and stir until it smells nutty. In a separate pot, bring water to a boil and add toasted quinoa. Cover and simmer for 20 minutes.

Option 1: Pop toasted quinoa into your rice maker along with onions, garlic, and sesame oil and cook. Super yum!

Option 2: For one of my Real Food Makeovers, I chopped up the veggies listed at left and cooked 'em together with the quinoa in the pot of water. Everyone loved it!

RICE-COOKER BROWN RICE
Vegan, Dairy Free, and Gluten Free

MAKES 4–6 SERVINGS

WHATCHA NEED

1 cup brown rice, rinsed (short- or long-grain or brown basmati)

3 cups water

1–2 tablespoons sesame oil or olive oil

1 teaspoon sea salt

If you are in the midst of digestive distress be sure to cook your rice to an almost porridge-like consistency—the softer it is, the easier it is to digest. Cook 1 cup rice with 4 cups of water, add more water ($1/4$ to $1/2$ cup) toward the end if needed—the more water added, the softer and more porridge-like the rice becomes. You can also run the rice and other grains through a food mill. During the first three months of my digestive distress, I ate almost all of my grains this way.

Whatcha Do

A rice cooker has saved my life! When I don't have enough time to stand over the stove, I sho' do love this little machine. When making brown rice, be sure to add enough water. If you didn't, and the rice isn't soft enough, just add more water and rerun the cycle. I also add sesame oil or olive oil before starting the rice cooker. Since brown rice requires a lot of water, place a kitchen towel on top of the lid when making a full pot, so that the steam doesn't spray everywhere. Toward the end of the cycle check the rice, and if it is not soft enough add $1/4$ cup more water. The rice cooker will keep cooking until all the moisture is absorbed. During the last 10 minutes of cooking, add 1 teaspoon sea salt.

BREAKFAST DISHES

MAKES 12 PANCAKES

WHATCHA NEED

2 large eggs

1/4 cup coconut nectar

1 tablespoon vanilla extract

1/4 cup water

1 1/2 cups blanched almond flour

1/2 teaspoon sea salt

1/2 teaspoon baking soda

1 tablespoon arrowroot powder

2 tablespoons grapeseed oil

ALMOND FLOUR PANCAKES
Dairy Free and Gluten Free

These pancakes are dairy free and high in protein—a great way to start your day! Because they are made using coconut nectar for sweetener, they will not spike your blood sugar. For an extra-healthy boost, add blueberries to your batter or toss in a ripe banana and mix it in with a handheld blender.

I like to cook up a few extra so I can use them for snacks or the next morning (they are good in the fridge for three days), as opposed to buying a box of frozen premades loaded with who knows what!

Whatcha Do

In a blender combine eggs, coconut nectar, vanilla, and water. Process on high for 1 minute or until smooth. Add in almond flour, salt, baking soda, arrowroot powder, and grapeseed oil, and blend until thoroughly combined.

Heat oil in a large skillet over medium-low heat. Pour a heaping tablespoon of batter onto the skillet for each pancake. Flip when small bubbles appear on the top of each pancake. When fully cooked transfer to a plate and serve!

COCONUT OATMEAL
Vegan, Dairy Free, and Gluten Free

Whatcha Do

Pour 1 cup of oats and kombu into a saucepan and cover with 4 cups water. Cover with lid and let it rest all night. This makes the oats easier to digest, and the kombu also adds minerals! (NO, kombu does *not* taste fishy—it actually adds the needed salt.) In the morning, turn on the heat to medium-low and let the oatmeal cook for about 30 minutes. You can eat this as is, and if you have leftovers try this for extra yumminess:

Set stove to medium-low and add coconut oil to a skillet. When the oil bubbles add in leftover oatmeal, coconut milk, bananas, and salt (optional). Cook until heated and bananas are soft (6–8 minutes). Top with flax and get ready to grub! This recipe can be tweaked depending on how much oatmeal you are using—add more banana or more coconut milk. Also top with toasted and crushed pecans or ground flax meal!

MAKES 4 SERVINGS

WHATCHA NEED

1 cup organic whole rolled oats (not the quick-cooking type)

2 inches dried kombu sea vegetable

4 cups water

1 tablespoon coconut oil

1/2 cup organic coconut milk (nothing added; read the label)

1 banana, mashed

Pinch of sea salt

1 teaspoon ground flax

Oatmeal with Quinoa Flakes
Vegan, Dairy Free, and Gluten Free

Whatcha Do

Pour 1 cup of oats and kombu into a saucepan and cover with 4 cups water. Cover with lid and it let rest all night. In the morning, turn on the heat under the pot to medium-low and add quinoa flakes, fruit, cinnamon, and pinch of sea salt. Let the oatmeal cook for about 30 minutes. Remove kombu, chop into tiny bites, and stir back into oatmeal. Serve with almond milk and brown rice syrup and top with ground flax. The quinoa adds protein and calcium—this is fortifying your own food, y'all!

MAKES 4–6 SERVINGS

WHATCHA NEED

1 cup organic whole rolled oats—not the quick-cooking type

2 inches dried kombu sea vegetable

4 cups water

1/2 cup quinoa flakes

1 cup raisins or chopped dates

1 tablespoon cinnamon or a cinnamon stick

Pinch of sea salt

1/2 cup almond milk

Brown rice syrup—optional to taste

1 teaspoon ground flax

MAKES 4 SERVINGS

WHATCHA NEED

1 cup cornmeal

1/4 teaspoon salt

2 teaspoons baking powder

2 teaspoons vanilla sugar,
or use brown rice syrup

1/4 cup shredded unsweetened
coconut

4 chopped rehydrated* dates

1/2 cup coconut milk, or rice,
soy, or almond milk
(carrageenan free)

1 teaspoon coconut oil or ghee
for batter, plus 2 tablespoons
for saucepan

1 egg

CORNMEAL PANCAKES
Vegan, Dairy Free, and Gluten Free

Whatcha Do

Combine the dry ingredients, sugar or syrup, shredded coconut, and dates in a large bowl. Add the coconut milk and 1 teaspoon of coconut oil or ghee, and mix the batter until it's well combined. If it's too watery add a touch more cornmeal. Add the egg and whisk. Melt about 2 tablespoons coconut oil or ghee in a frying pan. Drop dollops of batter in the pan and fry on both sides, until pancakes are done.

*Soak dates in really warm water for 5 minutes while you prepare the batter—this makes them easy to chop and blend.

MAKES 2–4 SERVINGS

WHATCHA NEED

4 corn tortillas

1 teaspoon olive oil

4 eggs

salt to taste

1 cup rancheras salsa
(see recipe)

1 avocado, cut into wedges

Huevos Rancheras
Dairy Free and Gluten Free

Whatcha Do

Preheat oven to 500°F. Coat each tortilla in olive oil and place on cookie sheet. When oven is ready, cook for approximately 5 minutes, depending on how crisp you like your tortillas.

Heat oil in small frying pan and cook each egg slowly on one side until whites are firm and yolks are runny. Salt to taste. Transfer your tortillas to plate and place one egg on each tortilla.

Make your rancheras sauce and pour 1/4 cup over the top of each egg, which will further cook the top of the egg. Let eggs sit for about 1 minute before serving, then top with avocado wedges!

EGGS IN A MUSHROOM OVER HASH
Dairy Free and Gluten Free

Now, ain't this so nutritiously creative . . . and down-home good, too!

Whatcha Do

Preheat oven to 400°F. Coarsely shred the celery root and onion in a food processor or by hand, add 2 tablespoons of parsley, and season well with salt and pepper.

Place mushrooms on baking sheet and brush with 1 tablespoon of oil and season with salt and pepper. Bake for 12 minutes.

Heat 2 tablespoons of oil in a large skillet. Place 4 large handfuls of the celeriac mixture in the skillet, pressing with a spatula to flatten. Fry for about 10 minutes, turning once, until brown. Drain on paper towels and keep hot.

Meanwhile, beat the eggs with the milk, parsley, salt, and pepper. Heat the remaining oil in a small saucepan and cook the eggs, stirring until just set.

Place the hash browns on warmed serving plates; top each with a mushroom and spoon scrambled eggs over mushrooms.

MAKES 4 SERVINGS

WHATCHA NEED

10 ounces celery root, peeled

1 small onion, peeled

3 tablespoons fresh chopped parsley

4 Portobello mushrooms

4 tablespoons olive oil

4 eggs

2 tablespoons unsweetened nondairy milk

Salt and pepper

MAKES 8 SLICES

WHATCHA NEED

$1/4$ cup coconut milk

2 tablespoons brown rice syrup

4 large eggs

1 teaspoon vanilla extract

$1/2$ teaspoon salt

$1/2$ teaspoon ground cinnamon

8 slices gluten-free bread

2 tablespoons grapeseed oil

French Toast
Dairy Free and Gluten Free

This French toast is ohhh sooo good! I hook it up for dinner sometimes! Dairy free and gluten free, if you choose!

Whatcha Do

In a medium bowl, whisk together the milk, brown rice syrup, eggs, vanilla, salt, and cinnamon until thoroughly combined. Pour the mixture into a baking dish and soak the slices of bread for 5 minutes on each side.

Heat the oil in a large skillet over medium-high heat. Cook the bread slices in the oil for 3–5 minutes on each side, until golden brown.

MAKES 4–6 SERVINGS

WHATCHA NEED

$1^1/4$ cups millet

3 cups water

2 cups dairy-free almond milk or coconut milk

1 teaspoon ground cinnamon

1 teaspoon organic vanilla extract

a pinch of sea salt

$1/4$ cup dried cranberries

Brown rice syrup, for topping (optional)

Ground flax seed, for topping (optional)

MILLET WITH DRIED CRANBERRIES
Vegan, Dairy Free, and Gluten Free

My former cook made me this breakfast on our trip to Mexico. Her version was dry and bland. Determined to make it better, I can say I succeeded. Here you go! Give it a peep. Millet is great for diabetics and anyone suffering digestive acid issues.

Whatcha Do

In a saucepan combine millet, water, milk, cinnamon, vanilla, salt, and cranberries. Bring to a boil and then reduce heat and cover, cooking on low for 35 minutes. If you want the millet softer add more liquid. I prefer this porridge to be extra soft. If you are heating up leftovers, do so in a skillet with a little coconut oil and add in fresh coconut milk or almond milk.

I like to top it with brown rice syrup and ground flax seed!

Organic Cream of Brown Rice Cereal
Vegan, Dairy Free, and Gluten Free

Switching from Cream of Wheat to Cream of Brown Rice is an easy change. It's also something easy for the body to break down.

Whatcha Do

In a medium saucepan mix together 3 cups of water, kombu, blueberries, bananas, and coconut oil. Bring to a boil. This allows kombu, blueberries, and bananas to soften. Once the water is boiling, add in creamy brown rice cereal. I use a whisk so it's dispersed evenly. Allow the cereal to really cook on high for a few minutes while stirring, then reduce heat to low and add coconut nectar and coconut milk; mix and cover. I like for it to simmer for about 15 minutes while I pack the girls lunches. Top with ground flax seed!

MAKES 4 SERVINGS

WHATCHA NEED

4 cups water

1-inch piece dried kombu

$1/4$ cup dried blueberries, organic preferably

2 bananas, cut into bite-size pieces

$1/2$ teaspoon coconut oil

1 cup creamy brown rice cereal

2 tablespoons coconut nectar (has a low glycemic index of 35)

1 cup Native Forest Organic Coconut milk (it is the only one I've found BPA-free)

1 teaspoon ground flax seed, for topping

QUINOA CAKES
Dairy Free and Gluten Free

This is a meatless meal packin' much protein and vitamin C! The quinoa adds moisture and texture, making these pancakes a great choice for any meal! It is healthy and easy to make. You can make the batter the night before—leave it covered in the fridge, and you have one easy and yummy breakfast waiting for you the next day.

Whatcha Do

Mix up the flour, banana, baking powder, salt, and cinnamon together in a bowl. In another bowl, whisk together milk, coconut oil, vanilla, and eggs and add to dry ingredients. Whisk well till all the lumps are gone.

Add the cooked quinoa to batter. Heat an iron skillet to medium heat and coat with cooking spray to prevent sticking. Pour batter into the pan and cook these cakes up like you would a regular pancake!

MAKES ABOUT 15 SMALL PANCAKES

WHATCHA NEED

$1 1/2$ cups buckwheat flour

1 banana mashed (to avoid adding additional sugar)

6 teaspoons baking powder

1 teaspoon salt

1 teaspoon cinnamon

$1 3/4$ cups nondairy milk

3 tablespoons coconut oil

1 teaspoon vanilla extract

3 large eggs

$1 1/2$ cups cooked quinoa

Coconut cooking spray for pan

MAKES 6 SERVINGS

WHATCHA NEED

SAUCE

1 10-ounce package frozen
corn kernels, thawed,
or ³/₄ cup fresh corn kernels

³/₄ teaspoon fine sea salt

1¹/₄ cups plain unsweetened
soymilk

2 tablespoons fresh
lemon juice

1 tablespoon olive oil

¹/₈ teaspoon cayenne pepper

TOFU AND MARINADE

1 14-ounce container water-
packed extra-firm tofu

¹/₄ cup fresh lemon juice

2 tablespoons olive oil

2 tablespoons water

1 tablespoon red wine vinegar

1 teaspoon Dijon mustard

1 teaspoon ground turmeric

¹/₂ teaspoon ground cumin

¹/₂ teaspoon fine sea salt

1 tablespoon minced fresh dill

1¹/₂ teaspoons minced fresh
tarragon, or ¹/₂ teaspoon
crumbled dried tarragon

Nonaerosol, nonstick
cooking spray

Tofu Benedict with Roasted Corn Hollandaise
Vegan, Dairy Free, and Gluten Free

A corn-based vegan version of hollandaise sauce brings its creamy, rich texture to this delicious special-occasion breakfast dish. In the hollandaise, the sweetness of the corn is balanced with just a hint of heat from the cayenne. The sauce is ladled over savory tofu set atop a thick slice of sourdough bread and then topped with tomatoes and spinach, making this a perfect start to the day. Heirloom tomatoes are especially tender and flavorful and come in a variety of appealing colors, but any ripe, juicy tomato will do. You can also use this hollandaise sauce over regular poached eggs!

Whatcha Do

Sauce: Preheat the oven to 375°F. Line a large, heavy baking sheet with parchment paper. Scatter the corn kernels over the baking sheet and sprinkle with the salt. Roast until the corn is crisp and begins to brown, about 30 minutes.

Transfer the roasted corn kernels to a blender. With the machine running, slowly blend in the soymilk, lemon juice, oil, and cayenne. Allow the mixture to continue blending until it thickens to the consistency of a runny pudding, about 3 minutes. Strain the corn mixture through a fine-meshed strainer and into a bowl, pressing on the solids to extract as much liquid as possible. You should have about 1¹/₂ cups of sauce. Discard the solids.

Just before serving, warm the sauce in a small saucepan over medium heat.

Tofu and Marinade: drain the liquid from the tofu, then place the tofu on a plate lined with paper towels. Cover the tofu with a folded paper towel and place another plate on top of the tofu to weigh it down. Set aside while you make the marinade.

Whisk the lemon juice, olive oil, water, vinegar, mustard, turmeric, cumin, and salt in a medium bowl to blend. Whisk in the dill and tarragon.

Cut the block of tofu horizontally twice, then cut in half to get six 3½- by 2- by ½-inch slices. Place the tofu slices in an 8 by 8-inch baking dish. Pour the marinade over the tofu and marinate for at least 1 hour at room temperature or cover and refrigerate for up to 1 day.

Do-Ahead Tip

At this point, the sauce and the tofu can be prepared up to one day ahead. Transfer the sauce in a covered container and refrigerate separately. Rewarm the sauce before serving.

Heat a ridged grill pan over medium-high heat. Spray the pan with non-aerosol cooking spray. Grill the tofu, brushing with the remaining marinade, until char marks form and the tofu is heated through, about 2 minutes per side.

Assembly: Meanwhile, place the tomatoes in a medium bowl and sprinkle lightly with salt. Set aside until the tomatoes begin to exude their water, about 10 minutes. Drain the accumulated water.

Heat 2 teaspoons of the oil in a large, heavy sauté pan over medium heat. Add the garlic and sauté until fragrant and softened, about 30 seconds. Add the spinach and toss just until it is heated through and begins to wilt, about 1½ minutes. Season to taste with salt and pepper.

Lightly brush both sides of the bread slices with the remaining 2 tablespoons olive oil and grill on the grill pan until toasted, about 2 minutes per side.

Place a slice of toast on each of six plates. Top with the tofu, then spoon the sauce over the tofu and around the toast. Top with the tomato slices and spinach. Garnish with the scallions and serve immediately.

ASSEMBLY

3 medium heirloom tomatoes (preferably yellow and green tomatoes), thickly sliced

A pinch fine sea salt

2 teaspoons plus 2 tablespoons olive oil

2 cloves garlic, minced

1 6-ounce bunch fresh baby spinach, stems trimmed

Freshly ground black pepper

6 ½-inch thick slices sourdough or country white rosemary bread

2 large scallions, thinly sliced

MAKES ABOUT 4 DOZEN
STRIPS

WHATCHA NEED

1/4 cup maple crystals (these can be purchased at health food stores)

2 tablespoons sea salt

1 1/2 8-ounce packages tempeh

2 tablespoons sesame oil

TEMPEH BACON
Vegan, Dairy Free, and Gluten Free

Ok, y'all—this bacon is bangin'! By far, one of my favorites! It only has four ingredients, but you will need to invest in a stovetop smoker, which is available at most cooking stores, and a very sharp knife. The investment is worth it for many morning, noon, and night dishes, because this bacon is great with breakfast and dinner dishes, such as soup, wraps, or as a topping on a salad or potato. Add to your favorite dishes for an extra boost of flavor. It will be your new secret ingredient!

Whatcha Do

Mix the maple crystals and salt on a large plate. Dip the tempeh into water and then into the maple mixture, turning to coat both sides evenly; wrap the tempeh pieces with plastic wrap, and place them on a baking sheet. Place a small baking pan atop the tempeh to weigh it down. Fill the baking pan with about 3 pounds of weight, such as two 28-ounce cans of tomatoes. Keep in fridge for at least one day and up to two days.

Prepare your stovetop smoker; unwrap the tempeh and smoke over medium heat for 40 minutes or until golden brown. Cool the tempeh.

Preheat the oven to 350°F. Line two heavy rimmed baking sheets with aluminum foil. Lightly coat the foil with 2 teaspoons of the oil. Using a very sharp knife, cut the tempeh lengthwise into 1/8-inch strips. Arrange the tempeh strips in a single layer over the prepared baking sheets and brush with 2 teaspoons of the oil. Bake for 10 minutes, then turn strips over and brush with the remaining oil; bake 10 minutes longer or until crisp and golden brown.

This bacon will keep for one week! Cool it to room temp and store in an airtight container at room temp.

TOFU SCRAMBLE
Vegan, Dairy Free, and Gluten Free

My favorite restaurant in Malibu makes the most bangin' Tofu Scramble and inspired me to make my own! I always steam my tofu for at least 15 minutes, which makes the tofu even easier to digest and absorb—the purpose of eating! Any veggies will work—these just happen to be my favorite.

After taking some time off from eggs, I'm now able to eat them at least twice a week with NO problems. This recipe rocks with eggs, too!

Whatcha Do

While prepping your veggies, steam the tofu. Heat your pan and add the olive oil. Once the oil is hot, drop in your onions (the white parts only—save the green parts for garnish) and garlic, adding in water, mushrooms and zucchini as you go. Once these veggies are soft, add in the peas. Lastly, I blend up my steamed tofu with the electric blending wand in a separate bowl. Add the blended tofu to the veggies along with the rest of the ingredients. Allow the mixture to cook and absorb the water used with the veggies. Ten minutes is all you need for the flavors to blend.

Serve with corn tortillas.

MAKES 4 SERVINGS

WHATCHA NEED

1 14-ounce container firm tofu— washed and steamed for 15 minutes first

1 tablespoon olive oil

1 green onion, sliced

1 clove garlic, minced

1/4 cup shiitake mushrooms, sliced

1 small zucchini, sliced into thin circles with skin on

1/2 cup frozen organic peas

1/3 cup water

1 tablespoon Italian herbs

Tamari soy sauce (to taste)

1 teaspoon turmeric (This adds color and anti-inflammatory support!)

Pinch of sea salt and pepper (unless you have digestive issues)

6–8 corn tortillas

APPETIZERS

MAKES 4 SERVINGS

WHATCHA NEED

DRESSING

1/4 cup sesame oil

2 tablespoons black or white sesame seeds

2 tablespoons lemon juice

1 tablespoon tamari

1 tablespoon brown rice syrup or coconut nectar

Salt and pepper

AVOCADO

2–3 medium- to underripe avocados, halved, peeled, pitted, and thinly sliced

1 handful micro basil or other micro herb (for garnish)

Sesame seeds (for garnish)

Course salt and pepper (for garnish)

Avocado Appetizer
Raw, Vegan, Dairy Free, and Gluten Free

This is a beautiful dish to get things started, and your palate and body will agree with you! This starter dish is nutrient dense. Eating nutrient-dense foods is one of the healthiest ways to eat. Nutrient density is the measure of nutrients foods contain in comparison to the number of calories. Avocados contain nearly 20 essential vitamins, minerals, and phytonutrients. Avocados contribute good fat to the diet. They are free of trans fats, cholesterol, and sodium! And that's not all for this starter dish, y'all! We got sesame!

Whatcha Do

Whisk all ingredients for dressing until well combined. Season with salt and pepper to taste. Fan out half an avocado per plate and drizzle with dressing. Garnish with micro basil, sesame seeds, and coarse salt and pepper. Serve immediately.

BLACK-EYED PEAS CROQUETTES
Vegan, Dairy Free, and Gluten Free

OMG! I LOVE these, and so does everyone who has ever eaten them! They are a great way to introduce people to a real food life. They are also yummy party favorites. If you are in digestive distress, hold off on this one 'cause the gas is a kicker if you're not in optimal health.

MAKES 12–15 SMALL CROQUETTES

WHATCHA NEED

CROQUETTES

2 cups black-eyed peas, soaked overnight in spring water

$1/2$ teaspoon sea salt

1 teaspoon shoyu soy sauce

1 teaspoon ground cumin

2 cups safflower oil for frying

DIPPING SAUCE

$1/2$ cup barley malt

1–2 tablespoons organic Dijon mustard

Chopped parsley or cilantro (for garnish)

Whatcha Do

Place soaked beans in food processor. Add salt, shoyu, and cumin. Blend until you get fine shreds of bean, but don't blend into a pulp. The mixture will be slightly wet but can hold together. Form palm–sized croquettes with your hands.

Heat 1 inch of oil in a cast-iron skillet to about 350°F. To test the oil, drop in a tiny amount of the croquette mixture. If it bubbles furiously and rises to the top, the oil is ready. Do not let the oil get so hot that it smokes. You may need to make little adjustments to the heat under the oil throughout the cooking process to avoid burning the croquettes.

Place 4 croquettes in the oil and let fry for about 4 minutes on each side. Place on paper towel and drain extra oil.

Heat barley malt and mustard over low heat until it bubbles. Pour over croquettes or into individual dipping bowls. Garnish with parsley or cilantro. Serve while still hot.

WHATCHA NEED

1 cup gluten-free self-rising flour

1 egg

³/₄ cup unsweetened nondairy milk

1 bunch green onions, thinly sliced

1 14-ounce can of chickpeas

Sunflower oil for frying

Salt and pepper

¹/₄ cup chopped cilantro (plus sprigs for garnish)

MAKES 6–12 WRAPS

WHATCHA NEED

HUMMUS

4 cups peeled and chopped zucchini

1 cup tahini

1 cup lemon juice

6 tablespoons olive oil

3–4 tablespoons water

Salt and pepper

WRAP

6–12 large lettuce leaves (Swiss chard or Romaine)

1 cup pitted, chopped, sun-dried olives

4 tablespoons chopped fresh herbs (parsley, basil, and mint)

Salt and pepper

Olive oil for garnish

CHICKPEA FRITTERS
Dairy Free and Gluten Free

When we were kids we had a babysitter who was the queen of corn fritters. When I found this recipe I was super excited 'cause it's not just comfy yummy food, but downright good fo'ya! These are less gassy than the black-eyed peas croquettes as they are not raw legumes.

Whatcha Do

Sift the flour into a bowl and make a well in the center. Add the egg and milk and stir into the flour, then beat to make a smooth batter. Stir in the scallions, chickpeas, and cilantro then season well with salt and pepper. Heat the oil in a large skillet and add tablespoonfuls of batter. Fry in batches for 4–5 minutes until golden brown, turning once. Serve the fritters stacked on warm serving plates and garnish with cilantro sprigs.

HUMMUS WRAP
Raw, Vegan, Dairy Free, and Gluten Free

Super easy and great to have on hand!

Whatcha Do

Hummus
Blend all ingredients in a high-speed blender until smooth and season with salt and pepper.

Wrap
Fill each lettuce leaf with hummus. Top with chopped olives and garnish with fresh herbs. To finish, season with salt and pepper and add a drizzle of olive oil.

JAMMIN' FALAFEL BALLS
Dairy Free and Gluten Free

Hook these falafel balls up for a nutritious meal packed with protein! Again, it's a relatively new thing that falafel balls are made with wheat. Originally they were just pure chickpea. So making them gluten free is easy—it's original! Cut the spice if you have picky eaters or are serving folks with digestive distress.

Whatcha Do

Falafel Balls

Place the chickpeas, onions and garlic, coriander, cumin, anise, chile, egg white, and salt and pepper in a food processor and process to form a firm paste with a texture. Stir in baking powder. Use chickpea flour on your hands to shape the mixture into 12 small balls.

Heat one inch of oil in a large saucepan to 350°F or until a cube of bread browns in about 30 seconds. Fry each ball for 2 minutes, turning until golden brown. Drain the falafels on a paper towel.

Salad

Cut all the peel and white pith off the orange and take out the orange pieces, saving the juice. Whisk the juice with the olive oil and season to taste. Lightly toss the orange slices and arugula with the dressing.

Serve the falafels with the salad.

MAKES 12 FALAFEL BALLS

WHATCHA NEED

FALAFEL BALLS

1 15-ounce can or 2 cups of cooked chickpeas, drained— or freshly cooked or leftovers

1 small red onion, chopped

2 garlic cloves, crushed

2 teaspoons ground coriander

1 1/2 teaspoons ground cumin

1 teaspoon ground star anise

1 red chili, chopped

1 egg white

Salt and pepper, to taste

1/2 teaspoon gluten-free baking powder

Chickpea flour for shaping

Sunflower oil or rice bran oil for frying

SALAD

1 large orange

2 tablespoons extra virgin olive oil

Salt and pepper, to taste

3 1/4 cups arugula leaves

WHATCHA NEED

1/2 cup chopped fresh cilantro

3 tablespoons freshly squeezed lemon juice

1 1/4 teaspoons sea salt

4 ripe avocados, peeled and pitted

GUAC'A MEEMEE!
Raw, Vegan, Dairy Free, and Gluten Free

Sweet and simple—the way I like it, and it's great for picky eaters!

Whatcha Do

Toss the cilantro, lemon juice, and salt in a bowl and set aside. Mash the avocados in a large bowl, stir in the cilantro mixture, and add more salt if you need to! Transfer to a bowl and serve fresh.

Keeps in fridge up to 4 hours, covered tightly. Stir before serving.

MAKES 2 CUPS

WHATCHA NEED

1 3/4 cup diced ripe tomatoes (about 2 large tomatoes)

1/2 cup finely chopped white onion

1/4 cup chopped fresh cilantro

1 small jalapeno chile, finely chopped

1 tablespoon freshly squeezed lime juice

1/2 teaspoon salt

PERFECT PICO DE GALLO
Raw, Vegan, Dairy Free, and Gluten Free

This pico de gallo is the best! It is great with tacos and better with cheddar nachos (see recipe). Seed the jalapeno chili for reduced spiciness.

Whatcha Do

Stir all ingredients in a bowl, blend, and use immediately. Cover and refrigerate up to 8 hours. Stir before serving.

POTATO PANCAKES
Dairy Free and Gluten Free

MAKES 4 SERVINGS

These pancakes are oh so good with the tempeh bacon (see recipe). My grandma was the queen of potato pancakes and just because I can't eat wheat doesn't mean I've given up one of my grandma's Sunday-morning treats!

WHATCHA NEED

1 cup of cold mashed potatoes

1 cup dairy-free milk

1/2 cup gluten-free self-rising flour

Pinch of salt

1 egg, beaten

3 tablespoons grapeseed oil

Whatcha Do

Put the mashed potatoes and milk into a food processor or blender and process to a thin puree.

Sift the flour and salt into a mixing bowl, make a well in the center of the flour, and add the potato puree and egg. Using a balloon whisk, gradually mix the flour into the liquid ingredients. Whisk the mixture to a smooth, creamy, and thick batter.

Heat a little oil in a large iron skillet, pour batter to fit up to 3 pancakes at a time, and cook for 2 minutes on each side or until golden brown.

Serve up with tempeh bacon (see recipe) or turkey bacon and organic maple syrup.

SLAMMIN' HUMMUS
Raw, Vegan, Dairy Free, and Gluten Free

Made with garbanzo beans and kombu seaweed, these protein-packed bean babies are super high in fiber and help lower cholesterol, y'all! I add kombu seaweed to all my beans to improve digestion and add nutrients. Kombu is packed with fiber, amino acids, selenium, and iodine. Cut your cooking time in half by using a pressure cooker!

MAKES 4–6 SERVINGS

WHATCHA NEED

- 1 1/2 cups dried garbanzo beans or 3 1/2 cups BPA-free canned beans
- 1 2–3 inch piece kombu
- 8 cups water
- 1/3 cup roasted tahini
- 1/2 cup fresh squeezed lemon juice (about 3 lemons)
- 3 tablespoons extra virgin olive oil
- 1 teaspoon minced garlic
- 1 1/2 teaspoons sea salt
- 1/4 cup freshly ground black pepper
- 1/8 teaspoon cayenne pepper
- 1/2 bag organic baby carrots
- 1 stalk organic celery, chopped into dipping-sized small stalks
- 1/2 organic cucumber, unpeeled, thinly sliced diagonally
- 1 tomato, cut into wedges

Whatcha Do

Soak dried beans and kombu overnight in a large bowl with enough water to cover by 3 inches. Drain and rinse the beans—keep that kombu!

Combine beans, kombu, and the 8 cups of water in a 4 1/4-quart pressure cooker and lock lid into place. Bring pressure to high over high heat. Decrease the heat to low and cook for 40 minutes. Remove from heat and let stand for 15 minutes to reduce pressure and then remove lid. Drain and reserve 1/3 cup of the cooking liquid. Discard the kombu and cool the beans completely so the heat doesn't mix with the other seasonings and change the slammin' flavor! (If you don't have a pressure cooker, cook the beans old-school style in a pot for 2–3 hours, adding more hot water as needed until they are tender.) If you want to use canned beans, skip all the above and take it straight to the next step, y'all!

Combine the cooked beans, tahini, lemon juice, olive oil, and garlic in a food processor and blend until smooth, adding enough reserved cooking liquid to form a creamy consistency. Blend in the salt, black pepper, and cayenne pepper. Serve with veggies! Keeps for two days covered in fridge.

SPINACH-ZUCCHINI PIZZA ROLLS
Raw, Vegan, Dairy Free, and Gluten Free

Move over microwave-processed pizza rolls, and hello, great finger food that's good for you!

Whatcha Do

On each spinach leaf, layer a few pieces of zucchini, then add a few dollops of marinara, pesto, and ricotta.

MAKES 12 SERVINGS

WHATCHA NEED

12 or more large spinach leaves or other dark green leaves, stems removed

1–2 medium zucchinis, peeled and julienned

1 cup raw marinara (see recipe)

1 cup Cilantro Walnut Pesto (see recipe)

1 cup raw ricotta cheese (see recipe)

VEGGIE CHEESE CHIPS
Raw, Vegan, Dairy Free, and Gluten Free

I love me some nachos! To get my nacho fix I hook up these chips for my girls and have a few, cause you just can't resist them! Who could when they are dairy free and gluten free and packed full of protein!

Whatcha Do

Heat the oil in a large, heavy frying pan over medium-high heat. Add the chips in batches, and fry up, turning occasionally with a tong for 2 minutes or until golden. Transfer to paper towel to drain oil and sprinkle with salt.

Arrange warm chips on plate and add warm melted cashew cheese, beans, pico de gallo, guacamole, and tofu sour cream. Top with green onion and serve pronto!

MAKES 6 SERVINGS

WHATCHA NEED

1 cup organic grapeseed oil

12 6-inch corn tortillas cut into wedges

Sea salt

$1/3$ melted cashew cheddar cheese (see recipe)

$1/2$ cup black beans warmed (see recipe)

$1/4$ cup pico de gallo (see recipe)

$1/4$ cup guacamole (see recipe)

2 tablespoons tofu sour cream

1 green onion, white and green parts, thinly sliced

MAKES 12 SERVINGS

WHATCHA NEED

SWEET PEA PUREE

6 cups fresh peas

1 avocado, peeled and pitted

1 tablespoon olive oil

1 tablespoon nutritional yeast

1 tablespoon brown rice syrup or coconut nectar

1 tablespoon lime juice

1/4 cup chopped cilantro

1 teaspoon nutmeg

1/4 teaspoon cayenne (a little goes a long way)

1 teaspoon sea salt

BLOSSOMS

1 dozen squash blossoms, rinsed, with stems removed

GARNISH

Nondairy sour cream

Pico de Gallo (see recipe)

Guacamole (see recipe)

SQUASH BLOSSOM TAMALES
Raw, Vegan, Dairy Free, and Gluten Free

Three words express this: beautiful, divine, and impressive.

Whatcha Do

In a food processor, process all the ingredients on puree until well combined and slightly chunky. Fill blossoms with a few tablespoons of puree. Before serving, drizzle with sour cream. Serve pico de gallo and guacamole on the side.

VEGGIE NORI RAW WRAP
Raw, Vegan, Dairy Free, and Gluten Free

Yo—Another raw wrap for you to choose from! This wrap is no joke! Rolled in nori and filled with all my favorites, it's an excellent way to get your sea veggies in and a great lunch-packing idea for eating almond butter in a non-sweet way!

Whatcha Do

Dressing and Slaw
Blend all the dressing ingredients until smooth and toss with cabbage.

Roll
On a mandoline slicer, slice daikon into paper-thin slices. Keep the slices as large and long as possible. Lay out half sheets of nori with the shiny side facing down. Coat nori layer with thin slices of daikon. (It is important to line the nori with the daikon so that it doesn't become soggy.)

On one end of the nori place a generous amount of slaw mixture. Layer in a few slices of carrot, red pepper, avocado, and sprouts. Gently roll nori at a diagonal to create a cone shape, ideally with veggies visible out of the top of the cone. Use water to seal cone together. Yum!

MAKES 12 WRAPS

WHATCHA NEED

DRESSING
1 cup almond butter

2 tablespoons nama shoyu

2 tablespoons grated ginger

1 tablespoon seeded and minced red chili

$1/2$ cup lemon juice

$1/4$ cup brown rice syrup or coconut nectar

2–3 tablespoons water

SLAW
Half a head napa cabbage, shredded

ROLL
6 sheets nori, cut in half

1 daikon radish, peeled

1 carrot, julienned

1 red pepper, julienned

1 avocado, thinly sliced

1 cup sprouts

SOUPS!

I am the QUEEN of soups. Not only is eating soup incredibly ancestral, soups are easy to make, an excellent way to get kids to eat veggies (by pureeing them), and easy on our digestion, giving our intestines a break from working so hard. Soups are warming to our bodies on cold days and a great way to stretch a buck! I make a fresh pot of soup at least once a week in the summer and twice fo'sho in the winter.

COCONUT-SWEET POTATO-LENTIL SOUP
Vegan, Dairy Free, and Gluten Free

MAKES 6–8 SERVINGS

WHATCHA NEED

1 cup lentils (soaked overnight in water with 3 inches of kombu sea vegetable)

5 cups water

2 tablespoons sesame oil

3 cloves garlic, chopped

1/2 sweet onion, chopped

1 tablespoon turmeric, fresh or dried

2 tablespoons curry powder— you can leave this out if you want, but I love it!

2–3 small to medium sweet potatoes

2 heaping tablespoons sweet white miso, diluted with soup broth

1 cup coconut milk

1 tablespoon sea salt

2 tablespoons mirin

2 tablespoons tamari

Whatcha Do

Rinse your soaked lentils and kombu. Chop kombu into small pieces and put them in your cast-iron soup pot along with the lentils and water. Bring to a boil and skim off the gassy foam that rises to the top. Lower your heat to medium low.

Add in sesame oil, garlic, onions, turmeric, curry, and sweet potatoes. The thing that makes this soup so yummy is when all the flavors merge together, so cook it slowly for an hour and a half, if you have time, by lowering the heat to simmer. If you don't have time, keep it on medium and cook for 45 minutes.

Once your sweet potatoes are soft the soup is ready for the miso, so dilute it in a small bowl with a couple ladles of broth and then add it in. Make sure heat is on low so you don't boil out the benefits of the miso. Add in the coconut milk. I use only organic because it doesn't have any added preservatives and sulfites. Sulfites irritate the intestines. I add the mirin and tamari the last 30 minutes of cooking. Mix it and enjoy!

BLACK BEAN AND BROWN RICE MISO SOUP WITH AVOCADO

Vegan, Dairy Free, and Gluten Free

Prepare your favorite brown rice recipe ahead of time. (See All About Grains for instructions.)

Whatcha Do

Rinse beans, place them in a bowl with a large piece of kombu sea vegetable, and soak overnight. When ready to cook, drain and rinse the beans and place them in a large pot and cover with at least 4 to 5 cups of water, add more water for more broth. Chop the kombu and add to the pot after you have removed the foam (see below).

Have a small bowl next to your pot and a large kitchen spoon—bring beans to boil. You will see a big 'ole pile of foam on top—scoop it off! This is the gas in the beans. Keep removing it until it stops forming. Lower the heat. Add turmeric, coriander, onion, garlic, basil, and 2 swirls of mirin. Continue to remove foam if it should reappear. Cover and cook on low heat for 1 1/2 hours. The beans are ready when they are soft but not too mushy. Add more water and cook a little longer if needed. In the last 20 minutes add salt and 2 swirls of tamari.

In a separate bowl, dilute the miso and pour into the beans. Heat through but do not bring pot to a boil.

For each serving: Place beans in a single serving bowl. Add a heaping spoonful of brown rice (as much as you like), and a wedge of avocado. Chilies can be added for spice if you do not suffer from digestive disease. Garnish with fresh cilantro.

MAKES 6 SERVINGS

WHATCHA NEED

1 cup black beans

4–5 cups water

1 large piece kombu sea vegetable

1/2 teaspoon turmeric

1/2 teaspoon coriander

1/4 onion, chopped

2 cloves garlic, chopped

1 tablespoon basil, dried or fresh (if fresh, use a little more to taste)

2 "swirls" mirin to taste

1 pinch sea salt

2 "swirls" tamari soy sauce to taste

2 large tablespoons sweet white miso

1 pot of prepared brown rice

1 avocado, cut in wedges

1 chili (optional)

Freshly chopped cilantro (garnish)

WHATCHA NEED

SOUP BASE

6 cups water

1/4 cup white miso

1 cup pine nuts

1/4 cup cashews

1 tablespoon brown rice syrup
or coconut nectar

1 tablespoon dulse flakes

Salt and pepper

SHIITAKES

1 cup shiitake mushrooms

1 tablespoon olive oil

1 tablespoon tamari

1 tablespoon lemon juice

GARNISH

1/4 cup hijiki, rehydrated
then drained

1/4 cup wakame, chopped,
rehydrated, and drained

Gomashio for garnish
(optional; see recipe)

CREAM OF MISO MUSHROOM SOUP
Raw, Vegan, Dairy Free, and Gluten Free

Take it to another level, y'all—this soup is all about supporting the body as it is PACKED with earthly medicine and vitamin D—and it's super easy to make! Shiitake mushrooms contain an antiviral substance, known as lentinan, that allows shiitakes to produce interferon, which is used to fight cancer and is found in some chemotherapy treatments. This is the reason that shiitake and maitake mushrooms have been recognized for their ability to enhance the immune system. In Western medicine, various extracts of shiitakes have been used to treat cancer, HIV, chronic fatigue syndrome, and other diseases.

Whatcha Do

Soup: Blend all ingredients in a blender at high speed until smooth and season with salt and pepper to taste.

Shiitakes: Mix them with olive oil, tamari, and lemon juice and marinate for 30 minutes.

Garnish: Before serving, stir shiitakes, hijiki, and wakame into the soup base; garnish with gomashio if desired.

GINGER-APPLE-BUTTERNUT SQUASH SOUP
Vegan, Dairy Free, and Gluten Free

My only childhood memory of butternut squash isn't such a good one. I was invited to a neighbor's house for dinner when I was five years old, and the lady of the house served hamburgers without a bun and a scoop of cottage cheese along with a side of blended butternut squash. Later that night, I threw up. To this day I am not sure if it was the bland food or the cold family dynamic of that household, but I avoided butternut squash for the rest of my life—until this past year.

It's funny how a food memory gets embedded in your brain, so I decided to find a way to create a new relationship with my squash. In LA, one of my favorite coffee shops and teahouses served an amazing carrot soup, so I had the idea of changing up the ingredients with squash and made this bangin' soup happen! Now I'm so psyched to share it with y'all—I promise, you're gonna LOVE it. The flavors are perfectly complementary: sweet and mild heat mixed with yum!

MAKES 6–8 SERVINGS

WHATCHA NEED

1 butternut squash, peeled and cut into medium-sized pieces

3 medium carrots, cut into medium pieces (the smaller the pieces, the faster they cook)

1 medium apple, peeled and cored

1 small onion, cut into medium half-moon slices

1 small piece of ginger, chopped (add more depending on how much heat you like!)

1 teaspoon grated turmeric*

3 cloves garlic, chopped large

1 tablespoon tamari/shoyu

5 cups water

1 cup leftover brown rice

1 large tablespoon sweet white miso

*I use fresh turmeric, but you can use powdered if that's all that is available to you.

Whatcha Do

Put everything except the miso into a soup pot. Cover with lid. Cook on medium low for about 20 minutes, long enough for everything to cook down. If the soup looks dry, add more water. I pull out some of the liquid broth to dilute my miso. Make sure to turn the heat down before adding the diluted miso. After everything is cooked, whip out your electric wand and blend this baby—if you don't have a wand use your blender.

KELP NOODLE SOUP WITH SEA VEGGIES
Raw, Vegan, Dairy Free, and Gluten Free

MAKES 2–4 SERVINGS

WHATCHA NEED

1 1/2 cups water

1 cup tamari

2 tablespoons dulce

1 tablespoon wakame

1 tablespoon sesame oil

1 tablespoon miso

2 tablespoons coconut nectar

1 tablespoon lemon juice

1 32-ounce bag kelp noodles, rinsed and drained

2 tablespoons chopped green onion

Gomashio (optional)

Next time you want to deliver chicken soup to your sick friend, serve them up some of this kelp noodle delight! This soup is loaded with dulse and wakame, sea veggies. Dulse is full of protein and contains all trace nutrients needed by humans. Wakame is full of calcium and omega-3s!

Whatcha Do

Blend everything except the noodles in a blender on high speed until smooth; strain through a sieve to remove any solids.

Equally portion out kelp noodles into bowls and fill with broth. Garnish with chopped scallions and gomashio (if using).

Lentils

Lentils stand alone 'cause they pack much punch to the bone! They are super high in fiber making our poop fuller. They "push" through the digestive tract, aiding in constipation problems. They also are great for diabetics because the soluble fiber in lentils traps carbohydrates. This slows digestion and absorption, helping to prevent wide swings in blood sugar levels throughout the day. Lentils also contain eight amino acids that help support brain chemistry. Give 'em to your youngin's to help them focus. I love to make lentils 'cause they're easy to cook and FAST. I soak them like I do beans, and skim off the foam. They give off the least amount of gas so they are quicker to cook.

LENTIL SOUP WITH VEGGIES
Vegan, Dairy Free, and Gluten Free

MAKES 6–8 SERVINGS

WHATCHA NEED

1 cup lentils soaked in water
with 3 inches of kombu
sea vegetable

5 cups water

4 chopped tomatoes (roasted
with skin removed, if you like)

3 tablespoons olive oil

1 onion, chopped

4 cloves garlic, chopped

1 teaspoon dried coriander

$1/4$ cup parsley, chopped

2 carrots, chopped bite-sized

2 potatoes (any kind), peeled
and chopped bite-sized

1 stalk celery with leaves*,
chopped small and bite-sized

2 cups chopped shiitake
mushrooms

1 teaspoon dried oregano

1 tablespoon dried basil

2 teaspoons dried hijiki
sea vegetable

2 heaping tablespoons sweet
white miso, diluted with
soup broth

*Celery leaves hold lots of flava'!

Whatcha Do

Rinse and drain your soaked lentils and kombu. Chop kombu into small pieces and put them in your cast-iron soup pot along with the lentils and water. Bring to a boil and skim off the gassy foam that rises to the top. Lower your heat to medium low.

Add everything else to the pot but the miso. I like to gently boil the soup for about 20 minutes, then bring the heat down to a simmer, covering with a lid. Once all the veggies are cooked add in the diluted miso and broth. Serve it up, shawty!

MISO SOUP
Vegan, Dairy Free, and Gluten Free

MAKES 4 SERVINGS

WHATCHA NEED

2 teaspoons dried wakame sea vegetable

2 dried shiitake mushrooms, hydrated, or you can use fresh too!*

1/2 medium onion, sliced in half moons

1/2 medium carrot, sliced in small circles or diced— your choice

Handful of daikon radish, sliced into matchsticks

5 cups spring water

4 teaspoons sweet white miso—it must be organic and aged for live cultures to benefit the body

1 teaspoon shoyu or tamari sauce or coconut aminos

1 scallion (green onion), sliced, for garnish

*If you don't have shiitake use any mushroom, especially maitake—these are the most powerful healing mushrooms of all. They contain interferon, an ingredient found in chemo treatments! Plus all mushrooms contain vitamin D!

Whatcha Do

Soak the wakame and shiitake mushrooms in 1 cup of spring water (be sure to rinse off your shiitake mushrooms first). Once the mushrooms are rehydrated, remove the hard stems (and discard), leaving the caps to be sliced into thin strips.

Place the onions, carrot, daikon radish, and remaining 4 cups of water in the soup pot along with the water you used to hydrate the wakame and the mushrooms. (This water is important 'cause it's got all the minerals from the wakame in it). Bring it to a boil, then reduce the heat and let simmer for 10 minutes.

Remove about a 1/4 cup of the broth and add the miso to it, mashing the miso into the water using a spoon (I use my soup ladle). Once it is blended and dissolved, add the diluted miso back into the soup and allow it to *SIMMER,* not boil, for less than 5 minutes. Add the shoyu (or tamari or coconut aminos) during the last 3 minutes. Serve and garnish with scallions.

TORTILLA SOUP
Vegan, Dairy Free, and Gluten Free

One of my all-time favorite soups—full of everything good, so I had to Mee-ify it fo'ya!

Whatcha Do

Heat the oil in a heavy stockpot over medium heat. Add the onions and garlic and sauté for 5 minutes. Add the jalapeno chili, tamari, cumin, salt, oregano, and pepper and sauté 1 minute longer. Stir in the stock, tomatoes, and tomato paste. Cover and bring to a simmer over high heat. Decrease the heat to medium low and stir occasionally for 10 minutes. Add tortillas, simmer 10 more minutes. Almost done, y'all!

Using your wand, blend the soup right in the pot until smooth. Stir in cilantro, garnish with avocado, tortilla strips, and pico de gallo, and get your grub on!

MAKES 4–6 SERVINGS

WHATCHA NEED

1 tablespoon olive oil

2 onions, coarsely chopped

3 cloves garlic, finely chopped

1 jalapeno chili, finely chopped (leave out the seeds and veins for less spice)

2 tablespoons tamari

2 teaspoons ground cumin

2 teaspoons sea salt

1 teaspoon dried oregano

1/2 teaspoon freshly ground black pepper

8 cups veggie stock (see recipe) or water

1 pound tomatoes, coarsely chopped

1/3 cup tomato paste

8 corn tortillas, coarsely chopped (for thinner soup use less)

1/4 cup finely chopped cilantro

1/2 cup crispy tortilla strips, for garnish (see recipe)

1 avocado, peeled and cut into cubes (optional)

1/2 cup pico de gallo (see recipe), for garnish

MAKES 2 CUPS

1 tablespoon organic
grapeseed oil

6 6-inch corn tortillas

1 teaspoon blended chili powder

$1/2$ teaspoon maple crystals

$1/4$ teaspoon sea salt

CRISPY TORTILLA STRIPS
Vegan, Dairy Free, and Gluten Free

Great crunchy strips to add to lots of Mexican dishes, especially the tortilla soup (see recipe). Or to chilliquilles—my favorite Mexican breakfast (see recipe)!

Whatcha Do

Preheat the oven to 350°F. Brush the oil over both sides of the tortillas. Cut the tortillas in half, then cut the halves crosswise into 8-inch-thick strips. Spread the tortilla strips on a heavy rimmed baking sheet. Stir the chili powder, maple crystals, and salt in a small bowl to blend. Sprinkle the powder mixture over the tortillas using a sieve. Toss the strips to coat, then arrange them evenly over the baking sheet. Bake, tossing occasionally, for 15 minutes until crisp. Transfer to a paper towel–lined plate to cool.

They will keep for two days in an airtight container at room temperature.

VEGGIE STOCK
Vegan, Dairy Free, and Gluten Free

If you like your soups to taste like a meal hook them up with this veggie stock instead of water. For a richer flavor, you can sauté your veggies or roast them coated with oil prior to adding them to stock. Avoid all cruciferous veggies; they are bitter when used in stock. Simmer the stock gently so it doesn't get cloudy.

Whatcha Do

Combine it all in a large pot and bring to a simmer over medium-high heat, then decrease heat to medium low. Simmer gently for 1 hour or until broth is flavorful. Strain into a large bowl and discard the solids. The broth will keep for two days covered in fridge.

Other good things to make veggie broth with: squash, parsnips, potatoes, tomatoes, corn on the cob, garlic, ginger, and herbs.

Veggies you definitely do not want to use: beets, broccoli, Brussels sprouts, leafy greens, cabbage, turnips, watercress, arugula, radishes, and vegetable stems.

MAKES 12 CUPS

WHATCHA NEED

14 cups water

2 onions, coarsely chopped

2 leeks (white and pale green parts only), coarsely chopped

4 stalks celery, coarsely chopped

1/4 bunch parsley

4 bay leaves

4 cloves garlic, lightly smashed

1 6-inch piece of kombu

6 whole black peppercorns

VEGGIE DISHES

MAKES 4 SERVINGS

WHATCHA NEED

1 cup dried arame or hijiki
seaweed

Water for rinsing and
hydration

1 tablespoon toasted
sesame oil

1 small onion, thinly sliced

1 large carrot, peeled and
julienned

2 tablespoons tamari
(or coconut aminos if you
are avoiding soy)

1 tablespoon mirin (rice wine)

2 green onions (white and
green part), thinly sliced

1 tablespoon toasted sesame
seeds (optional)

ARAME WITH CARROTS
Vegan, Dairy Free, and Gluten Free

Whatcha Do

Rinse arame or hijiki in a mesh strainer, removing any debris
and dirt, then hydrate in bowl of water for 10 minutes. Drain
well.

Heat sesame oil in a large heavy skillet over medium heat.
Add the onion and sauté for 5 minutes or until tender and
beginning to brown. Add the drained arame, carrot, 1 tablespoon of the tamari (or coconut aminos), and mirin. Decrease
the heat to medium-low and sauté mixture for 8 minutes. Stir
in remaining tablespoon of tamari. Transfer to a bowl, sprinkle
with green onions and sesame seeds, and serve.

The arame will keep for three days in the fridge covered.
Serve it warm or cold.

BOK CHOY AND PORTABELLA MUSHROOMS
Vegan, Dairy Free, and Gluten Free

I love bok choy because it has the softest taste, and it's a part of the cabbage family, providing my body with all those yummy health-fighting properties. It's known for being used in Asian dishes and can easily be found in most regular markets. Bok choy cooks up fast, so it is perfect for great last-minute meals!

Whatcha Do

Heat the pan, add the oil, and toss in the onions, garlic, ginger, tamari, and mirin. Once onions, garlic, and ginger have cooked to a clear color, add the mushrooms and allow them to cook for about 5 minutes. Lay the bok choy on top of everything and cover for 6 minutes. I like to serve this vegetable over leftover brown rice.

MAKES 4–6 SERVINGS

WHATCHA NEED

1 tablespoon sesame oil

1/2 sweet onion, sliced in half moons

1 clove garlic, chopped

1 teaspoon crushed ginger

2 tablespoons tamari

1 tablespoon mirin (rice wine)

3 large Portabella mushrooms

1 large or 2 small heads of bok choy (prepared as in Rules for My Greens on page 246)

1/4 cup hydrated hijiki or arame seaweed

MAKES 4–6 SERVINGS

WHATCHA NEED

1 large head broccoli,
stems and all

Juice of 1 lemon

2 cloves garlic, crushed

BROCCOLI WITH GARLIC AND LEMON
Vegan, Dairy Free, and Gluten Free

Whatcha Do

Steam your broccoli in a steamer pan for about 6 minutes, then move to a serving bowl and toss with lemon and crushed garlic.

Rules For My Greens

Kale, collards, turnips, and mustard greens—seriously old-school ancestral! Once again, I've got rules and simple instructions that can apply to almost *all* greens. Peep 'em and get cooking, 'cause once I started eating greens a couple times a week, my health majorly improved.

Cook a HUGE bunch since they cook down big time and then you'll have leftovers for the next day!*

- Wash 'em well.

- Chop 'em up, stems and all.

- Heat a big pan, add 2 tablespoons of olive oil, 1 tea-spoon of salt, and chopped up garlic. I like a LOT of garlic, so I hook 'em up! Four cloves at least.

- Add in your greens and salt toward the end.

- Add a few tablespoons of water to steam down the greens, and then add more greens as the first bunch cooks down. Toss in hydrated sea veggies.

- Garnish greens with umeboshi vinegar or lemon.

- Or just rinse your greens, blanch or steam 'em, top 'em with umeboshi vinegar and toasted sesame oil, and pack 'em up for lunch on the go!

*If you are suffering from digestive distress, cook your greens way down! If you do not have digestive distress cook 'em down any old way, 'cause greens are the one veggie that deliver more nutrition the longer they are cooked! What to do with leftover greens? Throw them into tomato sauce or tomato-free sauce or add them to miso soup!

BRUSSELS SPROUTS AND HIJIKI SAUTÉ
Vegan, Dairy Free, and Gluten Free

I love Brussels sprouts and knowing how good they are makes 'em better. Studies have shown that Brussels sprouts reduced the development of precancerous cells by 41 to 52 percent in the colon and by 27 to 67 percent in the liver—and they drastically diminished the size (85 to 91 percent) of precancerous lesions in the liver.

Whatcha Do

Blanch Brussels sprouts in boiling water for 5 minutes. Heat large skillet with olive oil, toss in onions, and cook until translucent (clear). Add the rest of the ingredients and blanched Brussels sprouts to skillet. Cook for 6 minutes and serve!

MAKES 4–6 SERVINGS

WHATCHA NEED

4 cups Brussels sprouts, washed and cut in half

$1/2$ sweet onion, cut in half moons

2 tablespoons olive oil

1 cup of chopped maitake mushrooms*

2 cloves minced garlic

1 tablespoon hydrated hijiki or arame seaweed

1 tablespoon coconut aminos or tamari soy sauce

$1/4$ cup diluted miso—sweet white or soy-free chickpea

*They come in a bunch like a head of broccoli.

CABBAGE, CARROTS, AND HIJIKI
Vegan, Dairy Free, and Gluten Free

Whatcha Do

Heat your pan. Add oil. Allow the oil to get warm, then toss in onions, cooking until soft. Add cabbage, carrots, hydrated hijiki, garlic, and miso and cover to steam on medium-low for 10 minutes. Cook for longer if suffering from digestive distress.

MAKES 6–8 SERVINGS

WHATCHA NEED

2 tablespoons olive oil or ghee

1 head white cabbage or Chinese cabbage, sliced

4 large organic carrots, grated

$1/2$ sweet onion, cut in half moons

2 tablespoons hydrated hijiki

3 cloves garlic, minced

$1/4$ cup diluted sweet white miso in water

CORN ON THE COB WITH UMEBOSHI SESAME
Vegan, Dairy Free, and Gluten Free

MAKES 4 SERVINGS

WHATCHA NEED

4 ears corn on the cob

1 tablespoon umeboshi vinegar

1 tablespoon toasted sesame oil

You will never miss butter on your corn again after trying this just ONCE! When I was a kid, I'd cover my gnarled-on cob with butter sucking the life out of it. I never imagined I'd enjoy myself while eating corn on the cob until I made this discovery one evening while having dinner with Carolyn Ross, M.D.

Whatcha Do

Boil or roast your corn on the cob and then sprinkle with the umeboshi vinegar and toasted sesame oil!

MASHED SWEET PAPAS
Vegan, Dairy Free, and Gluten Free

MAKES 4–6 SERVINGS

WHATCHA NEED

3–4 large sweet potatoes

Water to cover potatoes

1 teaspoon ghee (optional)

1/2 15-ounce can organic coconut milk

Brown rice syrup, to taste (optional)

A down-home dish, sweet and packed with vitamin and beta-carotene—two major fighters of cancer and immune-balancing goodies.

Whatcha Do

Wash the sweet potatoes off really good by using a veggie scrub brush, and then add them to a full pot of water. Simmer them until they are soft all the way through. Peel off the skins and put the cooked potatoes into a bowl with your coconut milk, ghee, and sweetener. Bust out your mixing wand and mash away!

KINPIRA GOBO
Vegan, Dairy Free, and Gluten Free

Kinpira gobo is a get-down good veggie dish that combines burdock root and carrots. There should be about four parts burdock root to one part carrot, which comes out to about one burdock root to one small to medium carrot. A half cup of this yummy dish is around 50–60 calories! Burdock is known to fight inflammation, to be a blood strengthener, and is excellent for teens with acne!

Whatcha Do

Cut the burdock root into about 2½-inch-long pieces. Cut each piece lengthwise into long thin slices, then cut the slices into matchsticks (this is called *julienne* slices). Or you can simply cut the root crosswise into circles. Put the burdock root pieces in a bowl with enough water and a bit of brown rice vinegar to cover, and let soak for a few minutes. Drain away the water, and refill the bowl with fresh water. Soak a few minutes more then drain again. Soaking burdock is optional. The benefit is that it will prevent discoloration and will give a milder flavor, but it's not necessary. Pat the burdock root dry with kitchen or paper towels.

Cut the carrot into matchsticks (or circles) about the same size as the burdock root. There's no need to soak the carrots.

Heat up a wok or large frying pan over high heat with the sesame oil. Add the burdock root and carrot pieces and sauté briefly. Add the chili pepper flakes and toss. Add the mirin and soy sauce and about ½ cup of water. Lower the heat to medium, and continue stirring until the moisture has disappeared. Taste a piece for doneness: it should be crisp-tender. If it's too crunchy for you, add a bit more water and cook some more. Kinpira gobo keeps in the refrigerator up to one week.

MAKES 4–6 SERVINGS

WHATCHA NEED

2 burdock roots, well scrubbed

Water mixed with brown rice vinegar to soak sliced burdock (optional)

2 small or 1 medium carrot, peeled and julienned

1 tablespoon sesame oil

1 teaspoon dry red chili pepper flakes, or 2 small fresh red chili peppers, finely chopped (optional)

1 tablespoon mirin (sweet rice cooking wine)

2–3 tablespoons soy sauce

½ cup water

Sea Vegetables

The value of sea veggies or seaweeds is through the roof—they are the last of the veggies to contain HIGH levels of trace minerals and the broadest range of minerals of ANY food. Folks in Asia and other coastal regions including Ireland, Scotland, Norway, Iceland, and New Zealand have been eating these veggies for 10,000 years.

The list of goodies they pack is extensive—from iodine (keeps the thyroid in check), magnesium, calcium (again, we don't have to drink milk to get it), and zinc to B vitamins, vitamin K, and a good amount of lignans (plant compounds with cancer-protective properties). Sea vegetables—especially hijiki, kombu, and wakame—also contain sodium alginate, which neutralizes and helps eliminate radioactive particles and heavy metals from the body.

The real "deal-io" is that folks who got started with seaweed have incredibly LOWER rates of colon cancer. If you've got a digestive situation, a cancer deal going on, or just plain old hormonal disruption—get to grubbing! There is just no greater source of minerals, vitamins, and phytochemicals on earth!

Sea vegetables are concentrated foods. You need to eat only small amounts of them—1 to 2 tablespoons per serving—to derive their enormous benefits. The easiest intro to seaweed is to add it to any miso or soup base. I always add kombu seaweed to my grains and beans while soaking and cooking them to add minerals to my food.

You can presoak seaweed, or cut it up and use it in soups as a vegetable, or in other dishes. There are over seventy-five species of sea vegetables eaten around the world. Following are some common varieties, their unique qualities, and cooking suggestions:

- **Agar-agar.** These crystal slices of algae are used as a thickener and base in custards, Jell-O, aspic, and mousses. Agar-agar is a natural gelatin, best used in flake form. The flakes have no taste or aroma. They simply need to be heated in the liquid of choice, and they dissolve. Usually 1 tablespoon of agar flakes per 1 cup of liquid is needed to create a gel state, or "kanten," as it is called. Agar-agar provides necessary bulk for regulating the intestines.

- **Arame.** Arame is a tasty black vegetable that comes in thin slivers or strands. It has a sweet, exotic flavor that is wonderful when cooked with other vegetables, such as carrots or onions. Prepare arame by soaking it to remove any sand or dirt. Once it is rehydrated, lift it out of the remaining water, and add a small amount of the arame to a stir-fry recipe, soup, stew, or pressed salad. Arame can also be cooked alone, or with carrots, onions, or lemon juice, for 30 minutes. Arame is rich in vitamins A and B, carbohydrates, calcium, many other minerals, and trace elements.

- **Dulse.** Dulse is high in iron, rich in protein and vitamins A, C, E, and B, and has iodine and trace elements. It has a tangy, salty flavor that complements vegetables, grains, stews, and fruit dishes. Dry roasted, it becomes a crunchy, savory condiment. Prepare dulse by wiping it with a damp towel to remove any excess salt and sand. Spread it on a cooking sheet and place it in a 250-degree oven for ten minutes.

- **Hijiki.** Hijiki has a robust flavor and bold appearance. It is a stringlike vegetable that is eaten as a side dish. Leftover hijiki is excellent in salads. Prepare hijiki by soaking a small amount in water for about 10 minutes, or until it is rehydrated and soft. Lift it out of the water, rather than pouring the water off, to allow any residues to settle to the bottom of the bowl. Then boil it alone or with carrots, onions, daikon radish, or beans for 1 to $1^1/_2$ hours. Hijiki is high in nutrients, especially protein, the B vitamins, vitamin A, calcium, phosphorous, iron, and many trace elements. It is traditionally used to strengthen the bones and to revitalize the skin and hair. It also helps build strong intestines.

- **Irish moss.** Irish moss is a sea vegetable used to thicken soups and stews. It is high in vitamins A and B, iron, sodium, calcium, and other elements.

- **Kombu.** Kombu is a stalklike sea vegetable used to add sweetness and hardiness to dishes. Use it in soups or cook it as a vegetable with carrots, onions, rutabagas, turnips, or daikon radish. When added to vegetables, beans, or grains, it greatly enhances their flavor, as well as softening them and increasing their digestibility. In addition, its nutrients leach out during the cooking and infuse the other foods. Prepare kombu by rinsing it in water. It can be used in whole form or chopped into small pieces. When soaked or added to soup, it will expand. When used in longer-cooked dishes, it usually will dissolve.

- **Nori.** Nori and sushi nori is the easiest sea vegetable to use and the one that newcomers to sea vegetables enjoy instantly. Nori, which comes in sheets, is commonly eaten in Japanese restaurants and used to wrap sushi. It can be roasted over an open flame in less than a minute and crumpled up to make a condiment. It is loaded with nutrients, including vitamins A, B, C, and D, calcium, phosphorous, iron, and trace elements.

- **Sea palm.** Sea palm is native to California and consists of strands of seaweed with a sweet flavor. It can be used raw, cut into strips, or added to salads. It can be boiled, both alone and with other vegetables. When added to soups and stews it has a softening effect similar to that of kombu. It can be roasted and ground with sunflower seeds for a delicious crunchy condiment.

- **Wakame.** Wakame is good in miso and other soups and stews. It enriches the flavor of other vegetables, such as carrots or onions. It can also be used as a sweetener. It is leafy and slippery in texture and expands when it is soaked, so one "square" is enough. It is best when soaked, chopped, and added to soups. When boiled, it is fully cooked in twenty minutes. Loaded with nutrients, wakame is high in calcium, thiamine, niacin, and vitamin B. It is traditionally used in Oriental medicine to purify the blood and strengthen the skin, hair, and intestines.

MAKES 4 SERVINGS

WHATCHA NEED

2 large parsnips, washed
and cut into long, diagonal,
French-fry shapes

2 tablespoons olive oil

1/2 teaspoon sea salt

PARSNIP FRIES
Vegan, Dairy Free, and Gluten Free

All I have to say is OFF THE HOOK! I'm not a huge root vegetable fan, but I know that eating root veggies supports our roots—the intestines—so I have found my favorite way to prepare them, and this recipe is so dang kid friendly it's crazy!

Whatcha Do

Wash and slice your parsnips. Heat the oven to 400°F. Using a large cookie sheet, spread out your fries and toss with olive oil and sea salt. Pop 'em in the oven for 15 to 20 minutes. Serve with veggie burgers or fish burgers or just as a yummy snack!

MAKES 2–4 SERVINGS

WHATCHA NEED

2 cloves garlic crushed

1 tablespoon mirin

1 tablespoon brown rice syrup

2 tablespoons tamari or
shoyu sauce

1 lotus root*, peeled, sliced,
and washed

2 tablespoons sesame oil

*When selecting lotus roots, it is a good idea to look for a firm texture and roots that appear to be plump and juicy with few exterior blemishes or soft spots. Generally, the lotus root should be prepared within a week of purchase in order to ensure the best taste and texture. The lotus root also works well in soups, stews, and as a steamed side dish for a meal.

SAUTÉED LOTUS ROOT
Vegan, Dairy Free, and Gluten Free

All I can say is that THIS IS SO DANG GOOD! Plus it's great for any type of congestion—may it be sinus, lungs, or intestinal. Lotus root is similar in texture to potatoes but not considered a heavy starch. You can find it in most Asian markets. My kids LOVE it!

Whatcha Do

Mix all ingredients except lotus root and sesame oil in a mini food processor. This creates a well-blended sauce for sautéing. When you wash the lotus root, be sure to clean inside the lace-like holes. When you're ready to go, heat the pan and add sesame oil. Once the oil is heated, add the lotus root and pour your sauce over it. Cover and cook on medium-low for 15–20 minutes—until the lotus root is tender yet crispy.

You can add hijiki seaweed or arame to this too! Hydrate it and add it in just before adding in the garlic.

STEAMED CAULIFLOWER WITH UMEBOSHI VINEGAR
Vegan, Dairy Free, and Gluten Free

This is Lola and Bella's favorite way to eat cauliflower, and it's a weekly staple in our house.

Whatcha Do

Rinse cauliflower, cut into pieces, and place in a steamer basket/pan. Cover and steam for 12 minutes or until desired softness.

Toss in a serving bowl with umeboshi vinegar.

MAKES 6–8 SERVINGS

WHATCHA NEED

1 large head of cauliflower, cut into medium pieces

2 tablespoons umeboshi vinegar

SUMMERTIME SQUASH WITH ARAME
Vegan, Dairy Free, and Gluten Free

Whatcha Do

Heat pan, add oil and ghee, add your half-moon sliced onions, minced garlic, and arame. Once the onions are clear, add in the squash and water. Cover squash for about 5 minutes until it's soft. Then add brown rice syrup and allow the veggies to caramelize a bit and the water to evaporate.

MAKES 6 SERVINGS

WHATCHA NEED

1 tablespoon olive oil

1/2 teaspoon ghee (optional)

1/2 Vidalia onion, chopped into half moons

1 large garlic clove, minced

1 tablespoon hydrated arame seaweed

4 yellow summertime squash, unpeeled*

3 tablespoons water

1/2 teaspoon brown rice syrup (optional)

*Sometimes I add 1 or 2 small zucchinis as well.

MAKES 4 SERVINGS
(About 8 Pancakes)

WHATCHA NEED

VEGGIE CURRY

3 medium carrots, cut into chunks

2–3 medium potatoes, quartered

2 tablespoons oil

$1^1/_2$ teaspoons cumin seeds

Seeds from 5 green cardamom pods

$1^1/_2$ teaspoons mustard seeds

2 onions, grated

1 teaspoon ground turmeric

1 teaspoon ground coriander

1 bay leaf

$1^1/_2$ teaspoons chili powder

1 tablespoon grated fresh ginger

2 large garlic cloves, crushed

Scant $1^1/_4$ cups strained tomatoes

Scant 1 cup organic veggie stock

1 cup organic frozen peas*

Generous $1/_2$ cup frozen spinach leaves

Salt

*If you're lucky and can find them at a summer-time farmers' market, use fresh peas!

CHICKPEA PANCAKES

Generous $1^1/_2$ cups chickpea flour—you can buy it or blend up your own in a Vitamix (see recipe)

1 teaspoon salt

$1/_2$ teaspoon baking soda

$1^3/_4$ cups water

Olive oil for cooking

VEGGIE CURRY WITH CHICKPEA PANCAKES
Vegan, Dairy Free, and Gluten Free

Another curry, completely vegan, and soy free! These chickpea pancakes are great with this veggie curry, or you can hook them up and eat them alone!

Whatcha Do

Curry:

To make the curry, steam the carrots and potatoes until just tender. Heat the oil in a large pan over medium heat and add the cumin seeds, cardamom seeds, and mustard seeds. When they start to darken and sizzle, add the onions, partially cover, and cook over medium-low heat, stirring frequently for 10 minutes.

Add the other spices, ginger, and garlic and cook, stirring constantly for 1 minute. Add the strained tomatoes, stock, steamed potatoes and carrots and partially cover and cook for 10–15 minutes or until the veggies are tender. Add the peas and spinach and cook for 2–3 more minutes. Season with salt before serving, and serve with warm pancakes.

Pancakes:

To make the pancakes, sift the flour, salt, and baking soda into a large mixing bowl. Make a well in the center and add the water. Using a balloon whisk, gradually mix the flour into the water until you have a smooth batter. Let stand for 15 minutes.

Heat the oil to cover the bottom of a skillet over medium heat. Pour a small amount of batter into skillet for a small cake; if you want a larger cake, spread the batter. Cook one side for 3 minutes, then turn and cook the other side until golden brown. Keep warm while making the rest of the batch.

Corn and Ketchup Are Not Vegetables!

As a kid I ate veggies—or rather veggies with BPA plastic, the liner in cans that is tied to disease and cancer. My veggies consisted of canned peas, canned green beans, canned corn, potatoes, occasional broccoli, and of course, tomato marinara sauce. Looking back we did pretty well, considering most of my friends ate even less veggies. When I met with Ginny, my food counselor, for the first time she asked me about the real veggies, the ones that pack big punches in keeping our blood clean. I had NEVER thought about cleaning my blood. I've spent tons of cash buying products to clean my skin, but *never* for my blood. The truth is, if our blood is loaded with fats, toxins, chemicals, pesticides, additives, and color dyes, how can it do its job? How can it deliver nutrients to our organs? If our blood is acidic, how can it heal—doesn't acid destroy? Dang—I heard Ginny Harper and I am passing it on to you.

There are a few easy veggies to add to your diet that will immediately change your blood chemistry. Try collard greens, kale, cabbage, bok choy, green beans, green onions, garlic, shiitake mushrooms, and daikon radish. Just these veggies alone can have a big impact!

TOFU RECIPES

So, Just What Is Tofu?

Tofu is a soybean curd that originated in China thousands of years ago to improve the digestibility of the highly valued soybean. My favorite Japanese restaurants make their own tofu, and the process is an art that begins with soaking, blending, and cooking soybeans and then mixing in a natural solidifier, such as nigari (a coagulant produced from seawater) or lemon juice. Tofu is full of B vitamins and minerals, including calcium, phosphorus, iron, sodium, and potassium. The kicker is that it's inexpensive (about $1.75 a package, and it goes a long way), and if it is made right, the calcium levels can match those of MILK!

Tofu has healing properties, too. It is known to relieve inflammation of the stomach and neutralize toxins.

Cooking with it is a breeze since tofu is a flavor sponge. It's important to store leftover tofu covered in water in a sealed container in the fridge. I recommend using it within two days.

It wasn't just fish that intimidated me; tofu gave me a fear of its own, especially because so many folks have an opinion about soy. Again, a reminder: we do have *way* too much soy in our diets because it's become the fabric of processed foods. So if we eliminate processed foods and eat soy in its healthiest form—that is, non-GMO (genetically modified) and pesticide free—including miso, tofu, tempeh, tamari/shoyu sauces, and black soybeans, it can be good for us. (By the way, it is important to not only avoid soy in processed foods but also to avoid all estrogen mimickers known as phalates. These are found in plastic food containers that we use in our kitchens as well as the packages that the food is purchased in. Body products, lotions, shampoos, conditioners, and cosmetics are just a few other places where phalates are found, exposing our skin—our number-one organ—to these estrogen mimickers. Studies have found that this is our biggest danger.)

When I first changed my eating habits I couldn't eat soy at all, but after six months being totally soy free, I finally reintroduced tofu to my diet. For the longest time I thought tofu was for hippies or more granola-type folks. The only time I'd ever eaten it and not minded it was in miso soup served at a Japanese restaurant. Determined to learn what I didn't *know,* I dug deep and began to explore the unknown world of tofu!

First of all, NO MATTER what anyone says, STEAM your tofu! This makes it easier to digest and cuts down on the gas factor, *especially* if you have digestive issues of any kind.

STEAMED TOFU
Vegan, Dairy Free, and Gluten Free

MAKES 4–6 SERVINGS

WHATCHA NEED

1 package organic tofu

Water for steaming

Whatcha Do

I use my stainless-steel steamer. First, rinse off the organic tofu, then slice it into little blocks and place in steamer pot. Fill the steamer pot three-quarters of the way full with water. Cover with lid and steam away—for at least 15 minutes.

SAUTÉED TOFU
Vegan, Dairy Free, and Gluten Free

MAKES 4–6 SERVINGS

WHATCHA NEED

TOFU

1 package of organic tofu, washed and steamed

MARINADE

3 tablespoons tamari

2 tablespoons mirin (rice wine)

2 tablespoons grated ginger

1 tablespoon sesame oil

1 tablespoon brown rice syrup

1 clove garlic

Additional oil for sautéing; you can use more sesame oil, or organic peanut or coconut oil

Whatcha Do

In the morning, steam tofu for 15 minutes. Meanwhile, mix everything else together in a food processor and then pour it over the steamed tofu. Set it aside and marinate until you are ready to cook dinner. Or pop it in the fridge to sit. Sometimes, I leave it in the fridge for 24 hours 'cause I've not gotten to it or we are eating leftovers—the longer it marinates, the yummier it gets. However, eat it within three days of steaming.

When you are ready to make the meal, heat your skillet, add 3–4 swirls of oil, and sauté away! This is great served over udon noodles with cabbage and carrots, or the next day in a gluten-free wrap!

MAKES 4–6 SERVINGS

WHATCHA NEED

2 12-ounce containers water-packed extra-firm tofu—for grilling stability

1/2 cup extra virgin olive oil

1/2 cup freshly squeezed lemon juice

1/4 cup mirin

1/4 cup tamari

1/4 cup fresh chopped basil

1/4 cup fresh chopped parsley

1/4 cup minced garlic

2 tablespoons chopped fresh dill

1 tablespoon freshly ground black pepper

GRILLED HERB TOFU
Vegan, Dairy Free, and Gluten Free

This is one of the most scrumptulicious ways to hook up your tofu, and it's a great choice for a summer dinner on the grill, especially if you're going to a cookout and you can bring your own grill grub! Pair it with grilled veggies and you got yourself a 5-star spread!

Whatcha Do

Drain tofu and save containers. Cut it in half horizontally and pat dry with paper towels. Place the tofu on a baking sheet covered in dry paper towels; let tofu sit and drain for 2 hours. Change paper towels after 1 hour.

Whisk the olive oil, lemon juice, mirin, tamari, basil, parsley, garlic, dill, and pepper in a bowl and pour some into each reserved container. Place one tofu slice in each container and pour more marinade over tofu; repeat with any remaining tofu and marinade. Cover and pop in fridge for at least 4 hours or up to one day.

On a medium-hot fire in the grill or in a grill pan preheated over medium-high heat, grill the tofu, brushing with remaining marinade, for 4 minutes on each side or until the tofu is heated through and grill marks appear. If you're not grilling, you can bake the tofu too! All you do is preheat oven to 400°F, arrange tofu on baking sheet, and bake for ten minutes on each side or until golden brown and heated through. Drizzle any remaining marinade over the tofu and serve.

Will keep for one day covered in fridge.

ISRAELI SCHNITZEL TOFU
Dairy Free and Gluten Free

MAKES 4–6 SERVINGS

WHATCHA NEED

1 package organic tofu, washed and sliced

2 beaten eggs or almond milk

1/2 onion, sliced into half moons

5 tablespoons olive or coconut oil

1 cup gluten-free pancake mix or cornmeal

Seasonings to taste, such as grated garlic, salt, pepper, paprika, thyme, and oregano

The best part of my Israeli life was the food. I fell deep and hard for Middle Eastern cuisine, and the way those folks cook fried chicken was a huge hit with me. I've adapted it for tofu now instead of chicken, and it rocks!

When I first started cooking with tofu I was intimidated. How in the world was I going to get my girls to eat it? Well, here is a great way to introduce it, and it goes over well as a next-day, packed-lunch special!

Whatcha Do

Steam the tofu in steamer for 15 minutes; let it cool and add it to the beaten eggs. Or if you are going egg free, soak the tofu in a small bowl of almond milk for one minute. The almond milk makes it sweet and toasty tasting.

Heat a large cast-iron skillet with olive or coconut oil. Once the oil is heated add the onions and cook until they start to brown. Remove from heat. I like to grate garlic over the tofu then add the onion on top and let it sit with the tofu in the juice. I do this in the morning, come home later and cook it, or I let it sit with the juices while I prep the rest of my food.

In a bowl or dish mix 1 cup of gluten-free pancake mix or cornmeal mix with seasonings to taste. Place the tofu squares in the pancake mix to coat. Don't shake off the garlic or onion pieces before dipping into the pancake mix. Just let whatever sticks, stick. Plop them into a pan, and once they are browned on all sides you've got schnitzel!

MAKES 8 CAKES

WHATCHA NEED

CHILI DIP

3 tablespoons white distilled vinegar or rice wine

2 scallions, finely sliced

1 tablespoon brown rice syrup

2 fresh chilies, finely chopped

2 tablespoons fresh cilantro

Pinch of salt

TOFU CAKES

$2^1/_2$ cups firm tofu, drained and coarsely grated

1 lemon grass stalk (outer layer discarded), finely chopped

2 garlic cloves, chopped

1-inch piece ginger, grated

2 kaffir lime leaves, finely chopped

1 large shallot, chopped

1 seeded Serrano chile (optional)

4 tablespoons chopped fresh cilantro

Scant $2/_3$ cup gluten-free, all-purpose flour

$1/_2$ teaspoon salt

Preferred oil as needed for cooking

THAI TOFU CAKES
Vegan, Dairy Free, and Gluten Free

These cakes are fantastic little appetizers or lunchtime sides to soup and salad. You could swap the tofu out for leftover cooked boneless chicken or even leftover salmon!

Whatcha Do

Hook up the chili dip first. Mix all the ingredients in a bowl and set aside.

Mix the tofu with the lemon grass, garlic, ginger, lime leaves, shallots, chiles, and cilantro in a mixing bowl. Stir in the flour and salt to make a course, sticky paste. Cover and let chill in the refrigerator for 1 hour to let the mixture firm up slightly.

Form the mixture into large walnut-size balls. With floured hands, flatten into circles until you have 8 cakes. Heat the oil to cover the bottom of a large skillet over medium heat. Cook the cakes in two batches, turning halfway through, for 4–6 minutes or until golden brown. Drain on paper towels and serve with warm chili dip.

TOFU CRUMBLE TOPPING
Raw, Vegan, Dairy Free, and Gluten Free

This is another great five-star tofu creation! Works great as a salad topper.

Whatcha Do

Steam tofu for 20 minutes, or until cooked through, and pop in fridge till cold. Cut the tofu into $1/8$-inch cubes. In a medium-size glass bowl whisk the lemon juice, curry powder, thyme, cumin, salt, turmeric, and pepper. Add the tofu and toss to coat.

The crumble will keep for one day, covered in fridge.

MAKES 1 1/2 CUPS

WHATCHA NEED

8 ounces water-packed firm tofu, drained

2 tablespoons freshly squeezed lemon juice

1 teaspoon curry powder

1 teaspoon dried thyme

1 teaspoon dried cumin

1 teaspoon sea salt

$1/2$ teaspoon turmeric

$1/8$ teaspoon freshly ground black pepper

MAKES 4–6 SERVINGS

WHATCHA NEED

CRUST

$1/2$ cup spelt or any gluten-free flour

$1/2$ teaspoon fine sea salt

$1/4$ cup mild-flavored oil

FILLING

$1^1/2$ pounds tofu, steamed

2 tablespoons plus 1 teaspoon olive oil

3 cloves garlic, chopped small

1 onion, chopped small

$1/4$ pound shiitake mushrooms, destemmed and sliced

4 tablespoons tamari soy sauce

1 cup frozen peas

3 tablespoons tahini

Pinch of sea salt

TOFU QUICHE
Vegan, Dairy Free, and Gluten Free

One evening Ginny Harper came to my house for dinner. I made a slew of sides, and she brought her version of Tofu Quiche. This was my first time EVER cooking tofu! What I discovered was FABULOUSNESS at its best! In fact, I make it for non-tofu eating folks all the time, and they are shocked by just how much they LOVE it!

Whatcha Do

Crust:

Preheat oven to 375°F. Put all ingredients in a medium bowl and use a couple of forks to begin mixing it. Then mix with your hands, or use your food processor to make it even easier! The mixture will be sticky and thick. Shape the mixture into a ball, then flatten it down and press into a prepared pie tin or small iron skillet. You can also roll it out if you dare, but I personally prefer the lazy way since it doesn't hurt the crust one bit. I use a 6 x 2-inch round cake pan for a nice deep pie. Prebake crust at 375°F for 10 minutes.

Filling:

Steam tofu (see recipe) and set pan aside. In a hot skillet, heat 2 tablespoons olive oil, then add the garlic and onions. Once these guys are clear in color, add in the shiitake mushrooms and sauté to softness. Add tamari and frozen peas. Cook for 12 minutes more.

Toward the end of cooking, remove the steamed tofu from its pan and place in the food processor. Add tahini and 1 teaspoon of olive oil and blend until smooth and creamy. Add the tofu sauce to the veggies and heat mixture.

Pour filling into the piecrust and bake for 40 minutes.

SALADS, DRESSINGS, AND SAUCES

For at least twelve years I avoided eating salads. I believed that I'd NEVER be able to digest them, and in truth I lived in fear of them. Proof that my intestines are doing well is I eat a couple salads a week. In fact, I'm always finding new ways to prepare them. It's as if I'm making up for all "our" lost time together.

CORN AND BLACK BEAN SALAD
Raw, Vegan, Dairy Free, and Gluten Free

This salad brings protein to any noodle or grain dish. Plus it's fresh and yummy, travels well, and folks dig it! The added perk is if you're at a picnic and eating out the cilantro kills salmonella, so toss in some extra! (Do not eat corn kernels until you are out of digestive distress. For me, this meant the first two years.)

Whatcha Do

Whisk the lemon juice, tamari, mustard, and pepper in a large bowl to blend. Gradually whisk in the olive oil to blend. Add the beans, corn kernels, bell peppers, green onions, and cilantro. Toss to coat. The salad will keep for one day in the fridge.

MAKES 12 CUPS

WHATCHA NEED

$1/4$ cup freshly squeezed lemon juice

3 tablespoons tamari

2 tablespoons whole-grain mustard

$1/4$ teaspoon freshly ground pepper

3 tablespoons extra virgin olive oil

$1 3/4$ cups cooked black beans (see recipe) or 1 can of organic beans, drained

1 cup yellow corn kernels

1 cup chopped bell peppers

10 green onions, white and green parts, sliced

$1/2$ cup chopped fresh cilantro

MAKES 4–6 SERVINGS

WHATCHA NEED

$^3/_4$ cup vegan mayo

4 ounces vacuum-packed firm silken tofu

$^1/_4$ cup minced onion

$^1/_4$ cup unsweetened soymilk or any other nondairy milk or REAL MILK!

2 tablespoons freshly squeezed orange juice

2 teaspoons Dijon mustard

1 teaspoon minced garlic

1 teaspoon onion powder

1 teaspoon vegan Worcestershire sauce

$^1/_4$ teaspoon celery seed

$^1/_4$ teaspoon sea salt

$^1/_4$ teaspoon ground black pepper

2 tablespoons finely chopped fresh chives

RANCH DRESSING
Raw, Vegan, Dairy Free, and Gluten Free

Tastes better then the real ranch to me! But if you are able to digest dairy, then, shawty, have at it and use it here in this real food recipe!

Whatcha Do

Blend the vegan mayo, tofu, minced onion, soymilk, lemon juice, mustard, garlic, onion powder, Worcestershire sauce, celery seed, salt, and pepper in a blender until smooth. Transfer to a bowl and whisk in the chives. Cover and refrigerate at least 2 hours and up to 2 days to allow the flavor to blend. Store in a recycled glass jar for 3–4 days in the refrigerator.

CLASSIC SIMPLE CAESAR SALAD
Vegan, Dairy Free, and Gluten Free

Whatcha Do

Slice romaine head lengthwise in quarters. Remove base and chop lettuce into 1-inch pieces. Place in a mixing bowl and toss with Caesar's vegan dressing and croutons. Arrange avocado slices with salad on individual plates or in a serving bowl, and garnish with lemon slices. Eat alone or serve with tempeh, organic chicken, or fish.

MAKES 4 SERVINGS

WHATCHA NEED

1 head romaine lettuce

1/2 cup Caesar's Vegan Dressing (see recipe below)

1 cup croutons—gluten free (see recipe)

1 avocado, sliced

4 lemon slices

CAESAR'S VEGAN DRESSING
Vegan, Dairy Free, and Gluten Free

Whatcha Do

Puree all ingredients in a blender. Store in a recycled glass jar for 3–4 days in the refrigerator.

MAKES 2 CUPS

WHATCHA NEED

1 cup olive oil

3/4 cup water

1/4 cup miso

1/4 cup lemon juice

2 garlic cloves, chopped

1 tablespoon capers

3/4 teaspoon sea salt

1/4 teaspoon black pepper

1/8 teaspoon white pepper

MAKES 4 SERVINGS

WHATCHA NEED

1 cup chopped tomatoes

1 cup peeled and chopped cucumber

1 cup chopped red bell pepper

1/2 cup chopped red onion

1/2 cup pitted Kalamata olives

1/2 cup Greek Lemon Garlic Dressing (see recipe)

1/4 teaspoon dried oregano

1/4 teaspoon sea salt

11/2 cups Tofu Feta (see recipe)

1/2 cup chopped fresh parsley

GORGEOUS GREEK SALAD
Vegan, Dairy Free, and Gluten Free

Whatcha Do

In a bowl, combine all ingredients except Tofu Feta and fresh parsley. Portion into four bowls, and top each with Tofu Feta and chopped parsley.

MAKES 4–6 SERVINGS

WHATCHA NEED

11/2 cups Tofu Feta (see recipe)

1 cup olive oil

1/2 cup lemon juice (juice from about 2 lemons)

2 garlic cloves, minced

1/2 teaspoon salt

1/4 teaspoon black pepper

GREEK LEMON-GARLIC DRESSING
Vegan, Dairy Free, and Gluten Free

Whatcha Do

Put all the ingredients in a jar, blender, or bowl, and shake, puree, or whisk. Store in a recycled glass jar for 3–4 days in the refrigerator.

GREEN GODDESS SALAD
Raw, Vegan, Dairy Free, and Gluten Free

The green goddess salad is all about broccoli and watercress topped with the most good-for-you dressing you've ever had—green goddess dressing! This dressing can be used on all of your favorite salads or dishes made of hearty ingredients that can withhold its weight. Watercress seems like a gentle leafy green, but, shawty, they are mean when it comes to packing a healthy punch; watercress contains significant amounts of iron, calcium, and vitamins A and C. At home on the ranch, I just walk down to the creek in front of our house and pluck 'em for lunch!

Whatcha Do

Dressing:
Blend everything in a blender on high speed until smooth and creamy.

Salad:
Toss salad with dressing with enough to generously coat. Season with salt and pepper to taste.

MAKES 2–4 SERVINGS

WHATCHA NEED

DRESSING
1 avocado

3 tablespoons olive oil

1 tablespoon lemon juice

$1/2$ tablespoon cider vinegar

1 tablespoon brown rice syrup or coconut nectar

1 tablespoon minced fresh chives

1 teaspoon minced fresh tarragon

1 tablespoon chopped dulse or dulse flakes

$1/2$ teaspoon salt

$1/4$ teaspoon pepper

1 cup water

SALAD
1 head broccoli, broken or chopped into small florets

3 cups fresh watercress

$1/2$ cup sunflower seeds

Salt and pepper

MAKES 4 SERVINGS

WHATCHA NEED

1 cup chopped tomatoes

1 cup peeled and chopped cucumber

1 cup chopped jicama

1 cup chopped avocado

$1/2$ cup chopped red onion

2 tablespoons lemon juice

$1/2$ teaspoon sea salt

2 cups mixed salad greens

4 cups cooked quinoa, cooled

1 cup Mango-Lime Vinaigrette (see recipe)

GARNISH

$1/2$ cup fresh cilantro leaves

4 tablespoons roasted or toasted pumpkin seeds

4 tablespoons currants, raisins, or chopped dates

4 slices fresh mango

1 teaspoon chipotle powder or cayenne pepper (optional)

MECCA AZTECA SALAD
Vegan, Dairy Free, and Gluten Free

Another one of my favorite spots in Los Angeles, Native Foods is a totally vegan restaurant that serves up amazing meals. This salad is so dang good I had to share.

Whatcha Do

In a bowl, combine tomato, cucumber, jicama, avocado, and red onion. Toss with lemon juice and sea salt. Divide salad greens on four plates or in bowls. Top each with 1 cup of cooked quinoa. On each serving, drizzle quinoa with about 2 tablespoons of the Mango-Lime Vinaigrette. On each serving, place $1/4$ of the tomato mixture on top of the quinoa. Drizzle a bit more Mango-Lime Vinaigrette on top of the tomato mixture. Garnish each serving with cilantro leaves, pumpkin seeds, currants, fresh mango slice, and chipotle powder.

MANGO-LIME VINAIGRETTE
Vegan, Dairy Free, and Gluten Free

MAKES I CUP

1 cup chopped fresh or frozen mango

$1/2$ cup safflower or sunflower oil

$1/4$ cup maple syrup

$1/4$ cup lime juice

1 tablespoon rice vinegar

$1^1/_2$ teaspoons sea salt

$1^1/_2$ teaspoons grated fresh ginger

This dressing is thick, so you may need to drizzle it on salads using a spoon.

Whatcha Do

Place all ingredients in a blender and puree. When I use frozen mango, I sometimes put it in frozen, since blending defrosts it. But you may defrost the mango first.

Variation: Substitute tangerine juice for lime juice, and call it Mango-Tango Vinaigrette.

Toasting Nuts, Seeds, and Coconut

Nuts and seeds are food for our brains! They give us energy and are full of antioxidants, calcium, omega-3s, vitamin E, iron, and potassium! They help cut heart attack and cancer risks. Peep how super easy it is to toast them up and add them to our meals!*

Preheat oven to 350°F. Place raw, unsalted nuts on a baking sheet and bake in oven for 5 to 10 minutes, stirring them occasionally and checking on them fre-quently so you don't scorch 'em! You can also heat up a cast-iron skillet on the stove and toast your seeds and nuts this way. I keep a freshly toasted batch of pumpkin seeds on my counter and chow on them all day long. They are great added to salads too!

Nuts are done when they are golden brown and fragrant. Cool completely and serve with salads, grain dishes, breakfast cereals—or eat alone!

*If you are on a healing diet, it is recommended to avoid nuts that tend to have more fungus and yeast, such as peanuts, pistachios, pecans, and cashews. Also, if you are suffering digestive distress avoid nuts until your free and clear of discomfort.

MAKES 4 SERVINGS

WHATCHA NEED

Water

Pinch of sea salt

1/2 cup thinly sliced carrots

1/2 cup thinly sliced daikon

1/2 cup finely chopped kale

1 teaspoon umeboshi paste

1/4 teaspoon brown rice syrup

BOILED SALAD
Vegan, Dairy Free, and Gluten Free

This is an excellent salad if you are going through any digestive distress or are on a healing diet. It's yummy, sweet, and salty, and easy on your body!

Whatcha Do

Put about 4 inches of water and the salt in a medium-sized saucepan and bring to a boil over a high flame. Add the carrots and cook for 2 minutes or until the color intensifies and the vegetables have softened. Remove the carrots with a slotted spoon and place in a medium-sized bowl. Repeat with the daikon and finally the kale. Ladle out 1/2 cup of the cooking water and place in a small bowl. Add the umeboshi paste and brown rice syrup, and stir until dissolved. Drizzle over the vegetables and toss before serving.

MAKES 4 SERVINGS

WHATCHA NEED

2 carrots, cut into matchsticks

1 onion, halved and sliced

1 cup presoaked hijiki

3 tablespoons rice syrup

2 tablespoons tahini

2 tablespoons fresh ginger juice

2 tablespoons shoyu or tamari sauce, or coconut aminos

2 teaspoons lemon juice

HIJIKI SALAD WITH TAHINI SAUCE
Vegan, Dairy Free, and Gluten Free

Whatcha Do

In a large skillet, water-sauté the carrots, onion, and hijiki for 10 minutes. In a small bowl, combine the rice syrup, tahini, ginger juice, shoyu (or tamari or coconut aminos), and lemon juice. Stir into the skillet, cover, and cook for 5 minutes. Remove from the flame and allow to sit until excess liquid evaporates.

MEXICAN LAYER SALAD
Raw, Vegan, Dairy Free, and Gluten Free

Everyone loves this colorful salad, and it is super easy to make, not to mention BEAUTIFUL!

Whatcha Do

Set aside guacamole, pico de gallo, and sour cream queso for assembly.

Corn Layer
To prepare the corn layer, toss corn, bell pepper, and cilantro with remaining corn layer ingredients. Season with salt and pepper and let marinate in fridge for about 5 minutes before assembling.

Dressing
To prepare the dressing, place all ingredients except the olive oil into food processor and blend. Once blended, slowly add oil. Store in recycled glass jar in the fridge for 3–4 days. I use leftover dressing as a marinade for tofu and then sauté or schnitzel it.

Assembly
In a 2-quart bowl or glass serving bowl, layer the corn, toss chopped lettuce/salad with dressing before layering guacamole, pico de gallo, and sour cream.

MAKES 2–4 SERVINGS

WHATCHA NEED

1 cup guacamole (see recipe)

1 cup pico de gallo (see recipe)

1 cup sour cream queso (see recipe)

CORN LAYER

3 cups fresh corn cut from the cob

1 red bell pepper, chopped

1/2 cup cilantro

1 tablespoon lemon juice

1 tablespoon lime juice

1 tablespoon olive oil

2 teaspoons cumin

Salt and pepper

CILANTRO-LIME DRESSING

1 cup cilantro

1/2 cup extra virgin olive oil

1/2 cup lime juice

1 tablespoon apple cider vinegar

2 tablespoons honey

1 teaspoon salt

Pinch of pepper

SALAD

6 cups romaine lettuce, coarsely chopped

MAKES 2 CUPS

WHATCHA NEED

2 cups cashews

1 cup water

1/4 cup lemon juice

1 tablespoon nutritional yeast*

1 tablespoon salt

*If you are avoiding yeast, use 1/2 teaspoon of sweet white miso instead.

SOUR CREAM QUESO
Raw, Vegan, Dairy Free, and Gluten Free

Okay, y'all, dairy-free sour cream is in the house!

Whatcha Do

Blend all ingredients in a blender at high speed until completely smooth.

MAKES 3 CUPS

WHATCHA NEED

3 cups thinly sliced cucumbers

3 tablespoons salt

1/4 cup brown rice syrup
or coconut nectar

1/4 cup apple cider vinegar

1 tablespoon celery seed

1 tablespoon mustard seed

QUICK CUCUMBER PICKLES
Raw, Vegan, Dairy Free, and Gluten Free

Swap out your crunchy, dried snacking habits for a yummy crunch that adds water to your digestive tract—plus it's great on salads.

Whatcha Do

Slice cucumbers on a mandoline slicer and then toss with remaining ingredients. Allow to marinate for 30 minutes before serving.

SEAWEED SALAD
Raw, Vegan, Dairy Free, and Gluten Free

Can't go wrong with this salad choice! Wakame and hijiki sea veggies are rich in fiber and essential minerals, and tahini—a sesame seed paste—is rich in calcium.

Whatcha Do

Seaweed:

Soak seaweed for 5 minute in warm water. Drain and strain out excess water.

Dressing:

Blend the tahini, lemon juice, sesame oil, ginger, miso, and water (along with sweetener, if using) until smooth.

To finish, toss seaweed with dressing and marinate for 30 minutes. Garnish with sesame seeds.

MAKES 2–4 SERVINGS

WHATCHA NEED

SEAWEED

$1/2$ ounce wakame seaweed, cut into small pieces

$1/4$ ounce hijiki

DRESSING*

$1/2$ teaspoon tahini

3 tablespoons lemon juice

1 tablespoon sesame oil

1 tablespoon miso

1 teaspoon grated ginger

$3/4$ cup water

Sesame seeds for garnish

*Adding 1 teaspoon agave, brown rice syrup, or honey can make this a touch sweet (optional).

MAKES 4 TO 6 SERVINGS

WHATCHA NEED

DRESSING

$3/4$ cup vegan mayonnaise

4 ounces vacuum-packed firm silken organic tofu

$1/4$ cup minced onion

$1/4$ cup unsweetened soymilk or any nondairy milk

2 tablespoons fresh lemon juice

2 teaspoons Dijon mustard

2 teaspoons minced and hydrated chipotle chili's and use organic adobo seasoning to season

1 teaspoon minced garlic

1 teaspoon organic vegan Worcestershire sauce

$1/2$ teaspoon celery seed

$1/2$ teaspoon fine sea salt

$1/4$ teaspoon freshly ground black pepper

3 tablespoons finely chopped fresh chives

SOUTHWESTERN SALAD WITH CHIPOTLE RANCH DRESSING AND AGAVE-CHILI TORTILLA STRIPS
Vegan, Dairy Free, and Gluten Free

Back in my old-food days, I loved a southwest chicken salad. When I found this recipe I knew all was right in the world. I Mee-ified it to make it even better! This salad is abundant in whole grains and plant protein, making it a meal in itself. The variety of fresh vegetables adds color and just the right amount of crunch texture. When I have guacamole on hand, I use a dollop of it instead of the fresh avocado. The ranch-style dressing has a kick from the chipotle chilies, chives, and garlic, plus the tanginess of the lemon. Chipotle chilies not only add heat, they also lend a distinctive smoky favor. If they're not available in your area, simply substitute a chipotle-flavored hot sauce, starting with about one-half teaspoon and slowly adding more to achieve just the right amount of heat.

Whatcha Do

Dressing:
Blend all the ingredients except the chives in a blender until smooth. Transfer the tofu mixture to a bowl. Whisk in the chives. Cover and refrigerate for at least 2 hours or up to 2 days to allow the flavors to blend. Season the dressing to taste with more salt and pepper.

Salad:

Toss all the ingredients except the tortilla strips in a large bowl with enough of the dressing to coat. Season the salad to taste with salt and pepper. Mound the salad on 4 plates, dividing equally. Garnish with Agave Chili Tortilla Strips (see next recipe) and serve immediately.

SALAD

1 head romaine lettuce, trimmed and cut into 1-inch pieces (about 10 cups)

2 cups cooked organic long-grain brown rice, cooled

1 15-ounce can Eden black beans, rinsed and drained well (or leftover beans)

$1/2$ small jicama, peeled and cut into $1/2$-inch cubes (about $3/4$ cup)

Kernels from 1 ear of yellow corn (about $1/2$ cup) or frozen organic corn

1 large red bell pepper, diced

1 cup cherry tomatoes, cut in half (quartered if large)

2 small, firm but ripe avocados, peeled, pitted, and cubed

3 scallions, chopped

12 cups grated cheddar-style vegan cheese (optional; see recipe)

3 tablespoons minced fresh cilantro

Fine sea salt and freshly ground black pepper to taste

$1/4$ cup agave-chili tortilla strips (optional; see recipe)

MAKES 3 CUPS

WHATCHA NEED

1 tablespoon neutral cooking oil*

2 teaspoons agave nectar
or brown rice syrup

1½ teaspoons chili powder

½ teaspoon fine sea salt

6 6-inch corn tortillas

*Neutral means has no flavor. Rice bran oil
works great!

AGAVE-CHILI TORTILLA STRIPS
Vegan, Dairy Free, and Gluten Free

Whatcha Do

Preheat the oven to 350°F. Mix the oil, agave nectar, chili powder, and the ½ teaspoon salt in a bowl to blend. Brush the mixture over both sides of the tortillas and stack the tortillas as you coat them. Cut the tortillas in half, and then cut the halves crosswise into ⅛-inch-thick strips.

Arrange the tortilla strips in an even layer on a heavy rimmed baking sheet. Bake, tossing occasionally, for 28 minutes, or until the tortilla strips are crisp. Set aside to cool. The strips will continue to crisp up as they cool.

The tortilla strips will keep for two days in an airtight container at room temperature.

MAKES 4 SERVINGS

WHATCHA NEED

1 cup quinoa, or 3 cups leftover

2½ cups water

10 vine-ripe cherry tomatoes,
seeded and chopped

3-inch piece of cucumber, diced

3 green onions, chopped

Juice ½ lemon

2 tablespoons extra virgin olive oil

4 tablespoons chopped fresh mint

4 tablespoons chopped fresh
cilantro

4 tablespoons chopped fresh
parsley

Salt and pepper

TABBOULEH
Vegan, Dairy Free, and Gluten Free

Traditionally tabbouleh is made with bulgur wheat, but if you're avoiding it or have a batch of leftover quinoa, then get your Mediterranean on with a new spin! This quinoa dish is delish! Again, packing all these fresh herbs gives your body a boost—they aren't just for flavor but have jobs, too!

Whatcha Do

Put quinoa into a medium pan and cover with water. Bring to a boil, then reduce the heat, cover, and let simmer over low heat for 15 minutes. Drain if necessary.

Let the quinoa cool slightly, then mix it up with the rest of the ingredients in a large bowl. Season with salt and pepper before serving.

BANGIN' BASIL PESTO
Raw, Vegan, Dairy Free, and Gluten Free

MAKES I CUP

WHATCHA NEED

2 cups fresh basil leaves

$1/2$ cup pine nuts, toasted (see recipe)

$1/4$ cup extra virgin olive oil

8 cloves garlic

3 tablespoons yellow miso

1 teaspoon freshly ground black pepper

I was so stumped when I thought about making pesto without cheese, not because it's hard or won't taste good, but because I was accustomed to eating and preparing it with dairy. The miso gives it a total cheesy feel and adds a natural probiotic—double win!

Combine this pesto with gluten-free pasta and no one will question or feel as if you've left anything out! Toasting the pine nuts is the secret to the deliciously rich and nutty flavor. Another option is to stir in a little vegan mayonnaise and use it for a sandwich spread.

Whatcha Do

Blend up everything in the food processor until smooth! That's it! Cover tightly and chill for a few hours before serving. Leftovers will last in the fridge for 2 days.

DILL DRESSING
Raw, Vegan, Dairy Free, and Gluten Free

MAKES 4–6 SERVINGS

WHATCHA NEED

2 cups vegenaise (vegan mayo)

1 tablespoon dried turmeric or about 2 inches fresh*

Juice of 1 lemon—and you can use some of the zest too!

1 tablespoon dried dill (I prefer fresh, so I add about $1/4$ cup)**

1 clove garlic

1 tablespoon olive oil

1 teaspoon each salt and pepper, to taste (with digestive disease skip the pepper)

I use this on lots of things—salad, tofu schnitzel, and fish tacos. Good for the croquettes too.

Whatcha Do

Put all ingredients in a food processor, or put in a bowl and use your handheld blending wand. Blend till everything is smooth.

*Turmeric fights inflammation.

**Use $1/4$ cup of cilantro if you want to mix up your flavors!

MAKES 4 SERVINGS

WHATCHA NEED

4 tablespoons olive oil

3 tablespoons organic ketchup

2 tablespoons organic apple cider vinegar

1 tablespoon brown rice syrup

$1/4$ teaspoon crushed garlic

FRENCH DRESSING
Vegan, Dairy Free, and Gluten Free

When I was a kid the only salad dressing I liked was French. Once I started reading labels I found it tough to find a French dressing without tons of additives and fructose corn syrup. Then my sister Nicole came to visit and with her determination to Mee'ify a French dressing recipe—here is what she came up with—and dang, it's good!

Whatcha Do

Combine all the ingredients in a bottle or jar and shake until dressing is thoroughly mixed.

MAKES 1$1/2$ CUPS

WHATCHA NEED

1$1/4$ cups water

1 cup raw pumpkin seeds

2 teaspoons umeboshi plum paste

PUMPKIN-PLUM DRESSING
Vegan, Dairy Free, and Gluten Free

A serious way to cut acid reflux is by incorporating umeboshi plums into your diet. This recipe is the perfect combo of sour and salty and eases digestive discomfort too!

Whatcha Do

Puree all ingredients in a blender until creamy.

THAI PEANUT SAUCE
Vegan, Dairy Free, and Gluten Free

When we moved back to Malibu I was thrilled that within the city of Los Angeles there were so many places for me to eat out! My favorite is a place called Real Food Daily. This sauce below is from their restaurant—I just Mee-ified it!

Whatcha Do

Blend the peanut butter, vinegar, maple or brown rice syrup, water, tamari (or coconut aminos), ginger, garlic, sesame oil, and crushed red pepper in a food processor until smooth and creamy. Add the cilantro and blend just until they're finely chopped. The dressing will keep for two days, covered and refrigerated.*

---

*This sauce will thicken when placed in the refrigerator, so add a little water to thin. I LOVE to use this sauce on leftover grains or mix it into grain or bean burgers. Also a *favorite* tossed with soba noodles and freshly steamed veggies.

MAKES 4–6 SERVINGS

WHATCHA NEED

$1/2$ cup creamy peanut butter or almond butter

$1/3$ cup brown rice vinegar

$1/4$ cup maple syrup or brown rice syrup

3 tablespoons water

2 tablespoons tamari or coconut aminos if you are avoiding soy

1 tablespoon fresh ginger, peeled and minced

2 cloves garlic

$1^1/2$ teaspoons toasted sesame oil

$1/4$ teaspoon crushed red pepper flakes (optional; I use less for the kids)

1 cup lightly packed fresh cilantro leaves

THOUSAND ISLAND DRESSING
Vegan, Dairy Free, and Gluten Free

I love this stuff on a burger, and it makes my bean burgers really hum!

Whatcha Do

Mix all ingredients together in a bowl.

MAKES 4–6 SERVINGS

WHATCHA NEED

1 cup vegan mayonnaise

2 tablespoons minced onion

1 tablespoon sweet pickle relish

$1/4$ cup organic catsup

MAKES 4–6 SERVINGS

WHATCHA NEED

2 tablespoons sesame oil
(olive oil works great too!)

$1/2$ onion, chopped fine

2 cloves garlic, minced

1 cup shiitake mushrooms

2 tablespoons shoyu or
tamari sauce

1 tablespoon mirin

2 cups water

1 tablespoon sweet white miso
or barley miso (diluted)

2 tablespoons kuzu (diluted
with about 2–3 tablespoons
cold water)

KUZU GRAVY
Vegan, Dairy Free, and Gluten Free

Kuzu Gravy is easy to make and is so good fo'ya it's hard to believe! When making gravy with kuzu (or cornstarch, flour, or arrowroot) being exact about the dilution is a little tricky. So trust your instincts, and never turn your back on the gravy while it's cooking—stick close so it doesn't stick to the pan.

Whatcha Do

Start by heating a frying pan on medium-low heat. Then add sesame oil, onions, garlic, and mushrooms. Season with shoyu or tamari and mirin and add 2 cups of water. Cover and allow this to cook together. Remove a ladleful of the hot broth and use it to dilute the miso in a separate bowl. Add diluted miso to the pot and let cook for a few minutes. Do not bring it to a full boil—this maintains the live cultures in the miso. Lastly, add the diluted kuzu.

To dilute the kuzu, add cold water to kuzu in a separate bowl. Make sure it is cold because kuzu can only be diluted in cold water. Once it becomes a white liquid, add it to the pot. Stir constantly to avoid clumps.

This gravy is perfect for mashed potatoes, grains, or pastas. Sometimes I add frozen green peas, too. Celery can also be added for flavor, and if you are not a vegetarian or vegan, than by all means use beef broth or chicken broth to replace the 2 cups water for extra richness.

Kuzu Is the Bomb, Baby!

I fell hard for this edible heartthrob! Kuzu is a root from Asia, and its starch is widely used in Asian cooking as a thickener. It is very low in calories, contains no fat, and is an easily digestible source of complex carbohydrates—only 8 grams per serving. Kuzu root is so strong that it can grow through concrete and rock. When eaten, it lends its strength to healing the intestinal lining in our bodies.

The intestines are the roots of our bodies, and *all* health issues stem from weakened intestinal walls because that is where the body receives nutrition. If the tissue there is damaged, our bodies can't get the nutrition they need. Eating root vegetables brings "core" strength and aids in balancing our health. Ancestral peoples claim that if the intestinal wall is weak, then kuzu will strengthen it. If the wall is too tough, kuzu will soften it. Kuzu is a natural ulcerative Band-Aid, easing intestinal sores while the body heals.

CHEESE (DAIRY AND NONDAIRY)

Once I got hooked into cheese it was crazy how much I missed it. Learning how to bring the cheesy back to the table was a huge feat! I keep some cashew cheese stashed in the freezer for grating! I'm also now able to digest a little bit of goat cheese, which I eat—and will only ever eat—as a treat. If you are a healthy person and able to digest dairy, than by all means add a little cow cheese. But if you are healing your body, give it a break and try some of these yummy alternatives!

RAW CASHEW CHEESE
Raw, Vegan, Dairy Free, and Gluten Free

If you plan ahead a day and allow the cheese to "set up," this cheese is super scrumptious! You soak the raw nuts first. This makes them super soft and easily digestible.

MAKES ABOUT I CUP

WHATCHA NEED

1½ cups raw cashews

⅓ cup water

2 teaspoons freshly squeezed lemon juice

2 cloves garlic

½ teaspoon sea salt

Whatcha Do

Soak these nuts in cold water ideally overnight or for a minimum of 6 hours, covering them by 2 inches, then drain. Combine soaked nuts, water, lemon juice, garlic, and salt in food processor and blend, scraping down the sides of bowl, for about 5 minutes until smooth.

Transfer to small bowl, cover, and keep at room temperature for one or two days. Or refrigerate until ready to use; it will keep for five days covered in fridge.

RAW RICOTTA
Raw, Vegan, Dairy Free, and Gluten Free

I love ricotta, and not being able to eat dairy while having to watch my soy intake makes this raw ricotta a great option. Plus it's easy peasy since you plop it all in your food processor. I use it in my lasagna!

Whatcha Do

Pulse everything in a blender at high-speed until smooth and fluffy.

MAKES 2 FULL CUPS

WHATCHA NEED

2 cups pine nuts or cashews

3 tablespoons lemon juice

2 tablespoons nutritional yeast

1 teaspoon sea salt

1 teaspoon black pepper

TOFU RICOTTA CHEESE OR CASHEW RICOTTA CHEESE
Vegan, Dairy Free, and Gluten Free

When blended, the tofu gives this vegan cheese a creamy consistency that resembles ricotta. This recipe is borrowed from my first book, The Real Food Daily Cookbook—when you have a good recipe, why change it?

Whatcha Do

Blend all the ingredients in a food processor until smooth. The cheese will keep for two days, covered and refrigerated.

MAKES ABOUT 3 CUPS

WHATCHA NEED

1 14-ounce container water-packed firm tofu, drained and cut into quarters*

$2/3$ cup yellow miso

$2/3$ cup water

$1/2$ cup tahini

$1/4$ cup olive oil

5 large garlic cloves

$1 1/2$ teaspoons dried basil

$1 1/2$ teaspoons dried oregano

$3/4$ teaspoon sea salt

*Alternatively, use 1 cup soaked cashews (overnight is ideal) in place of tofu.

ROCKIN' FAUX CHEDDAR
Raw, Vegan, Dairy Free, and Gluten Free

MAKES 4 CUPS

WHATCHA NEED

1$\frac{1}{4}$ cups raw cashews

$\frac{1}{2}$ cup nutritional yeast

2 teaspoons onion powder

2 teaspoons sea salt

1 teaspoon garlic powder

$\frac{1}{8}$ teaspoon ground white pepper

3$\frac{1}{2}$ cups unsweetened soymilk or other dairy-free milk

1 cup agar flakes (about 2 ounces)*

$\frac{1}{2}$ cup olive oil

$\frac{1}{4}$ cup yellow miso

2 tablespoons freshly squeezed lemon juice (about 1 lemon)

*If you are not happy with how your cheese turned out, blame it on the agar flakes! It is best to measure these by weight instead of volume, because flake cuts differ from brand to brand.

Can't have nachos without the cheese, baby! I use this cheese to whip up my childhood favorites, like good ol' mac and cheese and grilled cheese, and as a sauce over peas! Made with cashews this cheese is not only antioxidant rich but also packed full of the same heart-healthy fat found in olive oil.

Whatcha Do

Without allowing cashews to turn into paste, finely grind them in a food processor using the pulse button. Pulse them babies up, then add in the yeast, onion powder, salt, garlic powder, and white pepper. Pulse it up a couple more times to blend. Set aside and keep in food processor.

In heavy saucepan combine nondairy milk, agar, and oil and bring to a simmer over high heat. Decrease the heat to medium-low and cover and simmer. Stir occasionally for 10 minutes or until agar is dissolved. With the food processor running, dump the soymilk mixture through the feed tube into the cashew mixture. Blend for 2 minutes, then add in the miso and lemon juice.

Use the cheese immediately as melted cheese. Store in fridge and remelt in saucepan, adding more milk for a thinner consistency. For grated or sliced cheese, refrigerate for 4 hours or until firm, then grate or slice!

TOFU FETA
Vegan, Dairy Free, and Gluten Free

Toss in salads, use on pizzas or in a wrap.

Whatcha Do

Cut tofu into $^1/_4$-inch cubes or crumble into pieces about that size. In a mixing bowl, toss tofu with dressing, salt, and oregano. Let marinate at least 30 minutes. Store in the refrigerator, and use within a week.

WHATCHA NEED

1 pound firm, Chinese-style tofu (not silken)

$1^1/_2$ cups Greek Lemon-Garlic Dressing (see recipe)

$^1/_2$ teaspoon sea salt

1 teaspoon dried oregano

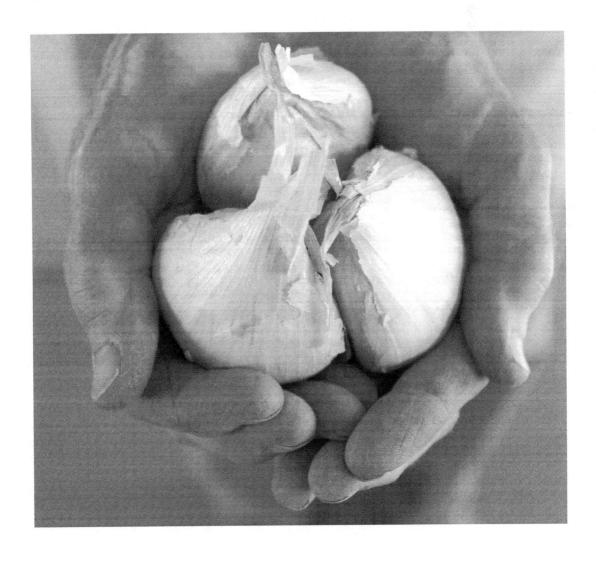

BURGERS

I luv me some burgers, fo'sho! My love runs all the way back to Wendy's single with cheese and my momma's memory. When I'm hungry and searching for snacky comfort food, nothing is more satisfying to me. Since I'm mindful of how often I eat meat—maybe once every six weeks tops!—I have become the master of veggie, bean, and grain burgers. I serve 'em up with all the traditional works.

MAKES 4 BURGERS

WHATCHA NEED

1 pound organic grass-fed beef, ground

1 huge handful fresh cilantro, chopped

2 carrots, grated

1 tablespoon hydrated hijiki seaweed minced

1 tablespoon shoyu or tamari soy sauce

1 leftover sweet potato (or regular potato)

1 zucchini, chopped small

$1/8$ cup finely chopped red pepper

$1/4$ cup grated onion

2 cloves garlic, minced

Salt and pepper to taste

Daikon to be sliced and served as a condiment

GRASS-FED BEEF BURGERS MEE-IFIED!
Dairy Free and Gluten Free

I don't know what came over me, but I was craving a hamburger, so I listened to my body and got myself some beef! I asked my housekeeper from Guatemala what to do with the beef and her eyes lit up. She said, "Watch!" This recipe can also be turned into a bangin' meat loaf by adding even more veggies, such as collards or kale, and topping with marinara sauce or the tomato-free marinara (see recipe). This recipe also makes great meatballs. Substitute oregano for cilantro, and add parsley, an egg, and breadcrumbs. If you cannot eat breadcrumbs, use leftover quinoa or brown rice!

Whatcha Do

Mix all ingredients together. Let mixture sit in the fridge all day to blend the flavors. When it's time to eat, whip it out and make some patties. Grilling is the best, but a skillet is old-school cool! I serve this up with a side of collards or kale!*

---

*Always eat animal meat with grated daikon, as it is known to aid in digestion and flush fats. It is commonly served in traditional Japanese restaurants whenever fish or fried food is consumed.

SALMON-DILL BURGERS
Dairy Free and Gluten Free

You can hook these burgers up with your favorite fish! I love to get down on the salmon. Even if you don't care for salmon, you will love this recipe—it is a great way to get your omegas! If you cut the salmon up into small chunks and toss all ingredients into a food processor, you can leave the eggs out of this recipe. Ground-up salmon is easily formed into shape. If you have only a small amount of fish and lots of guests, toss in a cup of leftover grains—this works as filler!

Whatcha Do

Rinse salmon, pat dry, and cut into $1/4$-inch cubes. Combine with flour, eggs, lemon, dill, and salt. Make into four patties about 2 inches thick.

Heat the oil over medium-high heat and cook each patty 4–6 minutes per side until golden brown. Transfer to paper towel–lined plate and serve it up, baby!

MAKES 4 SERVINGS

WHATCHA NEED

1 pound wild skinless salmon

$1/2$ cup blanched almond flour

2 eggs

1 tablespoon lemon zest

1 tablespoon chopped fresh dill

$1/2$ teaspoon salt

2 tablespoons grapeseed oil

THAI TUNA BURGERS
Dairy Free and Gluten Free

Whatcha Do

Put all ingredients in a big old food processor and grind it up. Make patties, and then dust them in your almond meal, corn-meal, or breadcrumbs. Heat skillet, add in sesame oil, and cook patties for about 4 or 5 minutes per side.

*Any fish works with this recipe, as do beans, grains, and veggies.

MAKES 4 SERVINGS

WHATCHA NEED

1 6-ounce filet fresh ahi tuna*

1 cup chopped cilantro

1 cup Thai basil (regular basil works, but Thai basil has more flavor)

2 tablespoons chopped ginger

Juice of 1 lime

1 tablespoon mirin

1 tablespoon tamari soy sauce or coconut aminos

1 teaspoon crushed red chilies (optional)

1–2 cups almond meal, cornmeal, or gluten-free bread crumbs

4 tablespoons sesame oil

MAKES 4 GENEROUS
SERVINGS

WHATCHA NEED

2 tablespoons olive oil

$1/4$ onion, chopped small

2 cloves garlic, chopped

1 tablespoon hydrated arame or hijiki (If you are using beans that you soaked and cooked with kombu, then chop that kombu into tiny bite-sized pieces and use it instead of the arame or hijiki)

1 stalk celery, chopped small

$1/4$ cup carrots, grated or chopped small

$1/4$ cup shiitake or maitake mushrooms, chopped fine

2 cups cooked adzuki beans or 2 15-ounce Eden canned beans*

$1/2$ cup leftover grain, such as millet, quinoa, or brown rice (white rice will work fine, too)

1 teaspoon chickpea miso diluted in $1/4$ cup of water

1 tablespoon organic adobo seasoning

1 tablespoon organic Worcestershire sauce**

1 tablespoon organic tahini

1 cup rice bread crumbs

Organic grapeseed oil or olive oil—just enough to coat the bottom of your skillet

*Always strain and wash beans to remove gas-causing carbohydrates.

**If you are avoiding yeast, substitute 1 teaspoon mirin and 1 teaspoon tamari for the Worcestershire. If you are avoiding soy, then replace tamari with coconut aminos.

BLACK BEAN BURGERS WITH VEGGIES AND SEA VEGGIES
Vegan, Dairy Free, and Gluten Free

For a healthy detoxing meal that supports the kidneys, use adzuki beans (or you can substitute any other beans you have). I like to use my leftover beans, but if you don't have any on hand then I recommend using canned Eden Organic Adzuki beans. The reason I use Eden is because they cook the beans with kombu seaweed and there is no BPA in the can's liner.* I love using kombu because it adds trace minerals and selenium. If you want, try a combination of chickpeas (garbanzo beans) and adzuki beans in this recipe. Together they are really good! I like to make plenty of these because they are wonderful little lunch-packers for the next day!

*BPA is controversial because it is a compound that exerts weak but detectable hormonelike properties, raising concerns about its presence in food.

Whatcha Do

Heat olive oil in a pan. Add onion, garlic, sea veggies, and celery and sauté for 5 minutes. Add carrots and mushrooms and cook for 5 more minutes. Mix in cooked beans and leftover grain with the veggies and add the diluted chickpea miso. Cover and cook for 5 minutes. Add seasoning, Worcestershire sauce (or alternatives), and tahini and mix well. Place cooked mixture into a mixing bowl. Using a handheld blender wand, lightly blend mixture, leaving it slightly chunky—not completely pureed.

Spread bread crumbs onto a plate. In a separate skillet, heat oil on medium heat while you are making the patties. Make your patties any size you like. I make big ones for adults and little ones for kids. Dust both sides of each patty with breadcrumbs then put them into your oiled and heated pan. Do not crowd the pan. Cook on medium-low heat until both sides are browned. I serve this dish with a side of cooked greens or a salad.

MEATY MEAT DISHES (VEGAN & NON-VEGAN)!

The thing about meat is that we don't need to eat it every day or even every week. If we look at how folks survived ancestrally, they barely ate meat. If you had a chicken, you didn't cook it all up at once. You took care of it and used the eggs. I always think about the slaves and the way they ate back in the day—plant-based. Occasionally, they'd get a hold of a bone to make a soup out of, and bits of fat were added when available. But never did they eat an entire chicken breast in one sitting. They also worked harder than anyone today under incredibly stressful conditions. Our thing with needing bacon for breakfast, turkey at lunch, and chicken or beef for dinner is certainly partly to blame for why we are all suffering from illness. It's out of balance, and there is no moderation. I can buy one organic chicken breast, chop it into bite-size pieces, and my family has food for three days! That's how you support your health and your pocketbook! Moderate what goes into your body and your grocery cart.

MAKES 4 SERVINGS

WHATCHA NEED

2 tablespoons olive oil

4 organic, skinless, boneless chicken breasts cut into 1-inch pieces

1¹/₂ teaspoons cumin seeds

1 large onion grated

2 fresh green chilies, finely chopped

2 large garlic cloves, grated

1 tablespoon grated fresh ginger

1 tablespoon ground turmeric

1 tablespoon ground coriander

1 tablespoon garam masala

1¹/₄ cups organic coconut milk in a can

Generous 1 cup canned, chopped tomatoes

2 teaspoons lemon juice

Salt, to taste

2 tablespoons chopped fresh cilantro to garnish

Freshly cooked basmati rice to serve

CHICKEN CURRY
Dairy Free and Gluten Free

My kids still enjoy chicken about once every six or eight weeks. Of course I use only organic chicken. The major benefit of chicken is that it is a complete amino-packed food.

Chicken Curry is a great chicken dish. Curry is a spice you want to have in your diet fo'sho as it is packed with natural anti-inflammatory properties. If you are not a chicken eater, steam tempeh for 15 minutes, slice into bite-sized pieces, and use it in this recipe in place of the chicken!

Whatcha Do

Heat the oil in a large, heavy pan over medium heat. Add chicken and cook about 5–8 minutes, turning frequently until lightly browned and cooked through. Remove from pan and set aside. Add cumin seeds to pan and cook until they start to darken and sizzle. Stir in the onion, partially cover pan, and cook over medium-low heat, stirring frequently, for 10 minutes. Add chilies, garlic, ginger, turmeric, coriander, and garam masala and cook for 1 minute.

Return the chicken to the pan and stir in the coconut milk and tomatoes. Partially cover and cook over medium heat for 15 minutes until the sauce has reduced and thickened. Stir in the lemon juice and season to taste with salt. Garnish with cilantro and serve with the rice!

ORGANIC BEEF STEW AND DUMPLINGS
Dairy Free and Gluten Free

Grass-fed beef is loaded with omega-3 and is not acidic like nonorganic beef is, due to the diet of grains. Always do your best to eat a balanced diet of mostly alkaline foods, with acidic foods making up 20% or less of each meal. An optimal pH-balanced body is disease free and cancer free! An overload of acid in our bodies over time causes inflammation, which leads to chronic disease.

Whatcha Do

Beef Stew:

Preheat oven to 325°F. Toss beef in flour seasoned with salt and pepper.

Heat 1 tablespoon oil in a large ovenproof casserole dish over medium-high heat. Add $1/3$ of beef and cook for 5–6 minutes, turning occasionally until browned. Remove the beef with tongs and repeat with another tablespoon of oil and cook another round of meat until finished. Set aside.

Add remaining oil to dish with the shallots, carrots, parsnip, and herbs, and cook for 3 minutes, stirring occasionally. Pour in the cider and bring to a boil. Cook over high heat until the alcohol has evaporated and the liquid is reduced. Add the stock and tamari and cook for 3 more minutes.

Stir in the chestnuts and beef and cover. Cook in preheated oven for 1 hour and 35 minutes.

Dumplings:

Meanwhile, to make the dumplings, combine all the ingredients in a bowl and season to taste with salt and pepper. Mix in enough water to make soft dough. Divide dough into walnut-size pieces and using floured hands, roll each piece into a ball.

Add dumplings to the casserole dish and bake covered for an additional 25 minutes. Once the dumplings are cooked, the stock has formed a thick, rich gravy, and the meat is tender, season to taste with salt and pepper and serve!

MAKES 4–6 SERVINGS

WHATCHA NEED

BEEF STEW

3 tablespoons gluten-free, all-purpose flour

1 pound grass-fed organic beef (round steak, cubed, works best)

3 tablespoons olive oil

12 shallots, peeled and halved

2 carrots, cut into thin sticks

1 parsnip, sliced into circles

2 bay leaves

1 tablespoon chopped fresh rosemary

2 cups hard cider

Scant half-cup organic beef stock

1 tablespoon tamari

7-ounce can of chestnuts, drained

Salt and pepper

DUMPLINGS

Scant 1 cup gluten-free self-rising flour

$1/4$ cup gluten-free shortening

2 tablespoons chopped fresh thyme

MAKES 6 SERVINGS

WHATCHA NEED

$^1/_2$ onion, chopped small

$^1/_2$ cup carrots, chopped small

2 cloves garlic, chopped small

1 tablespoon hijiki or arame (seaweed), hydrated

$^1/_2$ teaspoon chickpea miso

1 tablespoon organic Worcestershire sauce

1 tablespoon mirin

2 tablespoons tamari

1 pound ground, organic grass-fed beef (15% fat)

$^1/_2$ cup leftover quinoa (or any leftover grain)—add more if needed to absorb extra moisture

$^1/_2$ tablespoon organic adobo seasoning

3 shakes black pepper

Sea salt to taste

$^1/_4$ cup fresh maitake or shiitake mushrooms, chopped small

1 cup kale or collards, chopped or pureed (or you can use any leftover greens)

1 egg, beaten (optional)*

*I add a beaten egg, but the grain will keep the mixture together pretty well if you don't eat eggs.

MEAT LOAF
Dairy Free and Gluten Free

In the depths of winter I crave meat loaf. Knowing that the only way I could eat it was to Mee-ify it, I set my mind on the task and this is what I came up with. I don't always make it with beef; I also use grains, beans, and tempeh, pureeing it all and adding eggs or tahini as an emulsifier.

Whatcha Do

Heat oven to 325°F. In a food processor bowl combine the onion, carrots, garlic, sea veggies, miso, Worcestershire, mirin, and tamari in the food processor. Pulse until the mixture is finely chopped, but not pureed. Combine the vegetable mixture and organic grass-fed ground beef with the leftover grain mixture. Season the meat mixture with the adobo seasoning, sea salt, and pepper. Add the mushrooms, greens, and egg (if using), and combine thoroughly, but loosely. Avoid squeezing the meat.

Pack this mixture into a 10-inch loaf pan to mold the shape of the meat loaf. Line a baking sheet with parchment paper. Turn the meat loaf out of the pan onto the center of the parchment-lined tray. Insert a temperature probe at a 45-degree angle into the top of the meat loaf. Avoid touching the bottom of the tray with the probe. Set the probe for 155°F. Bake for about an hour or until meat is cooked through.

Top with Meat Loaf Topping (see recipe) for a tasty, tangy treat.

MEAT LOAF TOPPING!
Dairy Free and Gluten Free

My favorite meat loaf topping to use in a pinch is left over marinara sauce (see recipe)! But for a yummy ketchup glaze, try this recipe.

Whatcha Do

Combine the ketchup, cumin, Worcestershire sauce, hot chili sauce, and brown rice syrup. Brush the glaze onto the meat loaf after it has been cooking for about 10 minutes.

WHATCHA NEED

1/2 cup organic ketchup

1 teaspoon ground cumin

Dash organic Worcestershire sauce

Dash hot chili sauce

1 tablespoon brown rice syrup

GINGER-GARLIC LAMB
Dairy Free and Gluten Free

Until it was recommended to eat this lovely little creature, I had never tried lamb before. Now I know that it is actually easy to digest! As long as it is prepared well and not greasy, my body does well with it. Plus, the sweet potatoes mixed with this ginger-garlic lamb are bangin'!

Whatcha Do

Preheat oven to 325°F. Toss all your spices (ginger, turmeric, pepper) and flavorings (tamari sauce and mirin) into the mini food processer—blend all into a pastelike rub. Cover the leg of lamb with this mixture, rubbing it all over. Pour the water into the bottom of the roasting pan, place the leg of lamb in the water, and surround the lamb with all the veggies (garlic, onion, celery, carrots, potatoes) and cover. Roast in the oven for 6 hours, adding more water as needed.

MAKES 6 SERVINGS

WHATCHA NEED

1 tablespoon crushed fresh ginger

1 tablespoon turmeric

1 teaspoon black pepper

2 tablespoons tamari or shoyu soy sauce

2 tablespoons mirin

1 leg of lamb

1/4 cup water

5 cloves garlic, chopped (not minced)

1 onion, sliced in half moons

1 celery stalk, cut into large pieces

4 carrots, cut into large long pieces

4 sweet potatoes, washed and unpeeled

MAKES 4 SERVINGS

WHATCHA NEED

LAMB

9 ounces organic lamb

1 onion, finely chopped

1 tablespoon chopped
fresh coriander

1 tablespoon chopped
fresh parsley

$1/2$ teaspoon ground
coriander

$1/4$ teaspoon chile powder

Salt and pepper

CHICKPEA MASH

1 tablespoon olive oil

2 garlic cloves, chopped

14-ounce can of chickpeas,
drained and rinsed, or leftover
freshly cooked chickpeas

2 tablespoons fresh
chopped cilantro

Salt and pepper

LAMB SKEWERS WITH CHICKPEA MASH
Dairy Free and Gluten Free

Use organic grass-fed lamb and serve these skewers up with some chickpea mash! It's a great way to mix things up! Plus this is an easy menu to whip up—folks will love it, and you can serve it with your quinoa tabbouleh (see recipe). By pureeing the lamb, it makes it easier to digest for someone with a healing intestinal tract and is an added perk for all of us, as the point of eating is to absorb— and when something is easily digested, it's a win-win!

Whatcha Do

Lamb:

Blend the lamb, onion, herbs, spices, and salt and pepper to taste in a food processor until mixed. Divide the mixture into 8 portions and with wet hands shape each portion into a sausage shape around a wooden skewer. Cover and chill the skewers in the fridge for 30 minutes.

Preheat a grill pan over medium heat and brush with oil. Cook skewers in 2 batches, turning occasionally for 10 minutes or until cooked through.

Chickpea Mash:

Heat the oil in a pan and sauté the garlic for 2 minutes. Add chickpeas and heat for a few minutes. Transfer to a food processor or blender and process until smooth. Season with salt and pepper and stir in fresh cilantro. Serve with lamb skewers.

TEMPEH MEAT LOAF
Vegan, Dairy Free, and Gluten Free

Another one of my favorites, y'all! My sister made it, and dang, I was HOOKED. Lee loves to make leftover tempeh meat-loaf sandwiches—ketchup and all!

Whatcha Do

Preheat oven to 375°F. Lightly coat a heavy rimmed baking sheet with 1 teaspoon of olive oil. Shred the tempeh with a food processor fitted with the shredding disk, or use a hand-held grater. In a large bowl stir the ketchup, miso, nutritional yeast, and soymilk to blend. Stir in tempeh to coat and sprinkle flour evenly over all and stir just until blended (the mixture will be moist). Transfer to the prepared baking sheet. Cover with foil and bake about 15 minutes, stirring occasionally to ensure even heating, until heated through.

Oil a 9 x 5 x 2-inch loaf pan with sesame oil and set aside. Heat 1 tablespoon of the olive oil in a large heavy skillet over medium heat. Add the onion, celery, carrot, and garlic. Sauté for 8 minutes or until the vegetables are very tender. Add the tomato, oregano, rosemary, thyme, salt, and pepper. Sauté for 5 minutes longer or until the tomato breaks down. Add the hot tempeh mixture and stir to blend well.

Transfer the hot tempeh mixture to the prepared loaf pan and coat the top with the remaining 1 teaspoon of olive oil. Cover and bake for 25 minutes or until heated through. Uncover and continue baking for 20 minutes or until the top is golden brown. Cool for 5 minutes.

Invert the loaf onto a platter, cut crosswise into thick slices, and serve.

MAKES 6 SERVINGS

WHATCHA NEED

1 tablespoon plus 2 teaspoons olive oil

1 1/2 pounds tempeh

1/3 cup organic ketchup

1/3 cup yellow miso

1/4 cup nutritional yeast

2 tablespoons unsweetened plain soymilk or any dairy-free milk

3/4 cup gluten-free flour

1 teaspoon toasted sesame oil

1 cup finely chopped onion

1/2 cup finely chopped celery

1/2 cup finely chopped, peeled carrot

2 tablespoons minced garlic

1 tomato finely chopped

1 tablespoon finely chopped fresh oregano or 1 1/2 teaspoons dried

1 tablespoon finely chopped fresh rosemary or 1 1/2 teaspoon dried

2 teaspoons of finely chopped fresh thyme or 1 teaspoon dried

1 teaspoon sea salt

1 teaspoon freshly ground black pepper

MAKES 4 SERVINGS

MAKES 4 SERVINGS

WHATCHA NEED

1 tablespoon olive oil

$1/2$ cup minced carrots (or you can substitute chopped bell pepper)

1 cup chopped onion (about 1 medium onion)

1 ounce hijiki seaweed, hydrated and rinsed

2 tablespoons dried daikon, hydrated

$1/2$ cup chopped celery

2 cloves garlic, minced

Salt

$1 1/4$ pounds grass-fed ground beef

1 cup leftover quinoa (optional)*

$1/2$ cup organic ketchup

2 cups tomato sauce (or 1 15-ounce can organic whole tomatoes, puréed)

1 tablespoon organic Worcestershire sauce

1 tablespoon umeboshi vinegar or red wine vinegar

3 tablespoons brown rice syrup or 2 tablespoons agave syrup

Pinch of ground cloves

$1/2$ teaspoon dried thyme

Pinch of cayenne pepper

2 turns freshly ground black pepper

4 gluten-free hamburger buns

*If you use leftover quinoa, cut the beef by $1/4$ pound.

CLASSIC SLOPPY JOES— BOOSTED FOR OPTIMAL HEALTH!
Dairy Free and Gluten Free

The Mee-ify in this classic is adding hijiki seaweed and dried daikon radish. Hijiki adds fiber, selenium, iron, magnesium, and calcium. The daikon is believed to help break down fats during the digestive process, and raw, grated daikon on the side serves as a digestive enzyme. And the magic is that NO ONE will even know this recipe's been Mee-ified!

The trick to this recipe is to brown the meat well on high heat. Don't crowd the pan, work in batches, and don't stir the meat until it is well browned on one side—browning adds fantastic flavor. It helps to use a large cast-iron pan, because cast iron can handle the heat and is believed to add iron to your meal.

Whatcha Do

Heat olive oil in a large sauté pan on medium-high heat. Add the carrots and sauté for 5 minutes. (If you are using bell pepper instead of carrots, add those at the same time as the onions.) Add the chopped onion, hijiki, dried daikon, and celery. Cook, stirring occasionally, until onions are translucent, about 5 more minutes. Add the minced garlic and cook for 30 more seconds. Remove from heat. Remove vegetables from the pan to a medium-sized bowl and set aside.

Using the same pan (or you can cook the meat at the same time as the vegetables in a separate pan to save time), generously salt the bottom of the pan (about $1/4$ to $1/2$ teaspoon). Heat the pan on high. Crumble the ground beef into the pan. You will likely need to do this in two batches, otherwise you will crowd the pan and the beef won't easily brown. Do not stir the ground beef; just let it cook until it is well browned on one side. Then flip the pieces over and brown the second side.

Use a slotted spoon to remove the ground beef from the pan—you can add it to the set-aside vegetables—salt the pan again and repeat with the rest of the ground beef.

If you are using extra lean beef, you will likely not have any excess fat in the pan. If you are using 15 percent fat or higher, you may have excess fat, so strain off all but 1 tablespoon of the fat.

Return the cooked ground beef and vegetables to the pan. Add the ketchup, tomato sauce, Worcestershire sauce, vinegar and brown rice syrup to the pan. Stir to mix well. Add ground cloves, thyme, cayenne pepper and black pepper.* Lower the heat to medium low and let simmer for 10 minutes. Adjust seasonings to taste.

Serve with toasted hamburger buns.

---

*If you are using less beef and adding quinoa, then add it in along with your spices.

Sloppy Joes—Three-Ways!

When I was a kid, my momma served sloppy joes way more often than hamburgers 'cause it was a sho'nuff way to stretch a little meat. In the early days of my food journey, I was totally bummed thinking this was an American classic I would miss out on. That was until I learned to Mee-ify my food! In these recipes, you will find three takes on the traditional sloppy joe: I've immune boosted the classic beef version (above); I've vegetarianized and veganified the second version by using tempeh; and in the third version, I've pushed the envelope by creating a totally raw and vegan sloppy joe!

VEGETARIAN SLOPPY JOES
Vegan, Dairy Free, and Gluten Free

MAKES 6 VEGETARIAN
SLOPPY JOES

WHATCHA NEED

1 tablespoon olive oil

1 large onion, chopped

1 green bell pepper, chopped

1 red bell pepper, chopped

1/2 cup grated carrots

3 cloves garlic, minced

1 ounce or 1 teaspoon dried hijiki seaweed—be sure to hydrate and rinse

1 teaspoon ground coriander

1 teaspoon ground cumin

Pinch of ground cloves

1/2 teaspoon dried thyme

1 teaspoon cayenne pepper (optional)

2 8-ounce packages organic soy tempeh*

2 Roma tomatoes, diced, or 1 28-ounce can diced tomatoes, undrained

1/4 cup organic ketchup

1 teaspoon organic vegan Worcestershire sauce (I like Annie's)

1 cup water

1/4 fresh chopped cilantro

Hot sauce to taste (optional)

Serve on gluten-free hamburger buns or in lettuce cups!

Whatcha Do

In a large skillet, heat olive oil over medium heat. Add onion, peppers, and grated carrots and sauté until softened, stirring occasionally. Add garlic, hijiki, and seasonings and sauté 2 minutes longer.

The trick with tempeh is making sure that it has been thoroughly cooked so it's easily digested. I *always* steam it for 15 minutes while I'm prepping my veggies.

After the tempeh's been steamed, use your hands to break it up and crumble it into the skillet, breaking it up even more with the help of a wooden spatula or spoon. Add tomatoes, ketchup, vegetarian Worcestershire sauce, and water; mix well. Simmer, stirring occasionally, until heated through, about ten minutes.

Remove from heat; stir in cilantro and hot sauce.

---

*If you are avoiding soy, substitute tempeh with a combination of 1 cup cooked leftover quinoa and 2 cups leftover black beans or 2 cans black beans. Add the quinoa and beans at the same time you would add in the tempeh.

RAW-VEGAN SLOPPY JOES
Vegan, Dairy Free, and Gluten Free

I like to serve this raw sloppy joe "meat" as an appetizer at parties or as a meal with a side of soup for lunch! Dinner guests will totally be impressed, and you won't be stressed because you can KNOCK this out in no time flat. The key to raw food is that it's raw, and so there is no "cooking" time needed.

Whatcha Do

Add all of the veggies, except for the Portobello mushroom pieces, to a food processor and process until well chopped and combined. Put the veggies into a large bowl and stir in the Portobello mushroom pieces. Season with a splash each of nama shoyu and apple cider vinegar and drizzle with a little flax oil. Add dried oregano, a little fresh rosemary, sea salt (go easy on the sea salt; with the nama shoyu, it would be easy to make the dish too salty), pepper, and a little cayenne and chili powder. Serve on romaine leaves for maximum deliciousness.

MAKES 4 SERVINGS

WHATCHA NEED

$1/4$ cup soaked raw walnuts—soaked overnight for optimal digestion and rinsed well.

$1/2$ red bell pepper, roughly chopped

$1/3$ sweet onion, roughly chopped

1 carrot, sliced

1 celery stalk, sliced

4 sun-dried tomatoes—hydrated.

1 clove garlic

1 medium Portobello mushroom cap, washed and diced

Splash of nama shoyu*

Splash of raw apple cider vinegar

Drizzle of flax oil

Oregano (dried), to taste

Rosemary (fresh), to taste

Sea salt, to taste

Black pepper, to taste

Cayenne pepper, to taste

Chili powder, to taste

Romaine leaves

*If you are avoiding soy, then substitute coconut aminos for shoyu. If you are avoiding gluten, use tamari (gluten-free soy sauce).

FISH DISHES

Growing up in Ohio, the only fish that came our way was perch caught in Lake Erie. Of course, Long John Silver's also served up some frozen goodies. My momma wasn't much of a fish eater or cooker, so when I started this diet and made fish my main source of animal protein, I knew I had a lot to learn. I live in landlocked Nashville, so finding fresh cold-water fish isn't an option. I've learned that frozen fish that is caught and frozen right there on the boat works perfectly and is less expensive than fish that's been shipped via refrigeration. I tend to eat a lot of cold-water white fish, because it is less fishy tasting and low in fat and oils. When healing one's body from illness, cutting back excess oil is key. However, if you're feeling great then have some salmon or tuna.* I'm so psyched to share with you that fish isn't smelly, and it's EASY to prepare!

Note: Always serve your fish with tons of fresh veggies to help your body break down the fish and digest it with ease!

*Tuna is known to have higher levels of mercury, so be sure to eat it in small increments. Also, the darker meat tuna has less mercury than the white meat.

MAKES 4 SERVINGS

WHATCHA NEED

1¹/₂ pounds cod

1¹/₂ cups blanched almond flour

1 teaspoon sea salt

2 eggs

2 tablespoons grapeseed oil

2 tablespoons olive oil

FISH STIX
Dairy Free and Gluten Free

Long John Silver's was another one of my momma's favorite fast-food spots. She would have loved to eaten my version of their fish stix! These stix are gobbled up in my house till they are gone! Serve with veggies or a salad and your favorite dipping sauce for a dinner sure to be a hit!

Whatcha Do

Rinse cod, pat dry, and slice into 1¹/₂-inch-wide strips.

In a medium bowl, combine almond flour and salt. In a separate bowl, whisk eggs. Dip cod strips into the eggs, then coat with almond flour mixture.

Heat the grapeseed and olive oil in a skillet over medium-high heat. Cook 3–5 minutes each side until brown.

Transfer to paper towel–lined plate and serve!

CORNMEAL FRIED RUFFY
Dairy Free and Gluten Free

When I was a little girl, Nana and I would walk to the fish market every Friday during Lent. There was a guy who made a lightly breaded fish, and Nana would order a bunch. However, when it was time to pay, she'd curse him in English. She didn't think bad words spoken in English mattered since it wasn't her first language. I'd cringe as they bickered back and forth. But I always went with her, 'cause she'd give me a piece of fish to eat on the walk home. This fish is just like Nana used to buy!

Whatcha Do

If you are using frozen fish, soak it in salt water and then place it in a baking dish. In a mini food processor, throw in the onion, garlic, salt, and pepper and process until smooth.* Pour mixture over the fish to marinate. Cover the baking dish and let the fish sit in the fridge all day. When you get back from work, bust out your favorite cast-iron skillet and heat up either $1/2$ cup olive oil or coconut oil. Once it's hot, dip your fish into the cornmeal seasoned with salt and pepper for a light dusting and drop it in the hot oil. (If you have digestive issues, don't use pepper; black pepper stimulates the bowel.) The fish cooks up pretty fast—about 4–5 minutes per side depending on the size of the fillets—so watch 'em. Once the filets are golden brown on both sides remove them and get ready to grub!

This serves up real nice with sweet potato soufflé and collard greens!

---

*If you don't have a food processor, then you can just grate the onion and garlic.

MAKES 4 SERVINGS

WHATCHA NEED

3 large filets orange or white roughy*

1 onion, chopped medium

4 cloves garlic, chopped medium

Salt to taste

Pepper to taste

$1/2$ cup olive oil or coconut oil

1 cup organic cornmeal, seasoned with salt and pepper (You don't have to use organic cornmeal, but now you know it exists.)

*You can use any type of fish. A whitefish turns out the best and is my favorite!

MAKES 4–6 SERVINGS

WHATCHA NEED

1 pound crabmeat,
picked free of shells

$1/3$ cup leftover quinoa pilaf
or any grain—instead of
crushed crackers

3 green onions (green and
white parts), finely chopped

$1/2$ cup finely chopped
bell pepper

$1/4$ cup veganaise

1 egg or egg replacer
(see recipe)

1 teaspoon organic
Worcestershire sauce

1 teaspoon dry mustard

$1/2$ lemon, juiced

$1/4$ teaspoon crushed garlic
or organic garlic powder

1 teaspoon sea salt

Dash cayenne pepper

Gluten-free cornmeal,
for dusting

$1/2$ cup grapeseed oil

CRAB CAKES MEE-IFIED!
Dairy Free and Gluten Free

Oh, man, I love crab cakes and I adore Paula Deene—I just can't eat her food without digestive distress. My sister and I found this recipe and KNEW we had to hook it up so I could eat it. Peep it and rock it, 'cause y'all are fixing to love it!

Whatcha Do

In a large bowl, mix together all ingredients, except the cornmeal and grapeseed oil. Shape into patties and dust with cornmeal.

Heat oil in a large skillet over medium heat. When oil is hot, carefully place crab cakes, in batches, in pan and fry until browned, about 4 to 5 minutes. Carefully flip crab cakes and fry on other side until golden brown, about 4 minutes. Serve warm with preferred sauce.

LOLA'S PINKY FISH
Dairy Free and Gluten Free

Salmon is the way to get omega-3s, which help your body fight off inflammation that can lead to disease. My biggest problem with salmon is masking the "fishiness" that can sometimes be associated with it. Not only does this recipe have a great blend of flavors, but also each ingredient brings a bonus to your body. Turmeric is one of the number-one anti-inflammatory spices on the planet. Ginger breaks down food, and garlic is an antibacterial agent. Toss in Thai basil—it slams the taste buds, packs punch on the health charts, aids in digestion, and puts up a serious battle with cancer cells!

Whatcha Do

I love to use a wok for this, but a cast-iron skillet works great, too. I remove the skin from my salmon first, this cuts the fishy flavor—but it's a choice and not mandatory. Then I like to chop my salmon into medium pieces and sprinkle them with salt. I heat my pan and add the salmon pieces, sesame oil, ginger, garlic, turmeric, mirin, tamari, and water, and cover. Cook for 7 minutes, then stir in brown rice syrup and basil. Cover and let simmer 7 more minutes. DONE!

Top with cilantro and green onions—serve on top of cooked quinoa.

MAKES 4–6 SERVINGS

WHATCHA NEED

1 pound Alaskan wild salmon

1 pinch salt

1 teaspoon sesame oil

1 tablespoon minced ginger

4 cloves garlic, minced

1 teaspoon turmeric, dried or fresh minced

2 tablespoons mirin

2 tablespoons tamari

1/4 cup water

2 tablespoons brown rice syrup (optional)

1 large bunch Thai basil (regular basil is fine too)

1 cup chopped fresh cilantro, for garnish

1 cup chopped green onions, for garnish

WHATCHA NEED

2–3 medium-size pieces
of tilapia

2 cups cilantro

Juice of 2 limes

3 cloves garlic

1 teaspoon sea salt

1/4 cup olive oil

Lime wedges for garnish

CILANTRO GRILLED FISH
Dairy Free and Gluten Free

I came up with this number one day when I was having some last-minute company, and Lee was firing up the grill. One word—simple!

Whatcha Do

Put everything except the fish and olive oil into the food processor. Puree, and then at the last minute, add the olive oil slowly so you have a pesto-like consistency. Rinse your fish off and then coat with cilantro pesto.

I like to use a fish basket for the grill as it's easy to cook both sides evenly and it doesn't stick. Cook for about 5 minutes per side and serve with a wedge of lime!

WHATCHA NEED

Shoyu, to taste

Lemon juice, to taste

White-meat fish, rinsed

SIMPLE POACHED FISH
Dairy and Gluten Free

This is a great fish dish if you're under digestive distress.

Whatcha Do

In a baking dish, combine the shoyu and lemon juice, and stir. Add the fish and marinate for 20 minutes. The shoyu and lemon juice will draw some of the liquid out of the fish. Brush a large skillet with olive oil and heat over a medium flame. Add the fish and sear for 2–3 minutes. Flip the fish and drizzle with marinade, adding enough to half cover the fish. If more liquid is needed, add more shoyu mixed with water. Cover and cook for 15 minutes or until flaky in the middle.

NOBU MISO COD
Dairy Free and Gluten Free

All I can say is that this is the best recipe to get non-fish eaters to eat. It's so dang good, it's CRAZY! Plus this fish is low in mercury (a toxic element that occurs naturally in the earth's crust) and high in omega-3 fatty acids that have tremendous heart-health benefits. Wild Alaskan cod also contains as much of the essential fatty acids EPA and DHA as wild salmon.

Whatcha Do

For the marinade, mix the brown rice syrup, shoyu, and chickpea miso in a container (with lid) and set aside. Clean the fillets and pat them dry. Place the fish into the marinade and coat them well. Cover and refrigerate overnight.

Preheat the oven to 400°F. Remove the fish from the fridge and scrape off the marinade. Coat a grill pan with olive oil and set on high heat. Add the fish and cook until browned on each side, about 2 minutes. Transfer the fillets to the oven and bake for about 10 minutes, until nice and flaky.

MAKES 2–4 SERVINGS

WHATCHA NEED

1 tablespoon brown rice syrup

3 tablespoons shoyu

$1/2$ cup chickpea miso (it is soy free)

1 pound black cod fillets (about 2–3 fillets depending on size)

1 tablespoon olive oil

MAKES 2–4 SERVINGS

WHATCHA NEED

2–3 medium-size pieces of any white fish

2 tablespoons extra virgin olive oil

2–3 cloves of garlic, minced (amount optional)

1 tablespoon sweet white miso

1 bunch fresh dill, chopped

1 teaspoon tamari

1 teaspoon mirin rice wine

Juice of 1 lemon

LEMON-MISO FISH
Dairy Free and Gluten Free

This fish is again something I came up with last minute, when my fridge was down to its last bits of food and a grocery-store run was in order. It's now one of my favorite recipes, and I use any frozen fish I have in the fridge. It's also great over tempeh or chicken.

Whatcha Do

Heat a large cast-iron skillet, add oil and garlic and cook for 3 minutes. Add layer of chopped dill to skillet and lay fish on top of dill. Keeping heat on medium, dilute your miso with a $1/2$ cup of water or more depending on how thick you want your sauce, then add tamari, mirin, and lemon juice to your diluted miso. Pour diluted miso mixture sauce over fish. Cover fish with lid and cook for 12 minutes. Serve with brown rice and a side of broccoli or asparagus, and top with green onions—for an added dose of vitamin C.

ITALIAN-INSPIRED DISHES

Giving up Italian food was my greatest struggle and probably the reason I've mastered alternative methods of cooking it! Using tofu ricotta or raw ricotta, I now know how to make some seriously great lasagna. And fettuccine alfredo is so my friend the way I make it now, using almonds and brown rice to create a cheesy, creamy nutrient-boosted sauce. If you are avoiding nightshades, then I've also included my tomato-less marinara sauce. It's super yummy and a great way to get your kids to eat a wider array of veggies as they are blended into the sauce.

ALMOND ALFREDO SAUCE
Vegan, Dairy Free, and Gluten Free

I got this down, and you know why? 'Cause I miss me some serious cream sauce! It's so good, and my kids LOVE it!

Whatcha Do

Sauté the garlic in oil. Grind almonds finely in a mini food processor, then blend to a cream with water and rice, herbs, and miso. Mix cream in with your sautéed garlic and heat for 15 minutes—again you wanna blend the flavors.* Toss with fresh-cooked pasta and serve immediately.

---

*I like to add mushrooms and peas to my garlic before pouring the cream into the skillet!

MAKES 6–8 SERVINGS

WHATCHA NEED

$1/2$ teaspoon toasted sesame oil

4 cloves garlic, minced

1 cup almonds

$1^1/2$ cups water

$1/4$ cup leftover brown rice (for cheesy effect, use sweet rice)

$1/2$–1 teaspoon oregano

1 teaspoon minced celery leaves*

1 tablespoon mellow white miso

1 package any style brown rice pasta works for me— or quinoa spaghetti!

*This is where the flavor really is found!

BUTTERNUT SQUASH ALFREDO
Raw, Vegan, Dairy Free, and Gluten Free

MAKES 4–6 SERVINGS

This is one of my all-time favorites, y'all! Love me some Alfredo! This version is made with cashews and miso. A wonderful combination of natural probiotics, nut protein, and power-packed squash!

NOODLES

1 large butternut squash

Salt

WILTED SPINACH

5–6 cups baby spinach

2 tablespoons olive oil

2 tablespoons lemon juice

Salt and pepper, to taste

ALFREDO

2 cups cashews

2 tablespoons lemon juice

1 tablespoon white miso

1 tablespoon brown rice syrup, coconut nectar, or agave

1¹/₂ cups water

1 tablespoon thyme

¹/₄ teaspoon salt

¹/₄ teaspoon pepper

MUSHROOMS

2 cups stemmed and chopped mushrooms (shiitake, oyster, Portobello)

2 tablespoons olive oil

2 tablespoons tamari

1 tablespoon minced fresh savory

Whatcha Do

Noodles:

Run the squash through a spiral slicer on medium spiral. Toss squash with a few teaspoons of salt and allow wilting for at least 10 minutes. Rinse, drain, and dry noodles well before tossing with sauce.

Spinach:

With clean hands toss the spinach with remaining ingredients. Stir spinach to wilt it and season with salt and pepper.

Alfredo:

Blend all ingredients in a high-speed blender until smooth.

Mushrooms:

Toss mushrooms with olive oil and tamari. Marinate for 30 minutes before serving.

Toss drained noodles with spinach and mushrooms, gradually add in a generous amount of Alfredo, and toss more. Season with salt and pepper.

CARROT NOODLES WITH TOMATO SAUCE
Raw, Vegan, Dairy Free, and Gluten Free

Refreshing and light, beautiful dish! An excellent way to get veggies into your youngin's tummies! Again it's a quick fix, and wonderful for picnics or travel days!

Whatcha Do

Sweet Tomato Sauce:
Blend all ingredients except basil in a high-speed blender until smooth. Stir in basil and season with salt and pepper.

Noodles:
Toss the carrot noodles and tomatoes with the sauce and garnish with the basil and the pine nuts.

MAKES 4–6 SERVINGS

WHATCHA NEED

SWEET TOMATO SAUCE

$1/4$ cup olive oil

3 cups chopped tomatoes (heirlooms if possible)

$1/4$ cup brown rice syrup or coconut nectar

2 tablespoons lemon juice

2 teaspoons salt

$1/4$ cup basil, julienned

NOODLES

1 cup cherry tomatoes

8 cups chopped carrots, run through a spiral slicer

GARNISH

12 basil leaves

$1/4$ cup pine nuts

MAKES 4 SERVINGS

WHATCHA NEED

2 tablespoons olive oil

2–3 cloves garlic, chopped
small or minced

2 cups tomato sauce
(use either the tomato-less
or my granny's)

$1/2$ cup white beans

$1/2$ cup fresh Italian parsley,
washed and chopped

1 cup water

1 cup brown rice pasta shells
(cooked according to
package directions)

PASTA E FAGIOLI
Vegan, Dairy Free, and Gluten Free

This is a leftover hookup, shawty, and a great way to use your foundation foods! When we were kids my grandmother and my momma would make this on cold nights or when we had colds. Garlic is a natural antibiotic, the beans are protein, and parsley is a power plant! Plus, it's cheap and fast.

Whatcha Do

I heat up a soup pot, add my olive oil, toss in my garlic, and let it get yummy for a few seconds, and then I pour in my tomato sauce, beans, and parsley. I cook it on low for about 15 minutes until the beans and sauce are cooked through. In a separate pot, I boil my pasta shells, strain them, and set them to the side. When the soup is ready to serve, I add the pasta shells to each individual bowl. Get down good!

POLENTA
Vegan, Dairy Free, and Gluten Free

Oh man, this recipe is so very satisfying and inexpensive, and it goes a long way. My nana used to make it, and I've Mee-ified it. I tend to eat it when I need a fiber break, and my intestines just need a smooth meal.

Whatcha Do

Bring 6 cups of water to a boil in a heavy, large saucepan. Add 2 teaspoons of salt. Gradually whisk in the cornmeal. Reduce the heat to low and cook until the mixture thickens and the cornmeal is tender, stirring often, about 15 minutes. Turn off the heat. Add the olive oil or ghee, and stir until melted.

I like to eat this like porridge the first night. The second night, after it has set in the fridge and solidified, I cut it into squares and top with mushrooms and tomato sauce.

Variation: when cooking the polenta, add in chopped up carrots, onions, garlic, and mushrooms for a polenta stew!

MAKES 4–6 SERVINGS

WHATCHA NEED

6 cups water

2 teaspoons sea salt

1³/₄ cups organic yellow cornmeal

3 tablespoons olive oil or ghee

MAKES 12 ROLLS

WHATCHA NEED

2¹/₂ tablespoons olive oil

2 onions, thinly sliced

6 cloves garlic, minced

2 tablespoons chopped
fresh basil

1 teaspoon fine sea salt

¹/₂ teaspoon freshly ground
black pepper

3 medium carrots, peeled
and cut into ¹/₄-inch pieces

2 zucchini, cut into
¹/₄-inch pieces

1 head broccoli, stems removed
and florets finely chopped

2 cups tofu ricotta cheese
or cashew ricotta cheese
(see recipe)

12 eggless lasagna noodles

3 cups Nana's Tomato Sauce
(see recipe)

LASAGNA ROLLS WITH TOFU (OR CASHEW) RICOTTA
Vegan, Dairy Free, and Gluten Free

This is a fun way to serve lasagna: Instead of the traditional layering, you top the individual noodles with a vegan ricotta cheese and vegetable mixture and roll it up. My tofu ricotta cheese is a blend of tofu, miso, and tahini, which creates a creamy consistency that easily spreads. The tomato sauce takes no more than 10 minutes to make; if there is any left over, use it the next day over rice or noodles.

Whatcha Do

Preheat the oven to 350°F. Heat 1 tablespoon of the oil in a large, heavy frying pan over medium-high heat. Add the onions, garlic, basil, salt, and pepper. Sauté until the onions are tender, about 10 minutes. Add the carrots, zucchini, and broccoli, and sauté until the carrots are crisp-tender, about 12 minutes. Let cool completely. Mix the vegetable mixture into the tofu ricotta cheese.

Cook the noodles in a large pot of boiling salted water, stirring often, until tender, about 10 minutes. Drain and rinse the noodles, then toss them with 1 tablespoon of the remaining oil to prevent the noodles from sticking together.

Coat a 13 x 9 x 2-inch baking dish with the remaining 1¹/₂ teaspoons oil. Spread 1 cup of the tomato sauce on the bottom of the dish.

Using a spatula, spread about ¹/₂ cup of the vegetable/tofu ricotta cheese mixture over each lasagna sheet, leaving about ¹/₂ inch of each end uncovered. Roll up each sheet tightly and place it seam side down in the baking dish. Pour the remaining 2 cups tomato sauce over the lasagna rolls.

Cover the dish with aluminum foil. Bake until the sauce bubbles, about 55 minutes. Remove the foil and continue baking for 15 minutes.

NANA'S TOMATO SAUCE
Vegan, Dairy Free, and Gluten Free

Now that I've got my body's acid level under control, I eat tomatoes! I spent a few weeks with my grandma and she schooled me on the old ways of "My People"—and they didn't have cans to open—so if you are feeling authentic, hit the kitchen and bring a little bit of Italy into your home. If you want to use canned tomatoes, then try to find tomatoes sold in jars, like Eden Organics. Why? Because the acid in tomatoes eats away at the lining of cans, the BPA lining in them is said to be necessary.

MAKES 6–8 SERVINGS

WHATCHA NEED:

10 red, ripe, whole tomatoes (use Roma) cut in quarters

2 cups of water

2 tablespoons extra virgin olive oil

1/4 cup chopped onion

Sea salt to taste

5 garlic cloves, minced

1 cup fresh basil

Whatcha Do

Toss tomato quarters in a large stainless-steel skillet with chopped onion. Add olive oil, garlic, and sea salt. Cook on medium to high heat, covered, for 10 minutes, stirring occasionally, until the steam that forms has softened the tomatoes and the peels have begun to pull away. Lower the heat to medium low, uncover the skillet, and gently crush the tomatoes into little pieces with a wooden spoon. Simmer until the thin juice has evaporated. This should take about 10 minutes, but it depends on your tomatoes. You can test your sauce by scraping a patch in the center of skillet with a wooden spoon. If the space stays clean for at least 5 seconds, your sauce is done. If the juice covers the space right away, continue to simmer on low, until done.

If you have a food mill, carefully pass all of the contents of the sauce through the smallest-size sieve.* It is very important to keep turning until all of the pulp has come off the skins. This is tomato paste and will thicken your sauce to the right consistency. Stir in the fresh basil leaves and your sauce is ready. Cooking basil can leave a bitter flavor.

---

*I recommend investing in a stainless-steel food mill, if you don't have one already. A food mill is a kitchen essential, and you can also use it to make homemade applesauce, mashed potatoes, and soups.

WHATCHA NEED

NOODLES

4–5 large parsnips

$1/2$ teaspoon Salt

PESTO

2 cups fresh cilantro, stems removed

$1/2$ cup walnuts, plus more for garnish

3 tablespoons lemon juice

1 tablespoon nutritional yeast

$1/2$ teaspoon seeded and chopped Serrano chili

$1/2$ teaspoon coarse salt

Dash pepper

$1/4$ cup of olive oil

PARSNIP AND WALNUT PESTO
Raw, Vegan, Dairy Free, and Gluten Free

Parsnips are an excellent root veggie to introduce to the family. They have a sweet flavor matched with the walnuts, which makes it a satisfying combination. Plus parsnips are packed with soluble fiber, giving your shadoobies a smooth ride out!

Whatcha Do

Noodles: Run parsnips through a spiral slicer and measure out 8 cups. Toss with salt and allow wilting for 10 minutes, then rinse, drain, and dry noodles well.

Pesto: Pulse everything in a food processor, leaving mixture a little chunky, then toss with noodles! Season with salt and pepper. Garnish with walnuts.

POTATO-BASIL GNOCCHI
Dairy Free and Gluten Free

Gluten-free gnocchi, y'all! Being an Italian hillbilly, I grew up with the combo of potatoes and pasta as a staple in my house. Again, once I realized I had to change my ways, I thought it was good-bye to the days of gnocchi. These potato-basil babies are sure to please the palate and do the body good!

WHATCHA NEED

1 pound potatoes

3 tablespoons basil, chopped

1/2 teaspoon ground nutmeg

Salt and pepper, to taste

3/4 cup gluten-free white flour

1 small egg, beaten

4 plum tomatoes, halved

1 medium red onion, halved

2 garlic cloves

Basil leaves for garnish

Whatcha Do

Peel and cut potatoes in chunks and boil in slightly salted water for 15–20 minutes or until tender, then drain. Press potatoes through a coarse strainer. Add basil to mixture, then season with nutmeg, salt, and pepper. Stir in flour and add enough egg to make a soft but not sticky dough.

Divide the dough into 4 pieces and roll each piece about 8-inches long and 1-inch wide. Cut each roll into 8 slices. Roll each slice into a ball and press over a floured fork with your thumb, making ridges on one side and an indentation on the other.

Place the tomatoes and onions cut side down onto a baking sheet with the garlic cloves and brush with oil. Broil for 8–10 minutes until the skins are charred. Remove the skins, roughly chop the flesh, and mix.

Bring a large saucepan of water to a boil and cook the gnocchi in batches for 4–6 minutes or until they rise to the surface. Lift out with a slotted spoon.

Serve the gnocchi hot, with the tomato mixture spooned over and garnished with basil leaves.

MAKES 6 SERVINGS

WHATCHA NEED

1 tablespoon olive oil

1 cup arborio rice

2 cups organic veggie stock

Scant $1/2$ cup coconut milk or any milk substitute

8 scallions, thinly sliced

8 ounces young spinach leaves

2 eggs, beaten

2 tablespoons chopped cilantro

Salt and pepper

SPINACH RISOTTO PIE
Dairy Free and Gluten Free

Get a dose of greens with a slice of pie! Gluten-free guests will be psyched you served it, and regular folks will appreciate the taste!

Whatcha Do

Preheat oven to 400°F. Brush a 9-inch round pan with oil and line the bottom with nonstick parchment paper.

Heat 1 tablespoon of oil in a large saucepan, add the rice and cook, stirring for 1 minute. Pour in some of the stock and cook, stirring often, until the liquid is almost absorbed. Continue to add the rest of the stock gradually until the rice is almost tender and there is no liquid. Stir in the coconut milk and scallions and season well. Remove from heat.

Place spinach in a saucepan and heat until the leaves are wilted. Drain spinach, pressing out any liquid. Stir into rice with the beaten eggs and cilantro. Stir the mix into the cake pan, smooth the top, and bake that baby for 25–30 minutes!

Turn out and serve hot or cold, cut like a pie!

What Is Umeboshi?

Umeboshi are dried, pickled ume fruits common in Japan. They are extremely salty with a very sour taste. They are often called plums but are actually in the apricot family. The umeboshi paste is made from the unripe plums that are brined and marinated with beefsteak leaves and used in a variety of dishes because of its versatility. It is believed that umeboshi help alkaline the body and cut acid. And for me they do—indigestion be gone! Eat one of these babies and suck on it for a few minutes after you've eaten the meat off . If you've got gas and bloating issues, open one up and poor one cup of boiling water over it and drink as a tea. When we travel I keep a bottle of condensed plum balls in the car; they taste like sugar-free sweet tarts, and my girls suck on 'em to help with carsickness. They are great for morning sickness, too. Also good to eat after dinner, as a digestive aid!

TOMATO-FREE MARINARA SAUCE
Vegan, Dairy Free, and Gluten Free

This is the sauce that is most excellent for those folks avoiding nightshades. It's so easy to make as you just put it all in a pot and puree. You can also doctor it up with even more herbs!

Whatcha Do

Use carrots and beet for a red sauce. Put big veggies—carrots, beet, 1/2 of the onion, celery, and 3 cloves of garlic in 3 cups of water to boil. Boil until veggies are super soft—about 30 minutes. Puree in blender or use your handheld blending wand in the pot. Add more water if needed to give mixture a tomato-sauce texture.

Heat oil in a pan. Sauté 3 more cloves of garlic, minced onion, and herbs for 5 minutes. Add optional mushrooms and sauté 10 minutes more. Next, add sauce and bring to a boil. Then cover and simmer for an hour—just like real sauce. The longer it cooks together, the better! Season with miso or tamari and add the vinegar. Add kuzu, stirring until thick and shiny. Remove bay leaf before serving.

Serve with any type of brown rice pasta, but be careful not to overcook or undercook the rice. Like all things, when you make this for a while, you'll get a rhythm, and you'll know how you like it.

MAKES 6–8 SERVINGS

WHATCHA NEED

THE BASE

6 carrots, cut in 2-inch pieces

1 small beet, quartered

1 large onion, quartered

1 stalk celery, sliced

3 cloves garlic

3 cups water

THE FLAVOR AND FUN

1–2 teaspoons olive oil

1 teaspoon basil

1 teaspoon oregano

3 cloves garlic

1 onion, minced

1 bay leaf*

1/4 cup Italian parsley, minced

2 tablespoons miso or tamari soy sauce

1 teaspoon umeboshi vinegar**

2 heaping tablespoons kuzu, dissolved in 1/2 cup cool water

1 cup mushrooms, sliced or chopped (optional)—add to sauce for a meaty texture

*Important because it gives the sauce a meaty taste.

**For this, you gotta use your taste buds to get it right, as this ingredient is key to bringing in that tangy tomato flavor

"MEXICAN I AM!" DELECTABLES

I'm always asked, "What nationality are you?" Bella put it into perspective when she said, "Momma, I know we are Italian, but we've never lived there and we have lived in Mexico, so I think we are Mexican, Tennessean, and Californian." I agree—as our family favorites prove it!

RANCHERO SAUCE
Vegan, Dairy Free, and Gluten Free

This sauce rocks! You can use it instead of tomato sauce for pasta dishes, on tacos, and with burritos and enchiladas. Gina Portillo, my Mexican Momma, gets down on this salsa, and I had to find a way to keep it in my real food life.

MAKES 5 CUPS

WHATCHA NEED

2 tablespoons olive oil

1 large onion, chopped

1 large red bell pepper, chopped

1 jalapeno chile, chopped

4 cloves garlic, chopped

1 1/4 teaspoons ground cumin

1 teaspoon sea salt

3/4 teaspoon freshly ground black pepper

1/3 cup tomato paste

1 28-ounce jar diced tomatoes

1 cup vegetable stock or water

1/4 cup packed fresh cilantro leaves

Whatcha Do

Heat up that olive oil in a large, heavy saucepan over medium heat. Add the onion and bell pepper and sauté for 5 minutes or until tender. Add the jalapeno chile, garlic, cumin, salt, and pepper, and sauté 2 minutes longer. Stir in the tomato paste and cook for 2 minutes, stirring often. Add the tomatoes with their juices and the veggie stock. Bring it up to a boil. Turn the heat down to medium-low, cover, and simmer, stirring occasionally for 30 minutes or until all the veggies are tender and liquid has reduced slightly.

Using your handheld wand or regular blender, puree the sauce until smooth. Add the cilantro and blend just until the cilantro is finely chopped. Add more salt if you feel it needs it!

Sauce will keep for two days covered in fridge.

BEAN TACOS
Vegan, Dairy Free, and Gluten Free

WHATCHA NEED

Corn tortillas

Black beans or aduki beans
(see recipes)

Brown rice

Salsa (see recipe)

Guacamole (see recipe)

Whatcha Do

I take a corn tortilla and fill it with black beans (or any bean I have left over), brown rice, salsa, and guacamole. Fold tortilla over filling and eat it! You can heat up the tortillas in a pan, or microwave if you like 'em hot!

RAW TACOS!
Raw, Vegan, Dairy Free, and Gluten Free

WHATCHA NEED

$1/2$ cup almonds (you can also substitute pecans or any other nut)

$1/2$ cup walnuts

1 tablespoon ground cumin

1 tablespoon ground coriander

$1/3$ cup olive oil

$2/3$ teaspoon sea salt

1 teaspoon nama shoyu or coconut aminos

This is the very first raw-food dish I ever made. I was so blown away by how easy it was to make, and of course, by how yummy and similar to tacos it tasted! It's a great dish to serve as an appetizer or to pack up for lunch!

Whatcha Do

In a food processor, process almond and walnuts and put aside in a bowl. Add other ingredients and mix well with a spoon. Keeps for 4–5 days in the fridge. Top with guacamole, tofu or cashew sour cream, and pico de gallo (see recipes)!

SALSA VERDE
Vegan, Dairy Free, and Gluten Free

WHATCHA NEED

1¹/₂ pounds tomatillos, husked, rinsed, and coarsely chopped

1 white onion, coarsely chopped

1 jalapeno chile, coarsely chopped

³/₄ teaspoon sea salt

¹/₄ teaspoon freshly ground black pepper

1 cup coarsely chopped fresh cilantro

A great green salsa!

Whatcha Do

In a large heavy saucepan over medium-heat, combine chopped tomatillos, onion, jalapeno chile, and salt and pepper. Cover and bring to a boil. Reduce heat to medium-low and simmer for 15 minutes or until tomatillos are tender. Add the cilantro and bust out your wand if you have one—if not a blender will do—and blend this baby till smooth!

TOFU SOUR CREAM
Raw, Vegan, Dairy Free, and Gluten Free

WHATCHA NEED

12 ounces organic, vacuum-packed firm silken tofu

2 tablespoons umeboshi vinegar

1 tablespoon olive oil

1 teaspoon dry mustard

¹/₄ teaspoon minced garlic

1 teaspoon dried dill

ALWAYS USE ORGANIC TOFU! Nonorganic soybeans (from which tofu is made) are heavily sprayed with pesticides and are genetically modified. Umeboshi vinegar gives this nondairy sour cream a nice tang, plus it is excellent for digestion as the sour and salty taste stimulate the production of saliva and stomach acids, which help the body break down and assimilate the nutrients. The organic acids in the vinegar help the body to maintain the optimal pH balances. Although the vinegar is acidic, its effects on the body are alkaline.

Whatcha Do

Blend the tofu, vinegar, olive oil, mustard, and garlic in a food processor until smooth. Transfer the tofu sour cream to a container and stir in the dill. Cover and put in the fridge for 2 hours and up to 2 days.

DOWN-HOME MEE-IFIED HEALTHY SOUTHERN COOKIN'

My main goal has been to create yummy food that people will want to eat not because it's good fo' ya, but because it's also so good you crave it! My desire to teach publicly in a southern town inspired me even more to Mee-ify local food choices.

CRANBERRY CHESTNUT STUFFING
Vegan, Dairy Free, and Gluten Free

MAKES ABOUT 4–6 SERVINGS

Whatcha Do

Preheat oven to 350°F. Heat olive oil in a skillet and sauté shallots until transparent and lightly browned. Add cubed bread, chestnuts, cranberries, parsley, salt, and pepper, and sauté 2–3 minutes, combining well. Add soymilk and sauté another 2 minutes. Place in an oiled 9 x 13-inch baking dish and bake, uncovered, for 20 minutes.

WHATCHA NEED

$1/2$ cup olive oil

1 cup minced shallots

6 cups slightly stale gluten-free bread cut into $1/2$-inch cubes

2 cups chestnuts, cooked, peeled, and chopped

1 cup dried cranberries

1 cup fresh chopped parsley

$1^1/2$ teaspoons sea salt

$1/4$ teaspoon white pepper

$2/3$ cup soy milk

MAKES ABOUT 1¼ CUPS

WHATCHA NEED

¼ cup cayenne

¼ cup paprika

¼ cup chili powder

2 tablespoons dried oregano

2 tablespoon sea salt

2 tablespoon dried thyme

½ teaspoon black pepper

¼ teaspoon ground allspice

¼ teaspoon garlic powder

¼ teaspoon ground mace

BLACKENING SPICE—FOR TEMPEH, FISH, OR TOFU
Vegan, Dairy Free, and Gluten Free

Whatcha Do

Mix together all ingredients and store in a recycled jar in a cool dry place. I like to have this on hand so when I'm ready to use it all I have to do is coat my fish, tempeh, or tofu and toss it in the skillet.

MAKES 4 PORTIONS

WHATCHA NEED

¼ cup water

About ½ cup instant cornmeal

½ teaspoon salt

1 teaspoon fresh rosemary, chopped

Olive oil for brushing

CORNMEAL CROUTONS
Vegan, Dairy Free, and Gluten Free

Top your favorite soup with these delicious cornmeal croutons. They are so good and gluten-free, baby! Cornmeal is old school; back in the day, wheat flour was hard to come by to waste on cooking croutons with, so using cornmeal is straight-up, farm-to-table living!

Whatcha Do

Heat the water to a boil, pour in cornmeal, and cook, stirring constantly with a wooden spoon, for 15 minutes or until thickened. Stir in the salt and rosemary. Remove the polenta from the pot and pour it into a rectangular baking dish that has been sprayed with olive oil. Store in the fridge until cooled.

Preheat oven to 450°F. Remove cooled polenta from the fridge and cut it into ½-inch squares, placing them on a cookie sheet coated with olive oil in a single layer so they don't touch. Bake for 25 minutes, turning every 10 minutes until all the croutons are brown and crispy.

MEE'S MAC AND CHEESE
Vegan, Dairy Free, and Gluten Free (Goat Milk option)

Okay, y'all, here it is: the mac and cheese for Mee! One of the best parts of going to culinary school and learning the French and American classics is that I've learned to take these recipes and cook them so that non-dairy eaters and gluten-free folks can enjoy too! I can get down on this traditional favorite, Mee-ified of course!

Whatcha Do

Preheat oven to 325°F. Bring a large pot of salted water to a boil over high heat. Add the pasta and cook, stirring often, for 8 minutes or until tender but firm to the bite. Drain, reserving 3/4 cup of the water.

In a small saucepan melt vegan butter or ghee. Add minced garlic. Stir in brown rice flour, creating a roux. Then add vegan milk or goat milk, cashew cheese, and grated nutmeg into milk mixture. Allow your creamy sauce to thicken by bringing up the heat and stirring continuously. Once the sauce is thick, mix with pasta, season with pepper, and place in a baking pan coated with olive oil. Top with gluten-free breadcrumbs and bake for 15–20 minutes.

If you are able to digest goat milk then add a tablespoon to the sauce along with the cashew!

MAKES 6–8 SERVINGS

WHATCHA NEED

12 ounces gluten-free elbow pasta

16 cups or 4 quarts of water for boiling pasta

1/2 teaspoon of salt

2 1/4 cups melted cashew cheese (see recipe)

2 tablespoons of ghee or vegan butter

1 tablespoon of brown rice flour

1/4 cup of goat milk or vegan milk

Pinch of freshly grated nutmeg

1 clove garlic, minced

1/2 teaspoon freshly ground black pepper

MAKES 4–6 SERVINGS

WHATCHA NEED

4 medium sweet potatoes

2 eggs

1 tablespoon brown rice syrup
(optional)

1/2 cup organic coconut milk

1/4 cup shredded unsweetened
coconut

SWEET POTATO SOUFFLÉ
Vegan, Dairy Free, and Gluten Free

This is something I created in the beginning of my new food journey, as I was determined to find a healthy and supportive pumpkin pie replacement. This is now a winter staple in our house.

Whatcha Do

Preheat oven to 375°F. Scrub sweet potatoes and slice each one into 3 large pieces. Leaving the skin on them, place in a steamer on the stove. It usually takes about 15 minutes until they are totally soft. Check by poking with a fork. While the sweet potatoes are steaming, whip up the eggs in a large mixing bowl and add in your coconut milk. After steaming, peel your sweet potatoes using your fingers. (This is easy peasy!) Using a handheld blender or a mixer, blend together sweet potatoes, whipped eggs, coconut milk, and brown rice syrup. Pour into a glass baking dish, sprinkle shredded coconut on top, and bake for 40 minutes.

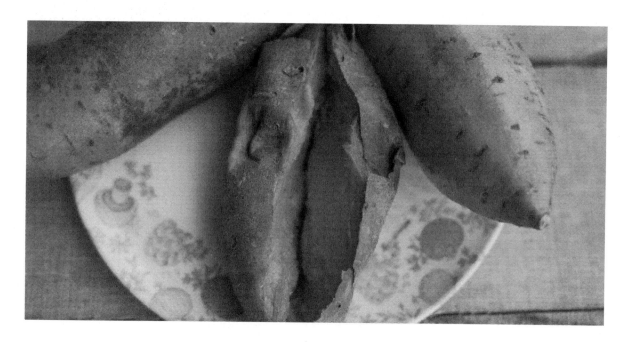

BAKED GOODS!

I was never much of a baker, unless it came out of a box or a roll that you popped open. I suppose I was intimidated and thought it all to be too time consuming. Oh, how I've matured in the kitchen! Below I've put together some of my favorite easy recipes that don't take up time and never hurt my tummy as I know exactly what's in them. (Be mindful with baked goods, whether gluten free or not, that they are still dry and absorb a lot of water from our digestive tracts, water we need to keep things flowing—moderation!)

Flours: So Many More Than Just Wheat!

Here in the U.S. the main flour we choose to use for baked goods is wheat, and as I wrote earlier, it's also the most common allergen. But all over the world, people have been using the flour from different grains and legumes for their baked goods.

- **Spelt** is considered a biblical grain as its use can be traced back to bible times. It has as much protein as high-protein wheat flour and tends to be less of an allergen than wheat flour. I was first introduced to spelt because it is easier to digest and good for those that don't have a wheat allergy but are wheat-sensitive. Spelt gluten can trigger a reaction so be mindful and introduce it in small amounts if you are sensitive. It requires about $3/4$ of the liquid that whole wheat requires in baking.

- **Amaranth flour**. I was first introduced to amaranth while living in Sayulita, Nayarit, Mexico, as its popularity there is great. A benefit of amaranth is that it offers calcium as well as calcium cofactors (minerals that help calcium to be absorbed), and is high in protein. Amaranth adds a slightly spicy, sweet, and nutty flavor to pancakes, waffles, or muffins, and is usually added in small quantities to leavened products; flat breads can have more amaranth (no gluten).

- **Brown rice flour** has a gentle, nutty taste. It is good in piecrusts or pizza crusts and can be used to make cookies, pancakes, and waffles. Health benefits are B vitamins and vitamin E (no gluten). Also an excellent choice for those with digestive distress as it's easy on the GI tract. I use this in my butternut squash pie (see recipe).

- **Buckwheat flour** has a very distinct flavor, almost floral. Mixing it with another grain will dilute the floral taste. The health benefits are more protein than many other grains, and it is typically added to pancakes, waffles, and pasta (no gluten). Peep my blueberry buckwheat pancakes.

- **Cornmeal**, an old-school farm kitchen grain, adds a hearty texture to muffins, breads, and polenta. It's the perfect replacer for bread crumbs as you can coat everything from fish to burgers with it. It contains its bran and germ. Blue cornmeal has a higher protein content than yellow cornmeal (no gluten). See the cornmeal fish recipe.

- **Millet flour** is the least acidic grain and an excellent choice for diabetics. It gives baked goods a subtle taste and works well with other gluten-free flours. For yeast breads, up to 30 percent millet flour may be used. It provides protein, calcium, iron, magnesium, potassium, and phosphorus (no gluten). My sister mixed this with oat flour in her famous strawberry pie (see recipe).

- **Oat flour** also contains its bran and germ, and is often combined with flours that contain gluten to aid rising. However, it does not need to be combined with gluten grains; you can balance it with rising agents. It offers a sweet cakelike crumb that makes it really nice in baked goods. It is naturally gluten free, but can have gluten if it is processed where gluten grains are also processed.

- **Oat bran** is a good source of soluble fiber and makes a good substitute for wheat bran. (Must be marked *gluten free* as it can be cross-contaminated with gluten.)

- **Quinoa flour** also has a nutty taste. It can be used as the sole flour when making crepes, pancakes, cookies, or muffins. It is a complete protein and contains calcium, iron, phosphorus, vitamin E, and lysine (no gluten).

- **Rye flour** also has low gluten content, so breads made with it can be dense but moist. To make rye breads less dense, add some spelt flour or whole wheat flour, if tolerated (gluten).

- **Soy flour** is a good source of protein. It has no gluten; so again, you will need additional flours if using it in a rising recipe (no gluten).

- **Tapioca flour** can be used as a thickener, much like traditional wheat flour. It is a great addition to gluten-free breads, giving them a better texture (no gluten).

- **Teff flour** has a flavor like malted milk and is rich in calcium, protein, and iron. It can be used to thicken soups and sauces as it adds a richness in taste. Combine it in a 1:5 ratio with spelt or wheat so that bread rises (no gluten).

ALMOND FLOUR BREAD
Dairy Free and Gluten Free—Eggs Are Optional

I've asked myself what has happened to "our daily bread," meaning we used to have bread maybe once a day, now we have bread all day long. When we made our own bread, it had value; we savored it and saved it for the next day. Fresh bread is what I missed the most when shifting my relationship with food. Finding fresh gluten-free and dairy-free breads that aren't frozen has been a hard hunt, especially when looking for ones that don't have yeast and don't cost $9 a loaf. This bread is so dang good, and it doesn't have ANY yeast! It's as fast as baking a cake 'cause you don't have to wait for it to rise. I use a 1-pound loaf pan and make this bread early in the morning or pop it in the oven just before starting dinner. It's ready in 45 minutes!

Whatcha Do

Preheat the oven to 350°F. Grease the loaf pan with grape seed oil, coconut oil, or even olive oil or Earth Balance. Then dust it with a little almond flour. (To dust means sprinkle a scoop onto pan, shuffle it around, and dump out what doesn't stick).

In a large bowl, mix the almond butter with a handheld blending wand until smooth, and then add in eggs, blending them together. In a medium bowl, combine the almond flour, arrowroot powder, salt, baking soda, and flax meal. Blend the almond flour mixture into the wet ingredients until thoroughly combined. Pour the batter into your loaf pan and bake for 40 to 45 minutes on the bottom rack of the oven. The time can vary depending on your oven's heat, so check your bread by sticking a knife into the center; when you pull it out and its clear, yo' bread is ready to take out. After baking, let it rest for at least 20 minutes before eating.*

---

*Let your bread sit a little while so that the baking soda and salt can merge; if you don't, it will taste salty.

MAKES 6–8 SERVINGS

WHATCHA NEED

Grapeseed oil, coconut oil, or olive oil to coat pan

1 1/2 cup creamy roasted almond butter—at room temperature; this makes it easy to work with

8 large eggs

1/2 cup blanched almond meal flour

1/4 cup arrowroot powder— this stuff is so good for the intestines, hence the word "root"

1 teaspoon sea salt

1 teaspoon aluminum-free baking soda

2 tablespoons ground flax

MAKES ONE 10-INCH
PIZZA PIE

WHATCHA NEED

1 1/2 cups blanched almond flour

1/4 teaspoon sea salt

1/4 teaspoon baking soda

1 tablespoon grapeseed oil

1 large egg

GREAT PIZZA CRUST
Dairy Free and Gluten Free

This pizza dough is super-easy to make and has only five ingredients! You know exactly what is going down your hatch when whipping up this delicious crust. Kids love making it as much as they do eating it! I love this pizza with my simple tomato sauce (see recipe), caramelized onions (see recipe), and kale. You don't even miss the cheese.

Whatcha Do

Preheat oven to 350°F. Cut two pieces of parchment paper the size of the baking sheet you will use. Combine flour, salt, and baking soda in a large bowl. In a medium bowl, whisk the oil and egg, then stir the wet ingredients into the dry until mixed. Put the dough in between the two pieces of parchment paper and roll with a rolling pin into a 10-inch circle, 1/8-inch thick. Take off the top piece of paper and transfer the bottom piece with the dough onto the baking sheet. Bake for 15–20 minutes, remove, add toppings, and eat pronto!

A Word About Eggs

For the first year on my new healing-with-food journey, I avoided eggs completely. Every time I'd eat anything containing eggs I'd get a tingling sensation in my mouth and a nauseous tummy. I was all about avoiding them, and now that I cook for folks with food allergies, I've mastered the egg replacer!

Egg Replacers (Equivalent to 1 Egg)

If you are baking without eggs, try these easy alternatives!

◆ For desserts or smoothies use 1/2 medium or large banana.

◆ For sweeter recipes use 3 tablespoons to 1/4 cup applesauce.

◆ Use a food processor on high to blend 1/4 cup soft or silken (pureed, pudding-like) tofu. I prefer soft.

◆ For breads and baking, use 1 tablespoon of psyllium seed husks* AND two tablespoons water.

◆ Buy an "egg replacer" found in most health food stores, and use 1 1/2 teaspoons with two tablespoons water.

---

*Psyllium seed husks are soluble fiber. Psyllium helps relieve diarrhea, constipation, and IBS. It helps maintain and improve GI transit. It also helps lower cholesterol and controls diabetes. Can be used in gluten-free baking and helps make the bread crumble less.

OLIVE-ROSEMARY BREAD
Dairy Free and Gluten Free

Scrumptious slices of soft bread, or baked-up in the oven crunchy slices served with your favorite olive oil and vinegar.

Whatcha Do

Preheat oven to 350°F. Grease a loaf pan with olive oil and dust with almond flour.

In a large bowl mix the almond butter and olive oil with a handheld mixer until smooth. Blend in eggs and nectar.

In a medium bowl, combine the almond flour, arrowroot, salt, and baking soda. Blend the dry into the wet until combined and add the olives and rosemary. Pour batter into pan and bake for 45–50 minutes on the bottom rack of oven until a knife poked in the center comes out clean.

Cool for one hour in the pan and then serve.

MAKES 1 LOAF

WHATCHA NEED

$3/4$ cup creamy roasted almond butter

2 tablespoons olive oil

3 large eggs

1 tablespoon brown rice syrup or coconut nectar

$1/4$ cup blanched almond flour

$1/4$ cup arrowroot powder

$1/2$ teaspoon sea salt

$1/2$ teaspoon baking soda

$1/4$ cup kalamata olives, pitted and chopped

1 teaspoon chopped rosemary

2 tablespoons of olive oil for coating baking pan

WHATCHA NEED

$^3/_4$ cups creamy roasted almond butter, room temperature

4 eggs

$^1/_4$ cup blanched almond flour

$^1/_4$ cup arrowroot powder

$^1/_2$ teaspoon sea salt

$^1/_2$ teaspoon baking soda

1 tablespoon ground flax meal

1–2 tablespoons of grapeseed oil for coating pan for baking

BEST BREAD EVER
Dairy Free and Gluten Free

Some gluten-free breads are better than others, and this one is the best one I have come across! No yeast, y'all! Now we are talkin'! Great for the French toast too (see recipe). When it is done, wrap it in a paper towel and store in a plastic bag in fridge. Store all homemade breads this way to make them last up to six days. I love this for sandwiches, too. Once a week I pack it on for my lunch— hummus, avocado, and tomato are my favorites. I also LOVE almond butter sandwiches!

Whatcha Do

Preheat oven to 350°F. Grease loaf pan with grapeseed oil and dust with almond flour.

In a large bowl, mix the almond butter with handheld mixer until smooth, then add eggs and blend.

In a medium bowl, combine almond flour, arrowroot, salt, baking soda, and flax meal. Blend the dry into the wet ingredients until combined.

Pour batter into pan and bake for 40–45 minutes on the bottom rack of oven until a knife poked in the center comes out clean.

Cool for one hour in the pan and then serve.

RED PEPPER CORN BREAD
Dairy Free and Gluten Free

WHATCHA NEED

1 large red bell pepper, seeded and sliced

1 cup fine cornmeal

$3/4$ cup gluten-free, white-bread flour

1 tablespoon gluten-free baking powder

1 teaspoon salt

2 teaspoons sugar

$1^1/4$ cups dairy-free milk

2 eggs, lightly beaten

3 tablespoons olive oil

The best part about southern cooking is that when it's done old school, it's downright good fo'ya!

Whatcha Do

Preheat oven to 400°F. Lightly grease a loaf pan. Arrange the red pepper slices on a baking sheet and roast in the preheated oven for 35 minutes or until tender. Set aside to cool, then peel away the skin.

Mix cornmeal, flour, baking powder, salt, and sugar together in a mixing bowl. Beat the milk, eggs, and oil together in a separate bowl and gradually add to the flour mixture. Beat with a wooden spoon to make a thick batter.

Chop the pepper and mix it into the cornmeal mixture, then spoon into the prepared pan. Bake for 30 minutes. Let cool in the pan for 10 minutes, then run a knife around the edges and turn loaf out onto a wire rack to cool.

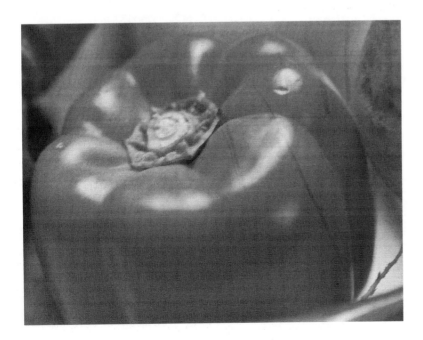

TEAS AND DRINKS

Not only is there a question regarding what we should eat, but what we should drink. I never drink more than 4 ounces of ANYTHING at a time. Dr. Sheng schooled me on this, as this is as much as our bodies are meant to absorb. I never drink with my meals—always after and usually warm tea. And when I drink fresh vegetable juices, I am sure to follow my 4-ounce rule. I sip on water or tea all day. This is most important if you are healing your body or suffering digestive distress.

About Tea Tonic

This tea was the first solution to get me off the couch. I had suffered for so long with constant burning and discomfort that when Ginny told me a simple tea concoction would help get me back on my feet, I found it hard to believe. But since I had decided to take my life back, I went home and made it.

Heads up: this is NOT a yummy tea—it's sort of salty and sour—but once you know it works, your body acquires a taste for it and now I kind of enjoy it! Within three days I was feeling much better. The following week I suffered a huge attack that usually would have sent me to the emergency room until Lee said, "Maybe we should go home and make the tea." I made this tea, and within thirty minutes, the spasms in my intestines stopped. I knew in that very moment that I would leave the land of pain and illness to find my way with a map of recipes and food as my vehicle.

This tea tonic is a combination of:

- **Umeboshi plum**. It is not really a plum so much as an apricot, but more tart and salty, like an olive.

The umeboshi plum is alkaline, balancing acidity in the stomach and blood.

- **Tamari or shoyu soy sauce**. This sauce is fermented soy that calms the digestion and helps with nausea. Like the umeboshi plum, tamari or shoyu soy sauce supports the blood by alkalizing it so that bacteria and viruses cannot live.

- **Twig or kukicha twig tea**. Although this tea is composed of the dark brown, roasted stems from the green tea plant, it contains VERY LITTLE caffeine. In fact, it is a "calming tea"—the taste is super mild yet satisfying.

- **Kuzu**. This serious root is all about balancing the intestinal walls—strengthening or softening them depending on the body's needs. Remember, it must be diluted in cold water to work. The amount of kuzu needed depends on your situation; if you are suffering from a lot of diarrhea, add more; if not, add less.

TEAS

The two main teas I drink are green tea and twig tea. Twig tea, also known as kukicha, is also from the green tea plant, but it is from the twigs and not the leaves; green tea is made from the leaves. Twig tea has substantially less caffeine and is actually seen as more calming and soothing to the nervous system. It is also packed with antioxidants, and big in the macrobiotic food culture.

ALOE VERA

Aloe vera juice has also been the one thing besides water that I still drink everyday. I see it this way: If you have a sunburn, aloe soothes it. Well, it does the same in the intestines, especially if they are inflamed. I see it as my Band-Aid and immune protector. You can make your own or buy it already pureed.

In Mexico I learned to make it myself. It's super easy to do. Buy a leaf, or if you live where there are aloe plants, cut one. Open it up with a knife and be careful to scoop only the clear center. The darker-colored flesh is bitter, and the clear is almost tasteless. I mix it in with a smoothie or add a little water and drink it straight. Two to four ounces at least twice a day during digestive distress, and once a day normally.

TEA TONIC
Vegan, Dairy Free, and Gluten Free

This tea combo is great for fighting oncoming colds and flus, as well as traveler's diarrhea. This tonic is also good for hangovers, but leave out the kuzu.

Whatcha Do

Allow twig tea to sit for 10 minutes, then pour it into a saucepan and bring to a gentle boil. Add the umeboshi and soy sauce. Then add in your kuzu to thicken the drink, making sure to stir often so the kuzu doesn't lump up. I keep this in a hot thermos and drink until my symptoms subside—sipping at times through the night! If it is for a cold or flu, drink once or twice a day for up to three days.

MAKES 1 SERVING

WHATCHA NEED

1 tea bag or tea ball of twig tea, made according to package directions

1/2 umeboshi plum, chopped up

1 teaspoon tamari or shoyu soy sauce

1/2 teaspoon kuzu,* diluted in 1/4 cup cold water

*If you've got runny shadoobies, add more kuzu.

MAKES 3 SERVINGS

WHATCHA NEED

$1/4$ cup grated carrot

$1/4$ cup chopped cabbage

$1/4$ cup chopped pumpkin
or squash

$1/4$ cup chopped large onion

4 cups water

SWEET VEGETABLE DRINK
Vegan, Dairy Free, and Gluten Free

*This drink is what helped me get off sugar, and it is yummy, too!
I keep it in the refrigerator for whenever the sugar calls my name.
Then I heat up a mug and sip. IT'S AMAZING!*

Whatcha Do

Add water to your grated and chopped vegetables and bring
to boil. Reduce heat and simmer for about 20 to 30 minutes.
Strain and drink only the liquid. You can eat the veggies too,
and store the broth in a covered container in the fridge so you
have it for a couple days. Be sure to drink a cup of broth at least
once a day, but the more times the better!

MAKES 6–8 SERVINGS

WHATCHA NEED

1 pot boiling water (enough to
fill an average-sized teapot)

$1^1/2$ teaspoons brown
rice syrup

1 large handful of cleaned
mint leaves—stems attached

TAY NANA!
Vegan, Dairy Free, and Gluten Free

*One of the best parts of living in Israel was meeting "Tay Nana."
After every meal in Israel, folks gather around to sit and talk while
aiding their digestion! Tay Nana is simply boiled water and fresh
mint leaves. Of course, folks love to sweeten this with sugar, but I
use brown rice syrup instead. The mint is calming and cooling,
while the hot water eases the digestive tract.*

Whatcha Do

Pour water into a clay or ceramic teapot and add brown rice
syrup. Mix it well, then add the mint leaves. I usually let it all
soak for about 10 minutes and serve it in tiny little coffee cups
or my favorite glass Moroccan-style tea set. Refrigerate leftover
tea and serve as a nice cool refresher, with or without ice, to
drink in the middle of the day. KIDS LOVE IT!

TURMERIC COCONUT MILK LATTE— INFLAMMATION FIGHTER!
Vegan, Dairy Free, and Gluten Free

Fighting inflammation is a big part of my daily routine. I'd long heard of an Indian milk tea made with turmeric, and then a few weeks ago I was out to lunch at a place called Hugo's—they serve amazing health-supporting cuisine—and on their hot beverage list I spotted turmeric latte. It was fantastic, and "those people" sucked it down. The real beauty is I had a terrible headache that afternoon, which was causing an upset tummy. A half hour after drinking the tea I felt 1,000 times better.* This morning I set out to replicate the tea, using fresh ginger, freshly grated turmeric, cardamom, nutmeg, cinnamon, and a splash of honey. Of course I'm dairy free, so I combined fresh almond milk with a quarter cup of coconut. Three more words: OFF THE HOOK! This is so creamy, rich, and YUMMY— kids are gonna flip fo' it!

---

*This tea is also excellent for preventing and fighting colds, flus, auto-immune diseases, cancer, joint issues, and so forth. It is recommended that you drink this upwards of twice a day.

MAKES 3 SERVINGS

WHATCHA NEED

2 cups almond milk*

1 cup coconut milk (the canned Native Foods brand contains no BPA or any additives)

1 cup of water

1 tablespoon fresh grated ginger (dried is okay, too)

1 tablespoon fresh grated turmeric (dried is okay, too)

Pinch of nutmeg

Pinch of cinnamon

Pinch of cardamom

*You can skip the almond milk and coconut milk and use just water, too—it's not as rich. If you like the taste of cloves, add a dash.

Whatcha Do

Combine almond milk, water, and coconut milk in a saucepot. Grate in or add your turmeric and ginger, add in dried spices, and simmer for 15 minutes. Turn mixture off and let it sit with a lid on it. Then pour tea through a tea strainer and serve. You can make a large pot and store in the refrigerator to be heated later.*

---

*Extras can be added to mashed sweet potatoes, too!

MAKES 2 SERVINGS

WHATCHA NEED

1 cup organic unstrained
apple juice

1 tablespoon kuzu, diluted
in $1^1/_2$ cups cold water

APPLE-KUZU DRINK
Vegan, Dairy Free, and Gluten Free

My girls LOVE this HOT COCOA replacement, and so do I! The combination of apples and kuzu calms the nervous system and the intestines. Known to calm hyperactive children, this is a must for all mamas and papas! This apple-kuzu drink is also known to fight fevers in little people as well as adults. If my girls start to come down with something, I serve this little drink up!

Whatcha Do

Bring apple juice to just under a boil, then pour in the diluted kuzu, stirring constantly to avoid lumps. Serve in tiny little coffee or teacups—carefully, because it's HOT!

MAKES 2–4 SERVINGS

WHATCHA NEED

2 cups beet juice
(3–4 medium beets)

1 cup orange juice

1 cup apple or pear juice

1 cinnamon stick

Pinch cayenne

$^1/_4$ cup agave (optional)

2 cups chopped fruit (apples,
oranges, limes, or melon)

RED BEET SANGRIA
Raw, Vegan, Dairy Free, and Gluten Free

This juice is off the chain; not only a five-star thirst quencher but a five-star blood-pressure reducer! The decrease in blood pressure is due to the chemical formation of nitrate from the dietary nitrate in the juice.

Whatcha Do

Mix it all up in a big ol' glass jug, add chopped fruit of your choice, and stir. Allow marinating and chilling for 30 minutes in fridge.

LEMON WATER AND CUCUMBER WATER
Vegan, Dairy Free, and Gluten Free

Yep, that old tale you've been told about a cup of warm water with a wedge of freshly squeezed lemon is true. This drink helps alkalinize the body first thing in the morning when it is most needed and aids in getting things moving! Both cucumbers and lemons are alkaline-aiding in reducing inflammation and balancing acid in the body. They are also hydrating and known to lower blood pressure. It only makes sense to add them to water because they detox and cleanse our bodies. Not to mention how yummy and cooling they are on a hot summer day or after a workout. I also serve lemon water at all of my Real Food Makeovers.

Whatcha Do

For lemon water or cucumber water, put slices into the pitcher of water and let sit a few minutes. Lemon water is alkalizing. Cucumbers are cooling to heat or inflammation in the body. And in the summer time, combining cucumber and lemon water is YUMMY for a great alkaline cocktail!

MAKES 6–8 SERVINGS

WHATCHA NEED

FOR LEMON WATER

1-gallon pitcher of water

3 lemons, washed and sliced into round circles

FOR CUCUMBER WATER

1-gallon pitcher of water

1 cucumber, sliced into round circles. (Do not peel as the skin is packed with vitamin C.)

Ginger Compress—A Serious Life Saver
(Not a Drink, but for Certain a Remedy!)

Ginger is a circulator—it moves things around. When healing ulcerations, stagnant gas, or blocked passageways, circulation is key. In fact, everyone who is going through some type of physical healing should take a look at ginger compresses. The belief is that when the intestines are full of stagnating mucus, the body can't receive nutrition via the intestinal villi. A ginger compress moves the blood and aids the regeneration of the cells. If you have ulcerations in the intestinal tract and are trying to use a diet change to clean your blood, ginger compresses help bring clean blood to the wound and heal it much more quickly.*

Before proceeding with instructions and treatment, take two terry cloth towels and fold each one in three folds, so that they cover the area on your abdomen that goes from the sternum of the rib cage to the pelvic bone and from one hip bone to the other. Once you have done this, sew each one along the loose edges to prevent them from falling open once you start the treatment.

Also, the treatment has to be done on an empty stomach, either an hour before you eat or two hours after you eat. It can be done at any time of day. However, a practical tip is to do the first treatment just before you go to bed. That night, leave the materials where they are after treatment. First thing in the morning, reheat the ginger water pot, making sure you do not actually boil the water, and then do the treatment again. If you proceed this way, you can do two treatments using the same ginger water.

If you use a gallon container, the ginger water should retain its heat long enough to do at least two treatments. If you want to ensure the ginger water remains hot, buy a hot plate and plug it into an electrical outlet near the place you choose to do the treatment.

---

*If you suffer from cancer, this is not recommended because some believe that the ginger compress would increase the blood flow to the tumor, aiding in its growth.

WHATCHA NEED

1 cup grated ginger with the skin left on

1 gallon saucepan boiling water

2 to 3 layers of cheesecloth cut into squares, large enough to wrap around the ball of grated ginger. Once it's done I call it a ginger ball, and I use a rubber band to seal it, or tie it in a knot with string.

1 pair of stainless-steel salad or cooking tongs

2 small towels

Whatcha Do

Bring 1 gallon of water to a boil and then drop in the ginger ball. Lower the heat, let simmer, and then turn off fire, allowing the ginger water to steep for 10 minutes. I also like to place 2 small washcloths or rags in the steeping water. After 10 minutes, ring out the washcloths/rags into pot, place a towel on the abdomen then the steeped washcloth/rag on top of that. Cover with the second towel to hold in the heat. Once it has cooled off, remove and use second washcloth/rag in the same manner. Return the used washcloth/rag to the pot to use over again. I do this treatment for 15 or 20 minutes.

The main purpose of this treatment is to bring circulation to the area. When I have gas and inflammation, this helps BIG time and has moved me through partial obstructions.

Nondairy Milks

Changing my milk intake from cow to alternative milk drinks wasn't hard at all. Even my little girls, who were hardcore cow-milk lovers, took to rice and almond milk. What I did have a problem with was finding one of these alternative milks that didn't include carrageenan. So I got in the kitchen and made my own! Peep how easy they are—and a perfect way to avoid any and all preservatives.

ALMOND MILK
Vegan, Dairy Free, and Gluten Free

When I lived in the jungle I was told by a man they call the "Frog Doctor" that I was in serious health danger and the best thing to do was change my diet to a plant-based, easy-to-digest meal plan. He thought almond milk was a great place to start as almonds are PACKED with nutrition.

Well, down there, almond milk was nowhere to be found on market shelves, so I soaked a cup of almonds, pinched the skin off in the morning, and ground them up, adding water, dates for sweetener, and vanilla. I ran the almond milk through cheesecloth, but you can use a tiny mesh strainer (I didn't have one then). My entire family LOVED it—seriously rich and yummy like a desert! So last week I was in Malibu, and there is a juice truck that sits in the park at Cross Creek. They sell small bottles of fresh-pressed almond milk—for $8 bucks a pop! I bought one, fell back in love, and immediately upon returning to Nashville made my own. However, this time I skipped the skin removal and blended it all up—grant it, this makes it a little more grainy, but it's super satisfying! Peep it y'all!

WHATCHA NEED

1 cup of raw, soaked almonds*

7–8 cups fresh, clean drinking water

6 dates**

2 tablespoons vanilla or fresh vanilla bean

*Soak overnight or for 24 hours or more for better absorption/digestion of nutrition; add a 2-inch piece of kombu seaweed to boost trace minerals. I chop up the kombu and put it in the blender with everything else. If you are someone who can't eat sea veggies then leave it out all together.

**Soaked in the 7–8 cups water; remove pits when soft and pour all into blender or Vitamix.

Whatcha Do

Blend all ingredients in blender, then pour through strainer into serving pitcher; I strain it a few times to remove the graininess. Drink or use to cook or bake. Right now I've added it to my brown rice breakfast cereal with apples and raisins!

MAKES 5 PINTS

WHATCHA NEED

1 cup uncooked organic
long-grain brown rice

2-inch piece kombu seaweed

8 cups water for cooking

1 vanilla bean—or 2 tablespoons
organic vanilla extract

6 pitted organic dates—
if you want to sweeten it

1 teaspoon salt

Additional water for diluting,
if desired

5 1-pint glass mason jars
for storage

BROWN RICE MILK
Vegan, Dairy Free, and Gluten Free

This is great if you are on a healing diet and having a hard time digesting fats or suffer from nut allergies. Making your own makes it easy to avoid all those extra and not so healthy ingredients.

Whatcha Do

Thoroughly wash the rice and soak for 20 minutes, adding in kombu. Put 8 cups of water in a big pot and bring it to a boil over high heat. Pour in the rice along with kombu. Cover the pot and lower the heat to let the water simmer. Cook for 3 hours. You'll end up with something that looks like a soupy rice pudding. Add the salt.

In batches, fill your blender halfway with the rice mixture and halfway with water.* Blend until very smooth. Strain twice through a fine-mesh strainer—I prefer a nut bag—into a mason jar. Continue on with the rest of the milk until you're finished, filling jars and screwing the lids on good and tight.

Even with the extra water, the homemade rice milk ends up thicker than the product you might be used to if you've always purchased Rice Dream rice milk. It's more like rice cream! You may want to dilute it further at the time of serving it. Just add a bit more water until it's the desired consistency.

*You can blend the kombu along with the rice or remove it.

Canned Coconut Milk

Choose fresh coconut milk over canned whenever possible. The only canned coconut milk that is free of BPA is Native Forest. Bisphenol-A (BPA) is a chemical that has been used in consumer goods since the 1950s. Animal studies and cell-culture research has linked low-level estrogenic activity, which is associated with BPA exposure, to all kinds of "fun" stuff like diabetes, ADHD, heart disease, infertility, and cancer. This chemical is found not only in canned goods but also in reusable drink containers, DVDs, cell phones, eyeglass lenses, food containers,

COCONUT MILK
Vegan, Dairy Free, and Gluten Free

MAKES 6 SERVINGS

WHATCHA NEED

4 cups water

1 1/2–2 cups unsweetened
coconut flakes

The health benefits of fresh coconut milk are through the roof; it's always an excellent choice. It's high in saturated fatty acids and medium-chain triglycerides (MCT), both of which are easily burned as fuel by the body. I have a hard time breaking down fats in my intestines so fresh coconut milk is super easy on me. MCTs are particularly beneficial in that they don't require bile acids for digestion, and they're directly thrust to the liver via the portal vein.

Whatcha Do

Heat water until hot (but not boiling). Add shredded coconut and water to blender (preferably a Vitamix!). If all the water won't fit, you can add it in two batches. Blend on high for several minutes until thick and creamy. Pour through a colander to filter out the coconut pulp, and then squeeze through cheesecloth or a nut bag (my favorite)* to filter the smaller pieces of coconut.

If you separated the water into two batches, put the strained coconut back into the blender with the second batch of water. Drink immediately or store in the fridge. Fresh coconut milk should be used within 3–4 days of making it for the best flavor and texture.

*You can order a reusable nut bag online.

baby bottles, some liquid juice cartons, automobile parts, and sports equipment. One of the highest sources of BPA are cash register receipts—a great reason to leave the paper train behind!

Guar gum is an additive that is found in all canned coconut milks. It is known to irritate the digestive tract and cause bloating and gas. If you are healing your gut or experiencing digestive distress, then be sure to avoid the guar gum by passing on the coconut milk. There are currently no brands of canned coconut milk that are free of both BPA and guar gum.

Smooth Smoothies for Smooth Moves

All of my smoothies are dairy free; however, feel free to add whatever you want. My goal is to get you blending, and then you can allow your creativity to take over! The difference between juicing and blending your vegetables and fruits is that you do not lose all the fiber. Pure juicing removes the fiber; that's why some folks prefer smoothies. I like both!

MAKES 3–4 SERVINGS

WHATCHA NEED

Scant 1 cup whole
blanched almonds

2$\frac{1}{2}$ cups almond milk or
any dairy-free milk

2 ripe bananas

1 teaspoon natural
vanilla extract

$\frac{1}{2}$ teaspoon cinnamon

$\frac{1}{2}$ teaspoon cacao

Ground cinnamon, for
sprinkling

ALMOND AND BANANA SMOOTHIE
Raw, Vegan, Dairy Free, and Gluten Free

Now here is a treat with benefits! This smoothie is packed with protein and potassium, and the topper, cinnamon, is a natural antibiotic. Toss in a teaspoon of cacao, and you get more anti-oxidants than a cup of green tea!

Whatcha Do

Finely chop the almonds in a food processor. Add milk, bananas, cacao, and vanilla and blend until smooth and creamy.

Pour into glasses and sprinkle with cinnamon.

BLUEBERRY-LAVENDER SMOOTHIE
Raw, Vegan, Dairy Free, and Gluten Free

WHATCHA NEED

5 cups organic blueberries,
fresh or frozen

2 cups almond milk

1 handful spinach

1 tablespoon brown rice syrup

1 tablespoon dried lavender

1 teaspoon vanilla

Pinch of salt

When I was pregnant with both of my babies I was addicted to lavender. I carried a bottle around hooting on it all day. Once I found this smoothie I was HOOKED, as it is packed full of cancer fighters and inflammation reducers—bring on those blueberries, baby! Toss in the antioxidant-, mineral-, and vitamin-rich spinach to get that extra kick in nutritional value and the lavender to aid in calming and soothing the body. Perfect treat to kick back and relax. Great for kids, too!

Whatcha Do

Throw it all in the blender at once and smooth!

PEAR AND ARUGULA SMOOTHIE
Vegan and Gluten Free

WHATCHA NEED

1 cup freshly squeezed
orange juice

2 cups arugula, tightly packed

2 tablespoons walnuts or
pecans, or your favorite nut

1 ripe pear, cored and peeled*

2 quarter-size pieces of
fresh ginger, peeled

4 tablespoons plain low-fat
yogurt (Can be omitted
if you are dairy free.)

6 ice cubes

This smoothie is a surprise! The arugula gives it a fresh taste, and the pear adds sweetness and perfume. This drink is best enjoyed right away.

Whatcha Do

Put everything in a blender and blend away for a full minute.

*If you can, get Comice pears, as they are wonderfully fragrant.

PINEAPPLE-KALE SMOOTHIE
Vegan, Dairy Free, and Gluten Free

WHATCHA NEED

1 cup fresh pineapple, chopped

1 medium apple, cored

2 cups kale, chopped

4–6 ounces filtered water

Whatcha Do

Toss the ingredients in your blender or Vitamix. Add a little ice if you want it extra cold—but no ice if you are suffering digestive distress. (Cold is hard on the intestines.) A pinch of apple juice will sweeten the smoothie, if you'd like.

Kale Makes A Great Smoothie!

Kale has a slightly stronger flavor than baby spinach, so if you are not used to green smoothies, you might want to include strongly flavored fruit, such as strawberries or pineapples, to help mask the flavor. You can also slowly introduce kale into your smoothie recipes and increase the amount to two cups per recipe over time. Kale has a firmer texture than spinach as well, so you might need to blend your shake slightly longer if you are not using a high-end Vitamix or Blendtec blender. I am a fortunate girl as I own a Vitamix, but if you don't have one, you can just blend longer on your regular blender.

How to Select Kale

When buying your kale be sure to pick deeply colored green leaves that are firm and do not show signs of wilting, yellowing, or browning. Kale is available year-round. Since kale ranks highly for pesticide residue (ranking 69 out of 100) according to research conducted by the Environmental Working Group, I recommend that you use organic kale whenever possible.

ORANGE-PEACH-KALE SMOOTHIE
Vegan, Dairy Free, and Gluten Free

I just bought some yummy peaches at the farmers market, so while they are in season, I'll be making this smoothie.

Whatcha Do

Toss the ingredients in your blender or Vitamix. Add a little ice if you want it extra cold—but no ice if you are suffering digestive distress. (Cold is hard on the intestines.) A pinch of apple juice will sweeten the smoothie, if you'd like.

MAKES 1 SERVING

WHATCHA NEED

1 orange, peeled

2 medium peaches, pitted

2 cups kale, chopped

4–6 ounces filtered water

BANANA-ORANGE-KALE SMOOTHIE
Vegan, Dairy Free, and Gluten Free

Whatcha Do

Toss the ingredients in your blender or Vitamix. Add a little ice if you want it extra cold—but no ice if you are suffering digestive distress. (Cold is hard on the intestines.) A pinch of apple juice will sweeten the smoothie, if you'd like.

WHATCHA NEED

1 medium banana, peeled

1 orange, peeled

1/2 teaspoon fresh ginger, grated

2 cups kale, chopped

4–6 ounces of filtered water

Juicing, Baby!

I'm not talking about fruit juice that is pure sugar; I'm talking about juicing veggies and eating a diet high in fiber. You see, everyone's first "I KNOW IT ALL" moment is when I tell him or her to add in veggie juicing. They say, "Oh, I heard it's too cooling to the body," or "It is too much sugar," or "But you've removed all the fiber." Well, yes, if all you are doing is juicing, of course. But the point is moderation and balance. Eat REAL food in its whole form, and all is good. I was slow to get on the juicing movement; in fact, I wish I'd known two years ago what I understand now regarding juicing. Having suffered a digestive disease, juicing is the best POSSIBLE thing for me to do while I'm undergoing digestive dis-ease. I put

full-on healing properties into my body instead of apple juice, milkshakes, and other things that lack powerhouse nutrients and anti-inflammatory ingredients. Now when I feel like my intestinal muscle needs a break, I give it one without starving myself.

You can't screw up juices. Use whatever you have in the fridge and it's a great way to not waste costly produce. On Sundays I make a batch of whatever I've got left in my fridge, including parsley, mint, cilantro. Hook it up and create your own combos!

Juicing is best in the morning; I make a large mason jar of juice and then drink it at three different times throughout the day. Be sure to seal the jar well and store it in the fridge.

GREEN LEMONADE
Vegan, Dairy Free, and Gluten Free

Kids love it. So maybe they won't eat the kale or collards, but they sure will drink em', especially if you allow them to be part of the process.

Whatcha Do

Wash everything and cut into sections where needed. Juice the apples and set aside. Juice everything else together and combine with the apple juice when done. Stir and enjoy! This delicious cocktail is a lean, green, healing machine.* Fresh-squeezed vegetable juice can work miracles in the treatment of any disease. The raw power of juice builds new healthy tissue, purifies the blood, removes waste from the large intestine, and rejuvenates the endocrine system.

*People with chronic, debilitating disease should undertake first-time juice therapy under the care of a qualified medical professional. There are tons of juicing books out there that believe that specific juices aid in healing and supporting different issues in the body. The recipes here are some good ones to get you started! They are not medicine replacements, but body supporters instead.

MONEY-SAVING TIP: You can purchase bulk-packaged vegetables from warehouse markets and food co-ops.

WHATCHA NEED

2 green apples—or red

4 stalks celery

8 stalks bok choy*

1/4 pound spinach

1 bunch parsley**

*Kale can be used in place of bok choy; in fact, I love kale in juices, as it's a smooth flavor. Cabbage can be used also, and cabbage is sweeter than carrots!

**I add one peeled lemon to tart up the parsley. You can also use cucumbers as they are cooling.

WHATCHA NEED

3 medium-sized carrots
(6 ounces)

1 large and 1 small celery stalk
(3 ounces)

3 ounces pineapple,
peeled

1/4 large lemon, peeled
(1 ounce)

ARTHRITIS-RELIEVING JUICE
Vegan, Dairy Free, and Gluten Free

This juice is great for reducing pain and inflammation associated with arthritis.

Whatcha Do

Cut all veggies into chunks and put through your juicer.

WHATCHA NEED

Juice of 1 lemon*

1 cup hot water

ACNE-FIGHTING JUICE
Vegan, Dairy Free, and Gluten Free

Fresh lemon juice purifies the blood by removing metabolic waste and by changing blood pH from acid to alkaline. Oh, and it also frees up yo' shadoobies, too, so if you need help getting un-constipated, this is your ticket!

Whatcha Do

Drink first thing in the morning on an empty stomach to battle that acne, shawty!

IRON-RICH JUICE
Vegan, Dairy Free, and Gluten Free

A fantastic juice for overcoming anemia. This is something I drank a lot of. Anemia is serious, and while I was getting iron transfusions from the hospital, I drank this juice to help my body along the way.

Whatcha Do

Cut all veggies into chunks and put through your juicer.

WHATCHA NEED

3 medium-sized carrots (6 ounces)

2 small beets or a 2-ounce piece of a larger beet

1 large celery stalk (2 ounces)

4 large leaves lettuce (2 ounces)

$1/4$ medium-large apple (2 ounces)

ALLERGY-RELIEF JUICE
Vegan, Dairy Free, and Gluten Free

Be proactive and support your body; prevent allergies or help to lessen the symptoms.

Whatcha Do

Cut all veggies into chunks and put through your juicer. Drink this anytime you want to feel relief from those annoying allergies! This is a great treatment for reducing inflammation and swelling of the nose, ears, and sinuses.

WHATCHA NEED

3 medium-sized carrots (6 ounces)

1 large celery stalk (2 ounces)

2-ounce piece pineapple, peeled

1 small beet or a 1-ounce piece of a larger beet

DESSERTS!

I love a yummy sweet, and once and in a while, I get my treat on. Now I'm mindful of how much sugar is going into my body I try to use low glycemic choices. Making my own desserts at home keeps me from sampling little bits of unhealthy bites when I'm out on the town.

MAKES I DOZEN

WHATCHA NEED

4 cups blanched almond flour

$1/4$ teaspoon baking soda

$1/4$ teaspoon salt

$1/3$ cup melted coconut oil

$1/2$ teaspoon coconut extract

$1/2$ cup brown rice syrup

2 eggs

1 tablespoon almond butter

$1/2$ cup raisins

$1/2$ cup coconut flakes

$1/2$ cup pecan pieces (optional)

ALMOND-COCONUT BUTTER COOKIES
Dairy Free and Gluten Free

I'm always in search of a quick, gluten-free, dairy-free, and low-sugar cookie! While hangin' out with my DFF (dear family friend) for our monthly week of cooking, we found this recipe online. The original called for butter, peanut butter, and honey. I swapped the butter for coconut oil and almond butter for peanut butter, and we used brown rice syrup instead of honey—brown rice syrup is easier for our bodies to process as it assimilates into our bloodstream slowly. We whipped these up in less than ten minutes!

Whatcha Do

Preheat oven to 350°F. Use two bowls: In a large bowl mix the dry ingredients, and in a small bowl mix the wet ingredients (including almond butter). Blend wet ingredients with a handheld blending wand. Fold wet ingredients into dry. Blend by hand until smooth. Add the raisins, coconut flakes, and pecans. Make dough into small balls. Place 'em on your cookie sheet and bake for 12 to 18 minutes, depending on size of cookies.

APPLE SOOTHY KUZU PIE
Vegan, Gluten Free, and Healing!

This is so yummy I can't believe it's so good for me—the combination of apples and kuzu are a natural calmer! I like making this pie in the wintertime. It's a great cold-weather treat and easy to serve up for guests!

Whatcha Do

Peel, core, and slice the apples. Heat pan and add ghee to saucepan with raisins, cinnamon, and two cups of water. Bring to a boil, cover, and simmer for 10–15 minutes, until apples are tender. Dissolve kuzu in cold water/apple juice mixture, add into pan, and stir until thick. For a cobbler taste and crunch, I top mine with ground flax!

MAKES 4 SERVINGS

WHATCHA NEED

4 apples

1 teaspoon ghee (optional; or use Earth Balance, coconut oil, or no oil)

1/4 cup raisins

1 tablespoon cinnamon

2 cups water or juice

1 heaping tablespoon kuzu

1 cup water and apple juice, mixed 50/50

2 teaspoons ground flax seeds

WHATCHA NEED

CAKE

1 generous cup gluten-free all-purpose flour

1 teaspoon gluten-free baking powder

Pinch of salt

$1/4$ cup organic sugar

6 tablespoons dairy-free milk

2 eggs, lightly beaten

$3/4$ cup dairy-free butter

2 bananas, mashed

FROSTING

$1/4$ cup vegan cream cheese

2 tablespoons dairy-free butter

$1/4$ teaspoon ground cinnamon

1 cup confectioners' sugar

BANANA CAKES WITH CINNAMON FROSTING
Dairy Free and Gluten Free

Even if you're not completely gluten free, but paying attention to how much wheat you're eating, give these beauties a whirl! You're using bananas, which are packed with natural sugar and major sweetness—in fact, you can cut the added sugar and toss in another banana! These cakes are super easy to whip up, and you don't need a lot of ingredients to make them completely from scratch. The frosting is off the chain! I've never tasted a dairy-free frosting so good.

Whatcha Do

Cake:

Preheat oven to 400°F. Place 8 large paper liners in a deep muffin pan. In a mixing bowl, sift the flour, baking powder, and salt, then stir in the sugar. Beat the milk, eggs, and butter together in a separate bowl until combined. Slowly stir in the flour mixture without beating. Fold in the mashed bananas. Spoon the mixture into the paper liners and bake in the preheated oven for 20 minutes until risen and golden. Turn out onto a wire rack and let cool.

Frosting:

To make the frosting, beat the cream cheese and butter together in a bowl, then beat in the cinnamon and confectioners' sugar until smooth and creamy. Chill the frosting in the fridge for 15 minutes to firm it up, and then top each cake with a dollop!

BANANA CHIA PUDDING
Raw, Vegan, Dairy Free, and Gluten Free

Chia seeds are amazing! Serving up a pudding like this to your kids beats the mess out of one from a box, especially when you KNOW what's in it!

Whatcha Do

Blend all ingredients except for chia seeds in a blender at high speed until smooth, making a cashew crème. Pour crème over chia seeds and allow to soak for at least 30 minutes, and up to 2 hours or more, until the chia becomes a tapioca consistency.

You can add fresh or dried fruit and nuts for a delicious breakfast!

MAKES 4–6 SERVINGS

WHATCHA NEED

$1/_2$ cup chia seeds

1 cup cashews

1 cup water

1 cup mashed banana

1 cup honey

1 tablespoon cinnamon

$1/_4$ teaspoon nutmeg

$1/_4$ teaspoon ginger

1 teaspoon vanilla

1 vanilla bean, scraped

$1/_4$ teaspoon salt

Amazing Chia Seeds

Chia is an edible seed that comes from the desert plant *Salvia hispanica,* a member of the mint family that grows abundantly in southern Mexico. You may have seen chia sprouts growing on the novelty planters called Chia Pets, but historically, the seeds have been the most important part of the plant. In pre-Columbian times they were a main component of the Aztec and Mayan diets and were the basic survival ration of Aztec warriors. I've read that one tablespoon was believed to sustain an individual for twenty-four hours. The Aztecs also used chia medicinally to stimulate saliva flow and to relieve joint pain and sore skin.

Chia is very rich in omega-3 fatty acids, even more so than flax seeds. And it has another advantage over flax: chia is so rich in antioxidants that the seeds don't deteriorate and can be stored for long periods without becoming rancid. And, unlike flax, they do not have to be ground to make their nutrients available to the body. Chia seeds also provide fiber (25 grams give you 6.9 grams of fiber) as well as calcium, phosphorus, magnesium, manganese, copper, iron, molybdenum, niacin, and zinc.

Another advantage: when added to water and allowed to sit for 30 minutes, chia forms a gel. Researchers suggest that this reaction also takes place in the stomach, slowing the process by which digestive enzymes break down carbohydrates and convert them into sugar.

MAKES 10 MUFFINS

WHATCHA NEED

2 cups blanched almond flour

$1/2$ teaspoon sea salt

$1/2$ teaspoon baking soda

$1/4$ cup arrowroot powder

1 teaspoon ground cinnamon

$1/4$ cup grapeseed oil

$1/2$ cup agave nectar
(you can cut the amount
of agave to $1/4$ cup)

1 large egg

1 tablespoon vanilla extract

2 medium apples, peeled, cored,
and diced into $1/4$-inch cubes

CINNAMON APPLE MUFFINS
Dairy Free and Gluten Free

These muffins are a great afterschool snack with a medium sweetness. I use agave sweetener here, and if you like you can cut it to half the amount, and they will still be a yummy treat!

Whatcha Do

Preheat oven to 350°F. Line 10 muffin cups with liners. In a large bowl combine the almond flour, salt, baking soda, arrowroot powder, and cinnamon. In a medium bowl, whisk together the oil, nectar, egg, and extract. Stir the wet ingredients into the almond flour mixture until combined then add the apples.

Spoon the batter into the cups and bake for 30–35 minutes until golden brown. Check with a toothpick for doneness (it should come out clean), and let cool in the pan for 30 minutes.

The Skinny on Agave

Agave nectar is a great alternative to sugar in most recipes that call for sugar. It holds up well with baking and it does not substantially raise glycerin levels as sugar and other sweeteners do. Agave is the actual nectar of the agave plant—a golden liquid available at health food stores, and now a lot of non-health food stores are starting to carry it due to its low level on the glycemic index. It comes in dark, amber, and light color. The light mostly resembles sugar in taste when baking. Purchasing it by the gallon gives you the best deal! Agave nectar is an excellent sugar replacement. Replacing sugar with honey is not a good swap in my opinion. Honey is more like a flavor, where agave is a sweetener and #1 choice for sweetener in my recipes!

Peep this Glycemic Index Chart:

Sugar 58.90

Maple Syrup 54.10

Honey 52.11

Agave Nectar 32.12

CHOCOLATE-AVOCADO MOUSSE MARTINIS WITH FRESH RASPBERRIES
Raw, Vegan, and Gluten Free

MAKES 4–6 SERVINGS

WHATCHA NEED

2 large ripe avocados

1/2 cup organic unsweetened cocoa powder*

1/4 cup coconut cream (the white cream when you open a can of coconut milk)**

1/2 cup agave nectar, plus more to taste

1/2 teaspoon pure vanilla extract

1/2 teaspoon almond extract

1/2 pint fresh raspberries, for garnish

*I like Green and Black's organic fair trade cocoa powder.

**You can swap out the coconut cream for half-and-half or cashew cream!

Whatcha Do

Cut the avocados in half, take out the seed, and scoop out the flesh. Put the avocado flesh in the bowl of a food processor with the metal blade. Using a spoon, break up the avocado a little in the food processor before processing. Add the cocoa powder, agave nectar, vanilla extract, and almond extract and process for 1 to 2 minutes. Scrape down the sides of the bowl and then process again until the mousse is very smooth—1 to 2 minutes longer.

Taste the mousse, and if it's not sweet enough, add more nectar, 1 teaspoon at a time.

Pulse to mix. Spoon the mousse into martini glasses or other pretty glasses. Cover with plastic wrap and refrigerate for at least 1 hour and up to 8 hours. Serve these yummy mousses chilled and garnished with raspberries.

MAKES 8 SERVINGS

COCONUT BERRY CRISP
Vegan, Dairy Free, and Gluten Free

MAKES 8 SERVINGS

WHATCHA NEED

Coconut oil and shredded coconut add a twist to this classic crisp. My guests are always pleasantly surprised by the complex flavors of this seemingly simple vegan dessert.

FILLING

2 10-ounce packages frozen strawberries

1 10-ounce package frozen blueberries

1/4 cup freshly squeezed lemon juice

1 tablespoon agave nectar

2 tablespoons arrowroot powder

TOPPING

1 cup blanched almond flour

1/2 teaspoon sea salt

1/4 teaspoon baking soda

1 cup unsweetened shredded coconut

1 cup walnuts, coarsely chopped

1/2 cup coconut oil, melted over very low heat

1/4 cup agave nectar

Whatcha Do

Preheat the oven to 350°F. Grease an 8-inch square baking dish with grape seed oil.

Filling:

To make the filling, place the frozen berries in the baking dish. Sprinkle with the lemon juice, agave nectar, and arrowroot powder, and then gently toss the ingredients to combine.

Bake for 40 to 50 minutes, until the mixture is slightly thickened.

Topping:

To make the topping, combine the almond flour, salt, baking soda, coconut, and walnuts in a large bowl. In a medium bowl, whisk together the coconut oil and agave nectar. Stir the wet ingredients into the almond flour mixture, until coarsely blended and crumbly. Sprinkle the topping over the fruit.

Bake for 20 to 25 additional minutes, until the topping is golden brown and the juices are bubbling. Let the crisp cool for 30 minutes, then serve warm.

FIG NEWTONS
Vegan, Dairy Free, and Gluten Free

MAKES 20 COOKIES

WHATCHA NEED

FILLING

1 cup dried figs

$1/4$ cup freshly squeezed lemon juice

1 tablespoon vanilla extract

DOUGH

$2^1/2$ cups blanched almond flour

$1/2$ teaspoon sea salt

$1/4$ cup grapeseed oil

$1/2$ cup agave nectar

$1/4$ cup yacon syrup

1 tablespoon vanilla extract

Whatcha Do

Preheat the oven to 350°F. Line two large baking sheets with parchment paper.

Filling:

To make the filling, blend the figs in a food processor until well chopped, about 30 seconds. Add the lemon juice and vanilla extract. Process until a smooth paste forms. Set the filling aside until ready to use.

Dough:

To make the dough, combine the almond flour and salt in a large bowl. In a medium bowl, whisk together the grapeseed oil, agave nectar, yacon syrup, and vanilla extract. Stir the wet ingredients into the almond flour mixture until thoroughly combined. Refrigerate the dough for 1 hour.

Divide the chilled dough into 4 parts. Place 1 piece of dough between 2 sheets of parchment paper and roll the dough into a 10- by 4-inch rectangle, $1/4$-inch thick. If the dough is wet, dust it with almond flour. Spread $1/4$ of the filling evenly down the long side of the rectangle. Fold the dough in half lengthwise, resulting in a 10- by 2-inch bar. Mend the seam where the two sides of dough come together so that the bar is symmetrical. Repeat this process with the 3 remaining parts of the dough and the filling.

Transfer 2 bars to each prepared baking sheet. Bake for 15–18 minutes, until lightly golden. Let the bars cool on the baking sheets for 30 minutes before cutting into 2-inch squares.

MAKES 6 SERVINGS

WHATCHA NEED

1$\frac{1}{2}$ cups cashews

$\frac{1}{2}$ cup pine nuts

$\frac{1}{2}$ cup maple syrup

$\frac{2}{3}$ cup coconut oil, melted

1 teaspoon lemon juice

$\frac{1}{4}$ teaspoon salt

2 vanilla beans, scraped

1 teaspoon vanilla

Maple syrup for topping

MAPLE CRÈME BRULEE
Raw, Vegan, Dairy Free, and Gluten Free

I love crème brulee, and this recipe is a fine substitute that will impress your guests!

Whatcha Do

Blend cashews, pine nuts, and $\frac{1}{2}$ cup maple syrup in blender at high speed until smooth. Add all other ingredients except remaining maple syrup and continue to blend until smooth. Do not overblend.

Pour mixture into a flan mold or small dish and put in freezer for 30 minutes. Once set, refrigerate. When firm, turn over and remove from dish to a plate. Drizzle each dish with 2 tablespoons of maple syrup.

ROSEMARY-HAZELNUT SHORTBREAD COOKIES
Vegan, Dairy Free, and Gluten Free

Whatcha Do

Preheat the oven to 350°F. Line two large baking sheets with parchment paper.

In a large bowl, combine the almond flour, salt, baking soda, hazelnuts, and rosemary. In a medium bowl, whisk together the grapeseed oil, agave nectar, and vanilla extract. Stir the wet ingredients into the almond flour mixture until thoroughly combined.

Roll the dough into a large log, $2^1/_2$ inches in diameter, then wrap in parchment paper. Place in the freezer for 1 hour, or until firm. Remove the log from the freezer, unwrap it, and cut it into $1/_4$-inch-thick slices with a wet knife. Transfer the slices onto the prepared baking sheets, leaving 2 inches between each cookie.

Bake 7–10 minutes, until brown around the edges. Let the cookies cool on the baking sheets for 30 minutes, and then serve.

MAKES 24 COOKIES

WHATCHA NEED

$2^1/_2$ cups blanched almond flour

$1/_2$ teaspoon sea salt

$1/_2$ teaspoon baking soda

1 cup hazelnuts, toasted and coarsely chopped

1 tablespoon finely chopped fresh rosemary

$1/_2$ cup grapeseed oil

5 tablespoons agave nectar

1 tablespoon vanilla extract

MAKES 12 CUPCAKES

WHATCHA NEED

1 cup leftover white beans *or*
1 15-ounce can unseasoned
Eden* white beans

5 large eggs

1 tablespoon pure vanilla extract
or one whole vanilla bean

$^1/_2$ teaspoon sea salt

4 tablespoons Earth Balance
butter (organic soy free) or
unrefined coconut oil**

$^1/_2$ cup brown rice syrup
or honey

6 tablespoons unsweetened
cocoa powder or organic
baking cacao (optional)***

1 teaspoon aluminum-free
baking powder

$^1/_2$ teaspoon baking soda

*Eden is the only bean company to use BPA-free cans and kombu sea veggies, which add trace minerals and selenium—a major ingredient that fights cancer and boosts the immune system!

**Or a mix of the two, which is what I do; that way you don't get so much of a coconut taste.

***Cocoa or cacao can be added to make cupcakes "chocolate"; or keep them "vanilla" by omitting this ingredient.

VANILLA WHITE BEAN CUPCAKES
Vegan, Dairy Free, and Gluten Free

These babies are flourless, gluten free, dairy free, and refined sugar free! These are "get down good" cupcakes for the heart. They are made out of white beans—seriously! The best part about these cakes is that they are totally budget-friendly, easy to make, and you will feel great while you are eating them—and after!

Whatcha Do

Preheat oven to 325°F. Drain and rinse beans in a strainer. Shake off excess water or pat dry with paper towels. Place beans, 3 of the eggs, vanilla, and salt into blender or food processor. Blend on high until beans are completely liquefied. No lumps! Whisk together cocoa powder (if making chocolate option), baking soda, and baking powder and set aside. Beat butter and/or oil with sweetener until light and fluffy with a hand-mixer, and add remaining two eggs, beating for a minute after each addition.

Pour bean batter into egg mixture and mix with hand-mixer. Finally, stir in dry baking soda and powder mixture and beat the batter on high for one minute, until smooth. Pour into cupcake tins almost to the top and bake for 25–30 minutes. Frost them with Whipped Coconut Cream (see recipe)! For BEST flavor, let cupcakes sit over night before frosting. These cakes will not have a hint of beaniness after letting them sit for eight hours. Try them, and let me know what you think!

WHIPPED COCONUT CREAM
Vegan, Dairy Free, and Gluten Free

MAKES 6–8 SERVINGS

WHATCHA NEED

1 14-ounce can coconut milk

2 tablespoons organic
powdered sugar

1/2 teaspoon vanilla

WHATCHA CAN ADD

1 teaspoon matcha, *or*

1 tablespoon cocoa powder, *or*

2 tablespoons pomegranate
juice—makes a pretty pink
and fruity whip!

Coconut milk makes a whipped cream just as thick and rich as whipping cream, if not more! And the only difference in preparation is to remember to put the coconut milk in the fridge long enough to chill.

An additional plus is that whipped coconut cream does not break down the way dairy does. This whipped cream can be covered and stored for up to a few days without separation taking place. That alone makes it a better option in my book!

Whatcha Do

Set can of coconut milk and mixing bowl in the fridge overnight. Set beaters in freezer for a few minutes before you begin. Open can and remove all the solid coconut cream (leaving about 1/4 can of coconut water). Mix cream in chilled bowl with chilled beaters until fluffy (3 minutes or so). Mix in powdered sugar and/or any other flavoring.

Use right away or cover and keep in the refrigerator for up to three days.

MAKES ABOUT 2 CUPS

WHATCHA NEED

1/3 cup apple juice

1 tablespoon agar flakes

Pinch of salt

12 ounces vacuum-packed extra-firm silken tofu

1/4 cup maple syrup or sweetener of your choice

1 teaspoon vanilla extract

WHIPPED TOFU CREAM TOPPING
Vegan, Dairy Free, and Gluten Free

I was a Cool Whip kinda gal. Talk about a food that has deep emotional roots and not much real anything in it. Now that I've found these alternative recipes, my Cool Whip craving has a means to satisfaction. Step aside dairy whip—meet tofu whip!

Whatcha Do

Combine the juice, agar, and salt in a small heavy saucepan. Bring to a simmer over high heat. Decrease the heat to medium-low, cover, and simmer, stirring frequently for 15 minutes or until the agar dissolves.

Meanwhile, blend the tofu, maple syrup, and vanilla in a food processor until very smooth and creamy. As soon as the agar is dissolved, pour the juice mixture through the feed tube with the food processor running and blend into the tofu mixture until well combined.

Cover and pop in fridge for 1 hour or until set. Return the chilled tofu mixture to the food processor and blend until smooth and creamy. It will keep two days covered in fridge. Whisk before using.

Resources

Autoimmune Epidemic, The by Donna Jackson Nakazawa (Touchstone, 2009)

Aveline Kushi's Complete Guide to Macrobiotic Cooking: For Health, Harmony, and Peace by Aveline Kushi and Alex Jack (Warner Books, 1988)

China Study, The: The Most Comprehensive Study of Nutrition Ever Conducted and the Startling Implications for Diet, Weight Loss, and Long-term Health by T. Colin Campbell & Thomas M. Campbell II (BenBella Books, 2006)

Complete Idiots Guide to Fermenting Foods, The by Wardeh Harmon (ALPHA, 2012)

Controlling Crohn's Disease: The Natural Way by Virgina Harper (Kensington, 2002)

Crazy Sexy Diet: Eat Your Veggies, Ignite Your Spark, and Live Like You Mean It! by Kris Carr (skirt!, 2011)

Dr. Andrew Weil's Mindbody toolkit: Experience self-healing with clinically proven techniques by Andrew Weil (Sounds True Inc., 2006) [Audio Book/CD]

The Farm as Natural Habitat: Reconnecting Food Systems With Ecosystems by Dana L Jackson & Laura L Jackson (Island Press, 2002)

Gerson Therapy, The: The Proven Nutritional Program for Cancer and Other Illnesses by Charlotte Gerson & Morton Walker D.P.M. (Kensington, 2001)

Gluten Free Almond Flour Cookbook, The by Elana Amsterdam (Celestial Arts, 2009)

Graphing Food and Nutrition (Real World Data) by Isabel Thomas (Heinemann-Raintree, 2008)

Healing Body Mind and Spirit: An Integrative Medicine Approach to the Treatment of Eating Disorders by Carolyn Ross, MD, MPH (Outskirts Press, 2007)

Healing with Whole Foods: Asian Traditions and Modern Nutrition by Paul Pitchford (North Atlantic Books, 2003)

It's Not the End of the World: Developing Resilience in Times of Change by Joan Borysenko, PhD (Hay House, 2009)

Omnivore's Dilemma by Michael Pollan (Penguin Books, 2006)

Power of the Mind to Heal, The by Joan Borysenko, PhD (Hay House, 1995)

Seeds of Deception: Exposing Industry and Government Lies About the Safety of the Genetically Engineered Foods You're Eating by Jeffrey M. Smith (Yes Books, 2003)

Self-Healing Cookbook, The: Whole Foods to Balance Body, Mind and Moods by Kristina Turner (Earthtones Press, 2002)

"The Power of Sourdough Bread" www.alive .com/368a1a2.php?subject_ bread_cramb =453?

"Sourdough Bread Has Most Health Benefits, Prof Finds" www.uoguelph.ca/news/2008/07/sour dough_bread.html

Learn more

www.dirtdoctor.com/Canola-Oil-Bad-Fat-News letter_vq4587.htm#nogo

www.breathing.com/articles/canola-oil.htm

Sources

Coconut Research Center: www.coconutresearch center.org/

"The Bomb Shell Truth About Canola Oil" http://healthwyze.org/index.php/ canola.htm

"The Real Story on Canola Oil (Can-ugly Oil)" www.diabetesincontrol.com/component/content /article/64–feature–writer–article/2570and Itemid=

"What Is Canola Oil" www.canolainfo.org/canola/ index.php

"The Truth About Canola Oil" www.tetrahedron .org/articles/health_risks/ canola_oil.html

"Olive oil: What Are the Health Benefits?" www .mayoclinic.com/health/food–and–nutrition/ AN01037

"What are EPA/DHA?" www.drhoffman.com/page .cfm/84

"Grass Is Greener: Buy Healthy Meat" www. womenshealthmag.com/nutrition/benefits–of– grass–fed–beef?page=2#ixzz1uao2oOmH

If you are interested in more info regarding GMO seeds check out *Seeds of Deception* by Jeffrey M. Smith.

Recipes by Category

Recipes by Title